SPATIAL AND TEMPORAL REASONING

Spatial and Temporal Reasoning

edited by

Oliviero Stock
IRST, Italy

KLUWER ACADEMIC PUBLISHERS
DORDRECHT / BOSTON / LONDON

A C.I.P. Catalogue record for this book is available from the Library of Congress

ISBN 0-7923-4644-0 (HB)
ISBN 0-7923-4716-1 (PB)

Published by Kluwer Academic Publishers,
P.O. Box 17, 3300 AA Dordrecht, The Netherlands.

Sold and distributed in the U.S.A. and Canada
by Kluwer Academic Publishers,
101 Philip Drive, Norwell, MA 02061, U.S.A.

In all other countries, sold and distributed
by Kluwer Academic Publishers,
P.O. Box 322, 3300 AH Dordrecht, The Netherlands.

Printed on acid-free paper

TABLE OF CONTENTS

Preface

Aim of this volume is to give a picture of current research on space and time focusing on both representational and computational issues. The title could have been *Spatial and Temporal Representation and Reasoning*, but double coordinations do not sound well, so "representation" has gone from it. The emphasis of the approach is on qualitative as opposed to thoroughly quantitative aspects of spatial and temporal reasoning. The picture is not exhaustive, but indicates some major lines of development in this multifaceted, constantly growing area.

The history of philosophy, physics, and some branches of psychology is permeated with the concepts of space and time. So what is new here? The point of view of this volume is one of artificial intelligence (AI) research. Within AI only recently has there been a strategic interest in addressing these topics within a unifying environment. The prospects are obvious at the ontological level (let us just think of the concept of *movement*), at the computational level (some techniques in the two areas have developed quite similarly and belong to a common class), and at the cognitive level (for example the areas of perception or language processing intrinsically require coping with spatio-temporal issues). Yet the task is not trivial because the background and state of the art research in spatial and temporal reasoning, including the specific communities of researchers, have different characteristics.

Temporal representation and reasoning are themes that have attracted quite a lot of interest in AI for a long time. Their importance is obvious for many possible applications of computer-based systems, for instance planning actions in the real world, scheduling within a complex system, or coordinating activities of different agents. Moreover, qualitative representations are necessary for humans to live in this world. Certainly, temporal reasoning is one of the cognitive capabilities we involve in communicating with other fellow humans. What if the computer has to communicate with us, understand stories, or produce understandable reports on facts and events that occurred in a certain period of time? The computer needs to have at least a "cognitively acceptable" capacity of reasoning about time. This desideratum has been acknowledged and has been at the core of the efforts of many AI practitioners. It may seem odd that an initial phase of research on, say, planning systems has not directly involved practical algorithms or representations for events, periods, durations and so on. Though it was clear that such concepts were of the highest importance as planning people were talking about actions (conditions for acting, ordering of actions and so on), the need to come out with constructive, practical results, outweighed the desire to include more problematic elements. Clearly enough, various formal systems at the crossroads of AI and logic had been proposed for a long time (and are currently being proposed). Yet true computational design has gone beyond that. Starting from the basic need to deal with the structure of time in computational systems, theories and techniques have been developed that take into account efficiency and the need to integrate time in a more extended reasoning apparatus. This road to contructive experimentation, in turn, leads not only to better and better systems but also to a deeper understanding of our conception of time. This field of research now appears technically sophisticated.

Research in *spatial representation and reasoning* developed much later, at least from an AI perspective. One can speculate that some systems that may actually benefit from sophisticated spatial reasoning modules (such as geographical information systems or CAD systems) have become widespread only with the advent of good–quality graphical interfaces, or that artificial vision has developed with much more interest for low–level perception (and geometry as far as space is concerned) than for high-level representations and inferencing. Besides, spatial reasoning is inherently more complex than temporal reasoning, if not for any other reason, because more dimensions are involved. The problems with space probably require a very subtle capacity for integration within the field itself: even more points of view seem to exist there and often they are jointly needed for addressing specific tasks. However, foundational issues had to be taken seriously if the field was to advance. Spatial representations constitute a delicate element. Consider the pervasiveness of spatial representations in many aspects of our interactions with our daily environment, including abstract worlds, metaphors (and – why not – dreams). What is the nature of the entities we are dealing with? From an AI, constructive point of view, what are the most suitable representations for a computational apparatus? What kind of perspective is feasible for the various reasoning needs? Currently, research on spatial reasoning still asks more questions of this kind than research in temporal reasoning, and many contributions from cognitive science and philosophy are welcome. Because the field took off later, it was in a position (and the spatial metaphor is purely accidental) to benefit from some computational ideas that originated in temporal reasoning (and also in more general areas such as knowledge representation).

With all this, qualititive reasoning about space and time – a reasoning at the human level – promises to become a fundamental aspect of future systems that will accompany us in daily activity. My own field of specialization, human-computer communication technologies, offers examples of this. Intelligent interactive multimedia systems will coordinate outputs that include images, both static and in motion, combined with linguistic outputs and sounds, and will allow the user to use language combined with gestures and sketching as input. Spatio-temporal reasoning will become a key factor in understanding references, retrieving relevant data (figures, videoclip fragments, and so on), giving rhetorical structure, and presenting the information (for example combining different videoclip fragments and coordinating them with explanations). Flexibility and decent quality of communication with a normal user will be possible only if the system is cognitively acceptable in the sense mentioned above.

This book reflects for the most part current research in these areas. The material in Part I helps set up the overall scene. The chapter by Laure Vieu is on the state of the art in spatial representation and reasoning, and the one by Alfonso Gerevini gives a similar survey on research in temporal reasoning. The specific contributions to these areas are then grouped in the two main parts. In Part II, Roberto Casati and Achille Varzi examine the ontological status of spatial entities; Anthony Cohn, Brandon Bennett, John Gooday and Nicholas Gotts present a detailed theory of reasoning with qualitative relations about regions; Andrew Frank discusses the spatial needs of geographical information systems; and Annette Herskovits focuses on the linguistic expression of spatial relations. In Part III, James Allen and George Ferguson describe an interval temporal logic for the representation of actions and events; Drew McDermott presents an efficient way of predicting the outcome of plan execution; and Erik Sandewall introduces a semantics based on transitions for assessing theories of action and change. Finally, in Part IV, Antony Galton's chapter stands clearly between the two areas of space and time and outlines the main coordinates of an integrated approach.

This volume grew out of two Advanced Schools held in Bolzano, Italy, that I had the honor and pleasure of directing. The Schools were instances of a long-term Bolzano initiative called International Schools on Philosophy and Artificial Intelligence coordinated by Roberto Poli and promoted by the Istituto Mitteleuropeo di Cultura/Mitteleuropäisches Kulturinstitut. Apart from Vieu's and Gerevini's introductory essays, all the chapters were written by lecturers at these Schools. I would like to thank them for their enthusiasm and the high quality of the contributions. Finally I would like to express a special thank to Achille Varzi for his advice when he still was at IRST and afterward, to Ileana Collini who was of fundamental help in the final preparation of the material and to Polly Margules of Kluwer, who helped make this project a reality.

Oliviero Stock

Abstracts

1. Spatial Representation and Reasoning in Artificial Intelligence

Laure Vieu

In this chapter, a presentation of the field of spatial representation and reasoning is given. Most of the chapter is dedicated to qualitative spatial reasoning, a main trend in this field. Basic issues in representing space are focused on. The different aspects of the ontology of space are discussed, particularly the nature of basic spatial entities and primitive spatial concepts. Primitive entities considered here are points, cells in arrays, tuples of intervals, and regions. Mixed ontologies, based on entities of various dimensions, are also considered. Spatial concepts are grouped into three clusters covering topology, orientation, and distance. In addition, a few morphological concepts and some spatiotemporal representational issues are presented. A number of well-known approaches illustrating these possible representational choices are reviewed, even though no comprehensive picture of the work done in the field is actually sought. The main problems in symbolic spatial reasoning are then briefly examined, and the different ways of handling spatial representations as a classifying factor are considered. Finally, some issues that may constitute interesting lines of current and future research in the field are emphasized.

2. Reasoning about Time and Actions in Artificial Intelligence

Alfonso Gerevini

Temporal reasoning has been a major research field in artificial intelligence since the beginning of this discipline, and it has been investigated in the context of many areas where time representation and reasoning are crucial. This chapter first illustrates fundamental issues concerning two major subfields of temporal reasoning: reasoning about time and reasoning about actions and change. Then it discusses the role of temporal reasoning in the important AI area of planning. Finally, reasoning about time is focused on, providing an overview of the main results in this subfield.

3. Spatial Entities

Roberto Casati and Achille C. Varzi

Ordinary reasoning about space, we argue, is first and foremost reasoning about things located in space. Accordingly, any theory concerned with the construction of a general model of our spatial competence must be grounded on a general account of the sort of entities that may enter into the scope of the theory. Moreover, on the methodological side the emphasis on spatial entities (as opposed to purely geometrical items such as points or regions) calls for a reexamination of the conceptual categories required for this task. In this work we offer some examples of what this amounts to, of the difficulties involved, and of the main directions along which spatial theories should be developed so as to combine formal sophistication with some affinity for common sense.

4. Representing and Reasoning with Qualitative Spatial Relations about Regions

Anthony G. Cohn, Brandon Bennett, John Gooday, and Nicholas M. Gotts

This chapter surveys the work of the qualitative spatial reasoning group at the University of Leeds. The group has developed a number of logical calculi for representing and reasoning with qualitative spatial relations over regions. We motivate the use of regions as the primary spatial entity and show how a rich language can be built up from surprisingly few primitives. This language can distinguish between convex and a variety of concave shapes, and there is also an extension that handles regions with uncertain boundaries. We also present a variety of reasoning techniques, both for static and dynamic situations. A number of possible application areas are briefly mentioned.

5. Spatial Ontology: A Geographical Information Point of View

Andrew U. Frank

Ontology is the science of objects. It is an ancient discipline, which has recently been rediscovered and overhauled for the purposes of artificial intelligence. Ontology has been concerned with the properties of objects, with their modes of existence, and with questions such as how they can be divided in parts and how they fill space. This presentation seeks to show not only that there is a 'production of ontologies' in the research literature, but also that these ontologies are useful and can be used. The article focuses on a particular area of application, namely that of geographic information systems (GIS). It answers the question, How can ontologies be used and how can they contribute to building better information systems? This will mostly be done by showing how the lack of a consistent ontology in a system causes difficulties for its users.

The chapter concludes with a set of recommendations as to how ontologies can be made more useful and how the connection between the producers and consumers of an ontology can be structured to make the exchange of ideas more effective. A number of broad general directions and specific topics are listed that may yield useful contributions both from scientific and engineering points of view.

6. Language, Spatial Cognition, and Vision

Annette Herskovits

This chapter investigates spatial language and the interface between language and spatial cognition. It first examines two essential properties shaping spatial language, schematization (which selects certain aspects of a referent scene to represent the whole) and the fluidity of lexical meaning, providing concrete illustrations through a detailed analysis of the semantics and use of the English spatial prepositions. Then work in computer vision and psychology on the role played by abstract spatial relations in perception is considered. On the basis of this review and the foregoing semantic analysis, several arguments are put forth that, contrary to claims in recent work on language and spatial cognition, (1) the language system has access to a variety of spatial representations such as cognitive maps and representations of the plane of view; and (2) visual representations do not automatically include the spatial primitives necessary to linguistic expression – apprehending spatial relations in visual scenes requires flexible, goal-directed, attentional, computational processes.

7. Action and Events in Interval Temporal Logic

James F. Allen and George Ferguson

A representation of events and action based on interval temporal logic that is significantly more expressive and more natural than most previous AI approaches is presented. The representation is motivated by work in natural language semantics and discourse, temporal logic, and AI planning and plan recognition. The formal basis of the representation is presented in detail, from the axiomatization of time periods to the relationship between actions and events and their effects. The power of the representation is illustrated by applying it to the axiomatization and solution of several standard problems from the AI literature on action and change. An approach to the frame problem based on explanation closure is shown to be both powerful and natural when combined with this representational framework. Features of the logic that are beyond the scope of many traditional representations are also discussed, as is an approach to difficult problems such as external events and simultaneous actions.

8. Probabilistic Projection in Planning

Drew McDermott

Temporal projection, defined as the prediction of what might happen when a plan is executed, is an important component of many planning algorithms. To achieve efficiency, it is desirable for a projection to be a totally ordered event sequence. To cope with uncertainty, the events must be generated using probabilistic rules. A rule language is required that allows us to specify what can happen when an event occurs, as well as what events can occur when certain propositions are true. The language has a formal semantics, which allows us to prove that a set of rules has a unique model (if it is "consistent"). This language supports a Monte Carlo style of projection, in which event sequences are sampled randomly using the probabilities in the rules. The output of the projector is a timeline that allows a planning algorithm to test the truth of propositions at arbitrary points. The algorithms for building and retrieving from the timeline can be shown to be correct. Experiments show that for a typical theory, the time to build a timeline is a quadratic function of the number of events in the timeline.

9. Underlying Semantics for Action and Change with Ramification

Erik Sandewall

This chapter reports on assessment results for several approaches to the ramification problem. Two types of assessments are reported: (1) assessment of soundness for one minimization-based method and one causation-based method and (2) relative range assessments for a number of minimization-based methods. Assessment of soundness is based on an underlying semantics for ramification. We propose, define, and use a causal propagation semantics for this purpose. Causal propagation means that an action is viewed as consisting of an initial state transition that represents the invocation of the action, followed by a succession of other state transitions that may be understood as representing links in a causal chain. The assessment of an entailment method specifies restrictions on the invocation and causation relations that guarantee that the entailment method is sound. Relative range assessments compare entailment methods pairwise and specify whether the set of selected models obtained by one is a subset of the set of selected models obtained by the other.

10. Space, Time, and Movement

Antony Galton

The phenomenon of movement consists of the same object occupying different positions in space at different times. A theory of movement must therefore incorporate a theory of time, a theory of space, a theory of objects, and a theory of position. The central thesis of this chapter is that movement events should be specified in terms of their occurrence conditions, necessary and sufficient conditions for the occurrence of a given species of movement at a given time. Movement is considered both in dense time and in discrete time, and both durative and instantaneous movement events are included in the analyses. The aim throughout is to approach the task in a systematic way, with a view to generality. Considerations of continuity play an important role in the treatment here, and we look in some detail at the implications of continuity for qualitative descriptions of motion. The outcome of this investigation is the introduction of the notion of a dominance space: with this notion, the properties of complex qualitative state-spaces can be derived systematically from those of smaller components, by means of a simple but powerful composition theorem.

About the contributors

James Allen is the John Dessauer Professor of Computer Science at the University of Rochester. He received his Ph.D. in Computer Science from the University of Toronto and was a recipient of the Presidential Young Investigator award from NSF in 1984. A Fellow of the American Association for Artificial Intelligence, he was editor-in-chief of the journal Computational Linguistics from 1983 to 1993. He is also the author of several books, including *Natural Language Understanding*, published by Benjamin Cummings in 1987 (second edition published in 1995).

Brandon Bennett is a Research Officer at the School of Computer Studies at the University of Leeds. He is a member of the Qualitative Spatial Reasoning group and is currently conducting researching into representations and efficient proof procedures for reasoning about spatial relations. Applications of this work include geographical information systems, specification of the behaviour of intelligent artificial agents and virtual world simulation. His first degree was in Computer Science and Physics and he has an M.A. in Philosophy.

Roberto Casati graduated in Philosophy from Milan University; he received a Ph.D. from Geneva University and one from Milan University. He holds teaching and research positions in Switzerland and in France, and is now researcher with French Centre National de la Recerche Scientifique. He published a number of articles in philosophical journals, and several books, including *Holes and Other Superficialities* (with A. C. Varzi, MIT Press 1994) and *La Philosophie du Son* (with J. Dokic, Chambon 1994). He is presently working with A. C. Varzi on a project on space representation.

Anthony Cohn is Professor of Automated Reasoning at the University of Leeds and leads a research group with a particular focus on qualitative spatial reasoning. He holds B.Sc. and Ph.D. degrees from the University of Essex where he studied under Pat Hayes. He now holds a number of grants in the area, and has published widely. He has been Chairman of the U.K. Society for Artificial Intelligence and Simulation of Behaviour and also of the European Coordinating Committee for Artificial Intelligence.

George Ferguson is a Research Associate at the University of Rochester. He received his Ph.D. in 1995 under the supervision of James Allen at the University of Rochester.

Andrew U. Frank is Professor of Geoinformation at the Technical University of Vienna since 1991 where he teaches courses in spatial information systems, representation of geometric data, design of geographic information systems (GIS) for administration and business, selection of GIS software, and economic and administrative strategies for the introduction of GIS. He leads an active research group, supported by industry and research foundations, focusing on problems of spatial cognition, user interfaces for GIS, and the collection, management and use of geographic information. He is also involved in several research projects of the European Community.

Antony Galton studied Mathematics at Clare College, Cambridge, and has a Ph.D. in Philosophy from the University of Leeds. He is now a Lecturer in Computer Science at the University of Exeter. His main research interests are in formal approaches to temporal and spatial reasoning in artificial intelligence and related disciplines. He is currently engaged in writing a book on qualitative spatial change.

Alfonso Gerevini is an Assistant Professor for Information Processing Systems at the University of Brescia (Italy). From 1988 to 1995 he worked as a research scientist at Institute for Scientific and Technologic Research (IRST) in Trento (Italy). Since 1992 he has been spending part of his time at the Department of Computer Science of the University of Rochester as a visiting research associate. His research activity in artificial intelligence focuses on temporal reasoning, constraint-based reasoning, planning, and knowledge-based systems, with an emphasis on computational issues. He has published several papers on these topics in the major international AI journals and conference proceedings.

John Gooday read Physics at University College London and studied Computing at Imperial College, where he gained an M.Sc. After completing his Ph.D. in nonmonotonic reasoning about action and change at the University of Exeter, he joined the Qualitative Spatial Reasoning Group at the University of Leeds. There he worked on qualitative spatial modelling, pictorial language semantics and general research related to the RCC spatial logic. Currently he heads the research and development team of Equifax Decision Solutions, applying AI techniques to credit risk management, fraud and marketing problems.

After a first degree in Psychology, **Nicholas Gotts** moved into artificial intelligence, concentrating on spatial reasoning and spatial skills. He has worked on human wayfinding, medical expert systems, modelling spiders' web-building procedures, automatic route-guidance systems, and logical and computational aspects of qualitative spatial reasoning. He recently moved to the University of Wales Aberystwyth as lecturer in Computer Science. His main research interests are now in the area of artificial life and complex systems, particularly cellular automata.

Annette Herskovits studied Electrical Engineering in France, then Computer Vision at MIT. She went on to earn a Ph.D. in Linguistics at Stanford University and has since concentrated on the semantics of spatial terms and its relation to vision and spatial cognition. She is the author of *Language and Spatial Cognition* (Cambridge University Press). She is currently a visiting scholar at the Institute of Cognitive Studies, University of California, Berkeley.

Drew McDermott is Professor of Computer Science at Yale University. His research is in artificial intelligence, specifically concerning reasoning about space and time, and sensor-guided planning. He has done seminal work in nonmonotonic logic and is the coauthor of two textbooks in artificial intelligence. He is on the editorial boards of Artificial Intelligence and the Journal of the ACM. He is a Fellow of the American Association for Artificial Intelligence.

Erik Sandewall is professor of computer science at Linköping University, Sweden, where he is also prorector and director of the Wallenberg Laboratory for Information Technology and Autonomous Systems (WITAS). He received his Ph.D. from Uppsala University (Sweden) in 1969, and has been in Linköping since 1975. His major research interest at present is logicist approaches to actions and change, and their applications to cognitive robotics. His monograph on this topic, *Features and Fluents*, was published in 1994. Erik Sandewall has also done research on programming environments and office information systems. He is a member of the Royal Swedish Academy of Sciences and the Royal Swedish Academy of Engineering Sciences.

Achille C. Varzi is Assistant Professor of Philosophy at Columbia University, New York. A graduate of the University of Trento (Italy), he received his M.A. and Ph.D. degrees in Philosophy from the University of Toronto (Canada) and has been a research scientist with the Institute for Scientific and Technologic Research (IRST) in Trento (Italy). His main research interests are in philosophical logic, model-theoretic semantics, and formal metaphysics, including applications to spatio-temporal reasoning. He is the author/co-author of some 30 papers and journal articles and co-author (with R. Casati) of the book *Holes and Other Superficialities* (MIT Press, 1994). With R. Casati he also edited the volumes *Events* (Dartmouth Publishing, 1996) and *Fifty Years of Events. An Annotated Bibliography 1947 to 1997* (PDC Press, 1997).

Born in 1964, **Laure Vieu** received her Ph.D. in Computer Science in 1991. After working as a research fellow in artificial intelligence at the Institut National de la Recherche Agronomique in 1991-1993, she has been a research fellow in computer science at Centre National de la Recherche

Scientifique since 1993. Her main research areas are representation of cognitive space, axiomatic theories of topology and geometry, formal semantics of spatial expressions, semantics and pragmatics of discourse.

SPATIAL AND TEMPORAL REASONING

Part I

Overview

1. Spatial Representation and Reasoning in Artificial Intelligence

Laure Vieu

1.1. Introduction

Space, like time, is one of the most fundamental categories of human cognition. It structures all our activities and relationships with the external world. It also structures many of our reasoning capabilities: it serves as the basis for many metaphors, including temporal, and gave rise to mathematics itself, geometry being the first formal system known.

However, space is inherently more complex than time, because it is multidimensional. In addition, even if unarguably less abstract than time, space is epistemologically multiple. Without going seriously into psychological studies, it is obvious that a larger number of knowledge sources (as vision, touch, hearing and kinaesthesis) contribute to establish mental representations of space. The multiplicity of spatial knowledge is also made evident by language. Space is grammaticalized in very few natural languages, and spatial concepts are spread over a wide range of syntactic classes: nouns (such as part nouns), prepositions, verbs (position and motion), adverbs, adjectives (shape).

Even though modeling spatial knowledge is clearly a crucial domain of artificial intelligence (AI), the difficulty of reducing all of it to a small number of primitive spatial concepts in an obvious or widely admitted fashion may explain why spatial representation and reasoning developed as an homogeneous clearly identified branch of AI much later than temporal representation and reasoning.

The earliest work appeared within other domains of AI and computer science, with a variety of objectives. Areas like robotics, physical reasoning, computer vision, natural language understanding, geographic information systems, and computer-aided design have contributed to the study of representing and reasoning with spatial knowledge, but space has not been really focused on as such there. A view widely held was that the ontology of space was unproblematic, topology and Euclidean geometry being the only mathematical models considered. This work then concentrated more on reasoning methods than on spatial representation, and, being closely linked to a variety of tasks, no real generic class of spatial problems and solutions emerged. It was even claimed that such a class does not exist (see Section 1.3.5). Only some of this work will be reported in this chapter, mostly in Section 1.4.

It is only during the last five years that fundamental studies on spatial representation and reasoning in AI, as such, have appeared in a significant number. A community has gathered now, as manifested by the recent increase in meetings and conferences (totally or in a great part) focused on the topic

(Mark and Frank, 1991; Frank et al., 1992; Aurnague et al., 1993; Frank and Campari, 1993; Guarino and Poli, 1993; Eschenbach et al., 1994; Amsili et al., 1995; Frank and Kuhn, 1995), and the series of workshops on spatial and temporal reasoning held in conjunction with major AI conferences such as IJCAI, AAAI, and ECAI since 1993. The main issues of the field have now begun to be identified, and a (still small) number of survey or field-defining papers and books have appeared (Davis, 1990; Freksa, 1991; McDermott, 1992a; Freksa and Röhrig, 1993; Hernández, 1994).

Although the term *spatial representation and reasoning in AI* still covers work toward the development of numerical algorithmic methods based on quantitative representations of space, the scope of this chapter is restricted to the symbolic approach, and it considers only qualitative spatial representations and symbolic reasoning methods. As a result, work more or less related to the field of computational geometry is completely left out here. For a survey of the field of computational geometry, the reader may refer to, for example, Preparata and Shamos (1985).

What remains in the scope of this chapter is the field that is now usually called *qualitative spatial reasoning*. This name was derived from the older field of qualitative reasoning, although at least two important differences should be stressed. First, the fields of qualitative reasoning and qualitative physics have in a great part dealt with scales discretizing quantitative domains or "quantity spaces" — that is, imprecise numerical values. Second, the representational problems raised by such quantity spaces being few, qualitative reasoning has then focused on reasoning methods. On the other hand, and however named, the field of qualitative spatial reasoning has given rise essentially to representational problems, which are far from being restricted to the discretization of a dense numerical space.

In the search for adequate spatial representations supporting genuine qualitative spatial reasoning, researchers in AI have started to give up the assumption that the ontology of space is straightforward and to address the issue of the nature of basic spatial concepts and spatial entities. Introducing several aspects of this ontological issue will constitute the core of this chapter. In the next two sections, some basic aspects of the ontology of space are discussed, and a number of approaches illustrating possible choices are presented. This presentation cannot thus pretend to cover exhaustively the work done in the field.

The subfield of spatial reasoning proper is then the subject of Section 1.4. Only a sketchy general picture of this field is given, considering the different ways of handling spatial representations as structuring factor. The very specific area of automatic geometric theorem proving is not examined there, even though algebraic geometry may in a sense be seen as symbolic and theorem proving techniques also. The interested reader may refer to Chou (1988) for a review of this area.

Finally, some issues that constitute interesting lines of current and future research in this field are emphasized in the last section.

1.2. Ontologies of Space and Spatial Knowledge Representation

1.2.1. GENERAL ASPECTS OF AN ONTOLOGY OF SPACE

The issue of the nature of spatial knowledge is certainly not a new topic raised by AI. On the contrary, it is an extremely old domain of research, investigated first in philosophy and mathematics, later in physics and psychology.

1.2.1.1. *Which Space?*

What is actually called *space* in all these disciplines varies significantly. It may be the real extent of the several dimensions in which we live. Physics postulates that we can observe and measure this physical space and then model it accordingly. It may be a cognitive representation of the physical space — that is, either the space human beings conceive from what they perceive, the space they store in memory and are able to recall through mental imagery, or the space they talk about. Modeling cognitive, mental, or commonsense space (or spaces) is here also an empirical enterprise, taken up by philosophy, psychology, and linguistics. Lastly, it may be an abstract construct, belonging to the class of mathematical structures that initially were built with the purpose of modeling the previous kinds of spaces.

Researchers in AI have intended to model either physical (for example, for robotics applications) or commonsense (for natural language processing purposes) space. In work aimed at giving general theories of space, this choice is sometimes left implicit. Moreover, arguments taken from both domains are often mixed. Confusion possibly arises from the fact that it is a widespread methodology in AI to rely on commonsense views for modeling physical as well as mental space. It might also be a sequel of the much held view that, even if the choice of primitives for an adequate representational framework is considered as debatable, the ontology of its *intended model* is still assumed to be unproblematic. For these researchers who perhaps adopt a Kantian view, space *is* Euclidean geometry without question. Reconsidering the classical distinction of goals in AI between obtaining efficient systems or cognitively accurate systems amounts here to distinguish clearly between physical space and mental space; and for both cases, we believe it useful not to take for granted that the ontology of space is a settled question. It is also plausible that in focusing on the differences between physical and commonsense space, one could find their commonalities and thus make further progress in the search for most general theories of space. Looking carefully at the properties of linguistic space with an AI perspective is, in these two respects, very important for the field. The chapter by Herskovits in this book (Chapter 6) contributes to this goal.

Whatever space is considered, the choice of a representational formalism of space and of its associated ontology is also based on several assumptions. The range of possible hypotheses is certainly not a novelty introduced by AI. These hypotheses recurrently appeared in the age-old philosophical debate on the nature of space.

1.2.1.2. *Absolute or Relative Space?*

The first choice to be made is between absolute and relative[1] space alternative made famous by the Newton-Leibniz controversy. An absolute space is a void, or "container," existing *a priori*, independently of the (physical or mental) objects that happen to be located in it. It is made up of purely spatial entities. In order to be used, such a space needs to be equipped with a location (or place) function giving each object its place. For its part, the relative approach denies the necessity of assuming the existence of an abstract independent space. A relative space is a construct induced by spatial relations over non-purely spatial entities — material bodies in the case of physical space, mental entities with more properties than just spatial ones in the case of cognitive space. The absolute option has been particularly fruitful in physics and is of course what mathematics deals with. The relative option seems to fit better with the cognitive approach, since the elements of an abstract space are not perceptible as such, but only through the existence of some material entities being located in it. It is also ontologically more parsimonious. Theories of relative space have, however, been much less developed than absolute ones.

If we assume the existence of an absolute space, we need next to choose between a space with a global structure or with only local properties. In what is here called a *global space*, each spatial entity is a location in a general reference frame so that its relative position with respect to all other spatial entities is already completely determined. An everyday example of a global space is a sheet of paper that serves as the backdrop for diagrams. In a *local space*, a spatial entity is situated through a number of explicit spatial relations with some, but not necessarily all, other spatial entities. The other spatial relations may be obtained by deduction, but some may be totally unspecified. An everyday example of local space is linguistic space, in which an object can be said to be close to another, without specifying in which direction. Thus, a global space is necessarily complete, whereas a local space can be either complete or incomplete.

This second question is closely related to the psychological issue of whether mental space is basically visual and constituted of images or depictions on which spatial relations between spatial entities have to be read (pictorial or analog or depictive representation) or whether mental space has a more linguistic flavor and is structured by propositions in which spatial relations relate spatial entities (propositional or descriptive representation) (Kosslyn, 1980; Paivio, 1986; Pylyshyn, 1985). A current position held is that (at least) both representational systems are present in the mind and involved in mental imagery processes (Kosslyn, 1980) or that, in fact, spatial cognition handles more complex structures covering both aspects (Tversky, 1993a).

Mathematically and computationally speaking, it amounts to choosing between a coordinate space, such as Cartesian geometry, or an axiomatic theory of space, such as Euclidean geometry, as in Hilbert (1971). In the former, spatial properties are implicitly given by the algebraic properties of numerical orders on several coordinate axes. Analytical geometry thus commits one from the start to standard analysis, as well as to a higher-order language, since a geometric figure is defined as a set of coordinate points. In the latter, usually called elementary geometry, axioms state fundamental properties of space. It does not commit to the use of number theory or set theory: congruence, determining distance, and order are not necessarily numerical; lines and planes are not necessarily sets of points.[2] Of course, there are strong links between the two kinds of structures. Cartesian geometry is a model of Hilbert's axiomatic system. But their underlying ontologies are very different, as are the reasoning methods applied to them.[3]

Since relative spaces are by definition theories of spatial relations, there is a strong similarity between relative spaces and local absolute spaces. At least two important aspects make the difference, however. First, they hold different constraints on possible basic entities. In a relative space, basic entities are constrained by the nature of the domain, so that their spatial properties depend on their other essential properties. For instance, in case of a physical relative space, the material constitution of physical bodies imply that they are all spatially extended. An absolute space is independent, so there is no other constraint than elegance, expressive power, and computational efficiency in the choice of basic entities. In a sense then, absolute spaces, in principle, are more general. However, to serve as an adequate representational framework, absolute spaces sometimes reflect some of the specific properties of physical or commonsense space. Second, their capacity to express motion is radically different. In an absolute space, the motion of a physical body is a change in value of the location function. In a relative space, the motion of a physical body is a change in spatial relationship with respect to some other bodies. Motion is then necessarily relative, which raises the question of the choice of adequate reference objects. More important, an absolute space is assumed to persist through time, so that expressing the continuity of motion amounts to stating that the location function is continuous. In contrast, a relative space is different at each different (spatial) state of affairs, so that continuity of motion depends on the identity of physical bodies through time, which is metaphysically problematic.[4]

For these reasons, or just because they were already more widespread in the literature, most authors in AI have chosen absolute spaces as representational frameworks. Classical mathematical global spaces (coordinate spaces) have been successfully used in computational geometry. In the knowledge representation area of AI, the necessity to cope with imprecision, incompleteness, and uncertainty of knowledge, both in physical space and cognitive space, led to drop this approach for a more qualitative one. As we will see, a number of authors still adopt a space that can be characterized as global. They keep the global axes for orientation and relax at least one of the undesirable characteristics of classical coordinate spaces, usually their metric, changing dense numerical orders for symbolic orders or discretizing them to deal with imprecision. However, local absolute spaces best fit these requirements. Being symbolic, they are particularly adequate for coping with imprecision and representing incomplete information. Gobal spaces require dealing either with disjunctions for the values of the location function or with numerical equations with free variables as in the algebraic geometry approach.

As a consequence, in the qualitative spatial reasoning community the kind of space adopted is generally local absolute space. This chapter focuses on local absolute spaces and describes only a few approaches based on global spaces.

Formal frameworks widely used for representing local spaces are of two types:

— Axiomatic theories, generally, first-order. These theories consist of a language (relation and function primitives) and a number of axioms.
— Relation algebras or "calculi." An exhaustive set of mutually exclusive primitive relations is given. The inferential behavior of these relations is given in transitivity tables, in the spirit of Allen (1983). These tables implement relation combination — the algebra of relations, a relation in the general sense being any disjunction of primitive relations.

Axiomatic theories are far richer in their expressive power. Indeed, only a small subclass of first-order axiomatic theories can be converted into relational algebras. On the other hand, reasoning in relation algebras, especially those based on binary relations, is made much easier by their good computational properties. Some authors use both versions of the same theory: they first present and discuss an axiomatic theory, more expressive, and then use an equivalent relational algebra for the implementation. It must be noted that, ideally, in both cases, a proof of which structures are the models of the theory should be given to fully characterize what the primitive concepts and entities are actually able to describe. Models, however, have been rarely worked out in the qualitative spatial reasoning literature.

The concrete elements of an ontology of absolute space actually are the basic spatial entities constituting the space, as well as the primitive spatial notions expressed over these entities. These two elements are actually interdependent, some notions being difficult, if not impossible, to express over some kinds of entities. We next introduce the kinds of basic entities and primitive notions that have been used for representing space. In the following section, we present several spatial representation frameworks developed in AI, classifying them according to these ontological criteria — first to the nature of spatial entities chosen as primitives, and then to the notions that are expressed.

1.2.2. ELEMENTS OF SPATIAL ONTOLOGIES

1.2.2.1. *Basic Entities*

As for time, for which there is an alternative between instant-based and period-based ontologies (van Benthem, 1983), basic spatial entities constituting absolute spaces can be of two types. On the one hand, space can be made of abstract lower-dimensional entities like points of classical geometry. On the other hand, basic entities can be extended portions of the same dimension than the whole space.

Choosing the first type of entities eases the development of theories because geometry has been investigated for a long time. Even though the objectives of AI are not those of mathematics, it helps to rely on well-known properties of the structures usually sought as intended models. Approaches based on points are presented in Section 1.3.1.

The second option does not benefit as much from mathematical results. The development of these theories is accordingly less advanced. Nevertheless, advantages are many, and much work is currently being done in this area. Extended entities are spatially more similar to the basic entities of physical or mental relative spaces. In particular, the argument of adequacy is often held by researchers aiming at modeling commensense (absolute) space. On the efficiency side, because extended entities are directly appropriate to serve as values of the location function, theories need not go higher order (for example, with sets of points as values) or be combined with an abstraction process (such as considering all objects as punctual). It is also possible for a theory based on extended entities to have a finite and still connected domain (space can be discrete without presenting gaps), thus facilitating their implementation.

The global-local option has an influence over the choice of basic entities. Point-based space can indifferently be local or global. To be accurate, in a global space points are no longer the real basic entities; these are the coordinates. Similarly, in a global space based on extended entities, the real basic entities are segments of the axes. This means that the shape of extended entities in a global space is fixed (in a Cartesian frame, rectangular or parallelipipedic), while in a local space, regions of any shape can be chosen. For extended basic entities, we then distinguish approaches where space is global and based on arrays of cells (Section 1.3.2) or tuples of intervals (Section 1.3.3), from approaches where space is local and based on regions (Section 1.3.4).

As for time, there are translation procedures between point-based ontologies and region-based ontologies. Defining one in terms of the other, for example, regions as sets of points and points as ultrafilters of regions,[5] requires the use of a higher-order language and thus is computationally unattractive. For this reason, when the knowledge to be represented bears on both kinds of entities, mixed ontologies are preferred. The domain of basic entities is then split into categories and the language includes incidence relations between them. The multidimensionality of space marks really the difference with time when more than two categories are considered, such as points, regions, lines and surfaces. As we already said, this is the case in some axiomatic theories of Euclidean geometry. Approaches based on mixed ontologies are presented in Section 1.3.5.

1.2.2.2. *Primitive Notions*
Spatial relations and properties are generally grouped into three domains: topology, orientation, and distance. Psychological studies have proved that these notions are acquired by the child successively, in this order (Piaget

and Inhelder, 1948). We now give a quick overview of these three groups of concepts. In this description, we heavily rely on mathematical concepts, principally introduced in different families of theories: topology, metric spaces, Euclidean geometry, and Cartesian geometry, which are what we have in mind when we talk about classical mathematical spaces. It must be noted that the orientation and distance groups are not clearly distinguished in these mathematical spaces. In Euclidean geometry, orientation and distance concepts are intimately related. From the standard axiomatics of Hilbert (1971), the axiom groups of incidence, order, and parallels deal only with orientation; but the other two groups, congruence and continuity, involve both orientation and distance. In metric spaces — which include the most standard mathematical spaces, as $\mathbb{R}^3$ — the real-valued distance function induces both an associated topology and orientation. Even if they are not so clearly marked out in mathematics, in AI it has proved to be fruitful to investigate topology, orientation, and distance separately, sometimes for different applicative purposes.

Of course, there are important spatial relations and properties that belong to none of these groups. These concepts are significantly more complex and accordingly much less treated in the literature. This is the case of shape properties, or morphology, which will be almost left out of the discussion because no systematic account has been proposed up to now in a qualitative manner. However, some morphological concepts have begun to be introduced on regions (see Section 1.3.4.3).

Topology.   Topological theories are generally seen as the most abstract spatial structures, the weakest geometries. Mathematically speaking, a topological space is a structure $\langle X, \Omega \rangle$ where:

 − X is a set (the points of the space)
 − Ω is a subset of 2^X (the *open* sets, or the topology)
 − Ω includes $\emptyset$ and X
 − the intersection of any two open sets (two elements of Ω) is an open set (belongs to Ω)
 − the union of any number of open sets is an open set.

A *closed* set is the complement in X of an open set.

There are several ways of looking at the spatial notions brought about by topology (Hocking and Young, 1961). Under one perspective, topology principally defines the notions of boundary and contact. An open subset of the topological space is seen as including none of its boundaries and a closed set as including all of them.[6] The *boundary* of a subset $x \subset X$, noted ∂x, is then defined as being the difference between its *closure* (the smallest closed set including it, noted $\bar{x}$) and its *interior* (the biggest open set included in it, noted $\overset{\circ}{x}$). The relation of contact or *external connection* between two subsets can be based on the sharing of boundaries. An interesting derived property is the one of being a connected subset — a one-piece space portion.

According to another view, topology essentially is the theory defining the notion of continuity. A function between two topologies is continuous if it maps an open set onto an open set. Since it characterizes invariants under continuous deformations, topology has been called the geometry of the rubber sheet. Algebraic topology defines the rank of the homology group of a subset — that is, the number of its "holes" or discontinuities in its boundary. It thus gives a somewhat rough notion of shape distinguishing a doughnut from a ball.

In representing spatial relations in other frameworks than classical topology (in particular in spaces not constituted of points as basic entities), some of these notions sometimes take a quite different meaning. For instance, in region-based spaces, contact may be modeled without calling for the notion of boundary or even that of open set. Nonetheless, theories axiomatizing contact may still be called topological because they retain most of the classical properties of contact.

In classical topology topological notions apply to subsets and imply a notion of extension[7] — contrarily to orientation or distance notions that classically apply to isolated points. As a consequence, in AI the set-theoretical notions of inclusion, overlapping, intersection, and union are often grouped with the topology cluster, even though strictly speaking these are not topological notions. What is more, they do not necessarily suppose the membership relation of set theory. When modeled directly on extended entities, they constitute what is called a *mereology* — a theory of part-whole relation (Lesniewski, 1931; Simons, 1987). Accordingly, theories modeling topological concepts without set theory, taking extended entities as basic entities, are known as *mereotopologies*.

Orientation.   We may distinguish two levels of basic orientational notions stemming from geometry. Relations of the first level are elementary in the sense that they enable the definition of relations of the second level, but in AI most authors treat orientation from the perspective of the second level only, introducing directly a complex system of relations.

First are the concepts of elementary geometry related to the notion of straight line (sometimes called arrangement): alignment between three points or incidence of a point on a line, betweenness of one point with respect to two other points and order on a line, congruence and comparisons of angles (pairs of lines or triplets of points), parallelism and orthogonality between lines. Betweenness is the primitive relation axiomatized both in Hilbert (1971) and Tarski (1959) as the basis of orientation. These concepts of elementary geometry are not easily transposed to ontologies that are not based on points.

Second, are the concepts of vectorial geometry enabling an axis (a directed line or *direction*) to establish an order throughout the space, not just on a line. This order presupposes implicitly the notion of orthogonal projection on an axis. Vectorial geometry is not restricted to point-based spaces. In global spaces, this orientational process is given a particular prominence, since the entities themselves depend ontologically on a *reference frame*, usually composed of several axes as in Cartesian geometry. Actually, reference frames are often used in local spaces as well, only implicitly through the use of binary relations. Two or three orthogonal axes (for two- or three-dimensional space) are frequent, thus yielding relations such as *is right of*, *is front-left of*, or *is Northwest of*, depending on the labeling of the reference frame axes. But more generally, a system of any number of axes dividing the space into several sectors or cones may be conceived.

In local spaces, considering orientation relations generated by a reference frame raises the problem of choosing a specific reference frame together with a labeling. Which reference frames are used? When are they appropriate? Even though it is not possible to answer them on purely spatial grounds, these questions have been debated to some extent, maybe because of their great importance in human communication, reference frames being often left implicit. These and other aspects of linguistic space are discussed in this book in Herskovits's chapter (Chapter 6). Here, let us just recall that literature distinguishes between three types of orientation:

- *Absolute orientation.* A unique, more or less arbitrary, reference frame is used. The two-dimensional reference frame of cardinal directions ⟨north/south, east/west⟩ is common in representing geographic space. The inherent reference frame of a global space yields, of course, an absolute orientation.

- *Intrinsic orientation.* The intrinsic reference frame of the reference entity (the second argument in a binary relation like *is left of*) is used. Intrinsic reference frames exist only for extended entities and originate in a variety of inherent properties of the entity: shape (particularly symmetry), motion, typical position, functional properties etc. The most common intrinsic reference frames in three dimensions consist of three axes: up/down, front/back, and left/right.

- *Contextual, extrinsic and deictic orientation.* The intrinsic reference frame of another entity, contextually salient but distinct from the reference entity, is used. When this entity is the speaker or the observer, we have a case of deictic orientation. When it is neither the speaker, nor any of the arguments of the spatial relation, orientation is called extrinsic.

Distance. In elementary geometry, the notion of *relative distance* is introduced through the relation of congruence between segments — that is, through a quaternary relation of equidistance on points: *x and y are as far apart as are z and t* (Hilbert, 1971; Tarski, 1959). Relative distance can also be introduced symbolically with the ternary relation *x is closer to y than it is to z*. This is the kind of distance most easily expressed in local spaces, whether point-based or region-based. However, what is usually called distance is the numerical function on which metric spaces are defined. More precisely, a *metric distance* is a function d mapping pairs of spatial points onto $\mathbb{R}_+$ such that $d(x, x) = 0$, $d(x, y) = d(y, x)$, and $d(x, z) \leq d(x, y) + d(y, z)$ (triangle inequality). It is worth noting that a metric space is not necessarily Euclidean. For instance, curved spaces (where parallels meet) admit of other distances.

As already mentioned, in geometry there is an inherent link between distance and orientation. Classical global spaces, having dense numerical orders on the axes, enable the definition of distance functions (Euclidean or not — that is, preserving congruence or not) that makes them metric. On the other hand, because metric distance is properly additive, it induces orientation:

$$Between(y, x, z) \equiv d(x, z) = d(x, y) + d(y, z)$$

Similarly, betweenness could, in principle, be defined in terms of the relative distance relation *is closer to* on points, exploiting an equivalent of triangle inequality (van Benthem, 1983):

$$Between(y, x, z) \equiv \forall t (t = y \lor closer(y, x, t) \lor closer(y, z, t))$$

In qualitative representations of space, a metric distance is rarely used, and, when a valued distance function is sought, it is replaced by a *discrete distance*. In discrete spaces like occupancy arrays, distance is simply a function on $\mathbb{N}_+$. In these cases, the dependency between distance and orientation is altered, and, for instance, "circles" may become squares. Of a more qualitative flavor are theories modeling concepts such as *far* or *close* or, in fact, any qualitative scale discretizing the continuous real domain. These discrete distances are sometimes called *naming distances*. Like for any other "quantity space" of qualitative physics (Bobrow, 1984), general purpose theories accounting of fuzziness and granularity phenomena may be used. However, it is in general difficult to axiomatize properly the additivity of distance and triangle inequality, thus loosing essential spatial properties and the link between distance and orientation.

Even though they are most often modeled on point-based spaces, distance concepts can be transposed to spaces based on other kinds of entities, in a rather straightforward fashion.

1.2.3. ADDITIONAL FEATURES

After choosing the ontology of a space, there are still a number of other possible general assumptions on its nature. Any of these parameters may be left unspecified, giving a more general but incomplete theory, which is computationally a drawback.

Space can be assumed to be bounded or unbounded (for any pair of points there is always a third one situated further in the same direction, or there is no maximal region), discrete or dense (between any two points there is a third one, or between any two nested open regions there is a third one), or even continuous (betweenness on points satisfies the Dedekind-cut property), and, if basic entities are extended, atomic or dissective (any region has a proper part).

All of these parameters affect of course the finite nature of the domain of the resulting theory and thus the computational properties of its implementations. For this reason, sometimes a difference is made between the intended ontology of space and the space which is actually represented. For instance, space can be assumed to be dense but *represented* as being discrete (Habel, 1994). In this case, the choice of a granularity is not intrinsic but dependent of a specific task. To really capture the "density in intension" of the intended models, the capacity of integrating various granularities in the same theory (switching granularities or combining them) is then an important further parameter.

Finally, the dimensionality of space may be fixed (and is necessarily so in global spaces), whether two-dimensional, three-dimensional, or even four-dimensional if space-time is considered.

Still other aspects can be considered if one takes into account the kind of entities one wishes to locate in space. For instance, the distinction between *table-top* space, *small-scale* space, and *large-scale* space is often made in AI and in cognitive sciences in general. Some spatial notions are more or less relevant depending on these perspectives. More important perhaps, there are ontological dependencies between properties of located objects and properties of spatial entities that can be exploited. These aspects are more deeply discussed in this book in Casati and Varzi's chapter (ontological dependencies between the materiality of objects and space, Chapter 3) and in Frank's chapter (ontological constraints on the spatial properties of geographical objects, Chapter 5).

1.3. Overview of Approaches to Spatial Representation in AI

This section presents a number of well-known or representative approaches to spatial representation that take points, cells in arrays, tuples of intervals, and regions, as basic spatial entities. It then examines approaches based on mixed ontologies and finally briefly discusses the relationship between space and time.

1.3.1. POINT-BASED SPACES

Approaches to spatial representation based on points and defining local spaces typically focus on orientation and distance concepts, since dealing with topology would require going higher order.

1.3.1.1. *Orientation*

Elementary orientation relations applied to points are at least ternary. As was noted before, the usual relation is *between*, which yields the alignment of the three points plus an ordering. Such relations have been rarely used in AI. Betweenness is axiomatized as a primitive relation in Vieu (1993) along the lines of van Benthem (1983), and also in Borgo et al. (1996a) following Tarski (1972). In these two papers, however, points are not really the basic entities of the theories; they are introduced as sets of regions or (implicitly) as centers of spheres.

Representation of orientation concepts in AI is most often tackled from the vectorial geometry point of view, which has been widely restricted to two-dimensional local spaces.[8]

Local reference frames.   Hernández (1994), Freksa (1992b), and Ligozat (1993) all express the contextual orientation of a located point with respect to a reference point, as seen from a perspective point. They apply to the reference point a local reference frame in which the frontal direction is fixed by the direction ⟨*perspective point, reference point*⟩. These authors all take the relation algebra approach and describe the inferential behavior of the primitive relations in transitivity tables.

Their approaches differ according to the orientational structure of the reference frame. Hernández uses four axes for two-dimensional space, resulting in the segmentation of the plane around the reference point into eight cone-shaped sectors, each centered around an half-axis: front, right-front, right, right-back, back, left-back, left, and left-front, yielding eight possible relations over the triplet.

Freksa uses only two axes, which segment the plane into four quadrants falling between, not around, the axes: right-front, right-back, left-back, and left-front. In addition, Freksa distinguishes the four half-axes as possible positions: front, right, back, left. This also yields eight relations, but his are quite different from Hernández's, since in this approach exact alignment between the three points may be represented. Exchanging the roles of the reference and perspective points yields a new reference frame, with an opposed frontal direction and applied now to the original perspective point. Combining the two reference frames thus obtained, Freksa gets three axes making a double cross distinguishing six areas of the plane, six half lines, and the segment between the two points — that is, thirteen different relations, rising to fifteen if we add the two distinguished positions of the reference and the perspective points (Figure 1). Ligozat (1993) generalizes this calculus with any number of axes.

Figure 1.   Freksa's fifteen relations

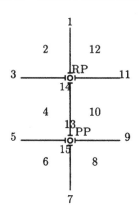

Order on angles.   Orientation relations can also be modeled with circular orders — that is, with angle comparisons in the plane. In the most basic of these orders (Schlieder, 1995), one compares the relative orientation of, again, a located point with respect to a perspective point and a reference point, through the characteristics of the angle A = ⟨*reference point, perspective point, located point*⟩. The located point is then situated either on the direction ⟨*perspective point, reference point*⟩ itself $(A = 0)$,[9] counterclockwise $(0 < A < \pi)$ from it, or clockwise $(-\pi < A < 0)$. This is nothing more than the, say, left-right orientation induced by a reference frame with a single axis. One can add the further distinction that the angle is either acute $(|A| < \pi/2)$ or obtuse, corresponding then to a reference frame with two axes, distinguishing the four quadrants left-front, left-back, right-back, and right-front (Latecki and Röhrig, 1993).

Schlieder (1993) generalizes the approach. Going around the perspective point in a predefined sense (say, counterclockwise, the positive sense), starting from the reference point (or the direction ⟨*perspective point, reference point*⟩), any number of located points (or directions ⟨*perspective point, located point*⟩) may be ordered. This order correspond to the comparison of several angles of the form ⟨*reference point, perspective point, located point*⟩. The orientational information contained in these generalized circular orders is not equivalent to the straightforward use of a local reference frame.

A representation system equivalent to circular orders is achieved by an axiomatic theory of directions in the plane (Aurnague, 1995). This theory takes directions as primitive entities, but those can be seen as equivalence classes of pairs of points, considering pairs of the kind ⟨*perspective point, located point*⟩. A ternary primitive relation $Kd(D1, D2, D3)$ is axiomatized so as to express that $D1$ is "closer" to $D2$ than to $D3$ — that is, that the absolute value of the angle ⟨$D1, D2$⟩ is smaller than that of ⟨$D1, D3$⟩. Definitions of equal, opposite, and orthogonal direction to a direction and of median direction between two directions are introduced.

These last two approaches, based on angle comparison, are more general and more qualitative than those based on local reference frames or on distinguished angle values. Indeed, in the latter two, the number of qualitative distinctions that the theory is able to make is fixed a priori. What is more, these distinctions induce discontinuities in the space on the axes of the reference frame. In Hernández (1994), it is assumed that a located point cannot fall exactly on the lines dividing the sectors, thus excluding some positions, whereas in Freksa (1992b) the same status is given to a half axis and to full quadrant, which amounts to give infinitely more precision to some positions than others. On the other hand, in generalized circular orders as well as in the theory of directions, the number of angles that can be distinguished is not fixed and rather depends on the number of located points to be compared. In other words, the precision of the theory adapts itself to the knowledge to be represented, and all points of the space are treated homogeneously. If the importance of the upper, frontal, and lateral axes in cognition justifies the use of a priori axes in a particular application, then it is easy to add some particular points or directions corresponding to these axes in the representation. To be fully general, though, these calculi still require to be extended to three-dimensional or even n-dimensional space.

1.3.1.2. *Integrating Orientation and Distance*

Qualitative distance notions have been significantly less treated than orientation, and they are usually considered together with orientation notions. According to the terminology introduced earlier, we distinguish between approaches based on relative and discrete distance.

Relative distance. It is surprising that very little work has been done modifying axiomatic Euclidean geometry, dropping some possibly undesirable properties such as continuity (Archimedes' axiom). In Vieu (1993) introduced above, betweenness for orientation is complemented by the relation of ternary relative distance relation *is closer to*. The quaternary equidistance relation may then be defined in the same theory, but the integration of orientation and distance requires further improvement.

Zimmermann (1993) adds to Freksa's orientation representation system a linear order on edges or line segments (point pairs) in order to compare their length implicitly. The division of the plane is successively refined, taking first into account the order between the three segments generated by the three points (located, reference, and perspective points), then adding the three segments generated by the orthogonal projections of the located point onto the three axes of the double cross, and lastly enriching the order along the lines of the so-called Δ-calculus (Zimmermann, 1995). It is claimed that the integration of orientation and distance is achieved. However, it is not clear exactly what the resulting system is. The relational algebra combining all distinctions is not fully described in these papers. The mapping between distance and orientation constraints — although introduced at the representation level of the relative position of the three located, reference, and perspective points — seems not to be exploited in the transitivity tables.

Discrete distance. In Frank (1992a) and in Hernández et al. (1995), qualitative "naming" distances are introduced. Both articles deal with granularity scales from the simple binary near-far scale to a totally ordered scale of n distance steps or ranges, partitioning $\mathbb{R}_+$ into n intervals. Addition (or subtraction) tables compute the distance between a and c ($d(a, c)$) from $d(a, b)$ and $d(b, c)$, where a, b, and c are aligned.[10]. Hernández et al. (1995) considers a variety of restrictions on the distance scales, such as monotonically increasing interval length along the scale, and thus obtains several composition tables. Distance addition in the general case can only be approximated by a disjunction of values. But even if triangle inequality is respected, its limit case, equality, cannot imply the collinearity of the three points. This is so because in a discrete scale, extreme values may absorb the others — for instance, $d(a, b) = $ *very close*, $d(b, c) = $ *very close* and $d(a, c) = $ *very close* are possible simultaneously, whether the three points are aligned or not. As a consequence, in these systems, full integration of distance and orientation is by definition impossible to reach.

In Hernández et al. (1995) the conditions when a particular granularity, or scale, has to be chosen are briefly discussed. Parameters such as the nature of the orientational reference frame and the size of the reference object are considered. However, the problem of how to switch granularities according to a change in perspective or how to combine information at various granularities is left aside in both approaches, while it is what is really at stake when modeling granularity.

1.3.2. SPACE AS ARRAYS

Occupancy arrays are widely used in computer vision as well as in spatial databases.[11] Arrays are nothing else but a discrete coordinate system. As global absolute spaces, they convey the three kinds of spatial information — topology, orientation, and distance (in this case, metric) — as a whole, and the relative position of any two spatial entities has to be calculated retrieving their coordinates.

This kind of spatial representation has been also been used in AI, modifying it so that a more qualitative flavor is gained, thus obtaining the so-called *symbolic arrays* (Glasgow and Papadias, 1992; Glasgow, 1993). In this approach, part of the metric and morphologic semantics of the grid is dropped, mainly preserving orientation (order) along the two or three axes and disregarding the rectangular shape and the size of the cells. Cell adjacency is interpreted in various ways depending on specific applications: it may denote the topological relation of boundary sharing but also immediate proximity, a distance concept. Inclusion is captured by a hierarchical nesting of arrays, which is also a way to capture granularity change. It is to be noted, though, that if cell adjacency denotes proximity instead of connection, then the spatial discontinuity significantly limits the possibilities of granularity refinement. The opposite process, aggregation, is also an important feature of this representational formalism: an object may be represented by several cells.

As explained earlier, arrays are, as global spaces, in a sense akin to mental images. This is developed at length in Glasgow's papers, as an argument in favor of the cognitive adequacy of symbolic arrays and their computational appropriateness to support reasoning methods analogous to mental imagery processes, like image construction, inspection, or transformation. Being a paradigmatic representation for mental images and pictorial spaces in general, arrays have been used in several works aiming at linking visual space and linguistic space (Habel, 1990; Habel, 1991; Latecki and Pribbenow, 1992). It has also been held that analogic spaces, and in particular arrays, are adequate to model what is called *diagrammatic reasoning* — that is, reasoning with diagrams or graphical representations (Glasgow et al., 1995). Constructive proofs in geometry are the paradigm of diagrammatic reasoning, but space is often taken as a metaphor for another realm (such as time or any ordered domain) so that a wide variety of application domains is considered for this kind of reasoning. In our opinion, it remains to be proved that the essential characteristic of a "pictorial" space, as opposed to a "propositional" space, which we take to be the property of being global, is indeed what makes a representation adequate to support diagrammatic reasoning (construction, combination, and transformation of diagrams), as opposed to deductive reasoning in logical frameworks. This may explain why the work covered by the term diagrammatic reasoning is actually very diverse — for instance, see Glasgow et al. (1995). In addition, it is not clear what exactly remains of the pictorial space, if metric aspects are dropped, as the authors intend. Surely, topological and orientation information remains, but it seems obvious that areas such as language and vision integration and diagrammatic reasoning should deal with some morphological aspects as well.

As a knowledge representational tool for space, the most important problem this approach encounters is that of any global space — namely, the difficulty to represent partial or vague information. The problem occurs with topology, which is dependent on orientation (for instance, to represent the fact that Spain and France share a boundary, it is necessary to know their relative orientation), as well as with orientation alone (for instance, it is impossible to store the information that Holland is north of France without also knowing that it is north of Belgium and east of Great Britain).

The representational expressiveness as well as cognitive adequacy and computational efficiency of this approach has been extensively commented in Narayanan (1993).

1:3.3. INTERVAL-BASED SPACES

After the great impact of Allen's interval calculus (Allen, 1983) in AI (see Chapter 7), there have been several (similar) intents of extending it to a multidimensional domain (Güsgen, 1989; Mukerjee, 1989; Mukerjee and Joe, 1990). In this approach, spatial regions are represented by tuples of intervals that are the projections of the regions on the axes of a given absolute reference frame. Spatial relations between rectangular regions are then expressed by a tuple of relations between two intervals for each axis, in the relation algebra formalism. Since the relations belong to the set of Allen's thirteen relations (*before, meets, overlaps, starts, started-by, during, contains, equals, finishes, finished-by, overlapped-by, met-by, after*), only topological and orientational information is accounted for.

Even though intervals are situated relationally with respect to each other, one can consider that space is more global than local. Indeed, using intervals as coordinates, vectorial orientation is given the priority, and topology depends on it. But mereotopology is more thoroughly accounted for than in symbolic arrays. Direct representation of region overlap is possible, and one distinguishes between inclusion in the interior (*during*) and inclusion at the border (*starts* or *finishes*). In a way, this approach extends the symbolic array one in dropping at the same time discreteness and any remaining metric aspect. Relational, possibly partial, orders along the axes replace numerical orders. However, since aggregation has not been considered, all regions are rectangular (or parallelepipedic) shaped. As in arrays, they are all aligned along the axes of an arbitrary reference frame.

For those applications domain meeting these restrictions, this theory has the advantages of Allen's calculus: topology and orientation information is freed from any distance and length information, and reasoning is eased by the existence of efficient algorithms and transitivity tables.

The extension to nonaligned rectangles has been considered in Mukerjee and Joe (1990) for two-dimensional space. Space is then local, as each rectangle creates its own local intrinsic reference frame based on the knowledge of which side is the "front" of the rectangle. The ease of reasoning, however, is lost because there are more possible relations between two rectangles that are nevertheless less precise, so that the transitivity table is bigger and presents more ambiguity. There is an important additional drawback at the expressivity level. The angle between the frontal axes of the two rectangles is determined with an inaccuracy up to $\pi/2$ degrees, which yields a high imprecision. Further, topological information is completely lost. The same relation between two rectangles may describe situations in which one rectangle includes, overlaps, touches, or is disjoint from the other. The usefulness of this extension is then really dubious.

1.3.4. REGION-BASED SPACES

Contrarily to tuples of intervals, regions are extended entities of any shape. This property makes the representational systems based on regions much closer to spatial cognition, as we already said. In addition, they constitute the only first-order theories that deal properly with topological concepts. For these reasons, region-based theories and calculi can be viewed as the right extension of Allen's calculus for dimensions higher than one, regions being to material objects and space portions such as "the inside of the glass" or holes, what intervals (or periods) are to events and states. Actually, the notion of region is independent from dimensionality, *extended* entity meaning only having a nonempty interior — that is, having the same dimension as the whole space. However, the word *region* is commonly used for spaces of dimension higher than one only.

Most existing axiomatic theories stem from the work of Whitehead and Clarke on mereotopologies in formal ontology (Whitehead, 1929; Clarke, 1981; Clarke, 1985). This area of research has regained attention lately (a good survey is present in Varzi (1994; 1996a)) and has become quite developed in AI as well, as evidenced by the chapters by Casati and Varzi (Chapter 3), Cohn, Bennett, Gooday and Gotts (Chapter 4), and Galton (Chapter 10) in this book.

Whitehead and Clarke's theories were based on a unique mereotopological primitive relation C (connection), axiomatized as symmetric, reflexive, and extensional. Some authors now choose to separate mereology from topology with two primitive relations, such as proper part and contact or external connection (Borgo et al., 1996a). Still some others introduce boundaries in their domain, thus obtaining mixed ontologies (see Section 1.3.5 below). In Clarke's theory as well as in most others, it is possible to isolate an exhaustive set of eight mutually exclusive mereotopological relations (DC, EC, PO, TPP, NTPP, TPP-1, NTPP-1, EQ) and thus transform the axiomatic theory into a relation algebra (Randell and Cohn, 1989). See Figure 2.

Figure 2. RCC eight relations

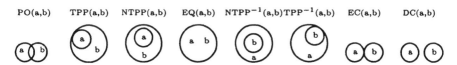

PO(a,b)   TPP(a,b)   NTPP(a,b)   EQ(a,b)   NTPP^{-1}(a,b)   TPP^{-1}(a,b)   EC(a,b)   DC(a,b)

For the mereological notions, Boolean operators of union, intersection, and complement are added, sometimes based on a general fusion operator (Clarke, 1981) as in standard mereology. For topological concepts on regions, two different approaches have been taken.

1.3.4.1. *Topology on Regions with and without Boundaries*
The first approach fully exploits the classical topological distinctions of open and closed regions. The introduction of interior and closure operators, in a way similar to that of Boolean operators, is made possible in theories where the complement definition and the axiomatics on C (or EC) are such that a region and its complement are not connected. This is the case in earlier theories such as Whitehead's and Clarke's.

Contrary to what Clarke seems to have thought, these theories do not capture just any standard topology restricted to extended regions — that is, without any region having an empty interior. Asher and Vieu (1995) have given the models of the theory presented in Clarke (1981). These are topologies restricted to nonempty *regular* regions[12]. However, as shown independently by several authors (Biacino and Gerla, 1991; Vieu, 1991), this theory, when extended with a certain definition of points as sets of regions (Clarke, 1985) (thus going higher order), has the unexpected result of having the same models as standard mereology (EC becomes an empty predicate). But it is still possible to give a more complex definition of points that preserves topological properties (Asher and Vieu, 1995).

With the topological notions of open and closed regions, different notions of contact may be defined: external connection between two closed regions or joint, contact between a closed region and an open one (as between a region and its complement), and weak contact or adjacency in which two closed regions touch without being connected. Contrary to the first two kinds of contact, weak contact implies a discontinuity — that is, the sum of the two regions is not connected[13] (Asher and Vieu, 1995). It must be noted that weak contact has an extension only in nondense models.

The same distinctions are introduced in Fleck (1996), which does not present an axiomatic mereotopological theory on regions but directly mathematical structures. The author shows how to constrain a classical topology on $\mathbb{R}^n$ and extract the right subsets corresponding to regions. In this work, weak contact is modeled as holding between two open regions whose common boundary has been deleted from the underlying space. The two regions are thus both not connected and zero distance apart. Two important differences can be noted between these structures and the structures that are models of the theory presented in Asher and Vieu (1995). On the one hand, even with deleted points, the remaining space may still keep the density of $\mathbb{R}^n$. On the other hand, a weak contact implies not only that the sum of the two regions is disconnected but also that the whole space is disconnected because space has gaps where objects touch. Change in touching is then difficult to cope with, and this solution seems to be more relevant for a relative space approach than for an absolute one. However, if the relative approach is in fact taken, then the appropriateness of $\mathbb{R}^n$ with its classical topological and metric structure needs at least to be discussed. For their part, pure mereotopological theories do not constrain the dimensionality of space, neither its Euclidean character. They thus have models that are classical topologies on $\mathbb{R}^n$, and models that are not (Lemon, 1996).

1.3.4.2. *Topology on Nondifferentiated Regions*

The second approach rejects the basic topological distinction of open and closed regions, on the grounds that there is no cognitive evidence of which regions corresponding to some location (for instance of physical objects) should be open and which closed. An additional concern regarding the theories of the previous approach is that, although they are not equal, there is no region that embodies the mereological difference between $\bar{x}$ and $\overset{\circ}{x}$ (the boundary). The best-known work in the approach based on nondifferentiated regions is the much developed axiomatic theory by Cohn's group in Leeds, the so-called RCC theory or calculus (Randell et al., 1992a; Gotts et al., 1996), although their first work belonged to the previous approach (Randell and Cohn, 1989). A special attention is given to computational issues, and the corresponding relation algebra is systematically derived. The chapter by Cohn, Bennett, Gooday and Gotts in this book (Chapter 4) thoroughly describes this work. RCC is also originally based on Clarke's theory, but a slight change in the definition of complement makes all regions (externally) connected to their complements. In the mereotopological part of the theory, the set of eight mutually exclusive relations described above is derived. The models are probably similar to those of Clarke's theory restricted to closed nonempty regular subsets, but no formal proof has been published.

Rejecting the open-closed distinction has a number of drawbacks. Different kinds of contact cannot be distinguished. More importantly perhaps, all models are then nonatomic, which is problematic on a computational point of view as well as on a cognitive one.

Quite similar results appear in Egenhofer and Franzosa (1991), taking the relation algebra perspective from the start. Observing that any subset x of a classical topological space can be represented with the pair of subsets $\langle \overset{\circ}{x}, \partial x \rangle$, the authors describe topological relations between two subsets through the emptiness or nonemptiness of the two by two intersections of their interiors and boundaries. This method defines sixteen relations between subsets that are reduced to eleven if the domain is restricted to (subsets corresponding to) closed extended regions and to nine if further restricted to regular regions — assumed in the paper to be what corresponds to relevant space portions of physical space. These nine are the eight relations described above, where partial overlap (PO) is split into two relations depending on the emptiness of the intersection of the boundaries of the two subsets. So, if the domain is further restricted to connected regions without holes,[14] the nine relations are reduced to the usual eight.

In the same approach that models contact without taking into account openness and closedness, there is the older work by Fleck on adjacency structures on "cells" and fuzzy spaces (Fleck, 1987). Cell structures differ from region structures in that, like in occupancy arrays, there is no mereological relations between cells — that is, no cell contains or overlaps another cell. Fleck shows that if adjacency sets (sets of cells sharing the same contact zone) are classified according to the dimension of the shared zone (point, line, surface, etc.), then adjacency structures over a cell partition of $\mathbb{R}^n$ fully characterize the topology of this space.

Actually, a recent trend tries to introduce distinctions between kinds of connections and to classify connectedness in mereotopological theories, whether with or without the open-closed distinction. The notions of "strong connection" (connection along a spatial entity of dimension $n - 1$ in n-dimensional space) and "simple" region or "well-connected" region (one-piece region such that any two halves of it are strongly connected) are introduced in Gotts (1994b) and Borgo et al. (1996a). In this last paper, mereological notions are introduced with the part primitive (P), and *simple region* is the chosen primitive predicate to introduce topological ones — without the open-closed distinction, thus this theory clearly belongs to the second approach.

The definition of topological shape (connectivity order, which distinguishes between "doughnuts" and "balls") has proven to be possible on the sole primitive of connection (Gotts, 1994b; Gotts et al., 1996); this definition is also independent of the kind of approach chosen.

If region-based ontologies are clearly well suited to represent mereotopological information, they seem to be less well suited for orientation and distance information; or at least these notions on regions have been much less investigated up to now.

1.3.4.3. *Orientation*

The direct modeling of the basic arrangement relations such as alignment or betweenness on any kind of regions is not straightforward. The extension of regions makes it difficult to consider a unique direction of alignment between three regions and establish properties such as the transitivity of alignment.

However, orientation is involved in morphology, at least implicitly. First attempts to model morphology on regions can be found in two approaches. First, the convex-hull operator has been axiomatized in RCC. It enables a number of other concepts based on orientation and topology, such as "inside" (Randell and Cohn, 1989), and morphological aspects based on the position and number of concavities (Cohn, 1995) to be defined. In principle, betweenness on regions should be definable in terms of convex-hull as well. It remains to be proved that its desirable properties can be recovered.

In another approach, spheres[15] are characterized on the basis of a primitive relation of congruence between regions (Borgo et al., 1996a). In this work, basic orientation notions on regions are then axiomatized in two steps. Exploiting the correspondence between a sphere and a point (its center), the authors first transpose Hilbert's classical axiomatic geometry on points to spheres. Geometrical notions are then extended to any kind of region.

Working out the models of these two theories remains to be done. In addition, it is not clear that all the desired properties of either convex-hull or congruence are captured — that is, that these morphological notions on which orientation depend are properly axiomatized. Indeed, in Lemon (1996), it is shown that the axiomatization of convex-hull in the language of RCC must be dependent on the dimension of the space, which is not the case in RCC theory up to now.

The application of vectorial orientation concepts originally introduced on points has also been transposed to regions. Approaches choosing this option are in a way similar to the local version of multidimensional extension of Allen's calculus. Nevertheless, since orientation is there added to topology instead of being the sole primitive notion, the shape of regions is not a priori constrained, and topological relations are correctly treated with their own primitives. In these works, regions are assumed to be connected. In Hernández (1994), the full relative position of two two-dimensional regions is given by a pair of one of the standard eight mereotopological relations and one of the eight sector orientation relations (cf. Section 1.3.1.1).[16] The local reference frame yielding the orientation relations is modified to take into account the extension of the reference object but not that of the located object. And, as regards orientation, regions are supposed to be approximated by rectangles. Even though interesting deductions can be drawn when mixing topology and orientation, this approach is still quite restricted and cannot be easily extended to deal with morphology. In Aurnague (1995), the algebra of directions presented above (cf. Section 1.3.1.1) is combined with Clarke's calculus on regions. The relative orientation between two regions, along one direction, is given by a ternary version of Allen's relations, thus implicitly comparing the intervals that would result from a projection of the two regions on a straight line oriented by the direction.

1.3.4.4. *Distance*

Distance on regions has received even less attention than orientation, and in particular, it has not been considered in RCC yet. A pseudo-metric space on regions has been proposed in Gerla (1990), but distance is not qualitative in this work.

A relative distance concept between points may be adapted to regions and linked to mereotopology. The ternary relation *is closer to* would then compare the shortest distances between regions. The null distance between regions may be defined either as the smallest distance or as occurring between regions in contact. It has to be noted that difficulties appear when trying to adapt triangle inequality, because the extension of the intermediate region has to be taken into account. Thus the link between alignment and distance is not easily recovered. This may explain why this approach has not been explored up to now.

In Borgo et al. (1996a) the notion of sphere, together with mereotopological primitives and the morphological relation of congruence (on which sphere is also defined), gives in principle a powerful means to deal with distance. At present, only granularity aspects have been integrated in the theory (Borgo et al., 1996b).

1.3.5. SPACES WITH MIXED ONTOLOGIES

Some approaches are based on entities of various dimensionality. Their spatial ontologies mix extended and nonextended entities, without assuming interdefinability — for instance, without assuming that regions are sets of points or points sets of regions. Incidence relationship between entities of different categories replace ontological dependency.

Mereotopology on regions and lower-dimension entities.   The motivations behind these approaches are twofold. On the one hand, some authors hold a cognitive justification before caring about ontological parsimony. They argue that humans unproblematically handle both real and abstract spatial entities in everyday spatial reasoning. In Gotts (1996b) and Galton (1996), any range of dimensions can be modeled. Gotts (1996b) chooses a unique asymmetrical primitive of incidence *includes a chunk of* holding between entities of possibly different dimensions, whereas Galton (1996) uses a part mereological primitive holding only between entities of the same dimension and a topological primitive *bounds.* Theories such as these should also in principle be able to define spatial concepts directly on the best-fit entities: topology on extended entities, and alignment and distance on points. It must be noted, though, that only mereotopological notions have been axiomatized in this approach up to now.

On the other hand, the ontological parsimony lost on the domain can actually be recovered on primitive concepts. Some authors are motivated by the ontological concern of having few, as general as possible, primitive notions. For instance, mereotopology can be axiomatized on regions and points with a mereological primitive only (Eschenbach and Heydrich, 1993; Eschenbach, 1994), assuming an additional primitive categorization (for example, with a *is a region* predicate). Another approach is taken in Smith (1993; ming). Smith axiomatizes mereotopology on regions and *boundaries* (entities of any lower dimension). His theory is based on two primitive relations, a mereological and a topological one, and no a priori categorization is made on the domain: *is a boundary* is a defined predicate. In these two theories, no attempt is made to model a range of dimensions of more than two categories.

Clementini and DiFelice (1995) mainly look for mathematical expressivity. Exploiting further the approach taken in Egenhofer and Franzosa (1991) (see Section 1.3.4.2), they consider the possible mereotopological relationships between two-dimensional regions and boundaries (lines) in classical point-set topology. Several representational methods are explored and compared, with set intersection, the three topological functions of interior, exterior, and boundary, and the dimension of the entities, as basic ontological primitives. The representation based on five primitive predicates (*touch, in, cross, overlap, disjoint*) and on two boundary functions is favored.

Geometry in the Qualitative Segmentation of Cartesian Space.   An older tradition in AI assumed a global space, in general Cartesian space, as the underlying ontology for space. There, points (actually, coordinates) were the basic primitive entities. Within this ontology of space, higher-dimension entities such as regions are in principle defined as sets of points. However, in practice, to be able to reason qualitatively, the representations include several classes of entities. Some spatial relations, like topological ones, are introduced directly over regions and are axiomatized more or less independently of the fact that they are sets of points and more locally than globally (without relying on the Cartesian frame of reference). In these approaches, the intended ontology of space is point-based, but the ontology of the representation actually is a mixed one. Forbus's and Davis's important work aiming at qualitatively modeling space and motion can be seen from this point of view (Davis, 1988; Davis, 1990; Forbus, 1983; Forbus, 1995).

In Forbus (1983; 1995), the duality of this ontology is made explicit by using both a *metric diagram*, which is a bounded piece of two-dimensional Cartesian space ($\mathbb{R}^2$), and a *place vocabulary*, which is a local space with a mixed ontology of points, line segments, and regions. The place vocabulary segments the underlying metric diagram into space portions that are qualitatively meaningful with respect to both the static objects occupying space and the mechanical characteristics of the motion to be described. The assumption that space, whether physical or perceptual, is global, point-based, and essentially metric and that qualitative spatial representations are necessarily approximations with specific points of view of this underlying space, seems to have led the author together with other researchers to hold the so-called *poverty conjecture*: *there is no problem-independent purely qualitative representation of space* (Forbus et al., 1987; Forbus et al., 1991). Fortunately, now that a lot of work has been carried out in AI on representations of space based on other ontologies, as this chapter and this whole book should show, such a pessimistic statement has become outdated. However, it would be very interesting to investigate how the process of constructing the right place vocabulary from a particular metric diagram and for a particular task, can be analyzed. Constructing Voronoi diagrams seems to be a possible solution in some cases (Edwards, 1993). More generally, this problem must be related to the design task in spatial reasoning (see Section 1.4.3).

In Davis (1988; 1990), the separation between the underlying global space and its qualitative representation is less clear. The choice of classical

Cartesian space (here $\mathbb{R}^3$) as the underlying space is motivated by the fact that, up to now, no alternative theory to Euclidean geometry has been proposed that thoroughly and consistently models all aspects of space. In reasoning qualitatively about space, this work indeed relies on a high number of more or less well-known topological and geometrical theorems, set in a logical framework. However, it does not clearly expound the axiomatic theory of space actually used. The logical language itself (the ontological categories, the primitive predicates and functions) is not clearly circumscribed. Nevertheless, we believe that there are at least two reasons to clearly give such a formal framework. First, there are several alternative axiomatizations of Euclidean geometry, semantically equivalent but not ontologically nor computationally equivalent. In order to be implementable, the theory actually used must be made explicit. Second, the author uses a number of restrictions on classical topology or geometry (such as spatial regions that can be occupied by material objects must be regular) which could be integrated in the theory, yielding a less general thus more efficient representational framework. Working out an appropriate axiomatics for a theory presenting spatial properties such as those used by Davis, without taking for granted topological and geometrical theorems, is in fact the main goal of the field we have been covering up to now.

1.3.6. SPACE AND TIME OR SPACE-TIME?

Lastly, let us say a short word about approaches combining space and time. As is shown in the next section, reasoning about space often involves reasoning about change in spatial configurations, thus reasoning about space and time. When used with this purpose, the representational frameworks above have usually been extended by a separate temporal dimension or a set of temporal relations, relying on previous classical works in temporal reasoning. This is the case in Galton's chapter in this book, for instance (Chapter 10). In this quite recent work, an essential aspect of space and time integration — namely possible transitions from one spatial configuration to another or continuity of motion — is analyzed and modeled qualitatively.

However, much more is to be said to thoroughly integrate space and time in qualitative representations. First, we believe that the very fact that space and time are two clearly separated realms should be discussed. Many motion concepts — like spinning, rolling, sliding, following, going around — do not involve just change or transitions between two spatial situations. They directly hold over trajectories or "histories" in Hayes's terminology (Hayes, 1985b) — that is, four-dimensional spatiotemporal entities. Some describe the intrinsic shape of a history; others describe complex spatiotemporal relations between two histories.[17] New theories based on spatiotemporal basic entities and spatiotemporal primitive relations could be obtained. It may then be possible to define space and time — that is, purely spatial or purely temporal relations. However, it is clear that constructing such theories is really a hard problem.

Second, even if one considers space and time separately, it seems that the question of the existence of some ontological dependencies throughout the two realms should be addressed. For instance, when is it sensible to keep the following "natural" correspondence? If space is point-based, then time will be instant-based; if space is region-based, then time will be interval-based; if space is global, then time will be just another dimensional axis. It must be noted that authors do not always adopt this kind of homogeneity. On the contrary, Galton's work shows that representing continuous motion on spatial regions requires a mixed temporal ontology of instants and intervals.

To the best of our knowledge, such spatiotemporal ontological questions have only begun to be addressed, and consequently, little work has been done on qualitative representations of space-time.

1.4. Classes of Spatial Reasoning

It must be noted from the start that there is no such a thing as a "spatial logic" field, that can be compared to the temporal logic field. Problems of spatial reasoning involving the change in truth value of a proposition according to a change in location in space have been rarely tackled. von Wright (1979) constitutes a notable exception and proposes a modal logic of spatial operators such as *somewhere* or *nearby*. A very recent work sets up some requirements for modal spatial logics of this kind (Lemon, 1996). In short, spatial reasoning has little to do with a three-dimensional equivalent of reasoning on persistence, action, and change or at least, this is the case up to now.

Nevertheless, spatial reasoning can be seen as a much older field of AI than spatial representation. Much work done in path planning, in motion prediction, and in shape recognition belongs to this field without any doubt. But on the other hand, spatial representation being a far younger issue, most work in spatial reasoning has been done without using the qualitative representations of space described above. As a consequence, the correspondence and the potential mutual enrichment between the two fields have not been fully exploited. And in fact, maybe because of not having carefully considered the ontological issue of spatial representation, spatial reasoning is a field that has not been systematically structured in a widely admitted fashion. This section aims only at describing a possible way of structuring the field of spatial reasoning and not at describing in detail the work reported. Whenever possible, the focus will be given to reasoning with respect to the representational frameworks described in the previous section.

The point of view adopted here tries to group approaches with respect to how they handle spatial knowledge and spatial representations. Only in a second step does it consider classes of problems linked to application domains. In this light, the main objectives adopted by a particular approach to reasoning over spatial knowledge may be

- Exploiting the spatial information and knowledge contained in a representation (deduction),
- Changing a representation into a different format (translation and interpretation), and
- Constructing a representation according to several constraints (design).

1.4.1. DEDUCTION WITHIN REPRESENTATIONS OF SPACE

The most basic reasoning task is to exploit the spatial knowledge and spatial information encoded inside a representational framework. Two cases can be distinguished according to the completeness or incompleteness of this knowledge and information.

1.4.1.1. *Simple Deduction*
The first case of deduction aims at making explicit a fact already implicit in the representation, by exploiting properties of spatial relations, often combining two or more explicit facts. This is necessary in local spaces, where not all information is explicitly encoded, but not in global spaces in which spatial relations can be directly "read" or at least calculated numerically. The paradigmatic case of this kind of deduction, if not the most simple case, is theorem proving in axiomatic theories of space. The efficiency of such a task lies mainly on the choice of an adequate ontology. From this standpoint, higher order representations are to be avoided. But first-order theories do not necessarily guarantee tractability. In order to significantly enhance the computational ease of simple deduction, the field has generalized the use of relational algebras and *transitivity tables* or *composition tables* (see Section 1.2.1.2). Transitivity tables encode all possible compositions of relations, which have been computed once and for all. Thus, they replace theorem proving by a simple look-up operation. This method, originally developed in the field of temporal reasoning, is described and applied in Cohn et al.'s chapter of this book (Chapter 4) as well as in Freksa (1992b), Randell and Cohn (1989), Randell et al. (1992a), Egenhofer (1991), Hernández (1994), Grigni et al. (1995), Zimmermann (1993), among others.

Another way to reduce the computational complexity of general theorem proving is to apply constraint satisfaction methods, as done also in Hernández (1994) and Grigni et al. (1995). Converting first-order theories into propositional intuitionistic or modal logics is still another method that has been applied to acquire decidability (Bennett, 1994b; Nebel, 1995).

1.4.1.2. Deduction on Partial or Uncertain Information and Extrapolation

When information or knowledge is incomplete or uncertain, one can try to infer possible facts on the basis of hypotheses on the structure of space or space-time.

In static space, one of the main problems concerns the vagueness or the uncertainty of region boundaries or, if the ontology is boundary-free, on the vagueness of the relationship between regions. Freksa (1991) first suggested applying *neighborhood structures* previously introduced in the temporal domain (Freksa, 1992a) to the spatial domain. These structures, which indeed have many applications (see below), were assumed to serve as a basis for reasoning under uncertainty. The so-called "egg-yolk representation" considers disjunctions of possible relations between regions, building on the RCC theory and indeed exploiting neighboring properties between possible relations (Cohn and Gotts, 1996a) (see also Cohn et al.'s chapter in this book, Chapter 4). Another approach applies nonmonotonic logic to spatial extrapolation, trying to "fill in" holes of uncertainty, in a fashion akin to persistence in time (Asher and Lang, 1994). This kind of work indicates a possible way to study spatial logics. Introducing the possibility of dealing with incomplete information in geographical information systems would be an important application domain.

Dealing with uncertainty in space-time has yielded a much more developed research trend — that of spatial envisionment or motion extrapolation. The aim is to simulate the spatiotemporal behavior of, in general, solid objects or more simply to predict the result of a motion. This domain of research exploits not only theories of space and time but also physical theories, such as mechanics. Three main approaches can be distinguished. The first, usually called *qualitative kinematics* adopts the general methodology of qualitative physics. State-graphs based on a particular segmentation of a Cartesian space (see Section 1.3.5) are exploited in several projects, each state-graph being highly task-dependent (Forbus, 1983; Forbus, 1995; Faltings, 1990; Forbus et al., 1991) No spatial or mechanical properties are applied in an explicit way, as the authors themselves claim to be impossible in the poverty conjecture. In addition to being thus a hardly generalizable approach, it must be noted that the complexity of simulation in the state-graphs increases rapidly with the number of static and moving objects.

The second approach applies the theorem-proving method. Davis (1988) does it in the framework of a logical model of topology, classical geometry, and mechanics (see Section 1.3.5). Nielsen (1988) exploits logical mechanical postulates in a similar framework but dramatically simplifies the coordinate space for vectors, using three values only (-,0,+), in the more classical spirit of qualitative physics. The logical approach is also adopted in naive physics, but with the aim to reason about the world in a similar fashion to how people do (Hayes, 1985b; Hayes, 1985a). The theory of mental space-time (the theory of spatial and temporal relations holding on *histories* that naive physics is supposed to use) has not been fully developed, though.

The third approach, more recent, tries to systematically capture in neighborhood structures, continuity graphs, or transition graphs, the continuity of motion as a general property of spatial relations (Hernández, 1993; Cui et al., 1992; Galton, 1993) (see also Cohn et al.'s and Galton's chapters in this book, Chapters 4 and 10). Two spatial relations are neighbors if a continuous change can yield a direct transition from one relation to the other. From these abstract graphs one can then derive the particular state-graph corresponding to a specific envisionment task. Even where orientation is taken into account, it must be noted that it is purely static orientation. Dynamic orientation is not represented, and as a consequence, reasoning on directions of motion, which is obviously a very important aspect of motion prediction, has not been tackled in this approach.

1.4.2. TRANSLATION BETWEEN SPATIAL REPRESENTATIONS

Converting information represented in one kind of spatial representation framework into another of another kind is another class of spatial reasoning.

1.4.2.1. *Language and Vision Integration.*

This area significantly overlaps the fields of computer vision, shape, and object recognition, which will not be discussed here because they are almost all based on global numerical representations of space and computational geometry algorithms (see, for example, Marr (1982), Ballard and Brown (1982), and Chen (1990). It is nonetheless interesting to mention here work aiming at integrating language and vision, an area that is growing lately (McKevitt, 1996). It draws on previous research done in both computer vision and natural language processing (understanding and generation). Clearly, the most important work on this topic has been done within the project VITRA over the last ten years (Wahlster, 1987; André et al., 1988; Herzog and Wazinski, 1994; Maass, 1995). There as in (Olivier et al., 1994), the numerical 2D representation of images is also used as the basic spatial representation for encoding the semantics of spatial expressions.

However, from a cognitive point of view as well as from a formal ontological point of view, language and vision integration raises its own classes of problems. Combining a global space, numerical or not, adequate to represent visual space, and a local space, more adequate for linguistic space, leads to interesting theoretical developments in spatial representation and, more generally, in hybrid reasoning (Habel, 1990; Latecki and Pribbenow, 1992; Habel et al., 1995; Borillo and Pensec, 1995). Work in this area, which we believe to have only begun to appear, exploits sudies on cognitive space — for instance, Herskovits's (Chapter 6) — in a systematic way. It will most probably in turn induce progress in the fields of high-level vision and the processing of spatial expressions.

1.4.2.2. *Change in Perspective or Granularity.*
It is also worth discussing here reasoning concerning change of point of view or granularity, although a single representational framework is sometimes used, and thus it could be considered as merely a special case of deduction.

Change in perspective is a frequent operation affecting orientation relations. In natural language, for instance, one often finds switches from an intrinsic reference frame to a deictic one (or the other way around), or if deictic orientation is maintained, the speaker may change in position so that the perspective point may change. These transformation are, of course, important as well in all domains where point of view is important. Hernández (1993; 1994) gives an account of how these operations can be modeled within the kind of representational framework presented in Section 1.3.1.1.

Dealing with granularity and granularity change is a very important aspect of qualitative reasoning. A few generic solutions have been proposed, and one of them applied to a (nonmetric) global space (Hobbs, 1985; Hobbs et al., 1987). In this approach, the grain is an explicit parameter. This is also the case in (Borgo et al., 1996b), where granularity is defined in a region-based local space (see Section 1.3.4.4). There, the "grain" is a particular entity chosen as a reference, identified by a predicate.

But there is another way to deal with granularity: implicitly, with operators switching between several subrepresentations. On the one hand, the domain of entities may vary in cardinality, as more or fewer spatial entities are distinguished in the different, discrete, subrepresentations. For instance, an atomic region may become nonatomic if one distinguishes several parts in it, and conversely, a nonatomic region may become atomic if its parts are no longer distinguished; the cells of the arrays may be subdivided into smaller cells or grouped into a unique bigger cell; in a nondense space of points, points may be added or removed. The hierarchical structures that have been introduced for array representations enable this kind of switch in granularity (Samet, 1984; Samet, 1989; Glasgow, 1993). A modal operator of refinement together with its converse has also been introduced on a region-based mereotopology, in particular to deal with the relativity of weak contact (Asher and Vieu, 1995) (see Section 1.3.4.1). In mereotopologies based on mixed ontologies, it would be interesting to try to model the abstraction process of seeing a region as a surface, line or point and, conversely, the refinement process of, for example, seeing a point as an extended entity. We believe that modal operators could be introduced in a similar fashion.

On the other hand, the domain of entities being fixed, the spatial relations may vary, some relations being considered as potentially coarser than others (for instance, contact taken to hold at a coarse granularity, is supposed to possibly disappear at a closer look). Euzenat (1995) exploits again neighborhood structures in an interval-based representation. Here, in fact, granularity is just another way to apprehend uncertainty.

1.4.3. DESIGN

Finally, it is impossible not to mention the class of problems related to the construction of spatial or spatiotemporal configurations filling certain requirements. This belongs to the general area of design and decision in AI and involves obtaining new spatial representations with additional entities.

This area includes one of the most important spatial problem humans have to solve a great part of their time — namely, route-finding. Indeed, for years most of the work in spatial reasoning has been done in this area. As said earlier, this large area cannot be covered here. Let us just recall that literature distinguishes between path planning at a small scale and route planning at a larger scale and add a word on the kind of spatial representations used to perform design in space-time. Path planning or motion planning uses numerical spatial representations, fitting the data robots are able to collect from their environment through sensors. Consequently, numerical global spaces are widely used. A variety of computational geometry algorithms and search algorithms operating on these representations have been developed. A classical, representative approach is based on a configuration-space representation — a dense coordinate space in which the robot's position is reduced to a point by appropriate transformations on the environment (Lozano-Pérez, 1983). Discrete global spaces (arrays) as well as local spaces based on cells and an adjacency relation, sometimes hierarchized to optimize search, have also been used (Slack and Miller, 1987; Fujimura and Samet, 1989). For a review of this area, see, for example, Latombe (1990) and Burger and Bhanu (1992). In route planning in a larger-scale environment, or navigation, the robot has to reason over spatial representations that do not need to directly match the sensor data. A classical approach is based on a *cognitive map* — a local spatial representation inspired by cognitive psychology results, whose mixed ontology combine regions, points and lines (or paths) into a network (Kuipers, 1978; Kuipers and Levitt, 1988; Levitt and Lawton, 1990). Search algorithms exploit the hierarchy created in the graph by part-whole relations over regions and incidence between points and regions. Besides route planning, gathering information to complete the cognitive map is an important issue addressed in this work as well.

Design in pure space, or space planning, is relevant to several domains of application, including architecture and land management. It covers a class of problems such as how to fit a room with furniture or how to design the plan of a new site. Here too, a variety of search methods have been applied to different kinds of spatial representations. Constraint satisfaction methods applied to local spaces have given interesting results (Baykan and Fox, 1987; du Verdier, 1993).

1.5. Conclusions

Much progress has been made in the search for new spatial ontologies and new spatial representational frameworks in the past few years, and we hope this chapter gives a good overview of this progress. Nevertheless, obtaining cognitively more adequate spatial representations is still essential for applications in natural language processing and multimodal interfaces. Constructing a complete representation of physical space in which a variety of qualitative reasoning tasks can be performed is still an open issue. What is more, reasoning on both kinds of spaces, commonsense and physical, is of a crucial importance — for instance, in geographical information systems. Looking for most generic theories of space or considering how to integrate several representations and looking for translation methods between different representations are possible ways to address this last issue. From these three points of view, new developments in spatial representation and in spatial reasoning are needed.

Several major directions of research already engaged toward this goal can be sketched:

- To look systematically for nonclassical theories of space, taking up theories already proposed in mathematics or developing new theories. This could be done with all kinds of ontologies, based on points, extended entities, and mixed ones. We believe that the full integration of topology, distance, and orientation concepts should be focused on. In particular, a first-order axiomatization of Euclidean geometry based on extended entities should be achieved. This may not guarantee that morphological concepts are easily handled in the theory, so systematic theories of shape should be developed, looking for adequate primitive concepts. With the aims of modeling mental space and obtaining a computationally effective theory, we must work out non-Euclidean geometries as well — for instance, dropping density or properly dealing with the variety of commonsense contact and boundary notions. This is one of the main lines of research adopted now in the field of qualitative spatial reasoning, of which the work described in Cohn et al.'s chapter in this book (Chapter 4) is an excellent representative. In this domain, there is an increasing awareness, if not a complete integration, of developments along a parallel line of research in formal ontology of space, for the great benefit of the discipline (see, for example, Varzi (1996a) and Casati and Varzi chapter, Chapter 3).

— To integrate and exploit non-purely spatial properties in theories of space. A way toward this goal is to consider seriously relative space — that is,theories of spatial relations on concrete entities — instead of abstract purely spatial entities. Alternatively, we could study the properties of the localizing function with respect to the properties of the entities located in an absolute space — that is to say, investigate the ontological dependencies between space and other realms such as matter. This approach may cast a new light on the choice of adequate ontologies of absolute spaces in the previous direction of research. Casati and Varzi's chapter in this book (Chapter 3) clearly opens this line of research, to which Aurnague and Vieu (1993) and Borgo et al. (1996b) have also contributed. Further investigating which ontological categories are worth considering (for instance, refining the dichotomy material-immaterial entities) may be done exploiting, for example, results in linguistics, cognitive psychology, or application domains involving physical space. Frank's and Herskovits's chapters in this book (Chapter 5 and 6) contribute toward this goal.

— To consider space-time as an integrated realm. Theories of motion based on histories as basic entities and genuine primitive spatiotemporal concepts must be developed. It is difficult to claim that this line of research has really begun, but work like that reported in Galton's chapter in this book (Chapter 10)could help start it.

— To develop spatial logics where connectives have a spatial (or spatiotemporal) meaning, not just to obtain more tractable version of first-order theories of space, but as frameworks for reasoning about space under uncertainty, or as frameworks for diagrammatic reasoning — that is, reasoning on constructing, combining, and transforming diagrams. As mentioned in Section 1.4, little work has been published in this area. We nonetheless believe it is of importance for the field in the future.

1.6. Acknowledgments

My deepest thanks go to Pascal Amsili, without whom this chapter would probably not exist. I also wish to thank Nicholas Asher, Michel Aurnague, Mario Borillo, Luis Fariñas, Nicola Guarino, Claudio Masolo, Achille Varzi, the members of the Langue, Raisonnement, Calcul group in Toulouse, and the members of the European HCM Network SPACENET, among others, for enlightening discussions or comments on an earlier version of this chapter that contributed to significantly improve it. Of course, all remaining errors and ambiguities are my own.

Notes

[1] The term *relational* is also found.

[2] The domain can hold three types of entities — points, lines, and planes — with an incidence relation (not membership) between them. In Tarski (1959), an axiomatic system of Euclidean geometry based only on points is proposed; in this same system, continuity axioms are freed from any reference to arithmetic.

[3] When transposed to AI, one can see reasoning in global spaces as model-based and reasoning in local spaces as deductive. However, model-based reasoning in global spaces is in general replaced by more efficient numerical algorithmic methods.

[4] Defining "good" identity criteria is very difficult. Spatiotemporal continuity is, however, often adopted as one of these criteria, which in this case would make the definition of continuity of motion circular.

[5] For a review of possible ways of defining points in terms of regions, see Gerla (1994).

[6] When there are no boundaries (as, for instance, for the whole space), the subset is both open and closed.

[7] For instance, in the standard topology of $\mathbb{R}$, $\mathbb{R}^2$, or $\mathbb{R}^3$, all open sets but the empty set are of the same dimensionality as the whole topological space.

[8] In the TACITUS project (Hobbs et al., 1987; Hobbs et al., 1988), a point-based global space is proposed, with independent "scales" or granular partial order relations (one for each axis).

[9] In all generality, the case $A = \pi$ should be distinguished.

[10] This means that these distance calculi require some underlying orientation system.

[11] To restrict memory size, they are sometimes compacted and hierarchically organized, as in Samet (1984; 1989).

[12] Regions extended throughout or, formally, regions x such that $\overline{x} = \overline{\overset{\circ}{x}}$ and $\overset{\circ}{x} = \overset{\circ}{\overline{x}}$.

[13] This way, a distinction can be made between jointing along a "fiat boundary" (Smith, 1995) (for example, the relation between two halves of a ball) and touching along real, objective, boundaries (for example, the relation between the ball and the ground).

[14] Note that Clarke's theory and RCC do not imply this last restriction.

[15] One may question the cognitive or physical plausibility of these particular regions. Indeed, perfect spheres may be seen as entities as abstract as points. As a consequence, a region-based geometry relying on the existence of spheres may be no more attractive than a point-based geometry.

[16] Except when there is a NTP relation between them or when they are equal, in which case orientation has no meaning. Notice that Hernández assumes that a TPP relation can be combined with orientation, considering the position of the common boundary, thus forbidding this shared boundary to be very long or to be scattered around the regions.

[17] This includes the case of the relation between one history and a static object, since immobility can be seen as being relative to a point of view.

2. Reasoning about Time and Actions in Artificial Intelligence: Major Issues

Alfonso Gerevini

2.1. Introduction

The ability to represent and manage temporal knowledge about the world is fundamental in humans as well as in artificial agents. Some examples of important "intelligent" activities that require time representation and reasoning include the following:

- Given that certain conditions, actions, and events occurred in the world prior to a time t, *predict* whether certain conditions will hold at t or whether certain actions can be executed or certain events will occur at or after t;
- Hypothesize conditions, actions, or events prior to a certain time t to *explain* why certain conditions, actions, or events occurred at or after t;
- Given a description of the world at a certain time t, *plan* a set of actions that can be executed in a certain order starting at t, to achieve a desired goal;
- *Schedule* a set of given activities to meet some constraints imposed on the order, duration, and temporal position or separation of the activities, such as a stipulated deadline;
- Given (possibly incomplete or uncertain) information about the temporal relations holding between events or facts in the represented domain, *answer temporal queries* about other implicit (entailed) relations; for example, queries about the possibility or the necessity that two particular future events will temporally overlap or about the shortest temporal distance separating two events that have occurred.

Temporal reasoning has been a major research field in artificial intelligence (AI) since the beginning of this discipline, and it has been investigated in the context of various AI areas where the tasks mentioned above are crucial. Such areas include knowledge representation (see, for example, Schmiedel, 1990; Miller, 1990; Schubert and Hwang, 1989; Artale and Franconi, 1994), natural language understanding (see Allen, 1984; Miller and Schubert, 1990; Song and Cohen, 1988), commonsense reasoning (for a survey see Sandewall and Shoham, 1995), qualitative reasoning (for a survey see Dague and MQD Group, 1995), diagnostic reasoning (e.g., Console et al., 1991; Nökel, 1991), plan generation (see Allen, 1991; Dean et al., 1988; Tsang, 1986; Vere, 1983), plan recognition (see Kautz, 1987, 1991; Weida and Litman, 1992; Song and Cohen, 1996), and scheduling (see Rit, 1986; Boddy, 1993; Frederking and Muscettola, 1992).

Since the field of temporal reasoning has been a central research topic in AI for many years, providing an exhaustive survey of all the results and proposed approaches would probably require an entire book by itself. The much less ambitious goal for this chapter is to serve as a base for orienting the reader in the field of temporal reasoning and as general background for further specific reading.

The first part of the chapter, after a short discussion on time models, introduces basic issues characterizing two major subfields of temporal reasoning: reasoning about time and reasoning about actions and change. Then the essential role of temporal reasoning in the important AI area of planning is discussed. Finally, the last part of the chapter focuses on reasoning about time, providing an overview of the main results.[1]

Note that the chapter mainly addresses reasoning issues, and says little about how temporal information is represented in a general language for knowledge representation. Also, the coverage of reasoning about time uses very restricted representations, where only disjunctions of basic relations between free variables are permitted. Syntax and semantics of more expressive sentential or quantificational temporal logics are not addresses. (The reader interested in first-order logics with temporal arguments, reified temporal logics, and temporal modal logic might consult the survey by Vila, 1994.)

2.2. Modeling Time

In order to build a time representation some ontological issues need to be considered.[2] For example, we have to choose the primitive *time unit*, which usually is either points or intervals.[3] Theoretically, this choice is not crucial, since it is possible to build a point-based theory of time that allows us to represent intervals in terms of points, or vice versa (see, for example, Galton, 1995b). However, the choice can be practically important. For instance, in building temporal reasoning system, a point-based representation supports efficient implementations of basic temporal database management (Dean and McDermott, 1987; Stillman et al., 1993; Gerevini et al., 1995; Barber, 1993).

Another fundamental issue concerns the topology of time. For example, we can model the direction of time by imposing on the basic time units either a total order or a partial order. In the former case we have a *linear-time* model, where for each pair of different time units one precedes the other. In the later case we have a *branching-time* model with multiple future times (or past times) lying on different time lines.

A time model can be either *discrete* (such as the integers), implying that given a pair of ordered time units there exists at most a finite number of time units lying between them, or it can be *dense* (such as the real numbers), implying that for each pair of ordered time units there exists a third unit lying between them. A time model is *bounded* when there exists a lower bound on times (such as the natural numbers), or there exists an upper bound on times (such as the negative integers). By contrast, a time model is *unbounded* when there exists no lower or upper bound on times (such as the integers).

Finally, another important issue in modeling time is *granularity* (see, for example, Hobbs, 1985; Leban et al., 1986; Ladkin, 1987a; Dean, 1989; Euzenat, 1995; Ciapessoni et al., 1993; Wang et al., 1995). Time units can be grouped into clusters of the same size (for example, seconds, minutes, hours) where these clusters are hierarchically organized to form "layers of time" with different granularities (seconds can be grouped into clusters of sixty elements to form a layer of minutes). This organization can be exploited in the reasoning process because it can allow us to abstract away details that may be irrelevant at a certain level of conceptualization.

Thus we have a variety of options in modeling time. From our perspective the "best" model to adopt in a AI application is mainly a practical issue, depending on the particular domain and application, rather than a philosophical or physical issue concerned with modeling what time actually is in the real world.

2.3. Reasoning About Time

In reasoning about time, temporal knowledge is typically specified in terms of a collection of qualitative or metric relations constraining time points or intervals. The main reasoning tasks are concerned with determining the consistency of this collection, deducing new relations from those that are given, and deriving an interpretation of the point (interval) variables involved that satisfy the constraints imposed by the given relations. For example, consider the following story in an imaginary trains transportation

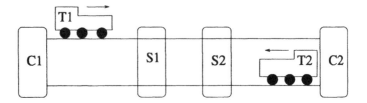

Figure 1. Pictorial description of the trains example

domain (see Figure 1):

> During its travel from city C1 to city C2, train T1 stopped first at the station S1 and then at station S2. Train T2 traveled in the opposite direction of T1 (i.e., from C2 to C1). During its trip T2 stopped first at S2 and then at S1. When T2 arrived at S1, T1 was stopping there too.

This simple story contains some explicit qualitative information about the ordering of the time intervals during which the events described occurred. In particular, from the first sentence we can infer that the intervals of time during which T1 stopped at S1 (at(T1,S1)) and at S2 (at(T1,S2)) are *contained* in the interval of time during which T1 traveled from C1 to C2 travel(T1,C1,C2); from the second sentence we can infer that at(T1,S1) is *before* at(T1,S2); from the third and the fourth sentences we can infer that at(T2,S1) and at(T2,S2) are *during* travel(T2,C2,C1) and that at(T2,S2) is *before* at(T2,S1); finally, from the the last sentence we can infer that the starting time of at(T1,S1) *precedes* the starting time of at(T2,S1) and that the starting time of at(T2,S1) *precedes* the end time of at(T1,S1).

Suppose that in addition we know that no more than one train can stop at S2 at the same time (say, because it is a very small station). Then we have that at(T2,S2) is *before or after* at(T1,S2). In performing the temporal reasoning tasks mentioned above in the context of the temporal information provided in the above story, we would determine that the story is temporally consistent. We would deduce new relations such as that travel(T1,C1,C2) intersects travel(T2,C2,C1), which are implicit in the story; we would strengthen explicit relations (e.g., we deduce that at(T2,S2) must be before at(T1,S2), ruling out the possibility that at(T2,S2) is after at(T1,S2)); and finally we would determine that the ordering of intervals in Figure 2 is consistent with all the (implicit and explicit) temporal relations in the story.

Note that if the supplementary information that T1 stopped at S2 *before* T2 were provided, then we would determine that the story is temporally

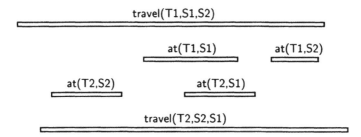

Figure 2.   A consistent ordering (scenario) of the time intervals in the trains example

*in*consistent. This is because the explicit temporal relations in the story imply that T2 left S2 before T1 left S1, which precedes the arrival of T1 at S2.

In many applications useful temporal knowledge is also available in the form of quantitative constraints such as durations, deadlines, and temporal distances between starting times or end times of events. For example, our simple transportation domain could provide the following additional quantitative information imposing duration constraints on the travel times and stopping times of the trains:[4]

> The durations of travel(T1,C1,C2) and of travel(T2,C2,C1) should be less than forty-eight hours; the trip of T1 (T2) from C1 to S1 (from S1 to C1) takes six to eight hours; the trip of T1 (T2) from S1 to S2 (from S2 to S1) takes eight to twelve hours; the trip of T1 (T2) from S2 to C2 (from C2 to S2) takes fourteen to twenty hours; both T1 and T2 stop at each station for at least two hours.

Furthermore, suppose that our story is extended with the following information about metric times:

> T1 left C1 at midnight on December 11. It stopped at S1 for six hours, and then it arrived at C2 at 4:00 p.m. on December 12. Regarding T2's trip, we have that T2 left C2 at 11:00 a.m. on December 10; that it stopped three hours at S2 and 4 hours at S1 and that it took nine hours to reach C1 from S2.

The resulting story together with the temporal information provided by the domain give rise to a rich set of qualitative as well as quantitative temporal relations between points and intervals. Such constraints can be represented in a knowledge base, and temporal reasoning is required in order to answer queries of the following form:

> Is the temporal information provided consistent ?
> What are the possible arrival times of T2 at C1 ?
> How long did it take for T1 to go from S2 to C2 ?

Did T2 arrive at C2 before T1 arrived at C1 ?
Is it possible that on Dec. 11 at 2:00 p.m. T2 had not arrived at S1 yet ?

Important issues in the research on reasoning about time concern the computational complexity of reasoning relative to the class of relations that can be expressed, the development of efficient representations and algorithms, and the implementation of domain independent systems that can be used as specialized temporal reasoners in larger AI systems (see, for example, Dean and McDermott, 1987; Koomen, 1988; Gerevini et al., 1995). Section 2.6 gives an overview of the main results obtained in this subfield of temporal reasoning.

2.4. Reasoning About Actions and Change

Formal methods for reasoning about change are used in AI to model the dynamics of the world (domain) represented, where changes can be determined by the effects of actions performed by an agent or of (possibly) unforeseen "external" events. Central reasoning tasks involve prediction and retrodiction of certain properties of the world represented.

More precisely, given a set of axioms formalizing the effects of the actions in a particular domain and the relevant preconditions (a set of *action laws*), an ordered set of actions (*a schedule*), a set of properties holding before the actions are executed (an *initial state*), and possibly a set of *observations* indicating that certain conditions hold (or do not hold) at particular times after the initial state, the prediction task regards determining whether certain conditions hold at a certain time after the execution of the actions in the schedule (in the *final state*). Similarly, a retrodiction task has a set of action laws, a schedule, a final state, and a possibly empty set of observations, and we have to determine whether certain conditions held (or did not hold) at certain times before the actions of the schedule are executed. This formulation of the prediction and retrodiction tasks can be extended by adding possible external events (see, for example, Allen and Ferguson, 1994).

2.4.1. THE SITUATION CALCULUS

One of the earliest and most widely used formalisms for reasoning about actions and change is the *situation calculus* (McCarthy, 1963, 1968; McCarthy and Hayes, 1969). In the situation calculus (SC) knowledge about the changing world is organized into a potentially infinite number of *situations*, each of which corresponds to one possible way that the world could be at a given time and is described by a collection of "facts" (McCarthy and Hayes, 1969, p.477):

A situation s is the complete state of the universe at an instant of time. Since the universe is too large for complete description, we shall never completely describe a situation; we shall only give facts about situations. These facts will be used to deduce further facts about that situation, about future situations and about situations that persons can bring about from that situation.

Situations are temporally represented as time points in a discrete branching (partially ordered) time model, and the performance of an action can change some properties (*fluents*) in the current situation, determining a transition to a new situation. Fluents can be seen as functions defined on situations whose value (either **true** or **false** for *propositional fluents* and a situation for *situational fluents*) is changed by the execution of an action or by the occurrence of an external event.

For example, in the context of the ever-popular *blocks world*, consider performing the action of moving block **A** on top of block **B** (**Puton(A,B)**) in a situation S1 where the blocks **A** and **B** do not have any block on the top of them (that is, where **clear(A)** and **clear(B)** are **true**, and **on(A,B)** is **false**). As a result of the execution of this action we transit from S1 to a new situation S2 in which **clear(B)** is **false** and **on(A,B)** is **true**, provided that the action **Puton** has been appropriately axiomatized. More formally, this can be represented by asserting

(1) **Holds(clear(x),s) ∧ Holds(clear(y),s) ∧ x ≠ y**
    → **Holds(on(x,y),Result(Puton(x,y),s)) ∧**
      ¬Holds(clear(y),Result(Puton(x,y),s))

(2) **Holds(clear(A),S1)   ∧   Holds(clear(B),S2)   ∧**
    ¬Holds(on(A,B),S1)

(3) S2 = **Result(Puton(A,B),S1),**

from which we can derive

(4) **Holds(on(A,B),S2) ∧ ¬Holds(clear(B),S2),**

where **Result** is a situational fluent mapping an action and a situation to another situation; **Holds(p,S)** is a fluent predicate indicating that the property **p** is true in the situation **S**; **x,y** and **s** are universally quantified variables of the appropriate sort.[5]

SC can be seen as a point-based temporal logic with a branching time model, where time is implicitly represented by the situations. In some alternative formalisms time it explicitly represented, and change is implicitly represented by asserting that a property holds at (during) a particular point (interval) of time, while it does not hold at another. In these formalisms knowledge about actions and properties of the represented world is formalized through various temporal logics based on different time models (see, for example, Allen, 1984; Allen and Ferguson, 1994; McDermott, 1982; Shoham, 1987; Galton, 1990; van Benthem, 1991).

Allen and Ferguson (1994) (see their chapter in this book, Chapter 7) discuss the need for explicit temporal logics to develop general representations that support a wide range of reasoning tasks including prediction, retrodiction, and planning and that can model complex realistic scenarios where actions and events take time, external unforeseen events may interact with planned actions, actions may overlap or occur simultaneously, and the knowledge of the world is incomplete and unpredictable in detail.

On the other hand, some researchers rely on SC as a theoretical and computational foundation for the ambitious ultimate goal of modeling autonomous agents acting in complex dynamic environments. Several extensions to the original SC have been proposed to accommodate in this framework some important features of reasoning about action and change. For example, some very interesting extensions have recently been proposed by Pinto (1994) and Reiter (1996), who enriched SC with concurrent actions, external "natural actions" that occur in response to known laws of physics, and continuous time.

2.4.2. THE FRAME, RAMIFICATION, AND QUALIFICATION PROBLEMS

The central problems in formalizing reasoning about actions and change are the so-called *frame problem*, *ramification problem*, and *qualification problem*. Shoham and McDermott (1988) describe these problems as intrinsic problems that are independent of the particular formalism used (either change-based or time-based). Here we choose to briefly illustrate them in the context of SC, despite the limited expressiveness of state-based approaches compared to time-based approaches argued by several researchers.

The frame problem was first described by McCarthy and Hayes (1969). Given a situation S in which an action A is performed, it concerns the formalization of those fluents that do *not* change value in the situation Result(A,S) relative to their original value in S. For example, suppose that in the previous simple blocks world we have an additional clear block C, and that in the initial situation S1 each block has a color associated with it, that is,

$$\text{Holds}(\text{color}(A,\text{blue}),S1) \land \text{Holds}(\text{color}(B,\text{red}),S1) \land$$
$$\land \text{Holds}(\text{color}(C,\text{blue}),S1).$$

Suppose also that the agent has the task of building a stack formed by at least two blocks of the same color. This can be accomplished by performing in S1 either Puton(A,C) or Puton(C,A). However, that these actions result in the desired final state cannot be formally proved because logically nothing ensures that while we move a block on top of another its color does not change. In particular, we cannot prove that color(A,blue) and color(C,blue) *persist* either if we perform Puton(A,C) or Puton(C,A).

In order to guarantee the persistence of the fluents unaffected by an action, McCarthy and Hayes proposed introducing a set of axioms that explicitly list the fluents that do not change their value when the action is performed. Such axioms are called *frame axioms*. The major problem with the frame axioms is that they can be quite numerous ($O(m \cdot n)$ for m fluents and n possible actions in the represented world), making the formalization tedious to specify and the (automated) reasoning computationally expensive. In general, the frame problem is the difficulty of formalizing the properties of the world that are unaffected by the performance of an action, without explicitly enumerating *all* such properties.

The ramification problem regards formalizing the effects of an action. In particular, in the situation calculus the ramification problem is the difficulty of formally specifying *all* changes in fluents to be expected in the resultant situation when an action is performed. This can be a problem because an action can have arbitrarily complex effects, since a particular change can give rise to further changes and so on, creating an arbitrarily long chain of changes.

For example, consider the action of driving a car from a location loc1 to another location loc2.[6] An obvious effect of this action is that the driven car is at loc2, and a consequence of this effect is that all the parts forming the car (the engine, the tires, and so on) change their original location from loc1 to loc2. In formalizing the driving action, instead of enumerating the changes of location for all the object forming the car, it would be more natural to be able to automatically derive such changes from the ("primary") effect that the car is in a new location. This requires solving the ramification problem, which in general is to avoid exhaustively enumerating as effects of an action *all* the changes determined by performing the action.

The qualification problem was identified in (McCarthy and Hayes, 1969; McCarthy, 1977) and concerns the formalization of the preconditions of an action. In fact, depending on the context in which an action is formalized, specifying the conditions under which an action is executable may require consideration of arbitrarily many cases. For example, the previous action of driving a car has many potential preconditions, such as that the battery is not dead, the gas is not empty, the tail pipe is not clogged up by anything, the engine works, the wheels have not been stolen, and so on. In general, the qualification problem is to avoid exhaustively enumerating all the preconditions of an action. This problem is related to the difficulty of making appropriate assumptions about what are the *relevant* preconditions for the formalization of an action in a specific domain.

A general concern of the research in reasoning about actions and change is the investigation of formalisms and inference methods based on non-monotonic logics (for a survey see Sandewall and Shoham, 1995), monotonic logics (see Schubert, 1990, 1994; Reiter, 1991; Morley et al., 1994), or probabilistic methods (see Pearl, 1988a; Dean and Kanazawa, 1989; Kanazawa, 1991; Dean and M. Wellman, 1991; Hanks, 1990a; Hanks and McDermott, 1994; Haddawy, 1996; McDermott's chapter in this book, Chapter 8) in which prediction, retrodiction, and other related reasoning tasks can be formalized without succumbing to the basic problems outlined above.

Two main methodologies have been followed: an *example-driven* methodology, which most of the researchers adopted, and a more recent *systematic* methodology.[7] Sandewall (1994a, 1994b) discusses the merits and the limits of the first, and proposes and uses the second as a methodology whereby one can obtain precise results on the *range of correct applicability* of several previously proposed theories of action and change, as well as new ones.

Various nonmonotonic logics for reasoning about actions and change were originally proposed in the context of the example-driven methodology, where the validation of the techniques proposed is usually restricted to the use of few representative examples, such as the famous *Yale shooting problem* (Hanks and McDermott, 1987). In this simple problem we have two possible actions, Wait and Shoot, and two fluents representing the properties that a gun is loaded (Loaded) and that the target is alive (Alive). In the initial situation S0 both Loaded and Alive hold. The problem is to derive the "intended" conclusion that if Wait and Shoot are performed in succession starting from S0, then in the resulting situation Alive will not hold. The difficulty of this example arises from the fact that the formalization of Wait has no effects, and the effect ¬Alive of Shoot is conditioned to the fact that Loaded holds in the situation where the action is performed. Hence, logically it is possible that in the situation Result(Shoot,Result(Wait,S0)) Alive still holds because during waiting the gun (spontaneously) became unloaded, that is, we have ¬Hold(loaded, Result(Wait, S0)).

The main distinguishing feature of the nonmonotonic logics proposed in the literature is the entailment method for selecting a more restricted subset of models (or a larger set of consequences) than those derivable in a classical logical framework. These models are selected according to some *preference relation*, and are designed to correspond to the set of models intended by a reasoner with common sense. Some prominent examples of these entailment methods are *circumscription* (see McCarthy, 1980, 1986;

Hanks and McDermott, 1987; Baker, 1989; Kartha and Lifschitz, 1995), *chronological minimization* (see Kautz, 1986; Lifschitz, 1987b; Shoham, 1988a; Sandewall, 1989; Lin and Shoham, 1991), *causal minimization* (see Haugh, 1987; Lifschitz, 1987a), *nonnormal defaults* and *autoepistemic logic* (see, Morris, 1988; Gelfond, 1989).[8]

An alternative approach to nonmonotonic logics that relies on the use of monotonic logics is *explanation closure* (Haas, 1987; Schubert, 1990, 1994; Reiter, 1991). We discuss this approach in the next section as an efficient method for dealing with the frame problem in planning.

The systematic methodology relies on a semantics that is used to define what the intended models are and to characterize scenario descriptions in terms of a taxonomy of (ontological and epistemological) properties that they may have. The range of correct applicability of a logic of actions and change (the ability to correctly infer change and nonchange) can then be identified in terms of classes of scenarios that can be handled by the logic. Sandewall (1994a, 1994b) evaluated several logics in the context of the systematic approach, using an underlying "inertial" semantics according to which the only changes that occur in a world are those known to be directly induced by an agent's actions, except for some limited cases of indirect changes.

More recently, Sandewall (see Chapter 9 in this book) extended his assessment results to some approaches for dealing with the ramification problem. For this purpose he proposes and uses an underlying *transition cascade semantics*, according to which "an action is viewed as consisting of an initial state transition which represents the invocation of the action, followed by a succession of other state transitions which may be understood as representing causal chains".

In this section and in the previous one we have given a general picture of the major issues concerning formal reasoning about actions and change, and reasoning about (qualitative or quantitative) temporal information. In the next section we discuss the important role of these subfields of temporal reasoning in the AI area of planning.

2.5. Temporal Reasoning in Planning

Planning is an important and challenging research area of AI in which a large variety of techniques have been proposed in the last three decades (for a review of the field see Tate, 1990; Georgeff, 1990; Allen et al., 1990; AIJ, 1995). Our goal in this section is to briefly introduce some fundamental aspects of domain-independent planning that are closely related to temporal reasoning. Similar issues can arise in domain-dependent planners as well, planners that concentrate on using domain heuristics to attain computational efficiency.

Planning, and especially *well-founded* planning, is a computationally very hard problem (Bylander, 1993, 1994; Erol et al., 1992; Nebel and Bäckström, 1994), which involves both reasoning about actions and change and reasoning about time. The emphasis in well-founded planning is on constructing planners that can be *proved* to have certain desirable properties, such as soundness and completeness for their intended class of problems, or the ability to find optimal or near-optimal solutions. On the other hand, practical planning research seeks to provide planning frameworks and tools that are sufficiently expressive, flexible, and efficient to be effectively usable in applications such as planning robot actions, transportation planning, factory scheduling, genetic engineering, and conversation planning. A considerable effort in current planning research aims at bringing well-founded approaches closer to practicality.

A domain-independent planner needs to cope with the frame problem and to manage the temporal constraints associated with the actions in the plan or with some conditions of the represented world (such as the period of time during which a certain resource can be consumed or an action can be synchronized with an external events). The rest of this section is dedicated to illustrating these issues.

2.5.1. THE FRAME PROBLEM IN PLANNING

STRIPS (Fikes and Nilsson, 1971) is one of the earliest domain-independent planning formalism on which several recent planners are still based. In STRIPS-based planners a state of the world is represented as a set of formulas, and the effects of an action are specified through a list of formulas to be removed from the state in which A is executed (a *delete list*), plus a list of formulas to be added to such a state (an *add list*). The execution of an action in a certain state determines a transition to another state, whose set of formulas is derived by the add list and delete list of the action.

In STRIPS, as well as in modern STRIPS-descendants such as UCPOP (Penberthy and Weld, 1992), the frame problem is "solved" by the adoption of some strong assumptions about the world represented and on the nature of the possible actions.[9] In particular,

- The planner has complete knowledge of the the relevant fluents and actions. For example, for any fluent f in the domain, the planner can decide whether either f or $not f$ holds in the initial state; typically this assumption is realized by using the so-called *Closed World Assumption* (Genesereth and Nilsson, 1987).
- The world is changed only by the actions of the agent executing the plan. Everything remains unchanged unless it is explicitly forced to change by the declared effects of the actions.

- Concurrent actions can never occur, and all the actions have only deterministic effects.

By exploiting these assumptions, from a logical point of view the planner can easily solve (without resorting to any frame axiom) the *temporal projection problem*. In general, given a description of an initial state of the world and a description of which events (actions) occur (are performed), the problem of temporal projection concerns determining the (possible or necessary) consequences of these events (actions). In particular, deciding whether a precondition P of an action A does or does not hold after execution of a certain sequence of actions is an instance of this problem.[10] Temporal projection can be very important during planning, for example, to determine whether an action may be executed (has all its preconditions satisfied) at a certain point in the plan under construction.

When some of the previous assumptions are relaxed to handle more complex domains, with more flexible representations of actions and domain knowledge, the frame problem can become an essential difficulty for efficient planning (Chapman, 1987). The simple STRIPS assumption that everything remains unchanged unless it is explicitly declared to change can no longer be maintained. In particular, the closed-world assumption implicit in systems like UCPOP breaks down in worlds with disjunctive ambiguity since it can give rise to inconsistent theories (Genesereth and Nilsson, 1987).

Furthermore, as pointed out by Schubert (1990), Pednault's preservation conditions (1988, 1989), asserting necessary and sufficient conditions for a fluent to change, also cannot in general be formulated when knowledge of the domain is incomplete.

As a simple example in which this difficulty arises consider the *next-to problem* analyzed by Schubert (1990, 1994). Suppose for simplicity that in a robot's world the only possible action is Goto(b), which has the only explicit effect of putting the robot next to a box b. However, in this world the robot going to a particular box B1 may "incidentally" also end up next to another box B2 that happens to be near B1. So, in general we cannot say that the condition nextto(ROBOT,b) holds *if and only if* Goto(b) is executed for some box b. Similarly, it can be seen that necessary and sufficient conditions for nextto(b) becoming *false* also cannot be given. In other words, without exact (geometrical) knowledge of the world in which the robot acts, we cannot infer whether a next-to condition *persists* in a state reached by the execution of some goto action(s).

An interesting and efficient solution to this problem is to use *explanation closure* (EC) axioms, which were suggested in Schubert (1990, 1994), building on (Haas, 1987) as a monotonic solution to the frame problem for worlds with fully specified actions. EC axioms are axioms complementary to the effect axioms, stating the necessary conditions for a fluent to change.

For example, in the previous simple scenario, we can assert the following EC axiom stating that nextto(ROBOT,b) becomes true only if the robot performs either action goto(b) or action goto(b') for some box b' near to b (assuming that nexto(b,b') implies that b is near b'):

$$\forall(a,x,s,s')[[Holds(nextto(R,x),s) \land \neg Holds(nextto(R,x),s') \land$$
$$s'=Result(a,s)] \rightarrow (\exists y)[a=Goto(R,y) \land Holds(near(x,y),s)]]$$

Using this EC axiom, if, for example, we happen to know that the robot is *not* next to B1, and then it goes to B2, which is *not* near B1, we can *deductively* determine that the robot still is not next to B1 after he has arrived at B2.

Two of the merits of the explanation closure method are that EC axioms can be specified in standard first-order logic and that the number of EC axioms required is comparable to the number of effect axioms (rather than being much larger, as in the case of frame axioms). Furthermore, this approach allows a planner to reason monotonically about *nonchange*. From a computational point of view this can be a significant advantage with respect to traditional approaches based on nonmonotonic techniques (Schubert, 1994; Allen and Ferguson, 1994). Ass argued by Schubert (1990) it is one of the reasons making explanation closure a potentially very powerful method for coping with the frame problem in planning and in reasoning about change in general.

Reiter (1991) supplies a method of automatically generating explanation closure axioms from effect axioms, under certain assumptions about the form and completeness of the effect axioms. He combines effect axioms with explanation closure axioms to obtain a single *successor-state axiom* for the truth of each fluent (or negated fluent) at the end of any action. Pednault (1988, 1989) had previously discussed the use of such axioms for formalizing and extending STRIPS.

Recently, Reiter (1996) proposed a generalization of Green's classical formulation of deductive planning (Green, 1969), which uses successor state axioms in the context of the situation calculus enriched to handle concurrent actions, external natural actions, and continuous time.

Schubert (1994) shows that explanation closure is a powerful method that allows monotonic solution of many problems in Sandewall's test suite (Sandewall, 1994a) for reasoning about change. He also argues that the completeness assumption on which successor state axioms rely is too strong and can easily break down, for example, when effects of actions are somewhat unpredictable, incompletely known, or expressed in terms of "vague" predicates such as nextto.

Allen and Ferguson (1994; see their chapter in this book, Chapter 7), show how to use explanation closure in the context of a representation of events and actions based on interval temporal logic.

2.5.2. TEMPORAL CONSTRAINTS IN PLANNING

During the search process the planner must (partially or totally) order the set of actions forming the plan by imposing a collection of appropriate ordering constraints. Such constraints are essential to guarantee the correctness of the resulting plan, that is, to guarantee that if the actions are executed starting at the initial state and consistently with these constraints, then the goal(s) will be achieved.

In nonlinear planning (see, for example, Chapman, 1987; Sacerdoti, 1975; Tate, 1977; Weld, 1994; Wilkins, 1988) the actions in a plan are partially ordered and reasoning about ordering constraints is required, for example, when the planner attempts to establish a subgoal G by "reusing" an action already in the plan under construction. In particular, the planner needs to determine the set of actions already in the plan that have an effect matching G and that can *consistently precede* the action whose precondition is G.

Moreover, in nonlinear planners such as UCPOP it is important to assert constraints that prevent an (instantaneous) action A from lying within a certain interval between two other actions $A1$ and $A2$, that is, $A < A1$ *or* $A2 < A$ and $A1 < A2$. In particular, this is required during planning to "protect" an established condition, when an earlier action ($A1$) serves to achieve the preconditions of a later one ($A2$), and no further action (A) should be inserted between them that would subvert those preconditions (because one of the effects of A falsifies some protected precondition of $A2$). An essential task of the planner is to determine whether the set of all the ordering constraints is consistent, which is an NP-complete problem (Gerevini and Schubert, 1994b). In UCPOP this is accomplished by a search that attempts to find a disjunct for each disjunctive constraint so as to obtain a consistent set of simple ordering constraints (if one exists). This search can be exponential since the problem is NP-hard.

Another planning framework where temporal reasoning is crucial is Allen and Koomen's planning system (1983). Their framework uses a richer temporal representation than (traditional) nonlinear planners that is based on an interval algebra formed from subsets of thirteen basic relations (Allen, 1983) (see the following section). By allowing for temporal constraints among properties of domain objects and actions available to a planner, they are able to reason effectively about simultaneous actions and to construct plans that take into account interactions among contemplated actions (such as disjointness constraints that prevent actions from overlapping because they contend for some resource.)

The reasoning task of checking the consistency of these relations is also essential in the planning algorithm presented by Allen (1991). Unfortunately, since the temporal relations used belong to the interval algebra, and reasoning with such an algebra is NP-hard (Vilain and Kautz, 1986), this task can be a bottleneck in the performance of the planning algorithm on large-scale problems.[11]

Other temporal constraints that a planner may need to manage concern the inherent duration of an action; goals with possible deadlines (as in the planners FORBIN (Dean et al., 1988) and ZENO (Penberthy and Weld, 1994)); and the coordination of an action with externally scheduled events (as in the DEVISER planning and scheduling system (Vere, 1983)).

Thus an important issue in designing an effective general planner is the efficient handling of a variety of qualitative and metric temporal constraints. Although in the worst case this often requires solving an NP-hard problem, recently some complete algorithms and data structures that work well in practice have been developed (see Gerevini and Schubert, 1995a; van Beek and Manchak, 1996; Ladkin and Reinefeld, ming; Nebel, 1996).

These techniques can manage a rich class of (qualitative) temporal constraints, including those mentioned above in connection with nonlinear planners, as well as those used in Allen and Koomen's framework. In particular, the techniques proposed by Gerevini and Schubert (1994a, 1995a) are very efficient in practice and are often able to decide disjunctions deductively by fast preprocessing techniques (linear or low-order polynomial time in the worst case). Their algorithms involve the use of a graphical representation of temporal information called *D-timegraphs* (where D stands for "disjunctive"), and unlike many complete temporal reasoning methods are *scalable* in the sense of being sufficiently economical in their use of storage and time to allow application to large data sets (say hundreds or thousands of relationships). The scalability of D-timegraphs makes them a promising approach for planning in temporally complex domains without sacrificing well-foundedness.

2.6. Reasoning About Temporal Relations

As mentioned at the end of Section 2.3, the research in AI on reasoning about time has mainly addressed computational issues. Our presentation in this section will adopt a similar perspective, focusing first on qualitative relations, then on metric constraints, and finally on a few prominent implemented reasoning systems. In the presentation we assume that time is linear, dense, and unbounded and that the basic time units are either points or intervals. Such models of time predominate in AI applications that involve reasoning about time. (Some interesting studies in the context of AI which investigate other kinds of time models are Vilain, 1982; Meiri, 1992, 1996; Ligozat, 1996b; Jonsson et al., 1996).

2.6.1. QUALITATIVE RELATIONS

Fundamental frameworks for reasoning about qualitative temporal relations are Allen's *interval algebra* (1983) and Vilain and Kautz's *point algebra* (1986, 1990). The interval algebra (IA) is a relation algebra (Tarski, 1941; Ladkin and Maddux, 1994; Hirsh, 1996) based on thirteen basic relations between intervals corresponding to all the possible ways in which the endpoints of two intervals can be ordered (see Figure 3).[12] By combining all possible sets of basic relations in disjunctive form, 2^{13} interval relations can be derived. For example, by combining *before* and *overlaps* we obtain the relation *before or overlaps*:

$$(I \ before \ J) \ or \ (I \ overlaps \ J) \equiv I \ (before \ or \ overlaps) \ J$$

The point algebra (PA) is a relation algebra based on the three basic relations between time points $<$, $=$, and $>$ and whose elements are the set of binary relations $\{<, \leq, =, \geq, >, \neq, ?\}$, where ? is the disjunction of the three basic relations.

Given a set of (assertions of) qualitative relations, fundamental reasoning tasks include *determining consistency* (satisfiability) of such a collection, *finding a consistent scenario* (an interpretation for all the temporal variables involved that is consistent with the information provided), and *deducing new relations* from those that are known (or computing their deductive closure).[13] These tasks are NP-hard problems if the assertions are in IA (Vilain et al., 1990), while they can be solved in polynomial time if the assertions are in PA (Ladkin and Maddux, 1988a; Vilain et al., 1990; van Beek, 1992, 1992; Gerevini and Schubert, 1995b). As a result of the latter fact, these problems are also tractable in a restriction of IA called simple interval algebra (SIA) by van Beek (1992). This consists of the set of relations in IA that can be translated into conjunctions of relations in PA between the endpoints of the intervals (Ladkin and Maddux, 1988a; van Beek, 1992; van Beek and Cohen, 1990). For example, the relation *before or overlaps* between the intervals I and J can be translated into

$$I^- < I^+ \ \wedge \ J^- < J^+ \ \wedge \ I^+ < J^+ \ \wedge \ I^- < J^- \ \wedge \ I^+ \neq J^-$$

where I^- and I^+ indicate the starting and the end time points of I (analogously for J).

Nebel and Bürckert (1995) identified a maximal tractable subalgebra of IA called the ORD-Horn subclass. This subclass subsumes SIA extending the percentage of IA relations that can be handled efficiently from 2.3 per cent (for SIA) to 10.6 per cent.[14] In particular, they proved that the consistency of a set of assertions of relations in the ORD-Horn class can be determined by imposing the *path-consistency* property on the set (Montanari, 1974; Mackworth, 1977). Such a property can be computed in

Relation	Inverse	Meaning
I before J	*J after I*	
I meets J	*J met-by I*	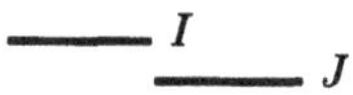
I overlaps J	*J overlapped-by I*	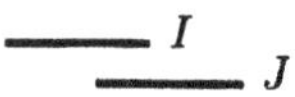
I during J	*J contains I*	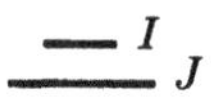
I starts J	*J started-by I*	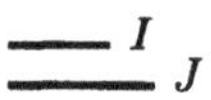
I finishes J	*J finished-by I*	
I equal J	*J equal I*	

Figure 3. The thirteen basic relations of the interval algebra

$O(n^3)$ time and $O(n^2)$ space, where n is the number of intervals involved in the input set of assertions.[15]

Recently, other tractable subclasses of IA containing more relations than those in ORD-Horn have been identified (Drakengren and Jonsson, 1996). However, such classes do not contain all of the thirteen basic relations, and hence they do not permit the specification of complete knowledge about the relation holding between two intervals of time.

A set of (asserted) IA-relations can be represented with a *constraint network* (Montanari, 1974) whose vertices represents interval (point) variables, and edges are labeled by the relations holding between these variables. Enforcing path-consistency for a given set of relations corresponds to enforcing path consistency for their network representation. This task requires deriving a (possibly) new equivalent network in which for every 3-vertex subnetwork formed by the vertices i, j, and k, the relation R_{ik} labeling the edge from i to k is "stronger" than the composition of the relations R_{ij} and R_{jk} labeling the edges from i to j, and from j to k, respectively.[16]

Allen (1983) originally proposed calculating the $2^{13} \times 2^{13}$ possible compositions of IA-relations dynamically, using a table storing the 13×13 compositions of the basic relations of IA. Other significantly improved methods have been proposed since then by Hogge (1987) and by Ladkin and Reinefeld (ming). Ladkin and Reinefeld compared these methods and showed that their method of storing all the possible compositions in a table (requiring about 64 megabytes of memory) is much faster than any alternative.

Table 1 summarizes the computational complexity of the best known algorithms for reasoning about relations in PA, PA^c, SIA, SIA^c, and ORD-Horn, where PA^c is the (convex) subalgebra of PA containing all the relations of PA except $\neq$, and SIA^c is the (convex) subalgebra of SIA formed by the relations of IA that can be translated into conjunctions of relations in PA^c.

The algorithm for determining the consistency of a set of relations in PA^c/SIA^c and in PA/SIA is based on methods for finding the "strongest connected components" in a directed graph (see Tarjan, 1972) and then examining the edges connecting vertices within such components (van Beek, 1992).

The algorithm for finding a consistent scenario for a set of relations in PA^c/SIA^c and in PA/SIA is based on first determining the consistency of the set and then topologically sorting the vertices of a directed acyclic graph (van Beek, 1992).

The algorithms for computing the deductive closure of a set of relations in PA^c/SIA^c and for deciding the consistency of a set of relations in the ORD-Horn class are based on algorithms that enforce path-consistency (see Allen, 1983; Vilain et al., 1990; van Beek, 1992; van Beek and Manchak, 1996).

The algorithm for finding a consistent scenario for a set of relations in the ORD-Horn class is based on two main steps (Gerevini, 1997). The first one checks the consistency of the set by imposing the path-consistency property on the set. The second step finds a consistent scenario for a particular set of relations in PA involving the endpoints of the interval variables of the input set of ORD-Horn relations.[17]

The algorithms for computing the deductive closure of a sets of relations in PA/SIA are based on first enforcing path-consistency and then examining

Problem	PA^c/SIA^c	PA/SIA	ORD-Horn
Consistency	$O(n^2)$	$O(n^2)$	$O(n^3)$
Consistent scenario	$O(n^2)$	$O(n^2)$	$O(n^3)$
Deductive closure	$O(n^3)$	$O(n^4)$	$O(n^5)$

TABLE 1. Time complexity of the best known temporal reasoning algorithms for PA^c/SIA^c, PA/SIA, and ORD-Horn.

some special four-vertex subnetworks to reduce certain implicit $\neq$ relations to $<$ relations (van Beek, 1992; Gerevini and Schubert, 1995b).

Finally, a simple algorithm for computing the deductive closure of a set of relations in the ORD-Horn class is based on using a path-consistency algorithm to determine whether any basic relation is a feasible relation between two interval variables.

The ORD-Horn class, though computationally attractive, is not practically adequate for all AI applications because it excludes disjointness relations such as *before or after*, which are important in planning and scheduling. For example, planned actions often cannot be scheduled concurrently because they contend for the same resources (agents, vehicles, tools, pathways, and so on). Similarly, reasoning about disjoint actions or events can be important in natural language understanding (for example, contrast "John reviewed a paper, practiced piano, and vacuumed the floor; he had no time left to cook dinner" with "John sprawled on the sofa, read a magazine, and listened to music; he had lots of time left to cook dinner").

Golumbic and Shamir (1993), and Drakengren and Jonsson (1996) have investigated some interesting subclasses of IA that contain interval disjointness relations. In particular, they provide the computational complexity analysis of their classes, as well as new graph-based algorithms. From these results it is clear that as long as we cannot refer to endpoints of intervals but only to intervals as a whole, we can handle interval disjointness in combination with certain other interval relations polynomially (for instance, when all we can say is that an interval I is disjoint from another interval J, or that I is before J).

However, as wasdiscussed in Section 2.5.2, the ability to refer to endpoints of intervals is useful in plan reasoning, where it is important to be able to say that a certain time points (perhaps an instantaneous action, or the beginning or end of an action) must not lie within a certain interval (another action, or the interval between two actions).[18] Unfortunately, it turns out that the minimal expressive power needed to express temporal nonoverlap in a point-based representation leads to intractability (if $P \neq NP$) (Gerevini and Schubert, 1994b). This is true even when we restrict ourselves to sets of statements asserting strict exclusion of certain time points from certain time intervals whose endpoints are unordered. It is thus important to formulate techniques that work well on average (or in practice), without sacrificing completeness.

Typically, the algorithms for handling classes of relations involving temporal nonoverlap (and more generally the full class of relations in IA) are based on search methods that use backtracking (Bitner and Reingold, 1975; Shanahan and Southwick, 1989). In particular, Gerevini and Schubert (1994a) propose a selective backtracking method for checking the consistency of a set of relations involving temporal nonoverlap that effectively addresses the problem of scalability and that can be extended to arbitrary disjunctions of point relations. Ladkin and Reinefeld (1992) proposed a method for finding a consistent scenario of a set of relations in IA that is based on chronological backtracking and that uses path-consistency algorithms as a pruning technique. At the time of writing their algorithm, recently also investigated by van Beek and Manchak (1996) and by Nebel (1996), appears to be the fastest known algorithm for relations in the full interval algebra.

2.6.2. METRIC TEMPORAL CONSTRAINTS

As was discussed in the trains example of Section 2.3, metric temporal informations of the form "the trip of train T1 from C1 to S1 takes six to eight hours" or "the travel time of T1 from C1 to C2 should be less than forty-eight hours" are practically very important.

A fundamental framework for reasoning about metric temporal relations is Dechter, Meiri and Pearl's (1991) TCSP (temporal constraint satisfaction problem) model. A TCSP consists of a set of temporal variables representing points in a continuous time domain and a set of distance constraints between temporal variables. Each constraint is of the form

$$y - x \in I_1 \cup I_2 \cup ... \cup I_n,$$

where y and x are point variables, I_1, I_2, ..., I_n are continuous closed intervals, and n is any integer.[19] As for the case of sets of qualitative relations, a TCSP can be represented through a constraint network where vertices represent the variables and edges the constraints. Given a TCSP the main reasoning tasks are similar to those in the qualitative case. They include *determining the consistency* of the set of constraints, *finding a solution* (an instantiation of all the variables that is consistent with the constraints), computing the *minimal network* representation (an equivalent temporal constraint network representation where the intervals of the constraints are the tightest possible);[20] and enforcing *global consistency* of the input set of constraints (making the set of constraints completely explicit, allowing for extension of the set of "partial" solutions of each subset of the constraints to "full solutions" for the whole set) (Dechter, 1992).

These problems are NP-hard for TCSP, but they become polynomial for a useful restriction of TCSP called STP (Dechter et al., 1991) that is based on constraints of the form $y - x \in I$ (STP-constraints), where x and y are point variables and I is a (possibly open or semiopen) interval in the time domain. For STP-constraints all the reasoning tasks mentioned above can be accomplished in $O(n^3)$ time and $O(n^2)$ space (Dechter et al., 1991; Gerevini, 1997), where n is the number of time points constrained.[21] Such complexity bounds refer to algorithms that are mainly based on traditional techniques for directed weighted graphs (see Floyd and Warshall's all-pairs shortest paths algorithm, and Bellman and Ford's single-source shortest paths algorithm (Cormen et al., 1990)), or on variants of them.

An interesting property of STP is that the minimal network of a set of STP-constraints is globally consistent. Another practically important related property of STP is that this class of problems allows efficient query answering, such as checking whether a given set of STP-constraints is consistent with the an existing (minimal) network of STP-constraints or whether it is necessarily satisfied in it (Brusoni et al., 1995).

Recently, an extension of STP to include inequations (that is, binary constraints of the form $y - x \neq d$, where d is any value in a dense time domain – such as the rational or real numbers) has been investigated. This extension, called STP$^{\neq}$ by Gerevini and Cristani (1995), was first studied in Koubarakis (1992).[22] STP$^{\neq}$ provides a useful increase of expressiveness for domains where both "instantaneous" (point) events and extended events can occur, without losing tractability. In fact, the task of determining the consistency and of finding a solution for a given set of STP$^{\neq}$-constraints can be accomplished in $O(n^3 + k)$ time (Gerevini, 1997), the task of computing the minimal network in $O(n^3 + kn^2)$ time (Koubarakis, 1995; Gerevini and Cristani, 1995), and the task of enforcing global consistency in $O(kn^4)$ time (Koubarakis, 1995).

Table 2 summarizes time complexity of known algorithms for STP, STP$^{\neq}$, and TCSP. As for STP the complexity bounds for STP$^{\neq}$ refer to algorithms that are based on traditional graph algorithms and in addition to some specialized techniques for dealing with the inequations. The algorithms for TCSP use complete techniques based on backtracking, or approximate methods (see Dechter et al., 1991; Schwalb and Dechter, 1993, 1995).

The integration of qualitative and metric information is a practically

Problem	TCSP	STP$^{\neq}$	STP
Consistency	NP-hard	$O(n^3 + k)$	$O(n^3)$
Solution	NP-hard	$O(n^3 + k)$	$O(n^3)$
Minimal network	NP-hard	$O(n^3 + kn^2)$	$O(n^3)$
Global consistency	NP-hard	$O(kn^4)$	$O(n^3)$

TABLE 2.   Time complexity of temporal reasoning for TCSP, STP$^{\neq}$ and STP. (n is the number of points constrained; k is the number of inequations.)

important issue especially in planning applications and in knowledge-based systems. Meiri's *general temporal constraint networks* (1996) and Kautz and Ladkin's *combined-metric-Allen* procedure (1991) are two prominent approaches allowing integration of STP-constraints with Allen's relations. Unfortunately, both of them are intractable, and Kautz and Ladkin's method is also incomplete.[23]

Very recently Jonsson and Bäckström (1996) proved the tractability of an interesting class of relations called *Horn disjunctive linear relations* (Horn DRLs). This class subsumes Nebel's ORD-Horn class as well as the STP$^{\neq}$-constraints. In particular, they proved that deciding the consistency of a set of assertions of Horn DRLs can be accomplished by using an algorithm based on linear programming. While this is indeed a significant result for the field, Jonsson and Bäckström's linear programming techniques can incur high computational costs.

It appears then that integration of qualitative and metric information is an aspect of temporal reasoning which deserves some further research. For example, such research might formulate new efficient representations and (complete or approximate) algorithms that work well in practice, or investigate other classes of relations that can express both qualitative and metric information (a recent related study on this subject is Hirsh, 1996).

2.6.3. IMPLEMENTED TEMPORAL REASONING SYSTEMS

The development of domain-independent temporal reasoning modules that can be used in AI applications as specialized reasoning engines is practically important. Several systems for representing and managing temporal relations have been implemented. Among them, two well-known examples are TIMELOGIC (Koomen, 1988), which is based on Allen's IA, and MATS (Kautz and Ladkin, 1991), which is based on both Allen's IA and on Dechter, Meiri, and Pearl's STP. These are two of the most ambitious systems, in terms of the relations they can handle. They implement polynomial constraint-propagation techniques, and their Lisp implementation is relatively simple. On the other hand, they have two drawbacks: they are incomplete, and they are very inefficient with large data sets (say, a set of input relations involving hundreds of intervals).

TIMELOGIC ensures completeness of consistency checking only when the input relations belong to the ORD-Horn subclass. MATS suffers the same limitation, and in addition its method for integrating metric and qualitative information is incomplete even when the input qualitative relations belong to SIA.[24] Some recently proposed techniques that improve previous methods for computing path-consistency could be used to improve the efficiency of these systems (van Beek and Manchak, 1996; Bessière, 1996; Ladkin and Reinefeld, ming).

Other systems based on graph algorithms have been developed with the aim of addressing scalability and supporting efficient reasoning with large data sets. Some important examples of such systems are TMM (Dean and McDermott, 1987; Dean, 1989; Boddy, 1993), IxTeT (Ghallab and Alaoui, 1989), Tachyon (Stillman et al., 1993, 1996) and TimeGraph I and II (Miller and Schubert, 1990; Gerevini et al., 1995; Gerevini and Schubert, 1995a).

TMM (time map manager) can handle the qualitative relations in PA^c (SIA^c) as well as metric temporal constraints expressing upper and lower bounds on the distance separating two time points, *dates* defined as offsets from a *global frame reference*, and *reldates* defined as offsets from a specified default date. TMM uses indexing techniques to efficiently manage large databases of temporal constraints (Dean, 1989). The system does not provide completeness guarantees, but it has the merit of being a more general reasoning tool than the other systems mentioned above. In particular, in addition to temporal constraints, it supports reasoning about change by managing *causal rules* of the form: *if a certain event occurs at time t, then a certain proposition becomes true at $t + \epsilon$.* Such rules are used by the system for accomplishing some temporal projection tasks. TMM has been used in planning and scheduling applications (Boddy, 1996).

Tachyon can manage STP-constraints as well as the qualitative relations in PA^c (SIA^c). It is based on a C++ implementation of the Bellman-Ford single source shortest-paths algorithm (Cormen et al., 1990), supporting consistency checking and the computation of the earliest or latest possible times of the point variables involved by the asserted constraints. Tachyon has a graphic interface for displaying and editing the temporal information represented through the constraint graph. It also has some diagnosis capabilities to detect negative cycles, when the set of the asserted constraints is inconsistent. This system has been used to support mixed-initiative planning in military applications (Stillman et al., 1996).

IxTeT (indexed time table) could originally handle only the qualitative relations in PA (SIA). Later it was extended to handle also metric constraints expressing upper and lower bounds on temporal distances between time points (Dousson et al., 1993). IxTeT uses a graph-based representation of the qualitative relations, which relies for efficiency on a maximum spanning tree, together with an indexing scheme of the vertices supporting very efficient computation of ancestor information. The system is not complete, since it cannot infer certain strict inequalities that are entailed by the relations represented in the graph. IxTeT has been used in the context of a situation recognition system for monitoring complex dynamic systems.

TimeGraph I was originally developed in the context of story comprehension and can efficiently manage large sets of relations in PA^c and SIA^c, as well as metric constraints such as upper and lower bounds on the temporal distance between two time points and absolute times (dates). TimeGraph II is a complete reasoning system that provides useful extensions to TimeGraph I, including an increase of expressiveness allowing the system to represent relations in PA, SIA, and disjunctive relations expressing point-interval exclusion and interval disjointness. On the other hand, the current version of TimeGraph II does not support metric constraints.

In TimeGraph I-II temporal relations are represented through a *timegraph*, a graph partitioned into a collection of *time chains* (sequences of time points) which in TimeGraph II are automatically structured for efficiency. Efficient query handling is achieved through a time point numbering scheme, and a *metagraph* data structure that guides the search processes on the same chain and across the chains.[25]

TimeGraph II also supports D-timegraphs, timegraphs augmented by a collection of disjunctions of relations of the form $x < y$ or $w \leq z$. Although reasoning with such disjunctive information is in the worst case NP-hard, experimental results given in (Gerevini and Schubert, 1995a; Yampratoom and Allen, 1993) show that the method implemented in TimeGraph-II for deciding consistency is in practice very efficient.

2.7. Conclusions

Time representation and reasoning is fundamental in many applications of AI as well as of other disciplines of computer science, such as computational linguistics (see Song and Cohen, 1991; Lascarides and Oberlander, 1993; Hwang and Schubert, 1994), database design (for a review on temporal databases see Snodgrass, 1990; Kline, 1993; Özsoyŏglu and Snodgrass, 1995; Orgun 1996), and computational models for molecular biology (Benzen, 1959; Golumbic and Shamir, 1993). In this article we have selectively surveyed some aspects of temporal reasoning, focusing on two subareas of particular interest to AI: reasoning about time and reasoning about actions and change. After introducing the basic concepts and techniques of both subareas, we briefly illustrated their essential role in the area of planning. We also provided an overview of the main results concerning reasoning about time.

The research conducted on reasoning about time in the last three decades has yielded a rich collection of results and techniques, ranging from computational complexity analyses to implemented reasoning systems. We believe that in general the state of the art in reasoning about time is relatively mature and has much to offer to the development of practical AI applications. However, at the time of writing some important aspects of temporal representation and reasoning still deserve further research. These include the following:

- New efficient representations and algorithms for managing combined qualitative and metric temporal information;
- New methods for representing and managing relations involving non-convex intervals, which for example can be useful in the representation of periodic events (see Leban et al., 1986; Poesio and Brachman, 1991; Terenziani, 1996);
- Extensions of the TCSP framework to represent stochastic temporal information such as "the travel of the train from Venice to Milan takes on average three hours with a standard deviation of five minutes" or other probabilistic temporal information;[26]
- Efficient methods for incremental maintenance of a temporal constraint network (or of any other kinds of representation), when new constraints are added or removed (some examples of the few studies conducted in this direction are Bell and Tate, 1985; Cervoni et al., 1994; Gerevini et al., 1996);
- Efficient (complete or approximate) algorithms for reasoning with disjunctive information in the context of the TCSP framework, possibly extended to represent relations expressing interval disjointness or point-interval exclusion (see Schwalb and Dechter, 1995);
- The integration of a temporal reasoner into a more general system of knowledge representation and reasoning, capable for example of using specialized temporal and spatial modules for representing movement information;
- The use of temporal constraint reasoning in the context of formal methods for reasoning about actions and change (see Schwalb et al., 1994).

Concerning formal methods for reasoning about actions and change, current techniques still appear to be far from practicality. Despite, significant recent progress in this subfield (see Pinto, 1994; JLC, 1994; Sandewall, 1994a; Lin, 1996; Reiter, 1996), current approaches cannot address all the ontological and representational characteristics of complex real situations, which include actions with nondeterministic effects, side-effects, or delayed effects; probabilistic or partial information about the scenario descriptions; external change and exogenous events; multiple agents; concurrent actions; continuous change.

However, some researchers (see Sandewall and Shoham, 1995) claim that the development of a general-purpose method should not be the ultimate goal of future research. Instead, the investigation of complementary methods, capable of addressing different phenomena which characterize restricted classes of scenarios (and their possible integration) is probably a more promising direction.

Similarly, computational methods for reasoning about actions and change are in general still inadequate for dealing with problems of the real world. In particular, in well-founded domain-independent planning the expressiveness of current planners is in general not yet fully satisfactory, and the performance of the algorithms and representation used is not yet adequate for problems of practical size. One very promising research direction concerns the development and use of techniques for *preprocessing* the specification of a planning domain (see Blum and Furst, 1995; Gerevini and Schubert, 1996; McDermott, 1996; Friedman and Weld, 1996). Such techniques can then be used to discover constraints on the structure of the search space, which can be exploited during planning in order to significantly cut down the search space.

Another intriguing recent development is the application of fast satisfiability testing techniques to planning (see Kautz and Selman, 1992, 1996; Kautz et al., 1996). The general idea is to convert a planning problem to a propositional satisfiability problem, and then using efficient (complete or stochastic) techniques to search for solutions (see Crawford and Auton, 1993; Selman et al., 1994).

Acknowledgments

I would like to thank Len Schubert for many helpful comments on an earlier version of this chapter. I am also grateful to George Ferguson for suggestions that helped to improve the quality of the presentation, to Peter Ladkin for some technical suggestions, and to the editor, for his invitation to contribute to this book.

Notes

[1] We choose to deepen this subfield, partly because the book does not contain a specific contribution on this subject and partly because this is one of the areas in which the author has conducted active research for several years.

[2] This section gives only quite a general introduction. For a more detailed treatment the interested reader is referred to Ladkin (1987b), Allen and Hayes (1989), van Benthem (1991), Galton (1995b), Galton's chapter in this book (Chapter 10).

[3] Other less commonly used primitive units are semintervals (Freksa, 1992a) and nonconvex intervals (Ladkin, 1986; Ligozat, 1990, citeyearLig91; Morris et al., 1993). Vilain (1982), Meiri (1996), and more recently Jonsson, Drakengren, and Bäcström (1996) studied frameworks where both points and intervals are primitive units.

[4] Suppose, for example, that the travel times of a train vary according to the kind and quantity of load transported.

[5] As observed in Sandewall and Shoham (1995) the predicate Holds is commonly used in the context of SC, though it was not used in the original formulation of SC.

[6] This example and the one that we will use to illustrate the qualification problem are borrowed from Shoham and Goyal (1988).

[7] Other methodologies are briefly reviewed in Sandewall's chapter of this book, Chapter 9.

[8] For a critical survey of these and other methods see Sandewall and Shoham (1995) and Sandewall (1994a).

[9] The actions that can be handled by UCPOP are a subset of those that can be expressed by Pednault's action description language (ADL) (1989), which is more expressive than the STRIPS's language. In particular, UCPOP operates with actions that have conditional effects, universally quantified goals, preconditions and effects, and disjunctive goals and preconditions (Penberthy and Weld, 1992).

[10] From a computational point of view, when the events (actions) are partially ordered, and their descriptions correspond to instances of STRIPS operators, temporal projection is NP-hard (Nebel and Bäckström, 1994; Dean and Boddy, 1988b).

[11] This is likely to be the case for instances of NP-complete reasoning problems that lie around critical values (a "phase transition", Cheeseman et al., 1991) of certain parameters of the problem space. Ladkin and Reinefeld (1992; ming), and more recently Nebel (1996) identified phase transitions for the problem of determining the consistency of a set of assertions of relations in the interval algebra.

[12] Allen and Hayes (1989) showed that one of these basic relations, meets, can be used to express all the others.

[13] van Beek calls the problem of computing the deductive closure computing the "minimal labels" (between all pairs of intervals or points) in van Beek (1992) and computing the "feasible relations" in (van Beek, 1992).

[14] IA contains $2^{13} = 8192$ relations, SIA contains 188 relations (Ladkin and Maddux, 1988a; van Beek and Cohen, 1990), and the ORD-Horn subclass is a strict superset of the relations in SIA containing 868 relations (Nebel and Bürckert, 1995).

[15] On parallel machines the complexity of iterative local path-consistency algorithms lies asymptotically between n^2 and $n^2 log\ n$ (Ladkin and Maddux, 1988a, 1994).

[16] Two networks are equivalent when the variables represented admit the same set of consistent interpretations in both the representations. A relation R_1 is stronger than a relation R_2 if R_1 implies R_2. Also recall that the relations of IA and PA form algebras, and hence they are closed under the operation of composition, as well as under the operations of converse and intersection. For more details the interested reader may consult (Tarski, 1941; Ladkin and Maddux, 1994; Nebel and Bürckert, 1995; Hirsh, 1996).

[17] Another algorithm for accomplishing this task has been proposed by Ligozat (1996a), without a worst-case complexity analysis.

[18] Note that two such relations used in conjunction can also express disjointness of two intervals.

[19] As discussed in (Dechter et al., 1991; Kautz and Ladkin, 1991), the TCSP model can easily be extended to the case where the intervals of the constraints are (semi)open, or have $-/+$ infinity as bounds.

[20] Two temporal constraint networks are equivalent when the corresponding set of constraints admit exactly the same solutions.

[21] Actually, the tasks of consistency checking and of finding a solution can be accomplished using $O(e)$ space, where e is the number of the input constraints.

[22] Another related study is Isli (1994).

[23] Combined-metric-Allen is not able to infer certain strict inequalities entailed by the input set of constraints.

[24] See Gerevini and Cristani (1995) for an example illustrating this source of incompleteness.

[25] Recently Delgrande and Gupta proposed an interesting extension to the chain partitioning of a timegraph that is based on "serial-parallel graphs" (Delgrande and Gupta, 1996).

[26] Some related studies on "fuzzy" temporal reasoning are 6Dubois and Prade 1989, Console et al. (1991), Godo and Vila (1995).

Part II

Spatial Representation and Reasoning

3. Spatial Entities

Roberto Casati and Achille C. Varzi

3.1. Introduction

Common-sense reasoning about space is, first and foremost, reasoning about things *located in* space. The fly is inside the glass; hence the glass is not inside the fly. The book is to the left of the glass; hence the glass is to the right of the book. Sometimes we may be talking about things *going on* in certain places: the concert took place in the garden; then dinner was served in the solarium. Even when we talk about "naked" (empty) regions of space — regions that are not occupied by any macroscopic object and where nothing noticeable seems to be going on — we typically do so because we are planning to move things around or because we are thinking that certain actions or events did or should take place in certain sites as opposed to others. The sofa should go right here; the aircraft crashed right there. Spatial reasoning, whether actual or hypothetical, is typically reasoning about spatial entities of some sort.

One might — and some people do — take this as a fundamental claim, meaning that spatial entities such as objects or events are fundamentally (cognitively, or perhaps even metaphysically) prior to space: there is no way to identify a region of space except by reference to what is or could be located or take place at that region. (This was, for instance, the gist of Leibniz's contention against the Newtonian view that space is an individual entity in its own right, independently of whatever entities may inhabit it.) It is, however, even more interesting to see how far we can go in our understanding of spatial reasoning without taking issue on such matters. Let us acknowledge the *fact* that space has little use per se in the ordinary representation of our environment (that is, the representation implicit in our everyday interaction with the spatial environment). What is the meaning of that for the theory of spatial reasoning? How does that affect our construction of a general model of our spatial competence?

These questions have both methodological and substantive sides. On the substantive side, they call for a clarification of the relevant ontological presuppositions. A good theory of spatial reasoning must be combined with (if not grounded on) an account of the sort of entities that may enter into the scope of the theory, an account of the sort of entities that can be located or take place in space — in short, an account of what may be collected under the rubric of *spatial entities* (as opposed to *purely spatial items* such as points, lines, regions). What are they? What exactly is their relation to space, and how are they related to one another? In short, what *special* features make them *spatial* entities?

On the methodological side, the issue is the definition of the basic tools required by a good theory of spatial representation and reasoning, understood as a theory of the representation of and reasoning about these entities. In fact, there may be some ambiguity here, as there is some ambiguity as to how "reasoning" and "representation" should really be understood in this regard. We may think of (1) a theory of *the way* a cognitive system represents its spatial environment (this representation serving the twofold purpose of organizing perceptual inputs and synthesizing behavioral outputs) or (2) a theory of the spatial *layout* of the environment (this layout being presupposed, if not explicitly referred to, by such typical inferences as those mentioned above: the book is to the left of the glass; hence the glass is to the right of the book). The two notions are clearly distinct; and although a comprehensive theory of space should eventually provide a framework for dealing with their mutual interconnections, one can presumably go a long way in the development of a theory of type 1 without developing a theory of type 2, and vice versa. On the other hand, both notions share a common concern; both theories require an account of the geometric representation of our spatial competence before we can even start looking at the mechanisms underlying our actual performances. (This is obvious for option 2. For option 1 this is particularly true if we work within a symbolic paradigm — if we favor some sort of mental logic over mental models of reasoning. For then the specificity of a spatial theory of type 1 is fundamentally constrained — if not determined — by the structure of the domain.) It is this common concern that we have in mind here. What are the basic tools required by a theory of this competence? How, for instance, should we deal with the interplay between truly spatial concepts — such as "contained in" or "located between" — and purely mereological (part-whole) notions? What are the underlying principles? And how do they relate to other important tools of spatial representation, such as topology, morphology, kynematics, or dynamics? Moreover, do the answers to these questions hold for all sorts of spatial entities? Or is there a difference between, say, material objects and events? Why, for instance, do spatial boundaries seem to play a crucial role for the former but not for the latter? Are there spatial entities whose spatial location is more than a contingent fact?

These and many other questions arise forcefully as soon as we acknowledge the legitimacy of the more substantive issues mentioned above. Our contention is that the shape of the theory of space depends dramatically on the answers one gives. Over the last few years there has been considerable progress in the direction of sophisticated theories both of type 1 and of type 2, particularly under the impact of AI projects involved in the design and construction of machines capable of autonomous interaction with the physical environment. We think at this point there is some need for a philosophical pause, so to speak. Our purpose in what follows is to offer some thoughts that may help to fulfil (albeit very partially and asystematically) this need.

3.2. Parts and Wholes

Much recent work on spatial representation has focused on mereological and topological concepts, and the question of the interaction between these two domains will be our main concern here.

There is, in fact, no question that a considerable portion of our reasoning about space involves mereological thinking — that is, reasoning in terms of the *part* relation. How is this relation to be characterized? How are the spatial parts of an object spatially related to one another? Traditionally, mereology has been associated with a nominalistic stand and has been presented as a parsimonious alternative to set theory, dispensing with all abstract entities or, better, treating all entities as individuals. However, there is no necessary internal link between mereology and the philosophical position of nominalism. We may simply think of the former as a theory concerned with the analysis of parthood relations among whatever entities are allowed into the domain of discourse (including sets, if one will, as in Lewis, 1991). This certainly fits in well with the spirit of type 2 theories, in the terminology of the previous section, but type 1 theories may also be seen this way. So mereology is ontologically neutral. The question is, rather, how far we can go with it — how much of the universe can be grasped and described by means of purely mereological notions.

We are going to argue that one cannot go very far. In our view (and this is a view we share with others, though we may disagree on how to implement it), a purely mereological outlook is too restrictive unless one integrates it at least with concepts and principles of a topological nature. There are several reason for this, in fact, and some of them will keep us occupied for quite a while in the second part of this chapter. However, one basic motivation seems easily available. Without going into much detail (see Varzi, 1994), the point is simply that mereological reasoning by itself cannot do justice to the notion of a whole — a self-connected whole, such as a stone or a rope, as opposed to a scattered entity made up of several disconnected parts, such as a broken glass or an archipelago. Parthood is a relational concept, wholeness a global property. And in spite of a widespread tendency to present mereology as a theory of parts *and* wholes, the latter notion (in its ordinary understanding) cannot be explained in terms of the former. For every whole there is a set of (possibly potential) parts; for every set of parts (that is, arbitrary objects) there is in principle a complete whole — its mereological sum, or fusion. But there is no way, mereologically, to draw a distinction between "good" and "bad" wholes; there is no way one can rule out wholes consisting of widely scattered or ill assorted entities (the sum consisting of our four eyes and Caesar's left foot) by reasoning exclusively in terms of parthood. If we allow for the possibility of scattered entities, then we lose the possibility of discriminating them from integral, connected wholes. On the other hand, we cannot just keep the latter without some means of discriminating them from the former.

Whitehead's early attempts to characterize his ontology of events provides a good exemplification of this difficulty. His mereological systems (1919, 1920) do not admit of arbitrary fusions, but only of wholes made up of parts that are attached or "joined" to each other. This relation is defined thus:

$$(3.1) \quad J(x,y) =_{df} \exists z(O(z,x) \wedge O(z,y) \wedge \forall w(P(w,z) \to O(w,x) \vee O(w,y)))$$

where P indicates parthood and O overlapping. This should rule out scattered wholes. But it is easily verified that this definition falls short of its task *unless it is already assumed* that the piece z overlaying two "joined" events (or things at large) x and y be itself connected (see Figure 3.1). In other words, the account works if the general assumption is made that only self-connected entities can inhabit the domain of discourse (i.e., be the values of bound variables). But this is no account, for it just is not possible to make the assumption explicit.

3.3. The Topological Option

Mereology can hardly serve the purpose of spatial representation even if we confine ourselves to very basic patterns. Not only is it impossible to capture the notion of one-piece wholeness; mereologically one cannot even account for such basic notions as, say, the relationship between an object and its surface, or the relation of something being inside, abutting, or surrounding something else. These and similar notions are arguably fundamental for spatial reasoning (for type 1 theories as well as for type 2 theories). Yet

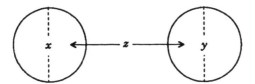

Figure 1. Whitehead's problem: x and y are not connected unless the overlaying piece z is itself assumed to be (self-)connected.

they run afoul of plain part-whole relations, and their systematic account seems to require an explicit topological machinery of some sort.

Now, in recent philosophical and AI literature, this intuition has been taken to suggest that topology is truly a more basic and more general framework subsuming mereology in its entirety. In other words, if topology eludes the bounds of mereology, then — so goes the argument — one should better turn things around: start from topology right away and define mereological notions in terms of topological primitives. For just as mereology can be seen as a generalization of the even more fundamental theory of identity (parthood, overlapping, and even fusion subsuming singular identity as a definable special case), likewise topology can be seen as a generalization of mereology, where the relation of connection takes over overlapping and parthood as special cases. This view was actually considered by Whitehead himself (1929), though it was only with Clarke (1981, 1985) that it was fully worked out. Recently it has been widely employed in AI, as reported in Cohn et al.'s contribution to this volume, Chapter 4.

The subsumption of mereology to topology proposed on this approach is straightforward: given a relation of topological connection (C), one thing is part of another if everything connected to the first thing is also connected to the second:

(3.2) $P(x, y) =_{df} \forall z(C(z, x) \rightarrow C(z, y))$.

Obviously, the reduction depends on the intended interpretation of C (which is generally axiomatized as a reflexive and symmetric relation). If we give C the same intuitive meaning as O, then (3.2) converts to a standard mereological equivalence: whatever overlaps a part overlaps the whole. But things may change radically on different readings.

Typically, the suggestion is to interpret the relation $C(x, y)$ as meaning that the *regions* x and y have at least one *point* in common. This means two things. First, the domain of quantification is viewed as consisting of spatial (or spatiotemporal) regions and not of ordinary things. Second, since points are not regions, sharing a point does not imply overlapping, which therefore does not coincide with (though it is included in) connection. In other words, things may be "externally" connected. There are, of course, some immediate complications with this account, for the absence of boundary elements in the domain means that things can be topologically "open" or "closed" without there being any corresponding mereological difference. In fact, various refinings are available that avoid this unpalatable feature, so we need not go into these details (see Varzi, 1997). Suffice it to say that with the help of C it becomes easy, on some reasonable interpretation, to capture various topological notions and to account for various patterns of topological reasoning. For instance, self-connectedness is immediately defined:

$$(3.3) \qquad \mathsf{SC}(x) =_{df} \forall y \forall z (\forall w (\mathsf{O}(w, x) \leftrightarrow \mathsf{O}(w, y) \lor \mathsf{O}(w, z)) \to \mathsf{C}(y, z)).$$

So if spatiotemporal regions are the only entities of our domain, then (3.2) yields important conceptual achievements: the basic limits of mereology are overcome. However, there is a second side of the coin. For if we really are to take an open-faced attitude toward real-world things and events, as we urged in the introduction (without identifying such entities with their respective spatiotemporal coordinates), then the reduction offered by (3.2) seems hardly tenable, as different entities can be perfectly colocalized. A shadow does not share any parts with the wall onto which it is cast. And a stone can be wholly located inside a hole without actually being part of it. The region that it occupies is part of the region occupied by the hole — but that's all: holes are immaterial and can therefore share their location with other entities. (See Figure 3.2.) For another example (from Davidson, 1969), the rotation and the getting warm of a metal ball that is simultaneously rotating and getting warm are two distinct events. Yet they share exactly the same spatiotemporal region because events, unlike material objects, do not *occupy* the space at which they are located. From here, intuitions diverge rapidly. And the notions of connection and parthood that we get by reasoning exclusively in terms of regions, no matter which specific interpretation we choose, just seem inadequate for dealing with the general case. This means, among other things, that the possibility of extending the theory to neighboring domains might suffer. For instance, a theory of events that reduces mereology to topology by mapping every event onto the interval or instant of time of its occurrence will not have room for cotemporal distinct events, let alone events occurring in the same spatiotemporal regions. (Compare Casati, 1995b, and Pianesi and Varzi, 1994, 1996a, 1996b.)

3.4. The Hole Trouble

These concerns may not be definitive. In particular, our examples of the shadow and of the stone in the hole presuppose a friendly attitude toward the ontological status of shadows and holes, which is far from

Figure 2. Clarke's problem: x is inside object y; but what is the relationship between object x and hole z? (and what the relationship between z and y?)

unproblematic. A nonrealist would simply say that such "things" do not exist (for shadows and holes are — after all — paradigm examples of *nothings*) — hence the above question would not even arise. However, this would require some radical eliminative strategy. It would, for instance, require some systematic way of paraphrasing every shadow- or hole-committing sentence by means of sentences that do not refer to or quantify over shadows or holes (the cheese is holed, but there *is* no hole in it; the wall is darkened, but there *is* no shadow). On the other hand, if we want to take common sense seriously, we should resist these ways out in favor of a realist, common-sense attitude. Holes and shadows are enigmatic. Yet if there is an ontology inherent in our everyday reasoning about the world, then this ontology comprises shadows and holes (and cognate entities such as waves, knots, cuts, grooves, cracks, fissures, smiles, grims) along with stones and chunks of cheese.

We have defended this view at large in previous work (especially in *Holes*, 1994), and we refer to it for further discussion of the underlying philosophical issues. In fact, we take this to be a good example of the sort of general ontological concern that we mentioned at the beginning: a general theory of spatial representation calls for a clarification of the relevant ontological presuppositions. It must be combined with (if not grounded on) an explicit account of the sort of entities that may enter into the scope of the theory. Be it as it may, it is apparent that the simplification introduced by (3.2) has critical consequences if our concern is with the foundations of general-purpose representation systems, *even if* we take a nonrealist attitude toward holes and shadows. For the basic issue of the relationship between an entity and "its" space (the space where it is located) is then trivialized: every entity is *reduced* to its space. Moreover, it yields a dull world in which every morphological feature is ignored, and the question of whether holes should be treated as *bona fide* entities next to ordinary objects, far from being left in the background, cannot even be raised. This, we maintain, is not only a source of conceptual poverty; it also may be misleading.

Let us focus on holes. Some recent work by Nick Gotts (1994a, 1994b) is indicative of the difficulties we have in mind. Gotts's concern is with the expressive power of Clarke's system and of its derivatives: How much can be expressed using the single connection predicate? In particular, Gotts sets out to address this question relative to the definite task of specifying the topological properties of a solid toroidal structure: Can we distinguish a doughnut from a sphere exclusively in terms of topological connection? Can we express the difference between holed and holeless objects without directly resorting to holes (that is, by referring exclusively to the connection properties of the objects)? Gotts shows that one can indeed go far in this enterprise. With the help of a minimal axiomatic apparatus, he shows how to describe the topology of a doughnut as well as the topology of an object with an internal void. These are the two main kinds of topologically relevant hole, so the achievement is remarkable. However, from our present perspective this result is necessarily partial.

For one thing, there are other kinds of holes that cannot be handled in the same way. Regardless of whether our primitive is C or something else, a purely topological account is bound to remain blind in front of superficial hollows, grooves, and other discontinuities of irreducible morphological nature. This is not an objection to Gotts; rather, it merely points out that topology is only one step ahead of mereology, and need be integrated by other notions and principles if we want to go beyond a world of spheres and doughnuts (and little else) without reflecting on the ontology. Second, and more important, an account in terms of connection is adequate only for capturing the intrinsic topology of an object. The *extrinsic* topology, the way the object is embedded in three-dimensional space, is ignored. To put it differently, the account is incapable of capturing the difference between a straight and a knotted hole. Now, of course knotted holes are just as important as straight ones, as it were. (And surely, you can hardly tell if the hole you are walking through is knotted or not.) But if a theory *has no room* for the difference, its classificatory power is deficient in an important sense.

Are there any ways of avoiding this outcome without reifying holes? One way would be to combine the analysis of the object's topology with that of its complement. Clearly, the complementary topology of an ordinary doughnut and that of a doughnut with a knotted hole are different, and presumably the difference can be expressed in terms of connection properties. But this shift (from the object to its complement) is crucial. If we are only talking about regions, then again all is fine: there is no significant difference between a region and its complement, and no reason to restrict oneself to one or the other. Gotts's results are quite telling then, provided we work out the complementary topology. But if, as we urged, we take an open-faced attitude towards ordinary spatial objects, then the

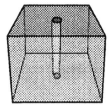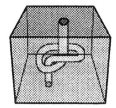

Figure 3.   We can't C well enough to tell a straight hole from a knotted one.

shift to the complementary topology is ontologically significant. An object's complement is, after all, just as immaterial as the hole. The complement includes the hole. So the complementary topology of the object is, to some extent, the topology of the hole. The expressive power of C is safe. But it doesn't save us from explicit reference to immaterial entities. In short, if we care about spatial entities, then we need to keep an eye upon the doughnut, and the other upon the hole.

3.5. The Compositional Approach

We take the foregoing to imply a threefold moral. First, it appears that one needs both mereology and topology as *independent* (though mutually related) frameworks. Mereology alone is too weak; topology alone is too strong (in a sense) but at the same time very limited (in another sense). Second, the limitations of topology are significant even at a fairly elementary level (a long way before functional features become important for classifying shapes or providing an analysis of such relations as containment, as urged, for example, by Vandeloise, 1994, and Aurnague and Vieu, 1993). Third, and perhaps more important, one had better abandon an approach to spatial representation and spatial reasoning in terms of spatial regions and consider from the very beginning an ontology consisting of the sort of entities that may inhabit those regions. As we said at the beginning, this is, of course, tied in with the difficult metaphysical issue of whether we can *dispense* with spatial items altogether. This is the controversy between spatial absolutism — the Newtonian view that space is an individual existing by itself, independently of whatever entities may inhabit it, and is in fact a *container for* the latter — and spatial relativism — the Leibnizian view according to which space is parasitic upon, and can be construed from, objects and relations thereof. But we believe one can remain neutral with respect to this issue at least at the beginning.

Let us consider one more example to illustrate the delicate interplay between ontological and representational issues. We are urging an open-faced attitude towards ordinary spatial entities, but we are also concerned exclusively in their spatial structure (and in their mereotopological structure to begin with), not in all of their properties. A certain degree of schematization in the way things are represented in the formal theory may therefore be appropriate, and perhaps also necessary in order to provide a realistic model of the way our cognitive systems operate. (To see whether the fly is inside the glass, say, we don't need to give a faithful representation of the insect's form, composition, and internal structure, but only a sketch of its contour, and a rather approximate one at that.)

An interesting proposal in this direction is Biederman's (1987) *recognition by components* (RBC) theory. This rather popular theory — whose primary concern is with shape recognition — is based on the primitive notion of a normalized cylinder, or geon, and offers a simple spatial syntax whereby every object can be viewed as composed out of cylinder-like components. (The basic idea has been used by several other authors and is usually traced back to the work of Thomas Binford; Biederman should nevertheless be given credit for formulating it in purely qualitative terms, without resorting to sophisticated abstract hyerarchies.) The related cognitive thesis is that the human shape recognition system is based on the capacity to decompose an object into cylinders. Thus, for instance, a coffee cup would consist of a main semiconcave cylinder (the containing part) with a small bended cylinder (the handle) attached to the first at both ends. In a more recent formulation (Biederman, 1990), both geons and relations among them are defined in terms of more primitive parameters, such as variation in the section size, relative size of a geon's axes with respect to its section, relative size of two geons, vertical position of a geon at the point of junction with another. The outcome is that with three geons one can theoretically describe over 1.4 billions distinct objects.

Also in this case, however, some problems arise immediately. For one thing, the theory is based on a general assumption pertaining to the cognitive dimension of part-whole reasoning that seems to be false. RBC is meant to do justice to the intuition that the mereological module is crucial to object recognition. However, recent data by Cave and Kosslyn (1993) show very clearly that a module for decomposition into parts does *not* generally act prior to, and is not a necessary condition of, object recognition. Their results indicate first of all that the recognition of an object depends crucially on the proper spatial relations among the parts: when the parts are scrambled or otherwise scattered, naming times and error rates increase. Second, Cave and Kosslyn's results show that the mereological parsing of an object affects the object's identificatiton "only under the most impoverished viewing conditions." This is not a disproof of the existence of a merelogical module per se (for instance, the way physical objects are partitioned tends to be rather robust across individuals). However, Cave and Kosslyn contend that such a module need not be activated for the purpose of object recognition, and their results leave little room for a rebuttal. (We tend to rely on data of this sort, for they dispose of the issue of object recognition in our discussion. In particular, the structure of the as yet putative mereological module should be considered independent of the pressures of object recognition.)

A second problem is more technical and, in a sense, further reaching. Take a flat object — say, a disc. In spite of the "generative" power of the notion of a normalized cylinder, it would seem that in cases like this its representational adequacy is at the limit: it seems unfair to represent a disc as a wide, short *cylinder* — a flat geon. It might be replied that this is an objection only if our concern is with type 1 theories, with *the way* a cognitive system represents its spatial environment. (Surely the fact that a certain object *can be* represented as a normalized cylinder does not imply that it actualy *is* represented that way by a cognitive system.) But if we are looking for a purely geometric theory of type 2, one could argue that this sort of artificiality is inessential. After all, for the purpose of spatial *reasoning*, it does not matter what we take a disc to be: the important thing is to keep the number of primitives to a minimum. If so, however, consider then a disc with a hole, or a doughnut for that matter. How is such an object to be represented? Here the problem is twofold (see Figure 3.4). On the one hand, we would again say that it is awkward to regard a disc or doughnut (an O-shaped object) as consisting of two joined handles (C-shaped cylinders), or perhaps of a single elongated handle whose extremities are in touch. This is the type 1 misgiving. But there is also a type 2 misgiving. For how do we choose between the possible decompositions? More generally, how do we go about decomposing an object with holes in terms of its nonholed parts? Is there any principled way of doing that? There isn't. And, of course, we wouldn't want to expand our primitives by adding doughnuts. Otherwise bitoruses — doughnuts with two holes (8-shaped objects) — should also be assumed as primitives. That would be necessary insofar as there seems to be no principled way within the putative RBC+torus theory to decompose a bitorus: as torus plus handle (C-shaped geon), or as handle plus torus? Since the same puzzle arises also for a tritorus, and more generally for arbitrary n-toruses, it therefore seems that by this pattern one would have to introduce an infinite amount of primitives — and *that* is unacceptable also from the perspective of a type 2 theory.

3.6. Negative Parts

Once again, the problem is that the theory under consideration aims to account for one *desideratum* but neglects the others. We welcome the suggestion of investigating a spatial compositional structure that is not simply a mereology of *space* but of spatial entities. This is as it should be.

Figure 4.   How do we decompose a doughnut into normalized cylinders? How do we
decompose a double doughnut?

But we already saw that a pure mereological module is not going to do all
the work; *a fortiori*, one can't go very far by reasoning exclusively in terms
of such well-behaved parts as geons.

However, here one might be tempted to reconsider our earlier conclusion:
perhaps *that* is precisely the problem; perhaps the problem is precisely that
the relevant notion of part (or component) is not broad enough to do all
the work. With a broader notion — not only broader than geons but at this
point even broader than the notion of part underlying standard parthood
theories — mereology might be enough after all.

One way of implementing this intuition could come from Hoffman and
Richards's original theory of parts (1985). Analyze a doughnut as consisting
of two parts — not just two ordinary parts but two "complementary" parts
(as it were): a *positive* part (in the shape of a disc) and a *negative* part
(the hole). This would be a solution to the above problem inasmuch as
both the disc and the negative part can be treated as RBC-normalized
cylinders. And the notion of negative part can be defined in relation to the
normalization of the solid (positive) body hosting it: the closest solid for a
doughnut is a cylinder; the negative part is the "missing" cylinder in the
middle (see Figure 3.5). The solution is obviously generalizable to arbitrary
n-toruses.

This proposal has some independent attractive features, which should
not be overlooked. One is that it deals neatly with complementary or
dual structures, such as those constituted by grooves (or notches, dents,
indentations) and ridges. A groove is a negative, intruding part just like
a ridge is an ordinary, protruding part. There is a rather obvious reason
for the desire to treat such dual structures on a par. A natural way to
produce an indent in a body is to act on it with another body's protrusion;
conversely, a natural way to produce a protrusion is to fuse some material
in anothers body's indent. We can immediately predict, by observing the
processes of fusion and of indentation, that the shapes of the notch and
of the protrusion will fit perfectly. (Are they actually one single shape?

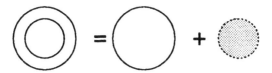

Figure 5.   Holes as negative parts

This is an interesting question, pertaining to the more general issue of the status of complementary shapes.) Another advantage of negative parts is that when it comes to holes the notions of *completion* of an object, or of a hole's being a lack in the object (a missing something), are immediately and rather nicely implemented. For holes are exactly there where some part of the object could conceivably have been; and as they *always* are where some part of the object could have been, it does not make a big difference if we have them coincide with some *actual* negative part of the object.

Let us stress indeed that these negative parts would exactly correspond to what we would treat as a hole. Wherever we have a hole, this theory would have a negative part, and vice versa. But the negative-part theory and our theory in *Holes* (the hole theory, hereafter) are false friends: they are not just notational variants. On the hole theory, a hole is not a *part* of its host. If you join the tips of your thumb and your index so as to form an O, you do not thereby create a *new part* of yourself, however negatively you look at it. On the negative-part theory, by contrast, a hole is precisely that: it is just a part, albeit of a somewhat special and hiterto neglected sort.

Now, this may well be a disadvantage of the hole theory. It requires a special primitive H (... is a hole in ...) logically distinct from the parthood primitive P. The two primitives are not only distinct; they stand for two relations that are totally disjoint: as we said, holes are never parts of their hosts. They don't even overlap, as reflected in the axiom:

(3.4) $H(x, y) \rightarrow \neg O(x, y)$.

By contrast, if holes are treated as parts (albeit parts of a special kind) the possibility is left open that the P primitive (perhaps combined with a suitable inversion functor) be sufficient for most purposes. The difference is important, of course. Conceptual economy may be very advantageous, especially from the perspective of a type 2 theory. (Ironically, this is not the perspective of Hoffman and Richards. But think of an expert system whose task is, say, to classify shapes. One may imagine using, in addition to several shape primitives, the P primitive and an inversion functor that maps (suitable) positive parts of an object's complement onto corresponding

Figure 6.   Problems with negative parts: is a semisphere composed of a whole sphere plus a negative half? What negative parts does a champagne glass consist of?

negative parts of the object itself, and viceversa — an idea that can be traced as far back as to the kinematic theory of Franz Reuleaux, 1875.)

At the same time, the price of this conceptual economy may be too high (see Figure 3.6). According to the hole theory a doughnut is just a doughnut — an object *with a hole*. According to the negative-part theory a doughnut is really the *sum* of two things: a disc *plus* a negative part. Is *that* what a doughnut is? More important, what does it mean to represent a doughnut in that way? What kind of mereology is required? And when are we allowed to speak of negative parts anyway? Are holes (and grooves, notches, etc.) the only sort of negative part? Take a sphere and cut it in half. According to one intuition, the closest approximation for each piece is the sphere itself; each half has a missing part. Yet surely it would be absurd to treat a semisphere as a *whole sphere plus a negative part* (the missing half). How can the negative-part theory rule that out? Perhaps in this specific case the difficulty might be dealt with simply by stipulating that objects must be approximated to their convex hulls. But that has the flavor of an ad hoc solution. An ordinary champagne glass would by that pattern involve two large negative parts — one surrounding the stem, and one inside the wine cup. It is hard to find satisfaction in that picture.

3.7. Hybrid Sums

Let us look at these questions more closely. If we are right, the answer will eventually be that no mereological module could function *reasonably* if it had to operate on negative parts. And this will be relevant to both a type 1 and a type 2 perspective on spatial reasoning and representation.

Consider how the mereological module can operate on holes if these are construed not as negative parts but as immaterial individuals that are *not* part of their material hosts. According to the hole theory, anytime there is a hole in an object, there is some mereological composition around. Not only because the theory implies that atoms are holeless. (A hole is always in some proper part of an object; therefore, if an object has a hole, it must have parts). There is also the trivial fact that a hole is a part of the mereological sum of the host and of the hole itself.

Now define a (cognitively) natural object as an object that is taken by the cognitive system as unitary (typically, a cognitively natural object is a unit for counting). As we said, not all mereological sums are natural objects. Think again of the sum consisting of our four eyes and Caesar's left foot. But even so, a large number of mereological sums are unitary; they have that cosy, peculiar naturalness and wholeness. Our question now is whether the mereological sum of an object and its hole(s) is a cognitively natural object, and, if it is, how it is related to a normal and holeless natural object. For topological connection plays a hand in the game, but exactly which hand it is unclear.

Mind the fact that such a sum — call it s — is not a mereological sum of the most obvious kind. It is a sum of two objects, one of which (the hole) *depends* existentially on the other (you cannot remove the hole from the doughnut), which in turn depends geometrically or conceptually on the former (you cannot have a doughnut without a hole). And these dependences are more than mereological: they involve a form of topological dependence too. The sum s is not decomposable into hole h and host o in the same sense in which the sum of two solid objects, a plus b, is decomposable into a and b. For the hole exists only insofar as it is topologically connected with its host. And if you *get rid of* the hole (for example, by elastically deforming the host or, if the host is a doughnut, by cutting it open), the host is no longer holed. Thus, even if the sum s of a hole h together with its host o is indeeed a sum of a hole and a *holed* object, metaphysically it has rather peculiar features. For instance, it does not behave as the ordinary sum of a holed object and of its perfect filler (imagining the hole to be filled).

Observe now that the hole theory allows us to express these facts by making a distinction between a hole's being *in* something and a hole's being *part of* something. The hole, h, is part of the hybrid sum s (hole + host) but it is not a hole in s. For h overlaps s, and by axiom (3.4) no hole overlaps its host. Moreover, the following principle of left-monotonicity holds:

(3.5) $H(x, y) \land P(y, z) \rightarrow O(x, z) \lor H(x, z)$.

That is, any object that includes the host of a hole is a host of that hole, unless its parts also include parts of that very hole. You can produce a holed object by taking just another holed object and by attaching a part thereto (in an appropriate way).

Connectedness (between a hole and its host) is thus mandatory for binding the salient parts of s. But one must add that the bind between a hole and its host is much stronger — topologically, not only ontologically — than the bind between two ordinary solid objects in touch with each other. (The bind resembles the one between the various non-salient, only-potential parts of an homogeneous, self-connected chunk of an ideal stuff. Any part of the chunk cannot but ideally be detached from the object — real detachment produces *two* new objects.) We do not see, in any case, how these facts should be related to the property of being a natural whole. We do not see any reason why the sum of an object and its holes should be a natural object. On the other hand, it seems that the negative-part theory requires that such a sum *be* a natural object, for this is where the cognitive system should start from when it comes to holed objects. The sum is assumed to be *cognitively prior* to the analysis into object + holes. But this is far from obvious. We are prepared to accept that in some cases a holed object is considered a sort of incomplete object (a statue with a perforation, say), but this is not the rule. And the proof is, quite simply, that in so many cases we would not be able to tell what parts are missing from what object.

3.8. Negative Parts of *What?*

We thus come to what seems to be the major problem of an ontology of negative parts. We have a number of characters here (see Figure 3.7). To begin with, there is an ordinary holed object; call it the *solid object, o.* Add to this its *hole* (or holes), *h.* The hole is not part of the solid object (which is impenetrable, and thus cannot have penetrable parts). It is nevertheless part of the sum of the solid object with the hole itself; call this sum the *holed sum, s.* Thus, $s = h + o$ and $o = s - h$ where '+' and '−' can be defined in the usual way:

$$(3.6) \qquad x + y =_{df} \imath z \forall w (O(w, z) \leftrightarrow (O(w, x) \lor O(w, y)))$$
$$(3.7) \qquad x - y =_{df} \imath z \forall w (P(w, z) \leftrightarrow (P(w, x) \lor \neg O(w, y))).$$

Then there are two relevant mereological complements: the complement of the solid object, $\sim o$, and the complement of the holed sum, $\sim s$, where in general we define

$$(3.8) \qquad \sim x =_{df} \imath z \forall w (O(w, z) \leftrightarrow \neg O(w, x)).$$

The hole is part of the complement of the solid object (which for the sake of simmetry may be called the *complement sum*), but it is not part of the complement of the holed sum. For the complement sum and the holed sum mereologically overlap: they share a negative part — the hole. In short, $\sim s = (\sim o) - h$ and $\sim o = (\sim s) + h$.

It is enough to formulate these distinctions to see a problem emerge. A pure mereological module founders because a negative part is at the same time part of the holed sum and of the complement sum. Now the theory of

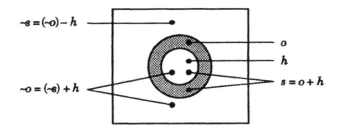

Figure 7. Doughnut, hole, sums, and complements

negative parts does not founder because of that. On that theory, the hole is not a negative part of the holed sum: it is a positive part thereof, and a negative part of something else. But of what, exactly?

More characters must be added to the picture (see Figure 3.8). First, in the negative-part theory we have this entity (partly solid and partly immaterial) that has h as a negative part. Call that entity o'. This is not to be confused with the holed sum s because h is a standard part of s, not a negative part. Nor is o' to be confused with o because h is not a part of o, whether positive or negative. Rather, o' is a third object, distinct both from s and from o. It is what, on the negative-part theory, the doughnut really is. Furthermore, the result of subtracting h from o' gives you another object still, distinct from all of s, o, and o': it give you a disc, the disc we *would* have in case our doughnut were holeless. Call this last character s'; we then have the following equations:

$$(3.9) \qquad s = o + h \qquad o = s - h \qquad s' = o' \ominus h \qquad o' = s' \oplus h.$$

The first two of these (on the left) are standard mereological equations, corresponding to (3.6) and (3.7). The last two (on the right) are not. The way h is added to o to yield s is not the same way h is added to s' to obtain o'; for the former operation yields a bigger object (in an intuitive, compositional, nonmetric sense) than the one we start with, whereas the latter — a form of negative sum — yields a smaller object. And the way h is subtracted from s to yield o is not the same way h is subtracted from o' to obtain s'; for the former operation yields a smaller object than the one we start with, whereas the latter — a form of negative difference — yields a bigger object. But is there any way to characterize the latter operations in terms of the former? Is there any way to characterize $\oplus$ and $\ominus$ in terms of standard mereological operations? It seems not, *unless* negative parthood is assumed as a primitive next to parthood simpliciter. But if we do so, then we have two mereologies, not one; that is, we have two mereological primitives. And one seeming advantage of the negative-part theory over the hole theory (conceptual simplicity) is lost.

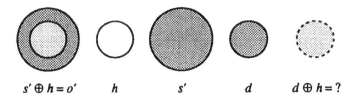

$$s' \oplus h = o' \qquad h \qquad s' \qquad d \qquad d \oplus h = ?$$

Figure 8. Spatial entities in negative-part mereology

Nor is this the whole story. Consider the complement operation, as defined in (3.8). How does it behave with respect to negative parts? We are not asking for the negative counterpart of the complement operation, which could presumably be defined as in (3.8) but using the negative counterpart of O. We are asking how $\sim$ behaves when its arguments are among the additional characters envisioned by the negative-part theory. For instance, how is the following table to be completed?

$$(3.10) \quad \sim s = (\sim o) - h \qquad \sim o = (\sim s) + h \qquad \sim s' =? \qquad \sim o' =?$$

Is h part of $\sim s'$? It would seem so, for surely h, a hole, does not overlap s', a solid disc; so it must be part of the complement. But then, what is the difference between s' and o? It can only be $s' - o$ — that is, the small *solid* disc in the middle of s' which is conceiled, so to speak, by the negative part of o'. However, that means that the list of entities at stake is still growing, giving rise to further questions. Call this new "invisible" part d. Is d also part of the complement of o? Of s? Of what entities? And what sort of entity is $d + h$? Finally, what sort of entity is $d \oplus h$ — the entity obtained from d by "adding" a perfectly congruent negative part? How does it differ from nothing at all?

3.9. The Need for Explicit Theories

The upshot of all this seems clear. If we don't take holes seriously, we end up with a theory that is formally just as rich, due to the need of two distinct mereological primitives, and ontologically much more dubious, due to the presence of such mysterious entities as s', d, $d + h$, and so on. Seen from another perspective, it is the notion of *complement* that founders conceptually. If the doughnut is really somewhat bigger than its edible part, if it also consists of a negative part, then *its* complement does not comprise the negative part. But if the mysterious negative parts are not parts of the complement — that is, if the negative parts of the doughnut are not parts of the doughnut's complement — then why are they negative? This intuition is not negotiable. And if the negativity does not lie in the complement, then why not allow for "negative" entities to begin with? Why not allow for holes?

We have thus reached again a general conclusion concerning the interplay between ontology, mereology, and topology. And the conclusion is that we need all of them. We need mereology because topology is mereologically unsophisticated. We need topology because mereology is topologically blind. And we need ontology because both topology and mereology — even if we try to relax or supplement the relevant primitives — are intrinsically incapable of making sense of important ontological distinctions.

It now goes beyond the aims of the present work to give specific indications of how these three domains can actually be combined into a systematic theory. Some developments can be found in *Holes* as well as in Casati (1995b, forthcoming), Casati and Varzi (1996), Pianesi and Varzi (1994), and Varzi (1993, 1994, 1996a, 1996b, 1997). By way of illustration, however, consider briefly how a mereotopological theory developed in this spirit can provide the foundations for some basic patterns of spatial reasoning of the sort mentioned at the beginning. The fly is inside the glass; hence the glass is not inside the fly. But under what conditions does a fly qualify as being *in* a glass? (Annette Herskovits gives a thorough analysis of this issue in her contribution to this volume, Chapter 6, examining all the intricacies allowed by the use of prepositions in natural language. Here we are interested only in the geometry of the problem, as it were — a much more modest task.)

Some authors have suggested that the answer could be given in terms of mereological inclusion in the convex hull of the containing object (Figure 3.9, left). But as Herskovits (1986) already pointed out, such an account would fail to appreciate the crucial role of containing parts as opposed to other nonconvex parts (a fly near the stem of a glass is not *in* the glass, though it may well fall within its convex hull: see Figure 3.9, middle). Nor can the problem be overcome by focusing exclusively on the convex hull of the object's containing parts, as initially suggested by Vandeloise (1986) (Vandeloise, 1994, defends a thoroughly functional approach): apart from the apparent circularity, it is not difficult to find counterexamples insofar as the outer boundaries of containing parts may themselves involve concavities (Figure 3.9, right; example from Vieu, 1991, p. 207).

Now, this problem is halfway between what we called the hole problem (a problem for a purely topological theory, which we discussed earlier in connection with Gotts's work) and Hoffman and Richards' problem (one of the problems for a purely mereological theory). It is similar to the former inasmuch as the relevant role of what really counts as a *container* (a "fillable" morphological discontinuity) cannot be explained in topological terms even if we extend the range of application of connection to the

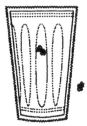 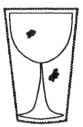 

Figure 9.   The fly problem: reference to the convex hull (dashed line) is of little use for the purpose of telling the flies inside the glass from those outside.

convex hull. And the problem is similar to the latter (and more generally to the crucial dilemma of the negative-part theory) insofar as it requires thinking about the *complement* of the object. By contrast, if we reason directly in terms of holes we get a radically different picture. Only the region corresponding to the hole — the one on the top, not the "groove" surrounding the stem or the top part of the glass in the right diagram — can reasonably be treated as the container. And to be contained *in* the glass is to occupy (perhaps partially) that region — that is, to fill (maybe partly) the hole. Mereology and topology give us the structure of the entities at issue (the glass, the hole, the fly, the corresponding regions); and containment is explained in terms of simple inclusion relations between the region of the fly and the region of the hole. We need the fly and the hole to begin with. *Then* we look at their regions. (See Casati and Varzi, 1996, for a closer examination of the structure of spatial location.)

Here the point is of course that the containing part of a glass determines a true hole — a hollow, in effect. No doubt there are other senses in which a glass can be said to be holed. However, *what* exactly counts as a hole or a containing part is not at issue: the account will be effective precisely insofar as the existence of independent criteria for holehood is presupposed — for example, insofar as the space around the stem of a glass is not taken to be a hole. So if we have holes in the ontology (along with corresponding identity and individuation criteria), the problem dissolves; whereas the lack of holes gives rise to the difficulties illustrated in Figure 3.9.

This is not to suggest that mereology + topology + explicit hole commitment will give us a complete account of the notion of spatial containment, or even a full solution of the fly-in-the glass problem. In fact it is not difficult to find instances where ordinary intuitions are not adequately captured by the above suggestion. For example, the two patterns in Figure 3.10 provide apparent counterexamples whose solution seems to call for a decisive step into other territories than purely geometrical reasoning. Most

Figure 10. Further difficulties with the relation of containment: in both cases the fly is in a hole hosted by the glass but not in the glass itself.

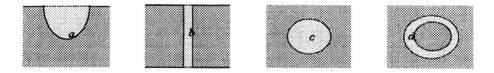

Figure 11. Holes come in superficial hollows (*a*), perforating tunnels (*b*), internal cavities (*c*), and some mixed cases, such as internal tunnel-cavities (*h*).

likely these include at least some pragmatics (as suggested, for example, by Aurnague and Vieu, 1993, and Vandeloise, 1994, forthcoming), or causal factors at large. Even so, several useful refinements can be introduced already at the geometrical level, including some applications to naive-physical reasoning about containment (see Varzi, 1993, 1996a, for details).

Moreover, the basic theory can be improved in various ways, by fully investigating the class of entities compatible with it. For instance, from a classificatory perspective the gist of the theory fragment presented in *Holes* is that holes come in three kinds: superficial hollows, perforating tunnels, and internal cavities (plus some significant mixed cases). The basic patterns are illustrated in Figure 3.11. There are, in fact, important distinctions among these three kinds of hole — more precisely, among the entities affected by such holes. And there is, correspondingly, a simple decision tree. This is illustrated in Figure 3.12 (left). But this basic taxonomy can then be extended. For example, Figure 3.12 (right) shows the result of including grooves. The idea is that grooves are a kind of hole, though geometrically rather bizarre. (We could say that a groove is a sort of "external" tunnel.)

In all of these cases, the same intuition is at work. To classify holes and hole-like entities, we need look at more than just the topology of their material host: we also need to look at their potential "guests," so to speak.

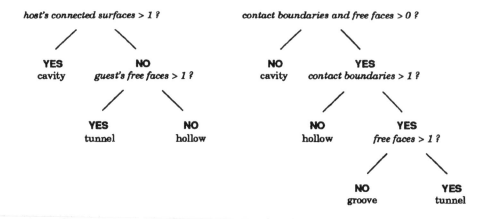

Figure 12. Basic and extended classification trees for holes. Here a free face is any (maximally connected) part of the surface of the hole's filler (the ideal object that can be used to perfectly fill the hole) that is not connected with the host's surface, and a contact boundary is any (maximally connected) boundary of such a free face.

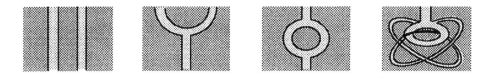

Figure 13. Some configurations that elementary topology cannot distinguish.

For holes are *fillable* entities, and much of our reasoning about holes and hole-like entities involves reasoning about how one can fill them. (In our view this is the only way to avoid two serious classificatory deficiencies of pure topology. One is the fact, already mentioned in connection with Gotts's work, that topology is blind against nonperforationg holes. The second is that it is also too strong, for it treats as equivalent holed objects — such as those in Figure 3.13 — that are clearly different from the standpoint of common sense, and which should be kept distinct for most purposes. By focusing on the patterns of interaction between host and guests (fillers), the hole theory aims at finer distinctions, as illustrated in Figure 3.14: the morphological complexity of a hole is reflected in the topological complexity of the host-guest contact surface.)

In a similar fashion, we also can extend our taxonomy by adding suitable *branching* and *knot* theories to account for further morphological

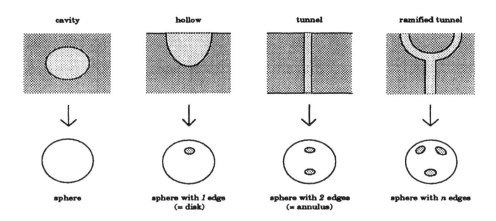

Figure 14.   The morphological complexity of a hole is reflected in the topologial complexity of the contact surface of its perfect filler.

complexities (see Figure 3.15). We may, for instance, wish to distinguish between an X-shaped and an H-shaped tunnel or groove by counting the relevant number of nodes or junction points. And we may want to distinguish between a straight I-shaped tunnel and a knotted one, between a simple O-shaped tunnel-cavity and a trefoil knotted one. (In all of these cases, the base theory is insensitive to what goes on inside the hole and considers only its relations with the external surface of the object. Thus, for instance, the basic principles underlying the decision tree illustrated in Figure 3.12 does not extend to the rightmost pattern of Figure 3.11.) Indeed, the possibility of relying on an explicit knot theory is an immediate and advantagious consequence of the main ontological choice of the hole theory: it is because holes are full-fledged entities — *that* type of entities, viz. immaterial spatial bodies rather than negative parts — that one can investigate the ways they can be knotted together. And with the help of this extended machinery, more complex patterns of spatial interaction between holed objects and their environment can be fruitfully studied.

3.10. Concluding Remarks

We have focused so much on holes and the problems they pose because we take them to be indicative of the issues involved in any spatial theory aiming to combine some affinity with common sense and a suitable degree of formal sophistication. This, we believe, is the main aim for a good theory of spatial reasoning and representation that will overcome the apparent discrepancy between "psychological" type 1 theories and "formal" type 2 theories. As

Figure 15.   Taking ramifications and knots into account

we proceed, we discover layers of problems that are recalcitrant to simple solutions and that are a sign of the presence of unresolved conceptual issues. And holes show how radical the need can be for a revision — or at least a reexamination — of the conceptual categories required for this task.

Holes are not an exception, though. Similar problems arise virtually for *every* spatial entity: not only holes or regions of space but even material objects have been the subject of philosophical dispute. And the particular strategy one is to adopt is often a symptom of wider philosophical concerns. Thus, one might choose to concentrate exclusively on the spatial entities and on their intrinsic properties (at the expense of the environment and of the relational ties linking the objects to their environment) and thereby neglect complementary reasoning or more generally holistic components in spatial reasoning. Or one can attend to global properties of spatial situations and fail to isolate relevant features of individual objects. To some extent this conflict (among others) can be seen as a sign of a deeper conflict between spatial absolutism and spatial relationism. But even so, we suggest the conflict may partly be resolved by integrating both perspectives: *common-sense* reasoning about space is, by one and the same token, reasoning about spatial entities.

Acknowledgments

The first part of this chapter includes revised material originally presented in Varzi (1993, 1994), Casati (1995a), and Casati and Varzi (1995). We also owe much to conversations we have enjoyed with people attending the Bolzano summer school on Spatial Reasoning.

4. Representing and Reasoning with Qualitative Spatial Relations About Regions

Anthony G. Cohn, Brandon Bennett, John Gooday, and Nicholas M. Gotts

4.1. Introduction

Qualitative Reasoning (QR) has now become a mature subfield of AI as its tenth annual international workshop, several books (e.g. (Weld and de Kleer, 1990; Faltings and Struss, 1992)) and a wealth of conference and journal publications testify. QR tries to make explicit our everyday commonsense knowledge about the physical world and also the underlying abstractions used by scientists and engineers when they create models. Given this kind of knowledge and appropriate reasoning methods, a computer could make predictions and diagnoses and explain the behavior of physical systems in a qualitative manner, even when a precise quantitative description is not available or is computationally intractable. Note that a representation is not normally deemed to be qualitative by the QR community simply because it is symbolic and utilizes discrete quantity spaces but because the distinctions made in these discretizations are *relevant* to high-level descriptions of the system or behavior being modeled.

Most QR systems have reasoned about scalar quantities, whether they denote the height of a bouncing ball, the amount of fluid in a tank, the temperature of some body, or perhaps some more abstract quantity. Although there have been spatial aspects to the systems reasoned about, these have rarely been treated with any sophistication. In particular, the multidimensional nature of space has been ill addressed until recently, despite some important early forays such as (Hayes, 1985a; Forbus et al., 1987).

The neglect of this topic within AI may be due to the *poverty conjecture* promulgated by Forbus, Nielsen and Faltings (Weld and de Kleer, 1990, page 562): "there is no purely qualitative, general purpose kinematics". Of course, qualitative kinematics is only a part of qualitative spatial reasoning (QSR), but it is worth noticing their third (and strongest) reason for putting forward the conjecture — "No total order: Quantity spaces don't work in more than one dimension, leaving little hope for concluding much about combining weak information about spatial properties." They point out that transitivity is a vital feature of a qualitative quantity space but doubt that this can be exploited much in higher dimensions and conclude: "we suspect the space of representations in higher dimensions is sparse; that for spatial reasoning almost nothing weaker than numbers will do."

However, there is now a growing body of research in the QR and, more generally, in the Knowledge Representation community and elsewhere that, at least partly, refutes this conjecture. A rich space of qualitative spatial representations is now being explored, and these can indeed exploit transitivity.

There are many possible applications of QSR; we have already mentioned reasoning about physical systems, the traditional domain of QR systems. Other workers are motivated by the necessity of giving a semantics to natural language spatial expressions, e.g., (Vieu, 1991), which tend to be predominantly qualitative rather than quantitative (consider prepositions such as 'in', 'on' and 'through'). Another large and growing application area is Geographical Information Systems (GIS): there is a need for qualitative spatial query languages for example (Cleméntini et al., 1994) and for navigation (Schlieder, 1993). Other applications include specifying the syntax and semantics of Visual Programming languages (Gooday and Cohn, 1995; Gooday and Cohn, 1996b).

This chapter is devoted largely to presenting one particular formalism for QSR, the RCC[18] calculus which has been developed at the University of Leeds over the last few years in a series of papers including (Randell et al., 1992a; Cui et al., 1992; Cohn et al., 1993; Cui et al., 1993; Bennett, 1994c; Gotts, 1994b; Cohn and Gotts, 1996a; Gotts et al., 1996; Cohn, 1995), and indeed is still the subject of ongoing research. One interpretation of the acronym RCC is 'Region Connection Calculus': the fundamental approach of RCC is that extended spatial entities, i.e. *regions* of space, are primary rather than the traditional mathematical dimensionless point. The primitive relation between relations is that of connection, thus giving the language the ability to represent the structure of spatial entities.

There are a number of reasons for eschewing a point-based approach to qualitative spatial representation and indeed simply using the standard tools of mathematical topology. Firstly, regions give a natural way to represent a kind of indefiniteness that is germane to qualitative representations. Moreover the space occupied by any real physical body will always be a region rather a point. Even in natural language, the word "point" is not usually used to mean a mathematical point: a pencil with a sharp point still draws a line of finite thickness! It also turns out that it is possible to reconstruct a notion of mathematical point from a primitive notion of region (Biacino and Gerla, 1991). The standard mathematical approaches to topology, general (point-set) topology and algebraic topology, take points as the fundamental, primitive entities and construct extended spatial entities as sets of points with additional structure imposed on them. However, these approaches generalize the concept of a 'space' far beyond its intuitive meaning; this is particularly true for point-set topology but even algebraic topology, which deals with spaces constructed from 'cells' equivalent to the n-dimensional analogues of a (2-dimensional) disc, concerns itself chiefly with rather abstract reasoning concerning the association of algebraic structures such as groups and rings with such spaces, rather than the kinds of topological reasoning required in everyday life, or those which might illuminate the metaphorical use of topological concepts such as 'connection' and 'boundary'. The case against using these standard point based mathematical techniques for QSR is made in rather more detail in (Gotts et al., 1996), where it is argued that the distinction between intuitive and counter-intuitive concepts is not easily captured and that the reasonable desire (for computational reasons) to avoid higher order logics does not mesh well with quantifying over sets of points.

Of course, it might be possible to adapt the conventional mathematical formalisms for our purposes, and indeed this strategy is sometimes adopted (see, for example (Egenhofer and Franzosa, 1991; Egenhofer and Franzosa, 1995; Worboys and Bofakos, 1993)). However, because we take the view that much if not all reasoning about the spaces occupied by physical objects would not, *a priori*, seem to require points to appear in one's ontology, we do not follow this route but rather prefer to take regions as primitive and abandon the traditional mathematical approaches.

In fact there is a minority tradition in the philosophical and logical literature that rejects the treatment of space as consisting of an uncountably infinite set of points and prefers to take spatially extended entities as primitive. Works by logicians and philosophers who have investigated such alternative approaches ('mereology'[19] or 'calculus of individuals') include (Whitehead, 1929; Lesniewski, 1931; Leonard and Goodman, 1940; Tarski, 1956; de Laguna, 1922) and more recently (Clarke, 1981; Clarke, 1985) — Clarke developed the the immediate 'ancestor' of RCC — (Simons, 1987; Casati and Varzi, 1994; Smith, 1993). Simons' book contains a review of much of the earlier work in this area.

Because RCC is closely based on Clarke's system, it is worth briefly presenting the main features of this system. Clarke 1981, 1985 presents an extended account of a logical axiomatization for a region-based spatial (in fact Clarke's intended interpretation was spatio-temporal) calculus; he gives many theorems as well to illustrate the important features of the theory. The basis of the system is one primitive dyadic relation $C(x, y)$ read as "x connects with y."

If one thinks of regions as consisting of sets of points (although we have indicated above that this is not our preferred interpretation), then in terms of points incident in regions, $C(x, y)$ holds when at least one point is incident in both x and y. There are various axioms which characterize the intended meaning of C (for example, two such axioms state that C is reflexive and that it is symmetric). In Clarke's system it is possible to distinguish regions having the properties of being (topologically) closed or open. A closed region is one that contains all its boundary points (more correctly all its limit points), whereas an object is open if it has no boundary points at all. Many topological relations (for example, regions touching or being a tangential or non tangential part) are defined in Clarke's system and many properties are proved of these relations. Clarke defines many other useful concepts including quasi-Boolean functions, topological functions (interior and closure), and in his second paper provides a construction for points in terms of regions following earlier work by Whitehead (1929). This, however, is faulty; a correction is provided by (Biacino and Gerla, 1991).

While on the subject of related work it is certainly worth mentioning the work done on interval temporal logics for two reasons; first, because the style of much of the work on QSR closely mirrors this work on interval temporal logic and indeed can be naturally seen as the extension of these ideas from the temporal to the spatial domain; secondly, of course it is possible to use this work directly by reinterpreting the calculus as a one-dimensional spatial calculus, though there are problems with doing so. Allen's interval calculus (Allen, 1983) is best known within AI; however, the credit for inventing such calculi is not due to him; van Benthem (1983) describes an interval calculus, while (Nicod, 1924, chapter 2) is probably the earliest such system. Allen's logic defines thirteen Jointly Exhaustive and Pairwise Disjoint (JEPD) relations for convex (one-piece)[20] temporal intervals (see Fig.1). Various authors including Mukerjee and Joe (1990) have used Allen's system for spatial reasoning, using a copy of the calculus for each dimension; however, although attractive in many ways, this has the fundamental limitation that it forces rectangular objects, and is thus not very expressive: consider the configuration in Fig.2.

The structure of the rest of this chapter is as follows. First we present the basic topological part of the calculus in some detail, although space

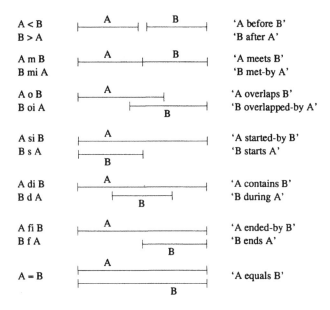

A < B B > A		'A before B' 'B after A'
A m B B mi A		'A meets B' 'B met-by A'
A o B B oi A		'A overlaps B' 'B overlapped-by A'
A si B B s A		'A started-by B' 'B starts A'
A di B B d A		'A contains B' 'B during A'
A fi B B f A		'A ended-by B' 'B ends A'
A = B		'A equals B'

Figure 1. Allen's thirteen interval-interval relations

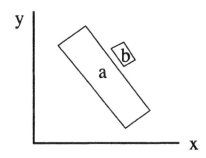

Figure 2. Allen's calculus can be used for reasoning about each spatial dimension, but it forces rectangular objects aligned to the chosen axes. In the diagram above, the two rectangles are not so aligned, and although the smaller one is part of the larger one when projected to each axis individually, this is not so in two dimensions; but this cannot be detected by comparing the one-dimensional projects.

precludes a full exposition. Then we turn to presenting some basic reasoning techniques including a qualitative spatial simulator. Following this we then extend the calculus with an additional primitive to allow a much finer-grained representation than a purely topological representation allows. Up to this point the representation is in a first-order logic; we then show how much of the calculus can be re-expressed in a zero-order logic to a computational benefit. A few possible application areas are then mentioned followed by an extension to handle regions with uncertain boundaries. We conclude by mentioning some current and future research and summarizing our work.

4.2. An Introduction to the Region Connection Calculus (RCC)

The original motivation for this work was an essay in Naïve Physics (Hayes, 1985b; Hayes, 1985a), We were interested in developing a theory for representing and ultimately reasoning about spatial entities; the theory should be expressed in a language with a clean well-understood semantics. Our desire was principally to create an epistemologically adequate formal theory (rather than necessarily a cognitively valid naïve theory).

We should make precise exactly what counts as a region. In our intended interpretation the regions may be of arbitrary dimension, but they must all be the same dimension and must not be of mixed dimension (for example, a region with a lower dimensional spike missing or sticking out is not intended). Such regions are termed *regular*. Normally, of course our intended interpretation will be 3D, though in many of the figures in this chapter, for ease of drawing, we will assume a 2D world (as is also usual in GIS applications). We will deal with the question of whether regions may be open, closed or both below. We also intend regions to *really* be spatially extended, i.e. we rule out the possibility of a region being null. Other than these restrictions, we will allow any kind of regions, in particular they may be multipiece regions, have interior holes and tunnels.

Our initial system was reported in (Randell and Cohn, 1989), which followed Clarke's system closely. However, in (Randell et al., 1992a) we presented a revised theory that deviates from Clarke's theory in one important respect, which has far-reaching implications. The change is to the interpretation of $C(x, y)$: Clarke's interpretation was that the two regions x and y share at least one point whereas our new interpretation is that the topological closures of the two regions share at least one point. Because we consider two regions to be identical if they are conected to exactly the same set of regions, so we could regard regions as equivalence classes of point-sets whose closures are identical. We also, require regions to be of uniform dimension and in terms of point-set topology this means that all the sets in these equivalence classes should have *regular* closures. From within the RCC theory it is not possible to distinguish between regions that are open, closed or neither but have the same closure, and we argue that these distinctions are not necessary for qualitative spatial reasoning. Such regions occupy the same amount of space and, moreover, there seems to be no reason to believe that some physical objects occupy closed regions and others open, so why introduce these distinctions as properties of regions? Moreover, Clarke's system has the odd result that if a body maps to a closed region of space then its complement is open and the two are disconnected and not touching! Another peculiarity is that, if a body is broken into two parts, then we must decide how to split the regions so formed: one will have to have be open (at least along the boundary where the split occurred) whilst the other must be closed and there seems to be no principled reason for this asymmetry.[21] Thus we argue that, from the standpoint of our naïve understanding of the world, the topological structure of Clarke's system is too rich for our purposes, and in any case appearing in this formal theory, it poses some deep conceptual problems. Furthermore, is it necessary to understand sophisticated topological notions such as interior and closure to create a theory of 'commonsense' qualitative space?

It should be noted that the absence of the open/closed distinction from our theory does not make it incompatible with interpretations in terms of standard topology. A particularly straightforward model is that the regions of our theory are the (non-null) elements of the *regular open Boolean algebra* over the usual topology on $\Re^n$. In such an algebra the Boolean product operation is simply set intersection, while Boolean complement corresponds to the interor of the set complement (hence, by DeMorgan, the (regular open) Boolean sum of two (open) sets is the interior of the sum of their closures). Thus all regions are identified with regular open sets.[22] We can then say that two regions are connected if the closures of the (regular open) sets identified with the regions share a point. So, although openness and closure figure in the model theoretic interpretation of the theory, they are not properties of regions and indeed have no meaning within the theory itself.

Hard-line critics of point-based theories of space might still argue that giving a point-set-theoretic semantics for our theory of regions is unsatisfactory. An alternative interpretation of C might be given informally by saying the distance between the two regions is zero. To do this formally would obviously require some (weak) notion of metric space definable on regions but we have not yet attempted to formally specify a semantics of this kind.

Insofar as openness and closedness are not properties of our regions, our theory is simpler than theories such as Clarke's, and hence, we believe that it will also prove to be more suitable for computational reasoning. Furthermore, we believe that the loss of expressive power resulting from our simplification does not restrict the utility of our theory as a language for commonsense reasoning about spatial information. It might be argued that without the open/closed distinction, certain important types of relation between regions cannot be differentiated. For example, Asher and Vieu (1995) have distinguished 'strong' and 'weak' contact between regions. In the former case the regions share a point, whereas in the latter they are disjoint but their closures share a point. Two bodies may then said to be 'joined' if the regions they occupy are in strong contact but merely 'touching' if their regions are in weak contact. Whilst we acknowledge that the distinction between bodies being joined and merely touching is important, we believe that these relations are not essentially spatial and therefore should not be embodied in a theory of spatial regions. They should rather be modeled within a more general theory of relationships among material substances, objects and the regions they occupy.

To formalize our theory we use a sorted first-order logic based on the logic LLAMA (Cohn, 1987), but the details of the logic need not concern us here. The principal sorts we will use are Region, NULL, and PhysOb. Notice that with this sort structure we distinguish the space occupied by a physical object from the physical object itself, partly because it may vary over time which we represent via a function space(x, t).[23] The sort NULL is true of regions that are not spatially extended and is used to model the intersections of disoint regions or the spatial extent of physical objects that do not exist at a particular time for example.

In fact, the axiomatic theory we have developed so far deals only with relationships between entities of sorts Region and NULL. Axiomatization of relations involving physical objects would be part of the more general theory of material substances in space, which was mentioned above. So, at present, the sort PhysOb and the space(x, t) merely serve to indicate how our theory would be incorporated into this much broader theory.

4.2.1. AXIOMS FOR C

Since our interpretation of C has changed, we need to re-axiomatize it and redefine many of the relations Clarke defined which we still want to use. The two main axioms expressing the reflexivity and symmetry of C in fact remain unchanged:

$$\forall x[C(x, x)] \tag{1}$$

$$\forall x \forall y[C(x, y) \rightarrow C(y, x)] \tag{2}$$

Using $C(x, y)$, a basic set of dyadic relations are defined (Randell et al., 1992a, section 4). Definitions and intended meanings of those used here are given in table 1. Unless otherwise specified, the all arguments to the functions and predicates we define are of sort Region. The relations P, PP, TPP and NTPP being non-symmetrical support inverses. For the inverses we use the notation Φi, where $\Phi \in \{P, PP, TPP, NTPP\}$, for example, TPPi.

Of the defined relations, those in the set {DC, EC, PO, EQ, TPP, NTPP, TPPi and NTPPi} (illustrated in Fig.3) are provably JEPD (Jointly Exhaustive and Pairwise Disjoint). We refer to the theory comprising this set of eight relations (and the quasi-Boolean functions to be defined below) as RCC8[25]. The complete set of relations described above can be embedded

TABLE 1. Some relations definable in terms of C

Relation	interpretation	Definition of $R(x,y)$
(3) $DC(x,y)$	x is disconnected from y	$\neg C(x,y)$
(4) $P(x,y)$	x is a part of y	$\forall z[C(z,x) \rightarrow C(z,y)]$
(5) $PP(x,y)$	x is a proper part of y	$P(x,y) \wedge \neg P(y,x)$
(6) $EQ(x,y)$	x is identical with y	$P(x,y) \wedge P(y,x)$
(7) $O(x,y)$	x overlaps[24] y	$\exists z[P(z,x) \wedge P(z,y)]$
(8) $DR(x,y)$	x is discrete from y	$\neg O(x,y)$
(9) $PO(x,y)$	x partially overlaps y	$O(x,y) \wedge \neg P(x,y) \wedge \neg P(y,x)$
(10) $EC(x,y)$	x is externally connected to y	$C(x,y) \wedge \neg O(x,y)$
(11) $TPP(x,y)$	x is a tangential proper part of y	$PP(x,y) \wedge \exists z[EC(z,x) \wedge EC(z,y)]$
(12) $NTPP(x,y)$	x is a nontang'l proper part of y	$PP(x,y) \wedge \neg \exists z[EC(z,x) \wedge EC(z,y)]$

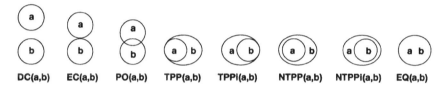

DC(a,b) EC(a,b) PO(a,b) TPP(a,b) TPPI(a,b) NTPP(a,b) NTPPI(a,b) EQ(a,b)

Figure 3. Illustrations of eight JEPD relations

in a relational lattice. This is given in Fig.4. The symbol $\top$ is interpreted as tautology and the symbol $\bot$ as contradiction. The ordering of these relations is one of subsumption with the weakest (most general) relations connected directly to top and the strongest (most specific) to bottom. For example, TPP implies PP, and PP implies either TPP or NTPP. A greatest lower bound of bottom indicates that the relations are mutually disjoint. For example with TPP and NTPP, and P and DR. This lattice corresponds to a set of theorems (such as $\forall xy[PP(x,y) \leftrightarrow [TPP(x,y) \vee NTPP(x,y)]]$) which we have verified.

Clarke axiomatized a set of function symbols in terms of C; the topological ones (interior, exterior, closure) we omit since (as already discussed) we do not wish to make these distinctions. However, he also defined a set of quasi-Boolean[26] functions which we will also require, though our definitions differ. The Boolean functions are: sum(x,y), the sum of x and y; u, the universal region; compl(x), the complement of x; prod(x,y), the product (intersection) of x and y; and diff(x,y), the difference of x and y (that is the part of x that does not overlap y). For brevity we will often use *, + and − rather than prod, sum and diff. The functions: compl(x), prod(x,y) and diff(x,y) are partial but are made total in the sorted logic

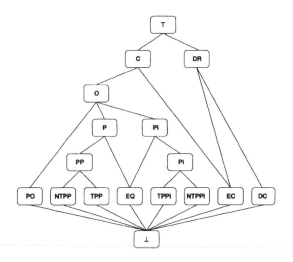

Figure 4. A subsumption lattice of dyadic relations defined in terms of C

by specifying sort restrictions and by letting the result sort of the partial functions be REGION ⊔ NULL. Our functions obey the following axioms:

$$\forall x C(x, u) \tag{13}$$

$$\forall x, y, z[C(z, \text{sum}(x, y)) \equiv C(z, x) \vee C(z, y)] \tag{14}$$

$$\forall x, y[[C(y, \text{compl}(x)) \equiv \neg \text{NTPP}(y, x)] \wedge [O(y, \text{compl}(x)) \equiv \neg P(y, x)]] \tag{15}$$

$$\forall x, y, z[C(z, \text{prod}(x, y)) \equiv \exists w[P(w, x) \wedge P(w, y) \wedge C(z, w)]] \tag{16}$$

$$\forall x, y[\text{NULL}(\text{prod}(x, y)) \equiv \text{DR}(x, y)] \tag{17}$$

$$\forall x, y, z[C(z, \text{diff}(x, y)) \equiv C(z, \text{prod}(x, \text{compl}(y)))] \tag{18}$$

As already mentioned, and will be clear from the fact that we have introduced the sum function, regions may consist of disconnected parts. We can easily define a predicate to test for one-pieceness:[27]

$$\text{CON}(x) \equiv_{\text{def}} \forall yz[\text{sum}(y, z) = x \rightarrow C(y, z)] \tag{19}$$

The following formula is also an axiom of the theory $\forall x \exists y[\text{NTPP}(y, x)]$. This formula mirrors a formal property of Clarke's theory, where he stipulates that every region has a nontangential part, and thus an interior (remembering that in Clarke's theory a topological interpretation is assumed) and is essential to ensure that the definition of P (x, yy) works as intended. The consequences of not having this axiom are explored in (Randell et al., 1992a) and further in (Gotts, 1996a) where atomic multi-region models are shown not to exist: the axiom defining compl (x) ensures that all regions will be C to a region without an NTPP - so only u can be without any NTPP s. Alternatively, if an axiom is included to rule out the model consisting of a single atomic region, then the formula above need not be an axiom since it would follow as a theorem.

4.2.2. THEOREMS OF RCC8

In (Randell et al., 1992a) we cite a number of important theorems which distinguish RCC8 from Clarke's system. First, note that for Clarke, two regions x and y are identical iff any region connecting with x connects with y and vice-versa (which in effect is an axiom of extensionality for $=$ in terms of C), that is

$$\forall xy[x = y \leftrightarrow \forall z[C(z, x) \leftrightarrow C(z, y)]] \ . \tag{20}$$

In the new theory, an additional theorem concerning identity,

$$\forall xy[x = y \leftrightarrow \forall z[O(z, x) \leftrightarrow O(z, y)]] \ , \tag{21}$$

($=$ is extensional in terms of O) becomes provable, which is not a theorem in Clarke's theory: any region z which overlaps a closed region x will also overlap its open interior (and vice versa), thus making them identical according to this axiom, but Clarke distinguishes open and closed regions so they cannot be identical, thus providing a counterexample.

Perhaps the most compelling reason that led us to abandon Clarke's semantics for C is the following theorem which expresses an everyday intuition about space, that, given one proper part of a region, then there is another, discrete from the first:

$$\forall xy[PP(x, y) \rightarrow \exists z[P(z, y) \wedge \neg O(z, x)]] \ . \tag{22}$$

This is provable in the new theory, but not in Clarke's: the interior of a closed region is a proper part of it, but there is no remaining proper part, since in Clarke's (and our) system the boundary of a region is not a region. A related theorem is the following:

$$\forall xy[PO(x, y) \rightarrow [\exists z[P(z, y) \wedge \neg O(z, x)] \wedge \exists w[P(w, x) \wedge \neg O(w, y)]]], \tag{23}$$

which again is a theorem in the new theory but not in Clarke's. A counterexample arises in Clarke's theory where we have two semi-open spherical regions, x and y (with identical radii), such that the northern hemisphere of x is open and the southern hemisphere is closed, and the northern hemisphere of y is closed and the southern hemisphere open. If x and y are superimposed so that their centers and equators coincide, then x and y will partially overlap, but no part of x is discrete from y, and vice-versa.

Another key distinction between our theory and Clarke's concerns the connection between a region and its complement. In the new theory,

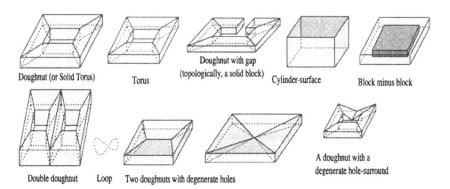

Figure 5.   It is possible to distinguish all these shapes using $C(x, y)$ alone.

$\forall x[\mathsf{EC}(x, \mathsf{compl}(x))]$ holds, that is regions are connected with their complements, which seems a very intuitive result, while in Clarke, a region is disconnected from its complement: $\forall x[\mathsf{DC}(x, \mathsf{compl}(x))]$.

restricted definable concept prove

Some further theorems expressing other interesting and important properties of RCC can be found in (Randell et al., 1992a) as can a discussion about how to introduce atomic regions into RCC. In the calculus as presented here, they are, of course, excluded because every region has a non-tangential proper part.

4.3. Expressing Topological Shape in Terms of C

So far, we have principally concentrated on binary predicates relating pairs of regions. Of course, there are also properties of a single region we would like to express, all of which, in some sense at least, characterize the *shape* of the region. Although we have only developed topological notions there is still quite a bit that can be said about the topological shape of a region. For example we have already introduced the predicate $\mathsf{CON}(x)$ which expresses whether a region is one-piece or not. We can do much more than this however, as (Gotts, 1994a; Gotts, 1994b; Gotts et al., 1996; Gotts, 1996c) demonstrates. The task set there is to be able to distinguish a 'doughnut' (a solid, one-piece region with a single hole). It is shown how (given certain assumptions about the universe of discourse and the kinds of regions inhabiting it) all the shapes depicted in Fig.5 can be distinguished.

Here we just give a brief idea of how the task is accomplished, as it also shows some of the range of predicates that can be further defined using C alone (and thus could form the basis of RCCn (for some $n > 8$)).[28]

The separation-number (SEPNUM) of a region is the maximum

number[29] of mutually disconnected parts it can be divided into:

$$\text{SEPNUM}(r, 1) \equiv_{\text{def}} \text{CON}(r) \qquad (24)$$

$$\text{SEPNUM}(r, N + 1) \equiv_{\text{def}} \exists s, t[[r = s + t] \land \\ \text{DC}(s, t) \land \text{CON}(s) \land \text{SEPNUM}(t, N)] . \qquad (25)$$

The finger-connectivity (FCON) of a CON region is defined[30] in terms of its possible *dissections*, Fig.6 illustrates three different finger connectivities. Making use of an easily definable predicate MAX_P (x, y), asserting that x is a maximal one-piece part of y, FCON can be defined as follows:

$$\text{FCON}(r, N) \equiv_{\text{def}} \text{CON}(r) \land \\ \exists a, x, b[[r = a + x + b] \land \text{CON}(a) \land \text{CON}(b) \land \\ \text{DC}(a, b) \land \text{SEPNUM}(x, N) \land \\ \forall z[\text{MAX\_P}(z, x) \to \text{EC}(a, z) \land \text{EC}(z, b)]] \land \\ \neg \exists a, y, b[(r = a + y + b) \land \text{CON}(a) \land \text{CON}(b) \land \\ \text{DC}(a, b) \land \text{SEPNUM}(y, N + 1) \land \\ \forall z[\text{MAX\_P}(z, y) \to \text{EC}(a, z) \land \text{EC}(z, b)]] . \qquad (26)$$

Gotts goes on to define a predicate to count the number of boundaries two regions have in common. Using these definitions a doughnut can be defined as a region with finger connectivity of 2 and a single boundary with its complement.

be a sphere or

surfaces,

Some of the initial assumptions made by Gotts can be weakened by introducing further defined predicates (which are interesting in their own right). For example, it is possible to define the notion of *intrinsic* TPP, which we term ITPP. Intuitively, x is an ITPP of y iff it is a PP of y that is not surrounded on all sides by the rest of y. The definition of TPP(x, y) itself is *extrinsic* since it makes reference to a third region, z, which is predicated to be EC to both x and y. The definition of ITPP avoids this third region. This has the result that u can have an ITPP but it cannot have a TPP: if u is 3-dimensional Euclidean space, any region of infinite diameter is an ITPP

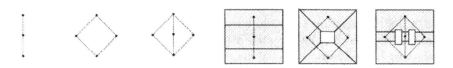

Figure 6. Dissection-graphs and dissections: finger-connectivities 1, 2 and 3

of u. ITPP is itself defined in terms of another predicates: FTPP(x, y) asserts that x is a *firmly* tangential proper part of y (not just point-tangential), which in turn is defined using FCON. These predicates are illustrated in Fig.7.

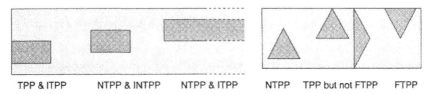

TPP & ITPP   NTPP & INTPP   NTPP & ITPP   NTPP   TPP but not FTPP   FTPP

Figure 7.   TPPs and ITPPs (left); TPPs and FTPPs (right)

Fig.8 illustrates another range of topological distinctions between CON regions that can be made (under certain assumptions) using C. A region, if it is connected, may or may not also be interior-connected (INCON), meaning that the interior of the region is all one piece. It is relatively easy to express this property (or its converse) in RCC terms.

However, INCON(r) does not rule out all regions with anomalous boundaries, and in particular does not exclude the region at the right of Fig.8, nor any of the final three cases illustrated in Fig.5, which do have one-piece interiors, but which nevertheless have boundaries which are *not* (respectively) simple curves or surfaces, having 'anomalies' in the form of points which do not have line-like (or disc-like) neighbourhoods within the boundary. (A region in which every boundary-point has such a neighborhood is called *locally Euclidean*.)

CON, INCON and WCON   CON, not INCON or WCON   CON and INCON, not WCON

Figure 8.   Types of CON Region

It appears possible within RCC (Gotts, 1994b), using the intrinsic ITPP and a similarly intrinsic INTPP, to define a predicate (WCON) that will rule out the INCON but anomalous cases of Fig.8, but it is by no means straightforward,[31] and it is not demonstrated conclusively in (Gotts, 1994b) that the definitions do what is intended. One source of the difficulties arising is the fact that within RCC, since all regions in a particular model of the axioms are of the same dimensionality as u , assuming u itself to be of uniform dimensionality (this follows from the fact that all regions have an NTPP), there is no way to refer directly to the boundary of a region or to the

R1(a,b) \ R2(b,c)	DC	EC	PO	TPP	NTPP	TPPi	NTPPi	EQ
DC	no.info	DR,PO,PP	DR,PO,PP	DR,PO,PP	DR,PO,PP	DC	DC	DC
EC	DR,PO,PPi	DR,PO TPP,TPi	DR,PO,PP	EC,PO,PP	PO,PP	DR	DC	EC
PO	DR,PO,PPi	DR,PO,PPi	no.info	PO,PP	PO,PP	DR,PO,PPi	DR,PO PPi	PO
TPP	DC	DR	DR,PO,PP	PP	NTPP	DR,PO TPP,TPi	DR,PO PPi	TPP
NTPP	DC	DC	DR,PO,PP	NTPP	NTPP	DR,PO,PP	no.info	NTPP
TPPi	DR,PO,PPi	EC,PO,PPi	PO,PPi	PO,TPP,TPi	PO,PP	PPi	NTPPi	TPPi
NTPPi	DR,PO,PPi	PO,PPi	PO,PPi	PO,PPi	o	NTPPi	NTPPi	NTPPi
EQ	DC	EC	PO	TPP	NTPP	TPPi	NTPPi	EQ

Figure 9. Composition table for RCC8

dimensionality of the shared boundary of two EC regions, or to any relations between entities of different dimensionalities.[32] The distinction between intrinsic and extrinsic topological properties, which is found in conventional mathematical topology, is of considerable interest. It demonstrates that at least in some cases, the distinction between properties inherent in an entity and those dependent on its relation with its environment is a real and fundamental one.

4.4. Reasoning with the RCC Calculus

4.4.1. COMPOSITION TABLES

So far we have not discussed reasoning with the calculus at all. Of course, since it is expressed in first order predicate calculus, a wide range of theorem provers are available and indeed we have used these (for example to check the theorems expressed[33] in the lattice of Fig.4 and those in section 4.2.2 above). However, often general theorem proving is too inefficient[34] and also is more than is required for many tasks. In his temporal calculus Allen introduced the idea of a transitivity table, which we term a *composition table* (following (Freksa, 1992a)). Such a table enables one to answer the following question by simple lookup: given $R1(x,y)$ and $R2(y,z)$, what is the relationship between x and z, where R1 and R2 are relations of the calculus?[35] This kind of computation is frequently very useful (for example, to check the integrity of a database of atomic assertions, as needed in the qualitative simulator described below). Fig.9 gives the composition table for RCC8. Where there are multiple entries this means that a disjunction of relations are possible. We have verified this table by checking that each disjunction has a possible model in the intended interpretation and by proving each entry is a theorem of the form $\forall x \forall y \forall z)[(R1(x,y) \wedge R2(y,z)) \rightarrow R3(x,z)]$. Our table coincides with that of (Egenhofer, 1991).

4.4.2. REASONING ABOUT CONTINUOUS CHANGE

So far we have concerned ourselves only with expressing the static properties of space rather than with developing a calculus for expressing how configurations of spatial regions evolve over times. However, such dynamic reasoning is clearly very important in many situations. In many domains, an assumption is made that change is *continuous*. The QR community has exploited this notion repeatedly (see, for example, (Weld and de Kleer, 1990)). In the context of qualitative *spatial* reasoning, assuming continuity means assuming that shape deformations are continuous in addition to assuming that movement is continuous. Fig.10 diagrams the possible next state descriptions, for RCC8, assuming continuity.[36] What we call 'continuity networks' turn out to be exactly the same notion as *conceptual neighbourhoods* (Freksa, 1992a). Galton, in the his chapter in this book and in (Galton, 1995a) has made a thorough analysis of continuity as it applies to RCC8. (Egenhofer and Al-Taha, 1992) builds similar (though not identical) structures for his calculus (there are fewer links in general) using a notion called *closest topological distance*. In the next section we discuss how these kinds of structures can be used to build qualitative spatial simulators.

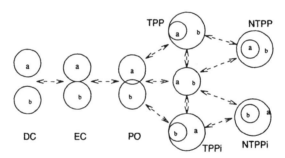

Figure 10.   Continuity in RCC8

We and others have noticed an interesting relationship between composition/transitivity tables and conceptual neighborhoods. For a variety of calculi, every entry in a composition table forms a connected subgraph of the conceptual neighborhood diagram. For example, an entry that included DC and PO would also have to include EC. Freksa (1992a) exploited this to generate a compact composition table for Allen's system. Freksa's reduced table gives compositions for set of relations (conceptual neighborhoods, in fact) rather than single relations. We have explored this approach in the context of Allen's calculus and the RCC system (Cohn et al., 1994). By slightly relaxing Freksa's conditions for choosing sets of relations upon which to base the tables, we managed to find compact representations for some RCC calculi; for example a 6×6 solution (44 per cent reduction in table size) for RCC8 and 8×8 solution for RCC15 (an extension of RCC8 described below) (75 per cent reduction in table size). We also investigated the construction of neighborhood graphs from information in composition tables and have had some success in this venture using a constraint-based approach.

4.4.3. QUALITATIVE SPATIAL SIMULATION

It is not difficult to build a qualitative spatial simulator based on composition tables and conceptual neighborhoods as described in (Cui et al., 1992).[37] A state is a conjunction of ground atomic atoms expressed in RCCn. Sucessor states are generated by forming the set of neighboring atoms (using the conceptual neighborhood diagram) for each atom in the state and forming the crossproduct of all these sets. Each successor state can then be checked for logical consistency by 'triangle checking' using the composition table.[38] It is useful to allow the user to specify domain-dependent inter- and intra-state constraints that further filter which next states are indeed allowable.

The implementation described in (Cui et al., 1992) also allows users to specify 'add' and 'delete' rules to introduce new regions under certain conditions, with specified relationships to existing regions, or to delete specified regions. Fig.11 illustrates two paths from envisionment generated by the program on a model of phago- and exco-cytosis (an amoeba eating a food particle and expelling the waste matter).[39]

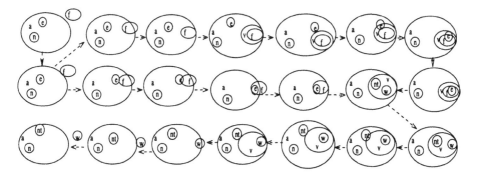

Figure 11. Two paths from the amoeba simulation; the amoeba is denoted 'a', its nucleus 'n', the food particle, 'f', an enzyme, 'e', the vacuole in which the food particle is trapped, 'v', the nutrient formed by digestion, 'nt' and the waste matter, 'w'.

4.5. Shape Representation using a Convex Hull Primitive

Looking at Fig.11, the reader will instantly notice the lack of similarity between the oval depicting the amoeba and a real-life amoeba which has a very irregular shape. However, thus far we cannot distinguish concave and convex shapes: the qualitative language of RCC8 is purely topological.[40] However it would clearly be very desirable to create more expressive languages for qualitative spatial reasoning but which still fall short of a fully metric descriptive language. An additional primitive (or primitives) clearly needs to be introduced since C is not sufficiently expressive to make such non topological distinctions. There are many possibilities for the choice of such primitive. The one we have so far explored in the context of RCC is the convex hull of a region, which we denote conv(x). Fig.12 illustrates the notion of a convex hull (which is defined mathematically in terms of points and lines as the region resulting from including every point on every line joining any two points in the region).

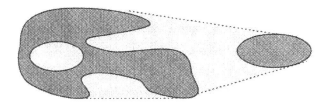

Figure 12.   An example of a convex-hull in two dimensions. The dark shading indicates the (concave) region; the sum of the dark and light shaded regions is the convex hull.

The problem we now face is to axiomatize conv(x). Since we have no notion of straight lines, the mathematical definition is of no help. The axioms below certainly capture many, if not all of the properties of conv that are expressible within RCC8. It is still an open question whether all relevant properties have been captured and whether any of the axioms are redundant.[41] First we define a predicate to test for convexity:

$$\mathsf{CONV}(x) \equiv_{\mathsf{def}} \mathsf{EQ}(x, \mathsf{conv}(x)) \tag{27}$$

Nine important properties of conv can then be axiomatized as follows:[42]

$$\forall x[\mathsf{conv}(\mathsf{conv}(x)) = \mathsf{conv}(x)] \tag{28}$$

$$\forall x[\mathsf{TP}(x, \mathsf{conv}(x))] \tag{29}$$

$$\forall x \forall y[\mathsf{P}(x, y) \;\rightarrow\; \mathsf{P}(\mathsf{conv}(x), \mathsf{conv}(y))] \tag{30}$$

$$\forall x \forall y[\mathsf{P}((\mathsf{conv}(x) + \mathsf{conv}(y), \mathsf{conv}(x + y))] \tag{31}$$

$$\forall x \forall y[\mathsf{conv}(x) = \mathsf{conv}(y) \;\rightarrow\; \mathsf{C}(x, y)] \tag{32}$$

$$\forall x \forall y [\text{CONV}(\text{conv}(x) * \text{conv}(y))] \tag{33}$$

$$\forall x \forall y [\text{DC}(x, y) \rightarrow \neg\text{CONV}(x + y)] \tag{34}$$

$$\forall x \forall y [\text{NTPP}(x, y) \rightarrow \neg\text{CONV}(y - x)] \tag{35}$$

$$\forall x \forall y \forall z [[\text{EC}(x, y) \wedge \text{CONV}(x + y) \wedge \text{EC}(y, z) \wedge \tag{36}$$
$$\text{CONV}(y + z) \wedge \text{DC}(x, z)] \rightarrow \text{CONV}(y)]$$

Axiom 28 simply expresses the fact that applying the convex hull operator a second time in succession is redundant. Axiom 29 states the obvious fact that a region must be a tangential part of its convex hull, as can be seen by inspection of Fig.12. Axiom 30 expresses a monotonicity property: taking convex hulls preserves parthood relationships (see Fig.13i). Axiom 31 asserts the distributivity of conv and + with respect to P(see Fig.13ii). Axiom 32 is perhaps more controversial; it states that any two regions having the same convex hull must be connected. We will return to why we want this axiom below. Axiom 33 asserts that the intersection of any two convex regions must itself be convex. The next axiom (34) expresses the obvious fact that the sum of two DC regions cannot be convex (as can be seen by inspection of Fig.12). The next axiom (35) expresses a similar property: that shapes with interior holes cannot be convex (see Fig.13iv). The final axiom (36) is more complicated; it expresses a property that can perhaps best be explained by reference to Fig.13v: there is no way to make y concave without violating the antecedents of the implication.

Given our new primitive of the convex hull, we can now start defining some new relations that exploit this function symbol. Perhaps the most obvious and useful distinction to make is to distinguish when one region is inside another, that is to say part of its convex hull but not overlapping the region itself. This notion is easy to define. We introduce three new predicates to test for a region being inside another (INSIDE), partly inside another (P-INSIDE) and outside another (OUTSIDE):

$$\text{INSIDE}(x, y) \equiv_{\text{def}} \text{DR}(x, y) \wedge \text{P}(x, \text{conv}(y)) \tag{37}$$

$$\text{P-INSIDE}(x, y) \equiv_{\text{def}} \text{DR}(x, y) \wedge \text{PO}(x, \text{conv}(y)) \tag{38}$$

$$\text{OUTSIDE}(x, y) \equiv_{\text{def}} \text{DR}(x, \text{conv}(y)) \tag{39}$$

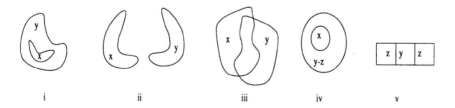

Figure 13. Configurations illustrating some of the convex hull axioms

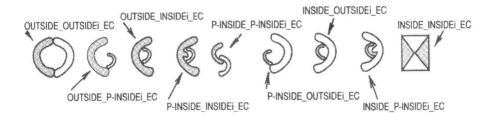

Figure 14. Nine of the new JEPD relations exploiting conv.

Each of these relations is asymmetric so they have inverses, denoted INSIDEi, P-INSIDEi and OUTSIDEi.

Obviously we have now moved beyond RCC8, but how many JEPD relations do we now have? It turns out that the above definitions naturally give rise to a set of twenty-three JEPD relations. The RCC8 relations of DC and EC no longer form part of the JEPD set; they are replaced by seventeen new relations nine of which are illustrated in Fig.14. The other eight are simply the DC versions of the first eight configurations. These seventeen relations can be schematically defined by

$$\alpha\_\beta\_\gamma(x,y) \equiv_{\text{def}} \alpha(x,y) \wedge \beta(x,y) \wedge \gamma(x,y) \tag{40}$$

where $\alpha \in \{\text{INSIDE, P} - \text{INSIDE, OUTSIDE}\}$, $\beta \in \{\text{INSIDEi, P} - \text{INSIDEi, OUTSIDEi}\}$, and $\gamma \in \{\text{EC, DC}\}$, excepting the case where $\alpha = \text{INSIDE}$, $\beta = \text{INSIDEi}$ and $\gamma = \text{DC}$.

It is worth commenting on why there is only an EC version of the final configuration in Fig.14. In fact, a DC version is outlawed by axiom 32 above. We believe that the only possible models that might satisfy a DC version involve strange and unintuitive infinite regions. For example, imagine two infinite corkscrews cut out of an infinitely long hollow cylinder out of phase and thus DC. Clearly they have the same convex hull and would thus be INSIDE_INSIDEi_DC. However, we outlaw such a possibility since we are trying to model the commonsense world which doesn't have infinite corkscrews! We have found other possible models for INSIDE_INSIDEi_DC, but they all involve similar infinite and counter-intuitive regions.

Fig.15 depicts an example of how these new relations can be used to advantage when describing the movement of one region from outside to inside and then overlapping another. However, labeling the final configuration simply as PO seems a little unsatisfactory: if x were partially overlapping y on the lefthand side, that is, if it were not within the convex hull of y, it would still be PO. The obvious solution to this is to define PO versions all the configurations in Fig.14. To do this requires the definitions of INSIDE, P-INSIDE and OUTSIDE to be changed slightly; the details are

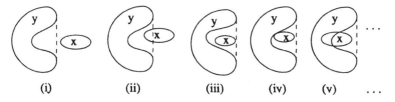

(i)　　　　(ii)　　　　(iii)　　　　(iv)　　(v)　　...

Figure 15. One region moving inside another:　(i): OUTSIDE_OUTSIDEi_DC(x, y),
(ii):　P-INSIDE_OUTSIDEi_DC(x, y),　　　　(iii):　INSIDE_OUTSIDEi_DC(x, y),
(iv): INSIDE_OUTSIDEi_EC(x, y),　　　　　　(v): PO(x, y).

in (Cohn et al., 1995). With this modification there are now thirty-two base relations (the original eight, less DC, EC and PO, plus the EC, DC and PO versions of the allowable combinations of INSIDE, OUTSIDE, P-INSIDE and their inverses).

There are many different reasons why a region may be concave as hinted at in the axioms for conv. In particular, regions might be multi-piece, or they may be missing an NTPP rather than having a simple depression in their surface; (Casati and Varzi, 1994)[43] is an excellent treatise on the different kinds of holes that might exist. In (Cohn et al., 1995) we provide definitions which distinguish many of these and more.

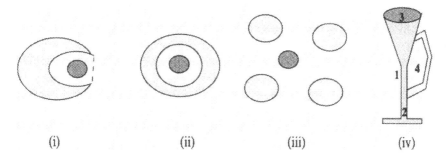

(i)　　　　　　(ii)　　　　　　(iii)　　　　　　(iv)

Figure 16. Different kinds of insides. In (i) the darker region is geometrically inside the lighter one; in (ii) it is topologically inside; in (iii) it's in the 'scattered' inside. In (iv) a fly in position 3 would be in the 'containable' inside (in that part of the whiskey glass that could contain a liquid); in position 2 it would be topologically inside (encased in the stem during the manufacturing process!); in position 4 it would be in the 'tunnel inside' (in the 'handle'), while in position 1 it would be inside the glass in a very weak sense: part of the convex hull but not any of the more specialized senses. Predicates can be defined to distinguish each of these notions of inside.

Fig.16 shows some of the different kinds of non convex regions which can be distinguished using C and conv. The first distinction to make is between one region, x, being *topologically* inside another region, y, and being *geometrically* inside: in the former case any one piece region touching x and the complement of the convex hull of y must connect with y, while in the latter case this need not be so. This is a very useful distinction to make in many practical situations: for example a marble contained in a jar with its lid on is topologically inside it cannot escape as it can when it is merely geometrically inside (once the lid has been taken off).

The notion of being geometrically inside can be further refined using the same two primitives of C and conv. It is possible to distinguish those geometrical insides which could contain a liquid, and those which are formed by being between components of a multi piece region for example. Still other possible relationships expressing further refinements are possible to define; for example does one region completely fill an inside of another region or does it only partly fill it? Again for many domains this may be a very useful distinction to be able to make easily.

{EC , $\beta \in$

In this section so far, we have concentrated on defining relationships between two regions that exploit the conv primitive. Of course, to a certain extent, these give rise to complementary techniques to describe the shape of one particular region. For example, if one region is topologically inside another, then the second region must have an interior void. In (Cohn, 1995) we focus explicitly on defining predicates which characterize the shape of a single two-dimensional region. Techniques are developed, using C and conv alone, which can, for example, distinguish all the different shapes in Fig.17. The principal idea is to distinguish the concavities of a region (which are the maximal one-piece well-connected parts of its inside) and then define predicates that are true of particular configurations of the concavities. Adjacent and non adjacent concavities can easily be distinguished for example. A particularly interesting idea (which turns out to have been long known about in the vision community (Sklansky, 1972)) is to apply the technique recursively: if a concavity is itself concave, then one describes the shape of its insides (this is how the first two shapes in Fig.17 are distinguished). Fig.18 illustrates this idea. It is also possible to define when a region is a triangle using C and conv and thus when a region is an arbitrary polygon.

Figure 17.   Qualitative predicates can be defined to distinguish all these shapes.

Of course, alongside simply defining new relations, it is interesting and important to isolate which particular extended sets of relations form JEPD sets and to define composition tables and continuity networks for these sets.

Figure 18. Finer shape descriptions can be obtained by recursively describing the shapes of the insides of a region.

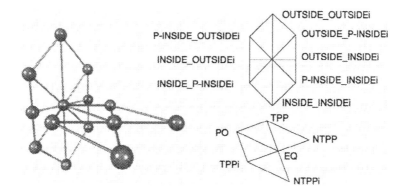

Figure 19. The continuity network for RCC-15. The unlabelled central node of the vertical plane is P-INSIDE_P-INSIDEi. PO has links to this and every other node in the vertical plane

In (Cohn et al., 1995) some sets of JEPD relations are distinguished. We have done some work on building the conceptual neighborhood diagrams for these sets. For example, Fig.19 is conceptual neighborhood for RCC15, which is the set of relations formed by taking RCC23 and collapsing the distinction between EC and DC. We return to the problem of building composition tables below.

As we have seen, a surprisingly rich and complex and expressive ontology for describing qualitative spatial relationships can be logically defined from just two primitives. It would be easy to define a set of well over a hundred JEPD base relations from the above predicates described above and many more could easily be defined such as JUST_INSIDE and JUST_OUTSIDE. The question arises: when to stop?[44] In (Cohn et al., 1995) we propose some criteria based on computational and predictive properties of the representation, but ultimately it must be a domain specific question: certain distinctions will be relevant for only certain domains, but for these domains they may be crucial.[45] Indeed, we have already noted in the introduction that the distinctions made in a quantity space should be *relevant* to the behavior being modeled.

4.6. Spatial Reasoning with Decidable Logics

The RCC spatial calculus is based on the primitives C and conv which are axiomatized in 1st-order logic. Although it is expressive it is hard to reason with. For example, even verifying the composition table for RCC8 using the Otter theorem prover (McCune, 1990) was a hard task requiring introducing various lemmas by hand (Randell et al., 1992b). It became clear that more efficient reasoning techniques were desirable. Our existing techniques for the composition table for RCC8 would not scale up to RCC23 or larger sets of relations. Initially, we experimented with a model-building program based on bitmap representations of possible spatial situations but this was only partly successful and was still fairly computationally intensive. We needed a more tractable logical representation.

The idea we pursued was to move from a first-order representation to a zero-order logic, which then provided a decision procedure (Bennett, 1994c). Here we summarize this approach to RCC. Zero-order logic is traditionally known as propositional logic; however, this is an inappropriate name for our purposes. We will not interpret the non-logical symbols as propositions (having truth values) but rather as symbols having sets as their values. If these sets are sets of spatial entities (points or atomic regions for example), then the non-logical symbols denote spatial regions, and logical connectives correspond to certain functions from regions to regions. Suppose we then assert that some formula denotes the universal region: this means that the regions denoted by the 'propositional' constants occuring in the formula must stand in some particular (spatial) relationship, determined by the logical structure of the formula. The formula can thus be used to represent that relationship. We say that such a spatial interpretation is *faithful* to a propositional logic if entailment among formulas in the zero-order representation mirrors entailment among the corresponding spatial relations. Such an interpretation can be used to reason about a certain class of spatial relationships.

For example, the classical formula $A \rightarrow B$ can be used to represent the relation $P(a, b)$ and the entailment $A \rightarrow B,\ B \rightarrow C \models A \rightarrow C$ reflects the fact that $P(a, b),\ P(b, c) \models P(a, c)$.

It turns out that classical zero-order logic is not sufficiently expressive to encode the RCC8 relations. Happily, this can be achieved in intuitionistic zero-order logic (Nerode, 1990), which we name $\mathcal{I}_0$. In fact, the idea of a topological interpretation of this logic was first introduced by Tarski (1938).

A model for $\mathcal{I}_0$ is a structure, $\langle \mathcal{U}, i, \mathcal{P}, d \rangle$, where

- $\mathcal{U}$ is the universe (a set of spatial entities in our intended interpretation).
- i is a function, $i : \wp(\mathcal{U}) \rightarrow \wp(\mathcal{U})$, obeying the standard axioms for an *interior* function.[46]

- $\mathcal{P}$ is a denumerable set of constants.
- d is a denotation function, $d : \mathcal{P} \rightarrow \mathcal{O}$, where $\mathcal{O}$ is the set of *open* subsets of $\mathcal{U}$ (that is $\mathcal{O} = \{X \mid X \in \mathcal{U}^* \wedge i(X) = X\}$).

The domain of d is extended to all $\mathcal{I}_0$ formulas[47] as follows:

- $d(\sim p) = i(\overline{d(p)})$
- $d(p \wedge q) = d(p) \cap d(q)$
- $d(p \vee q) = d(p) \cup d(q)$
- $d(p \Rightarrow q) = i(\overline{d(p)} \cup d(q))$.

This semantics associates each formulas of $\mathcal{I}_0$ with a term involving constants denoting open sets, the Boolean set-theoretic operators and the interior operator. We call this a set-term. If regions are considered as open sets, a formula can be used to represent a spatial relation holding between regions just in case the corresponding set-term has the value $\mathcal{U}$. This is a faithful interpretation of $\mathcal{I}_0$, which means that a standard theorem prover for $\mathcal{I}_0$ can be used to reason about spatial relations represented in this way.

An important point to notice in this semantics is the interpretation of negation: it is the interior of the complement, so the union of the denotation of a region with its complement is not the universe, $\mathcal{U}$. It is this that allows us to distinguish DC from EC, and TPP from NTPP. However, $\mathcal{I}_0$ is still not quite sufficient by itself to distinguish all the RCC8 relations. It turns out that we need not only conditions expressible by asserting that some set-term equals $\mathcal{U}$ but also conditions that require us to assert that some set-term does not equal $\mathcal{U}$. For example, although the part relation P(a, b) is straightforwardly represented by the relation $A \Rightarrow B$, because it holds whenever $i(\overline{d(a)} \cup d(b)) = \mathcal{U}$, representing the proper part relation PP(a, b) requires us, in addition, to ensure that the relation P(b, a) does not hold. To do this in the $\mathcal{I}_0$ representation we need some way of asserting that $i(\overline{d(b)} \cup d(b)) \neq \mathcal{U}$.

It turns out that this limitation can be overcome with a simple extension of $\mathcal{I}_0$, which we term $\mathcal{I}_0^+$, together with an appropriate meta-level reasoning algorithm. Expressions of $\mathcal{I}_0^+$ are pairs of sets of $\mathcal{I}_0$ formulas, $\langle \mathcal{M}, \mathcal{E} \rangle$. One set represents (positive) *model constraints*; the other (negative) *entailment constraints*. For example, PP(p, q) may be represented as $\langle \{p \rightarrow q\}, \{q \rightarrow p\} \rangle$. Actually, as we noted above that regions should be non null, we ought really to add *non-null* constraints on p and q: $\langle \{p \rightarrow q\}, \{q \rightarrow p, \neg p, \neg q\} \rangle$. We are now in a position to be able to define the complete set of RCC8 relations in $\mathcal{I}_0^+$, see Table 2.

Bennett (1994c) explains the $\mathcal{I}_0^+$ representation in detail and proves the correctness of the following algorithm to determine the consistency of sets of spatail relations represented in $\mathcal{I}_0^+$:

1. For each relation $R_i(\alpha_i, \beta_i)$ in the situation description find the corresponding propositional representation $\langle \mathcal{M}_i, \mathcal{E}_i \rangle$.

Relation	Model Constraint	Entailment Constraints
$DC(X,Y)$	$\sim X \vee \sim Y$	$\sim X,\ \sim Y$
$EC(X,Y)$	$\sim(X \wedge Y)$	$\sim X \vee \sim Y, \sim X,\ \sim Y$
$PO(X,Y)$	—	$\sim(X \wedge Y),\ X \Rightarrow Y,\ Y \Rightarrow X, \sim X, \sim Y$
$TPP(X,Y)$	$X \Rightarrow Y$	$\sim X \vee Y,\ Y \Rightarrow X, \sim X, \sim Y$
$TPPi(X,Y)$	$Y \Rightarrow X$	$\sim Y \vee X,\ X \Rightarrow Y, \sim X, \sim Y$
$NTPP(X,Y)$	$\sim X \vee Y$	$Y \Rightarrow X, \sim X, \sim Y$
$NTPPi(X,Y)$	$\sim Y \vee X$	$X \Rightarrow Y, \sim X, \sim Y$
$EQ(X,Y)$	$X \Leftrightarrow Y$	$\sim X, \sim Y$

TABLE 2. RCC relations defined in $\mathcal{I}_0^+$

2. Construct the overall $\mathcal{I}_0^+$ representation $\langle \bigcup_i \mathcal{M}_i,\ \bigcup_i \mathcal{E}_i \rangle$.
3. For each formula $F \in \bigcup_i \mathcal{E}_i$ use an intuitionistic theorem prover to determine whether the entailment[48] $\bigcup_i \mathcal{M}_i \models F$ holds.
4. If any of the entailments determined in the last step does hold, then the situation is impossible.

Nebel (1995) has shown that this algorithm applied to instances of the RCC8 relations has polynomial complexity in the number of instances (we do not yet have any complexity results for reasoning with larger classes of RCC relations). A slightly more complicated algorithm will test entailment rather than consistency.

4.6.1. ENCODING conv IN $\mathcal{I}_0^+$

A further layer of meta-level reasoning can be applied to the $\mathcal{I}_0^+$ representation in order to reason about RCC relations involving the convex-hull operator conv. For each region symbol P occurring in a set of $\mathcal{I}_0^+$ expressions describing some situation, introduce a new symbol $\mathrm{conv}(P)$ to represent convex hull of P. As regards the $\mathcal{I}_0^+$ reasoning algorithm $\mathrm{conv}(P)$ will simply be an atomic constant, but the meaning of conv will be enforced by meta-level constraints.

The form of the conv axioms is such that they can be put into clausal form without introducing Skolem functions and the relations constituting the atoms of these clauses are all representable in $\mathcal{I}_0^+$. If we instantiate these clausal conv(x) axioms in as many ways as possible using all the region symbols (including the newly introduced convex hull expressions) and then replace the atoms with their $\mathcal{I}_0^+$ representation we end up with an additional set of logical constraints on $\mathcal{I}_0^+$ expressions in the form of meta-level (classical) propositional clauses. In doing this we are treating the convex hull axioms as schemas and since there are only finitely many regions involved in the description of any spatial situation, there are only finitely many (zero-order) instances of these schemas.

Taking account of the meta-level constraints for the conv axioms is combinatorially explosive but quite manageable when small numbers of regions are involved. The most naïve method for testing for consistency is simply to search for a selection of one literal from each clause such that, when these are added to the $\mathcal{I}_0^+$ expressions describing the situation, the resulting set is consistent. (There is a much more effective method based on resolving constraint literals against consequences of the situation description.) We have used an implementation of $\mathcal{I}_0^+$ together with the required meta-level reasoning for conv to generate the complete composition table for RCC23 with little computational effort.

It is worth pointing out that this representation gives us a true spatial logic rather than simply a logical theory of space: the logical constants $(\wedge, \vee, \Rightarrow$ etc.) all have a spatial interpretation. We have also investigated other possible spatial logics, in particular modal ones where the necessity operator is interpreted as an interior operator (Bennett, 1995). Another investigation of the use of modal logics for RCC, interpreting C as the accessibility operator can be found in (Cohn, 1993). Moving away from modal logics to constraint languages, we have shown (Davis et al., 1997) that the constraint language of RCC-8 plus a predicate $CONV(x)$ is decidable.

4.7. Some Applications of RCC

The main focus of our work has been theoretical: to design logical calculi for qualitative spatial reasoning. However, we have also worked on applying RCC to some domains.

We have already mentioned the simple modeling of phagocytosis when describing the operation of our qualitative spatial simulator above. We are now constructing a new qualitative simulation system using Transition Calculus (Gooday and Galton, 1997), an event-based nonmonotonic temporal reasoning formalism. This simulator has a much more formal basis than our original qualitative spatial simulator described in section 4.4.3 above and has already been used to model a simple physical system. RCC continuity networks can be directly represented as event types in Transition Calculus' high-level modeling language making it well-suited to our simulation tasks. We intend to encode various continuity networks and explore a number of simulation problems with the new system.

Another application we are currently investigating is for the specification of the syntax and semantics of a visual programming language (Gooday and Cohn, 1995; Gooday and Cohn, 1996b). Visual programming languages are an important new weapon in the software engineer's armory, but while textual languages have benefited from work on providing appropriate mathematical semantics, there has been little work on providing suitable tools for visual languages. One visual language that can be specified almost entirely using topological concepts is Pictorial Janus (Kahn and Saraswat, 1990) and indeed RCC turns out to be quite suitable for this task. Fig.20 illustrates some basic Pictorial Janus elements and a program to append two lists.

A constant consists of a closed contour (the shape is irrelevant) containing a number or string (what the constant represents) and a single internal port. The internal port is represented by another closed contour abutting the constant but wholly inside it and acts as a handle for the entire object. Ports cannot themselves contain any elements. Functions are represented by closed contours containing a label and an internal port together with any number of external ports. In this case we have illustrated a list-constructor function, cons, which normally takes two arguments and thus requires two external ports. The final part of the figure shows how the cons function can be used to build up a list.

A Pictorial Janus agent is a closed contour containing rules, a call arrow to another agent contour, or a label. It may have any number of external ports but no internal ports. A rule is defined in exactly the same way as an agent but with the additional requirement that it must be contained within an agent. Agents may communicate via channels: directed curves linking two ports (an arrow is used to indicate directionality). Finally, links are undirected curves joining two ports. There is not space to fully specify Pictorial Janus here, but as a simple example we will give the definitions for internal and external ports that are defined in terms of ports, to show how RCC can be exploited in this domain:

$$\mathsf{Iport}(port, x) \equiv_{\mathrm{def}} \mathsf{Port}(port) \wedge \mathsf{TPP}(port, x) \qquad (41)$$

$$\mathsf{Eport}(port, x) \equiv_{\mathrm{def}} \mathsf{Port}(port) \wedge \mathsf{EC}(port, w) \qquad (42)$$

Using RCC we have successfully captured the full syntax of Pictorial Janus and are now working on completing our description of the procedural semantics. It is intended that these RCC descriptions will be used in conjunction with our spatial simulator to model the execution of Pictorial Janus programs.

Another application we have investigated is the application of RCC to help with the problem of integrating two different databases. In this case we are using a spatial metaphor: we think of a database class as a region, and the prototypical members as another region which is always a PP of the complete class.[49] The question addressed in this work is how can we obtain a measure of the reliability of the merge of two datatypes? For example, supposing firm A takes over firm B and they merge their

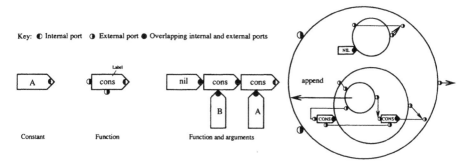

Figure 20. Some basic Pictorial Janus concepts and an append agent (containing two rules).

employee databases. They may have different definitions of employee. We use a spatial metaphor to develop a ranking to rate the relative goodness of fit in such cases. The final ranking we developed is a refinement of the run of our qualitative simulator. Further details can be found in (Lehmann and Cohn, 1994).

We also have considered the application of RCC to Geographical Information Systems (GIS) (Cohn et al., 1997; Bennett, 1996a). In fact, a parallel development of a system very similar to RCC8 has taken place within this field (Egenhofer and Franzosa, 1991; Egenhofer, 1991)[50] but firmly based on a point-set theoretic approach rather than our logic of regions approach. Addtionally the work on regions with indeterminate boundaries in Section 4.8 below was motivated primarily by applications in GIS.

A new application we are working on is real time event recognition from image sequences; our initial work in this area is reported in (Fernyhough et al., 1996; Fernyhough, 1997; Fernyhough et al., 1997).

4.8. Spatial Regions with Uncertain Boundaries

Much work in qualitative spatial reasoning is based exclusively on crisp regions and lines. But many domains, particularly GIS, have objects with indeterminate boundaries, such as clouds, urban areas, areas of a certain soil or vegetation type, marshlands, habitats and so on. The question is whether RCC theory as developed so far can be used or extended to model these kinds of entities.[51] In a series of papers (Cohn and Gotts, 1996a; Cohn and Gotts, 1994b; Cohn and Gotts, 1994a; Gotts and Cohn, 1995; Cohn and Gotts, 1996b) we have tackled this problem[52] from two sides: firstly we have added a further primitive and developed an axiomatisation and a series of definitions to help model such indeterminate spatial entities; secondly, we have applied the *egg-yolk* calculus, mentioned above, to represent such regions.

4.8.1. A PRIMITIVE FOR REASONING ABOUT INDETERMINACY

We need to say at least some of the same sorts of things about vague
regions as about crisp ones, with precise boundaries: that one contains
another (southern England contains London, even if both are thought of
as vague regions), that two overlap (the Sahara desert and West Africa),
or that two are disjoint (the Sahara and Gobi deserts). In these cases, the
two vague regions represent the space occupied by distinct entities, and we
are interested in defining a vague area corresponding to the space occupied
by either, by both, or by one but not the other. We may also want to say
that one vague region is a crisper version of another. For example, we might
have an initial (vague) idea of the extent of a mineral deposit, then receive
information reducing the imprecision in our knowledge. Here, the vagueness
of the vague region is a matter of our ignorance: the entity concerned
actually occupies a fairly well-defined region — though perhaps any entity's
limits will be imprecise to some degree. In other cases, vagueness appears
intrinsic: consider an informal geographical term like 'southern England'.
The uncertainty about whether particular places (north of London but
south of Birmingham) are included cannot be resolved definitively: it is a
matter of interpretational context. A contrasting example is the region
occupied by a cloud of gas from an industrial accident. Here we have
two sources of intrinsic vagueness: the concentration of the gas is likely
to fall off gradually as we move out of the cloud; and its extent will
also vary over time, so any temporal vagueness (for example, if we are
asked about the cloud's extent at 'around noon') will result in increased
spatial vagueness. In these cases of intrinsic vagueness, there is a degree
of arbitrariness about any particular choice of an exact boundary, and
often, none is required. But *if* we decide to define a more precise version
(either completely precise, or less vague but still imprecise), our choice of
version is by no means *wholly* arbitrary: we can distinguish more and less
reasonable choices of more precise description. Distinguishing ignorance-
based from intrinsic vagueness is important, but many of the same problems
of representation and reasoning arise for both.

This then motivates introducing an additional primitive: a binary
predicate $X \prec Y$,[53] read as "X is crisper than Y", which is axiomatized
to be asymmetric and transitive and hence irreflexive. Various useful
predicates can easily be defined in terms of $X \prec Y$. For example, Crisp(X),
which is true when no region is crisper than X, MA(X,Y), which is true
when X and Y are mutually approximate; that is, they have a common
crisping, and $X \prec\!\!\prec Y$ which is true when X is crisper than Y and is itself

crisp.

$$\text{Crisp}(X) \equiv_{\text{def}} \neg \exists Y[Y \prec X] \tag{43}$$

$$\text{MA}(X,Y) \equiv_{\text{def}} \exists Z[Z \prec X \wedge Z \prec Y] \tag{44}$$

$$X \nleftarrow Y \equiv_{\text{def}} X \prec Y \wedge \text{Crisp}(X). \tag{45}$$

Further axioms postulate the existence of a complete crisping of any region, and also of alternative ways to crisp and decrisp a region (for if this were not so, then one could hardly claim that indeterminacy existed about the region). Another possible axiom asserts the denseness of crisping: if $X \prec Y$, then there must be another region crisper than Y but less crisp than X. An interesting parallel can be drawn between the theory expounded in (Cohn and Gotts, 1996b) and the axiom-sets for mereology (theory of part-whole relations) discussed by (Simons, 1987); we will return to this below.

The question arises: how many JEPD relations are there between non crisp regions? For the sake of simplicity, our work so far our calculi for spatial regions with indeterminate boundaries has been based on extending RCC5 rather than any of the larger RCC systems. Figure 21 depicts the RCC5 relations and their conceptual neighborhood. Consider two non-crisp regions. Depending on the initial configurations, there may be different possible RCC5 relations between complete crispings of the two regions. We make the assumption that any set of complete crisping relations will be a conceptual neighborhood (a connected subgraph of the complete conceptual neighborhood graph). Although there are twenty-three such conceptual neighborhoods for RCC5, (see Fig.21) it is possible to argue that only thirteen[54] of these can form a set representing the possible complete crispings a pair of vague regions. However, in the next section we suggest that more than thirteen distinctions are, in fact, possible.

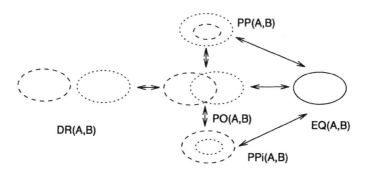

Figure 21. The RCC5 conceptual neighborhood.

4.8.2. THE EGG-YOLK THEORY

We have already mentioned the egg-yolk theory above when discussing
the application of RCC theory to database integration. Fig.22 depicts this
representation. The *egg* is the maximal extent of a vague region and the
yolk is its minimal extent, while the *white* is the area of indeterminacy.
Note that since RCC allows non connected regions, so yolks (and indeed
eggs themselves) could be multi-piece. Fig.23 shows the forty-six possible
relations between two non-crisp regions (assuming that RCC5 calculus is
used to relate eggs and yolks and that yolks are never null).[55]

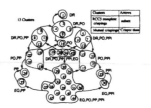

Figure 22.   The egg/yolk interpretation

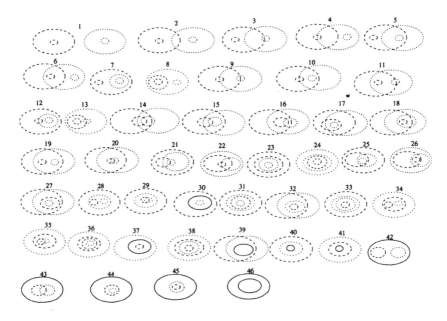

Figure 23.   Forty six egg-yolk relations between two eggs

At first glance, there is an apparent problem with the egg-yolk approach:
the most obvious interpretation is that it replaces the precise dichotomy
assumed in the basic RCC theory, where space is divided into what is in

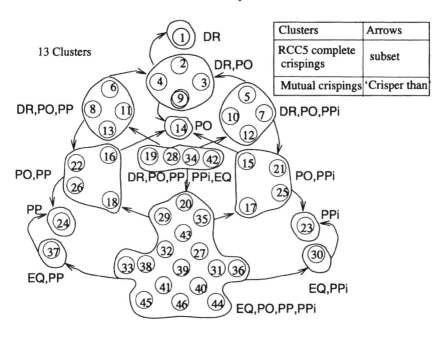

Figure 24. Clustering the forty six relations into thirteen groups.

a region and what is outside a region, by an equally precise trichotomy of yolk, white and outside. This appears contrary to a key intuition about vagueness: that not only is there a doubtful zone around the edges of a vague region but that this zone itself has no precise boundaries. Gotts and Cohn (1995) suggest a way of using the egg-yolk formalism that is consistent with this.

We link the OCregions of Section 4.8.1 (and the corresponding theory), with ordered pairs of RCC5 regions, the first of the pair being a part, but not necessarily a proper part, of the second. If it *is* a PP, then the pair is an egg-yolk pair in the sense of (Lehmann and Cohn, 1994), and the OCregion is NonCrisp. If not, the OCregion is Crisp. We now link the CR predicate of OCregion theory with the egg-yolk approach. We define a function ey to map an OCregion to an egg-yolk pair, and two functions eggof and yolkof, to map such egg-yolk pairs to the RCC5 region comprising its egg and yolk, respectively. We will normally write $ey(X)$ as $\hat{X}$ for notational convenience. We have the following axiom for egg-yolk pairs:

$$\forall X P(\text{yolkof}(\hat{X}), \text{eggof}(\hat{X})) \, . \tag{46}$$

We then assert the following additional axiom concerning CR:

$$\forall X, Y [X \prec Y \rightarrow$$

$$[[\mathsf{PP}(\mathsf{eggof}(\hat{X}), \mathsf{eggof}(\hat{Y})) \wedge \mathsf{P}(\mathsf{yolkof}(\hat{Y}), \mathsf{yolkof}(\hat{X}))] \vee$$

$$[\mathsf{P}(\mathsf{eggof}(\hat{X}), \mathsf{eggof}(Y)) \wedge \mathsf{PP}(\mathsf{yolkof}(\hat{Y}), \mathsf{yolkof}(\hat{X}))]]] \ .$$

$$(47)$$

This axiom links CR to the predefined RCC5 relations by an *implication*, not an *equivalence*: we do *not* specify that if the specified RCC relations hold between $\mathsf{eggof}(\hat{X})$, $\mathsf{yolkof}(\hat{X})$, $\mathsf{eggof}(\hat{Y})$ and $\mathsf{yolkof}(\hat{Y})$, the CR relation holds between X and Y, but these relations *must* hold for the CR relation to do so. We leave undefined what additional conditions, if any, must be met. This gives us the kind of indefiniteness in the *extent* of vagueness, or *higher-order* vagueness, that intuition demands. Consider the vague region "beside Nick's desk." This can be regarded in OCregion theory as a NonCrisp region. There are some precisely defined regions, such as a cube 10cm on a side, 5cm from the right-hand end of Nick's desk, and 50cm from the floor, that are undoubtedly contained within any reasonable complete crisping of this NonCrisp region. Others, such as a cube 50m on a side centred at the front, top right-hand corner of the desk, contain any such reasonable crisping. These two could correspond to the yolk and egg of an egg-yolk pair constituting the NonCrisp region "beside Nick's desk," forming a very conservative inner and outer boundary on its possible range of indefiniteness. However, some OCregions (Crisp and NonCrisp) lying between this pair would *not* make a reasonable crisping of this region: consider a volume including the 'yolk' of the pair, plus a layer one centimeter deep at the very top of the white. This meets all the conditions for a crisping of the specified OCregion, but is an absurd interpretation of "beside Nick's desk." In general, we need not precisely specify the limits of acceptability. For specific applications, we could add further conditions on acceptable crispings (such as preserving particular topological features or relative proportions in different dimensions), and perhaps assert that (for that application) these conditions are sufficient.

Configuration 1 in Fig.23, given the interpretation of OCregion region theory in terms of egg-yolk pairs of RCC5 regions outlined here, clearly shows a pair of NonCrisp regions such that any pair of complete crispings of the two must be DR. Taking the left egg-yolk pair as representing NonCrisp region X, and the right one NonCrisp region Y:

$$\forall V, W [[V \twoheadleftarrow X \wedge W \twoheadleftarrow Y] \rightarrow \mathsf{DR}(\mathsf{eggof}(\hat{V}), \mathsf{eggof}(\hat{W}))] \qquad (48)$$

Similarly, configuration 2 represents a pair of NonCrisp regions such that, for any complete crisping of either, we can choose a complete crisping of the other that is DR from it, and there are also some complete crisping pairs of the two that are PO. (Cohn and Gotts, 1994b) shows how each of the forty-six configurations can be distinguished in terms of the possible results of replacing one or both of the egg-yolk pairs with a single region-boundary lying within the white of the egg, a complete crisping of the vague region represented by the egg-yolk.

This way of interpreting OCregion theory explains why we found so many parallels with Simons' mereology. Under the egg-yolk interpretation, an OCregion amounts to a three-way division of u into yolk, white, and non-egg. If we consider a set of all such divisions where no part of space is in the yolk of one division and the non-egg of another, we have a mereological system with all the possible precise boundaries as atoms. Crisping expands yolk and/or non-egg at the expense of the white. One OCregion being a crisping of another is like one individual being a proper part of another because the white of the first is a proper part of the white of the second. We have a plausible candidate for the VCC (Vaguest Common Crisping) of two MA OCregions: the VCC 's yolk could be the sum of the yolks of its two blurrings, its egg the prod of the two blurrings' eggs (which, if the two are MA , must exist as a region). Similarly, the yolk of the CCB (Crispest Common Blurring) of *any* two OCregions might be defined as the prod of their yolks; its egg as the sum of their eggs.

The implications of these identifications remain to be explored. However, the egg-yolk model of the OCregion axioms does appear to provide a straightforward way to define OCregion extensions of the compl, sum, prod and diff functions defined within RCC. Moreover, egg-yolk theory gives us a way to reason with vague regions using the existing mechanism of the RCC calculus.

4.9. Final Comments

Work is still continuing on RCC and related formalisms, both at Leeds and elsewhere. We are still working on the formal semantics of RCC (Gotts, 1996a).[56] An interesting piece of work in this regard is (Dornheim, 1995), who has produced a point-set theoretic semantics for RCC8 and related it to the work of Egenhofer. RCC, as presented here, does not have sufficient existential axioms. In (Bennett, 1996b) some progress is made towards addressing this defficiency.

There is still further work to do with the axiomatization of conv and indeed in investigating other primitives that would enhance the expressiveness of RCC. We also hope to work further on our approaches to reasoning about indeterminate boundaries. The work on using zero-order logics seems promising, but there is still further work to do on the larger RCC calculi and in formally relating the zero and first-order representations. We are also looking to various applications to drive our work forward.

We have mentioned some related work in passing during this chapter. QSR is a growing field and there is not space to do it justice here. Hernández (1994) provides a slightly dated review in a final chapter; also see the survey in (Cohn, 1996). The proceedings of COSIT (such as (Frank and Campari, 1993; Frank and Kuhn, 1995)) contain many related papers. A spatial reasoning web site including a pointer to an online interactive bibliography can be found at: http://www.cs.albany.edu/~amit/spatsites.html.

In summary, we have presented a logical calculus for qualitative reasoning about spatial regions, with both a first-order and propositional subvariant. The system has remarkably few primitives, which is desirable not only from a theoretical viewpoint, but also from an implementational one: one need only implement these few primitives to interface to a perceptual component. RCC provides a rich vocabulary of qualitative shape descriptions and has extensions to handle uncertainty. We have provided some special-purpose reasoning techniques (composition tables and conceptual neighborhoods) that can be exploited in a qualitative spatial simulator. We have also sketched some possible application areas for RCC.

Acknowledgments

The support of the EPSRC under grants GR/G36852, GR/H78955 and GR/K65041 is gratefully acknowledged. This work has also been partially supported by a CEC ESPRIT basic research action, MEDLAR II, 6471, and by an HCM network. We gratefully acknowledge many discussions on qualitative spatial reasoning with many people, in particular the "Spacenet" HCM Network community. Special thanks are also due to two previous research fellows at Leeds, Zhan Cui and in particular David Randell who were involved in much of the earlier work reported in this chapter. John Gooday is now working at Equifax, London and Nicholas Gotts at the Department of Computer Science, University of Wales, Aberystwyth.

Notes

[18] This name is recent and is not used in many of our earlier papers.

[19] 'Mereology' is a term (first used by Leśniewski) to describe the formal theory of part, whole and related concepts.

[20] Ladkin (1986) has investigated temporal non convex interval logics. The spatial logic we present below will also allow non-convex spatial entities.

[21] This problem has already been noted in a temporal context (Galton, 1990).

[22] Alternatively, non empty regular closed sets of connected T_3-spaces have been proved to be models for the RCC axiom set (Gotts, 1996a).

[23] The argument sorts for space are Region and Period, respectively, while the result sort is Spatial ⊔ NULL. Period is a sort denoting temporal intervals.

[24] Note that this definition of overlap ensures that connection and overlap are different: if two regions overlap then they share a common region, while this need not be the case for connecting regions, which need only 'touch'.

[25] Actually, sometimes by 'RCC8', we will denote the logical theory (i.e. all the axioms and the definitions of the relations) and sometimes just the set of 8 relation names without necessarily presupposing the logical theory; context should make clear which we intend.

[26] Quasi, because the lack of a null region means the functions do not form a Boolean algebra.

[27] For notational convenience we will sometimes write $x = y$ rather than $EQ(x, y)$; technically the latter is preferable, since EQ is a relation defined in terms of C rather than true logical equality. However, for readability's sake we will ignore this distinction here.

[28] An interesting question arises: what is so special about RCC8? One answer might be that it is essentially the system that arises (in 1D) if one takes Allen's calculus and ignores the before/after ordering: the thirteen relations collapse to eight, which mirror those of RCC8. However, note that Allen's calculus assumes that all intervals are one piece and further relationships would exist if this were not the case (Ladkin, 1986). The 4-intersection model of Egenhofer and Franzosa (1991) also gives rise to exactly eight analogous relations under certain assumptions (such as zero co-dimension). In fact (Dornheim, 1995) shows that the interpretation of the RCC8 relations is slightly more general, but not in any practically interesting sense.

[29] In fact, this predicate formally requires the introduction of natural numbers; however, the usage made of SEPNUM in defining a doughnut could always be cashed out in terms of predicates that do not require these additional primitives.

[30] The corresponding definition in (Gotts, 1994b) is faulty.

[31] Note, however, that this task becomes almost trivial once the conv(x) primitive is introduced in Section 4.5.

[32] In cases where reasoning about dimensionality becomes important, the RCC system is not very powerful. To remedy this we have proposed a new primitive INCH(x,y), whose intended interpretation is that spatial entity x *includes a chunk of* y, where the included chunk is of the same dimension as x. The two entities may be of differing (though uniform) dimension. Thus if x is line crossing a 2D region y, then INCH(x,y) is true, but not vice versa. It is easy to define C(x,y) in terms of INCH, but not vice versa, so the previous RCC system can be defined as a sub theory. An initial exposition of this theory can be found in (Gotts, 1996b). Interestingly, a similar proposal was subsequently made independently by (Galton, 1996).

[33] Of course, this lattice allows certain kinds of reasoning involving subsumption and disjointness of relations to be performed efficiently as noted in (Randell and Cohn, 1992).

[34] As as simple corollary to (Grzegorczyk, 1951) we can show that RCC8 is undecidable (Gotts, 1996d).

[35] (Bennett, 1994a) discusses various other uses and aspects of composition tables.

[36] Note that the assumptions about what is continuous behavior are quite sophisticated here: imagine two regions, one that is two piece and has one component that is an NTPP of the other region and a second component which is DC from the other regions; thus the two regions are PO. If the component which was an NTPP disappeared (a puddle drying in the sun?), then there would be an instantaneous transition from PO to DC! However, we argue that becoming NULL is discontinuous.

[37] A newer, more principled implementation based on the *transition calculus* is described in (Gooday and Cohn, 1996a).

[38] An interesting open theoretical question is raised here: is this method for checking the logical consistency of a set of ground atoms with respect to the full first order RCC8 theory complete? We have not found any counterexample to this conjecture but equally have not been able to prove it.

[39] Fig.11 reveals a subtle difficulty with our analysis of state transition. In the first transition on the second row the food particle crosses the boundary and touches

the enzyme all in one step but in fact since the crossing of the boundary happens instantaneously it must precede the coming together of enzyme and food. The distinction between instantaneous and durative changes has been examined by Galton(1995c) and in Galton's chapter in the present work.

[40] As mentioned above when outlining how to define a doughnut, it is possible to describe some non-convex regions using C alone, but it is impossible to describe the holes themselves as regions. Moreover, not all kinds of concave shapes can be distinguished using C alone (for example, depressions in a surface cannot be distinguished).

[41] One possible line of attack would be to introduce an alternative primitive, "region y is between regions x and z" (see Tarski's axiomatisation of geometry which uses a point based betweenness primitive (Tarski, 1959)) and define conv in terms of this primitive. Linking this primitive to Tarski's point based betweenness relation may provide a way to verify the completeness of the axiomatization.

[42] It should be noted that these axoms are not all independent. It is quite easy to prove that axiom 28 is a consequence of axiom 33 and that axiom 30 is entailed by axiom 31; and it is probable that there are further dependencies.

[43] See also their chapter in this book and (Varzi, 1996c; Varzi, 1996b).

[44] It has been shown that using just the two primitives of conv(x) and C(x,y), any two 2D shapes not related by an affine transformation can be distinguished (Davis et al., 1997).

[45] In his chapter of this book, Frank discusses the general question of ontologies from a consumer's viewpoint.

[46] $\wp(\mathcal{U})$ means the power set of $\mathcal{U}$.

[47] Note that we use the connectives $\sim$ and $\Rightarrow$ to emphasize that the logic is intuitionistic.

[48] This explains the term *entailment constraint*.

[49] We termed this representation the the 'egg-yolk' calculus, for obvious reasons, and will meet it again when describing an extension to RCC to handle regions with indeterminate boundaries below.

[50] This system has been extended to allow for regions with holes, and relationships between regions of different dimensions, for example, see (Egenhofer et al., 1994; Egenhofer, 1994; Egenhofer and Franzosa, 1995).

[51] We are sceptical about the merits of 'fuzzy' approaches to indeterminacy, believing that their use of real number indices of degrees of membership and truth are both counterintuitive and logically problematic. We have no space to argue this controversial viewpoint here; see (Elkan, 1994) and responses for arguments on both sides.

[52] Note that we have addressed only the question of modelling indeterminate boundaries rather than indeterminate position.

[53] We will use upper-case italic letters for variables ranging over OCregions. These are optionally crisp regions, which may be crisp or not.

[54] Each cluster of Fig.24 represents one of these conceptual neighborhoods.

[55] (Clementini and DiFelice, 1994) have also produced a very similar analysis.

[56] Asher and Vieu (1995) have provided a formal semantics for Clarke's system.

5. Spatial Ontology:
A Geographical Information Point of View

Andrew U. Frank

Prima di essere ingegneri siete uomini!
Francesco de Sanctis

5.1. Introduction

The ancient philosophical discipline of ontology has been rediscovered for the purposes of artificial intelligence (Hayes, 1978; Hayes, 1985b). The importance of fixing exactly what is at the base of the things one talks about and of specifying how the different terms interact becomes evident when one attempts in a serious fashion to construct models of the real world. Above all, because in natural language different points of view are brought to bear, confusion and incompatibility can arise.

Ontology has been concerned with the properties of objects, with their modes of existence and with questions such as how they can be divided in parts and how they fill space (Smith, 1982). Ontology, topology and mereology (Simons, 1987) have thus been linked together (Smith, 1995). Recently an ontology of holes has been published (Casati and Varzi, 1994).

There is extensive literature proposing practical ontologies and discussing the finer points of difference between the schemes proposed by others (Hobbs and Moore, 1985). This literature is important in furthering the development of ontologies and it helps us to understand the consequences of different choices (Shaw, 1984). While some of my earlier papers can be understood as contributions to this tradition of proposing formal ontologies and exploring their properties (Frank and Kuhn, 1986; Frank, 1992a; Frank, 1994; Frank, 1996b; Frank, 1996a; Frank, 1996c), I would like here to proceed in a different direction by taking the position of a consumer of ontologies.

This assumes that there is a production of ontologies in the research literature and that these ontologies are useful and can be used. The chapter concentrates on the latter pair of issues, discussing a particular area of application, namely geographic information systems (GIS) (Maguire et al., 1991). It addresses how ontologies are used and how they can contribute to the building of better information systems (Kuhn, 1992; Mark et al., 1992). This is done mostly in relation to examples of problems that arise for the users due to the lack of a consistent ontology in the system (Kuhn, 1993; Kuhn, ress). Such problems become manifest at the user interface level, where the user is confused by two conflicting ontologies and has to learn when one and when the other applies.

The chapter concludes with a set of recommendations as to how ontologies can be made more useful and how the connection between the producers and consumers of an ontology can be structured to make the exchange of ideas more effective. I will also list a number of research directions and specific topics that I would think could provide a useful contribution both from a scientific and an engineering point of view.

This chapter is built on a simple *metaphor*: ontologies are products and are sold in the international *supermarket* of AI research. In this *supermarket* consumers with particular needs shop for ontologies. They must select a set of ontologies to describe the entities in their application domain, and these ontologies must form a consistent ensemble. Contradictions and other inconsistencies may later become apparent to the end-users of the information system. In consequence, the producers of ontologies need clear labels on the products, indicating the advantages and disadvantages of each ontology and potential conflicts with other ontologies. This is advocating truth in labeling for ontologies.

5.2. Geographic Information Systems Build on Ontologies

To make it easier to understand the focus of this chapter, it seems useful to clarify the position from which it starts. Geographic information systems (GIS) are systems that manage information about cities, rural areas, the environment for many different purposes (Antenucci et al., 1991; Laurini and Thompson, 1991). They integrate data about space collected from many sources and use computer technology for the processing, storage, and visualization of such data.

GIS have their origin in the analog method of overlaying different thematic maps to show combinations of features: if one map uses cross-hatching to indicate built-up areas, another uses hatching to indicate the areas zoned for residential buildings, and a third uses gray tone to mark

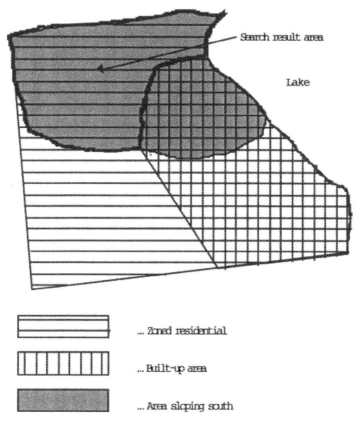

Figure 1.   Overlay search for an area where one can build a new family home facing
south

areas sloping south, then the combination makes it easy to spot areas where one could build a new family home facing south. It is necessary only to search for areas that are hatched and gray throughout (see Figures 1). In zones that are cross hatched and gray, one could search for homes that are for sale (Frank, 1987).

The traditional analog method points to a computer implementation and systems were constructed already in the 1960s (Schmidt and Zafft, 1975). The restrictions of the analog method (for example, only a few layers can be used at any given time) were eliminated. Tomlin proposed a closed algebra with a rich set of operators on maps (Tomlin, 1983a; Tomlin, 1983b; Tomlin, 1989).

Such systems are widely used in urban and regional planning, in the discussion of environmental problems, and for all geo sciences (see especially volume 2 in (Maguire et al., 1991)). They are useful but also limited as they are built around the map metaphor. In the analog system, human cartographers or planners drew the maps and interpreted the results. They applied their commonsense and professional understanding of the situation; They knew about the limitations of the process and separated the ontology of the process (map, color encoding, and so on) from the ontology of the application domain (land-use categories, soil types, and so on). They avoided unwarranted conclusions based on their understanding of the application domain.

Some of the limitations of the map algebra-based, layer, and overlay operations oriented systems are linked to the cartographic models from which they originate. In lieu of working with maps (graphical pictures of the world), a GIS attempts to construct a model of the world (Frank, 1984). Analytical functions can be applied to the model rather than graphical analysis applied to a graphical rendering stored in a computer. This approach was very fruitful, first and foremost for administrative systems, but then also for GIS used for scientific research and planning.

GIS today are widely used and their field of application is almost without limit: most human activities are linked to space and thus most administrative and political decisions are influenced and influence space. GIS are regularly used to plan political campaigns, to assess social disparities, to make regional and urban planning decisions, but also to study global change in climate. GIS software has a rapidly increasing market; for some regions of the world, rates of increase of 20 to 30% per year are currently observed.

The GIS industry is hindered by the capabilities of the software and its quality (Mark and Frank, 1991; Frank and Mark, 1991; Mark and Frank, 1996). This is similar to the state of affairs in other branches of the information technology industry (Joch, 1995), but the problems are more acute and thus better analyzed. In addition to the regular problems of software engineering and poor programming practice using current programming languages (Liskov and Guttag, 1986), a number of special issues can be detected that are directly linked to the ontologies used and thus of interest in the current discussion.

5.2.1. MODELS OF REALITY IN A GIS MODEL AN EXTERNAL INDEPENDENT REALITY

The GIS is built to present a model of some aspects of reality (Frank and Mark, 1991). This model must reflect observable properties of this reality, and the model is useless if there are substantial systematic deficiencies in the correspondence between observed reality and model.

This differentiates GIS and other reality-oriented information systems (such as systems designed for the steering of robots) from those administrative information systems where there is no other reality than the one created through the system so that the system is, by definition, correct. The stock example is banking, where the only operations possible are the ones built into the program, and there is no attempt to model connection to an independently existing external reality. The definition of a client of a bank is "a person listed in the database of bank clients". Systems that must correspond to some external reality are more difficult to build (Shaw, 1984). The most obvious consequence of modeling an exterior reality is that the closed-world assumption, which is at the foundation of any database query language, is not valid any more (Reiter, 1984).

5.2.2. A GIS IS A FORMAL SYSTEM.

Despite the fact that GIS are built following informal specifications and formal methods are not yet sufficiently developed to be used routinely for software development, the resulting set of programs is a formal system executed by the computer.

The formal properties of a GIS, which is a complex system of several million lines of code, are hidden in the mass of the programming code. It is difficult to see where different definitions are used and how they interact, but they will often interact in the most distracting manner, as an abundance of complaints from users demonstrate.

5.2.3. GIS MODEL SPACE

In GIS software some particular concepts for the representation of space are built in. The appropriate models for space have been central in much of the scientific discussion of GIS (especially the series of AutoCarto conferences and then Spatial Data Handling and Conference on Spatial Information Theory).

In GIS it is customary to use a three-level hierarchy of concepts for modeling space (Frank, 1992b; Goodchild, 1992):

- *Spatial concepts*, which reflect the *user's* conceptualization of space, can be informal and not directly implementable. Two fundamentally different views are necessary: a concept of space with attributes (commonly labeled as *raster GIS*) and one with objects that have spatial and non-spatial attributes (which is often called *vector GIS*). These two concepts can be traced back to ontological roots.
- *Spatial or geometric models* are implementable models of space with formal definitions. The major two contenders are models that model space using a raster and others that support geometric constructions based on points, lines, and areas.
- *Spatial data structures* implement geometric models in computer code, achieving optimal performance.

These three levels are comparable to the AI division in concept, knowledge, and data.

5.2.4. GIS ARE USED FOR HUMAN ACTIVITIES.

The results yielded by GIS are used in administrative and political processes, where they are the input in human decision-making processes. ¿From this it follows that the interpretation of output by humans matters. The goal is not primarily an objective scientific truth, but a commitment to consider human cognitive processes.

There is first and most obviously an effort to be made to produce output in a format human beings can digest, thus leading to efforts to visualize in graphical form but also using other media that are effective and easy to interpret by the application specialist.

There is also an effort necessary to construct user interfaces in the broadest sense that correspond to the abilities and concepts of the users to reduce the effort to learn to use the system. This is particularly important as today more than half of the cost of acquiring GIS software goes for efforts to train the user to use the system effectively.

5.2.5. GIS INTEGRATE DATA FROM DIFFERENT SOURCES BASED ON DIFFERENT CONCEPTS.

The fundamental tenet of GIS is the idea of integrating data from different sources with respect to spatial location. This reflects the human experience that different factors affect locations, from natural phenomena like southern exposure and soil type to factors created by human beings: distance from a railway station, noise effects from an airport, building zones, south-exposed slope, and so on.

Different data originate with different organizations and reflect different scientific backgrounds. It is surprising how the spatial concepts of different sciences differ. Scientific disciplines are often distinguished by the scale of spatial or temporal phenomena they consider: resolution of time for a geologist is in thousand-year units, whereas a wildlife biologist studies movement of animals during a day. Similar differences apply in the spatial scale.

Spatial concepts can be two-dimensional (possibly embedded in a three-dimensional space), three-dimensional, continuous or divided in discrete units, or restricted to a graph (as is typical for traffic and other communication studies). Despite several years of research effort, it has not been possible to find a single, unifying concept of space to which all the others can be reduced; the question of whether this is possible in principle is still open.

5.2.6. DIFFERENT CULTURAL GROUPS ARE INVOLVED IN PRODUCING AND USING A GIS.

GIS software is used to model many different kinds of geographic information. It is used in different circumstances and different countries (Campari, 1991). GIS users speak different languages (Campari, 1994). Differences in the concepts of land, ownership, nature, and the environment are easily detected (Campari, 1992). A less evident issue is caused by the fact that the designers and programmers of GIS software are predominantly from the United States and assume typical U.S. attitudes toward planning, land use,and so on (Guttenberg, 1992; Guttenberg, 1993), attitudes that rest on concepts distinct from those used in many other countries where GIS is used (Campari and Frank, 1994).

5.3. Problems with Ad-Hoc Ontologies in GIS

GIS are a typical, advanced, and demanding case of a complex information system about the spatial environment. They point to a number of difficulties in building such systems, difficulties that are, however, not unique. Observations made today in building GIS software can be generalized and applied to other fields. It is thus important to observe how such systems are advanced by the use of properly developed ontologies.

GIS are based on ontologies about objects, space, time, and many categories from law, technologies, and social structures. Until recently, these were mostly ad hoc or based on well-known mathematical abstractions like topology, Euclidean geometry and set theory.

Problems can be observed in today's use of GIS that can be traced back to the unsystematic use of ontologies (Guevara, 1985). The problem was not so much a lack of systems but rather a multiplicity of alternative systems combined with a neglect of serious work in the subject until around 1890 and then again between 1920 and 1980 (Smith, 1982; Simons, 1987).

5.3.1. INCONSISTENCY BETWEEN ONTOLOGIES BUILT INTO A GIS

The ad hoc construction of the ontology of a GIS will invariably lead to some choices that will not be compatible with each other. Galton discusses possible inconsistencies for time and motion (Galton, 1995c); in the rich domain on which GIS are based, many more inconsistencies are possible. The legal definition of a parcel in common law uses a *general boundary* concept, which is a fuzzy area not belonging exclusively to any of the two parcels. The GIS typically represents such a boundary area by a sharp line (which is the dominant legal concept in the European cadastres).

5.3.2. CONFLICT BETWEEN THE ONTOLOGICAL CONCEPTS AND THE IMPLEMENTATION

GIS software is often assuming continuous space and, if included, continuous time. The user interface is designed in these terms, and much of the code is written based on concepts of continuous space. The implementation, of course, must use finite representations for coordinate values and thus cannot truly manage continuous space. For at least fifteen years, GIS software was plagued with simple conflicts between geometric computations done with floating point numbers approximating real coordinate values and rules from topology: overlay computations produced erroneous values for regular input or could not complete a computation. After many years of gradual improvement, a consistent theory is available (Greene and Yao, 1986), and an ontology-like description of a consistent geometry that can be implemented is known (Gueting and Schneider, 1992).

5.3.3. CONFLICTS BETWEEN THE COMMONSENSE ONTOLOGY OF THE USER AND THE MATHEMATICAL CONCEPTS IN THE SOFTWARE

The concepts used by the different users of a GIS are often closer to commonsense theories than to objective scientific (physics-based) theories. Administrative rules and law, everyday ethics, and everyday planning decisions embody ontologies that which with scientific ideas but are highly useful nonetheless.

The difference between commonsense ontologies and the ones used in physics are surprisingly large. Equally surprising is the observation of how little the construction of our material technology (buildings, machines, cars, and so on) is based on strict physical laws. It was found that systems to diagnose real machines must use so-called naive physics that permits logical, often qualitative, but not strictly quantitative physical modeling of simple physical mechanism. Egenhofer and Mark (1995) apply similar ideas to geographic information.

5.4. Use of Ontologies in GIS and Similar Information Systems

Building application programs in this context means constructing an ontology for the application domain. This is normally done by the analyst in assimilating the ontology underlying the description given by the application specialist.

This partial information is then transformed in an abstract ontology by the software designer, usually relating it to standard mathematical concepts. These do not precisely capture the application notion; hence, they are then modified, and inconsistencies result. Sometimes it is not possible to implement these mathematical categories exactly, and approximations are used, again leading to inconsistencies.

A GIS uses quite a few ontologies, each of which poses serious problems, most of them have occasionally appeared in the literature. A survey of a few issues follows.

5.4.1. ONTOLOGY OF ENTITIES

What does it mean to be an entity? When are entities created, when do they end (Al-Taha and Barrera, 1994)? When does a piece of land become an entity in its own right? A typical example is provided by the legal system, which deals with land parcels: they are created and cease to exist, despite the fact that land can neither be created nor destroyed. New parcels emerge when previously existing ones are divided and cease to exist when merged with another one (Casati and Varzi, 1994).

5.4.2. ONTOLOGY OF SPACE

Space in today's GIS is always seen as Euclidean space, represented with Cartesian coordinates. To deal with the spherical surface of the earth (which is not a Euclidean plane) is often not necessary. But when it is necessary, for example, to construct a spatial sampling method that gives equal probability for any point of the sphere to be included, no good solutions exist (Goodchild and Shiren, 1990).

Data that are not related to a point with given position cannot be entered in a GIS. This limits the use of GIS for combining verbal reports about events, such as accidents. "The fire is on the left bank of the river", "The fire is north of the railway bridge", and "The fire is on route 451" together describe a precise location, but neither of the three pieces of information can be entered in a GIS independently (Frank, 1992a).

A separate issue is the representation of nonpoint data, for example, the representation of diffuse chemical contamination of an area. Either space is seen as a continuum, so that for each point (in principle) an attribute value gives the local concentration, which is then discretized to a regular raster. Alternatively, space is seen as consisting of a collection of spatial objects with uniform raster and proper boundaries. In some applications, these objects must form a partition and together constitute the space. In other applications, different objects may coexist at the same location, that is, objects may overlap. In both cases, space is modeled as a collection of spatial objects that describe the boundaries of these objects (Corbett, 1979).

A new idea is the use of constraints, which, in the simplest form, describe a semi plane but can be combined to limit the infinite set of points to the desired area. This represents the infinite number of points in an area by inequalities, that is, an infinity of coordinate pairs.

5.4.3. ONTOLOGY OF TIME

Most GIS do not include concepts of time; they describe an instantaneous picture. Indeed, they often give the data valid for different instants, depending when the last update for an area was made. Administrative uses demand at least that the date for which the data were valid is recorded, to avoid inconsistencies due to the comparison of data from different times. Often there is a legal need to record not only the current situation but also previous situations so that a complete documentation of all previous states, and of all the operations that led to the current state, can be reconstructed. This is typically the case for cadastral applications (Al-Taha, 1992) but will be increasingly included in others. For example, a commercial distributor of a road atlas in digital form documents all changes to his road databases to avert liability cases.

Natural sciences often study theories that describe change. GIS for scientific uses thus must deal with time series (instantaneous data related to regularly spaced moments in time). The national statistical bureaus collect and distribute snapshot data, collected in regular intervals (typically every ten years).

Not all models of time in science follow the familiar arrow concept: natural phenomena are often repetitive and thus their description is cyclic also (Frank, 1996a).

5.4.4. MEREOLOGY

The entities in a GIS appear single and uniform at one level of description, but they can be divided and further divided; each of these parts can again be an entity in the GIS. They seem to form hierarchies (such as the division of a country in smaller units), but often the relations are more complex and form a lattice. The prototypical case of hierarchies of two-dimensional areas form a part of hierarchy; but there are special cases. For example the *Gemeinden* (communes, counties) in Switzerland do not form a partition. There are areas that are jointly governed by two Gemeinden and there are others that are not in any Gemeinde.

Hierachies in linear networks are not built on a part of or inclusion relation, and a consistent ontology is an open problem (Car and Frank, 1994; Timpf et al., 1992). Considering maps of different scales, objects from the small-scale map are shown with more detail, more parts, on the larger scale-map. A detailed analysis of this relation is necessary to build comprehensive, multiscale cartographic databases (Frank and Timpf, 1994; Timpf et al., 1994; Timpf and Frank, 1995).

5.5. Two Different Types of Uses for Ontologies

The above list documents questions thta are typically dealt with in ontology and mereology, but current GIS use ad hoc solutions. The few cases where useful ontologies have been proposed in the literature demonstrate that formal ontologies, if applicable, are quickly assimilated by the GIS designers and built into the software. For example, Allen's time intervals (Allen, 1983) were generalized to two dimensions by Egenhofer (Egenhofer, 1989) to construct a classification scheme for topological relations. This scheme is implemented in GIS software, mostly in order to achieve formal semantics for spatial query languages.

5.5.1. CONSTRUCTION OF SOFTWARE

Ontologies are useful for the construction of software. Indeed, they are indispensable, and all application software contains some ontology of the domain it is applied to. Too often, however, these ontologies are not intentionally designed and are constructed in an ad hoc fashion. Tools exist today to describe ontologies formally and to check their consistency (Guttag et al., 1985; Frank et al., 1986; Frank, 1994).

5.5.2. CONSTRUCTION OF TESTABLE HYPOTHESIS ABOUT

COMMONSENSE THEORIES

Understanding the commonsense theories is very difficult, and several large-scale projects are underway (Lenat et al., 1990). Formal theories help to identify possible alternative theories, to construct alternative hypotheses, and to develop the experiments to decide the question (Stevens and Coupe, 1978; Mark, 1992).

5.6. How to Make Ontologies Usable

For a software engineer building basic GIS software, ontologies would be very helpful if they were ready made for use. What properties are important to make an ontology useful? Here, properties of the ontology and then properties of the presentation, which make the ontology easier to implement, are discussed.

5.6.1. SMALL THEORIES TO COMBINE

The guiding assumption here is that no single ontology can capture all aspects of reality but that we can build particular ontologies for specific aspects of physical, cognitive, administrative or legal reality. For example, in Frank (1994) different models for time from cognitive, natural science, and administrative points of view are presented. These small theories can be formally documented and must be described in a form that makes it possible to combine them with other similar small theories.

5.6.2. TYPED ONTOLOGIES

Combining small theories is likely aided by using a typed logic for their formalization. Typed logic avoids paradoxes and helps understanding. Most programming languages used today for GIS are typed, and thus the translation effort for the software engineer is reduced.

5.6.3. PRESENTATION FORMAT

Software engineers are at best fluent in first-order predicate calculus using standard notation. Any deviation from this *lingua franca* increases the effort necessary to understand. Indeed, other formalism makes a text nearly incomprehensible for the software engineer, and thus the ontology described is not consumable. I understand the reasons for continuing with the notational standards of traditional ontological research (Simons, 1987), but these must be weighted against the limitations of the potential users.

5.6.4. REVIEW OF FORMALLY DESCRIBED ONTOLOGIES IN A COMPARABLE FORMAT

The literature contains a large number of ontologies with some differences; these differences can be important for some applications or then can make certain combinations possible and rule out others. A systematic review, with identification of common parts, would be useful. In particular, a formal description perhaps in the form of a lattice of types, with inheritance relations and dependencies indicated would be most useful for software designers. Catalogs of "reusable parts" (Booch, 1987) were very successful in software engineering and have substantively influenced current practice.

5.6.5. ONTOLOGIES THAT ADMIT A FINITARY REPRESENTATION

Computers can deal only with finitary representations. Ontologies that assume a continuum are difficult to simulate on a finite machine. Users will detect effects of the approximations and in consequence be confused in their understanding of the operation of the GIS software.

   The translation from an ontology using an unbounded continuum to one that is based on a bounded and finite set, which can be represented in a computer, is non trivial and not purely an implementation problem but part of the problem of ontology construction.

5.6.6. COMPUTATIONALLY EFFECTIVE

The models must be computational and should lead to good practice. Models built or translated in constructive logic or even easily implementable subsets of logic (such as Horn clauses) are more easily assimilated by the designers of GIS.

5.7. Open Questions for Ontologies for GIS

In this section a number of questions for ontologists are posed from a GIS perspective. They are based on observation of current research in spatial information theory and point to areas where fundamental work at the level of ontologies would make a useful contribution.

5.7.1. ATOM-BASED THEORIES

There are good reasons to assume continuous space and time, but in many cases, reality presents itself as consisting of discrete pieces. The human senses do not allow us to differentiate spatial position when objects are less than $1/10$ mm apart or events in time when events occur less than $1/30$ sec after each other: a piece of paper cannot be torn in infinitely many pieces, and so on. There are limits to the subdivisions, but in practical experience we hardly ever reach that point: after cutting the paper into twenty pieces, further subdivisions are not attempted. Parcels of land are often subdivided beyond what is reasonable to allow economical exploitation, but they still remain at least several square meters large. Distances between boundary points of less than one meter would show the influence of measurement errors in cadastral surveying even to the layperson!

5.7.2. ONTOLOGIES THAT CAN COPE WITH IMPRECISION AND UNCERTAINTY

The common experience of all observation of reality demonstrates the presence of errors, imprecision, and uncertainty in the results. There are various reasons for these limitations of the observation process (physical, technical, and cognitive) but they are fundamental, and nearly nothing can be measured with absolute accuracy. Constructing ontologies that allow for these limitations of the perception of reality would be most helpful (Burrough and Frank, 1996).

5.7.3. DIFFERENT TYPES OF BOUNDARIES

Boundaries come in different kinds: some are sharp and well defined physically; others are undefined. There are several kinds, each with its own properties (Burrough and Frank, 1996). A family of consistent ontologies of boundaries and related phenomena would be most useful.

Human cognition has a tendency to move boundaries to areas where few difficult cases may appear: the boundary between Austria and Italy generally follows mountain ridges, where economic interest in land is extremely low and nothing hardly ever happens. This becomes apparent when something happens there; for example a mummified body of a Stone Age man is found, and the two countries become involved in a dispute of scientific ownership. Other boundaries are in the middle of lakes or rivers, where there is no land to discuss the ownership of. Similarly, boundaries between cognitive categories are such that few dubious cases arise: there are no questionable animals between dogs and cats, between fish and others (and the efforts of biologists to confuse us with the classification of sharks or whales do not constitute important cognitive counterexamples in this respect).

5.7.4. HIERARCHICAL STRUCTURES

Cognitive structures are often arranged in such a way that wide concepts are subdivided into more narrow ones, if necessary. At first, they seem to follow a hierarchical structure, where the elements of the upper level are subdivided in smaller ones, such that a group of smaller ones makes up exactly one unit at the higher level. But this is not necessarily the case, and in general a directed acyclic graph can be observed, sometimes forming a lattice or a structure that can be easily completed to form a lattice.

This can be observed for spatial areas (such as the political subdivision of a country in regions, provinces, and counties, but also others, for example, the subdivision in water catchment areas). It can be conceptual classification (e.g. the subdivision of plants according to the Linnaean system). It can be a division of a task in a subtask (driving from A to B consists of tasks like entering the car, starting the engine, and so on).

This is a particular case of a part-whole structure, where the parts do not have the same level in the genus-species tree (Smith, 1982). There is sufficient generality to warrant a systematic investigation.

5.8. Using Ontologies: Merging Multiple Theories

Assuming that ontologies are small theories with few axioms and few predicates (for example the RCC theory of Randell and Cohn, 1989 and Randell, Cui, and Cohn, 1992), how do we arrive from these small theories capable of modeling reality, as is required for an application? Assume that there are ontologies for solids, space, living things, persons, and buildings: how can we build from these the ontological base for a legal ontology (Frank, 1996c)?

It seems possible to build the prototypical case from the concrete classes of the physical world. The adaptations reflect metaphorical mappings in the sense of Lakoff and Johnson (Lakoff and Johnson, 1980; Johnson, 1987). From the simple case the more complex cases are then constructed through specialization of the classes in *is_a* hierarchies.

A difficulty stems from different viewpoints: we generally assume that the theories are treating different things, that is, an entity is either a person, a piece of land, or a building, with an "exclusive or", and follows the rules of the corresponding theory. But theories must also be combined if they consist of different viewpoints: a piece of land can be at the same time a parcel, a census track, a wildlife habitat, and so on. A person is owner of the parcel, is employee of the bank granting a mortgage on the parcel, and so on.

Last, but not least, the theories can be different in their approach: a legal (commonsense) theory of land applies at the same time as a physical theory of space or a technical construction based on Euclidean geometry. However, they may differ in the uncertainties or errors considered.

5.9. Research Topics

The previous list of major open questions indicates issues where concerted, multiyear efforts seem appropriate. In this section, a few questions are listed, to which interesting and useful results could be achieved with limited efforts, perhaps a single Ph.D. thesis.

The approaches proposed here are all case based. This stems from the conviction that the past years have developed all the results that can be found by theoretically considering and reconsidering the same general topics. New insight can be gained from detailed investigations in particular cases; the more concrete, the better. Later generalizations, if the same observations are made several times, can then lead to a better general theory.

5.9.1. LEGAL ONTOLOGIES

The law assumes ontologies for various things, from human beings to land parcels. The ontological bases of a specific national law would be a worthwhile project, but it seems also possible to build ontologies for certain legal areas, independent of specific national legislation. Different legislations must resolve the same problems, and thus the ontologies are likely similar, will reveal more about the problem area, and separate this from specific legal solutions. There is currently a need for such analyses for the new countries in Eastern Europe and Asia, which all must rebuild their legal systems and need, for example, legislation for land ownership.

5.9.2. ONTOLOGIES FOR TRADITIONAL GAMES

The traditional games are valuable artifacts that embody in an abstract and reduced form substantial parts of human cognition. Many of the board games (such as chess and go) include a spatial abstraction. To formalize these notions and to understand the differences in the concepts of motion, for example, in these games, would be useful and advance the understanding of the prototypical cases of human cognition.

5.9.3. SPATIAL ONTOLOGY FOR A SPECIAL CASE

The spatial situation of a town can be abstracted to an atomic theory of space, where the spatial atoms are much smaller than the objects to be modeled: buildings do have certain sizes (a building in Vienna holds the international record: it is less than 2 m wide!). Between-building spaces are left, again, with some minimal sizes, otherwise they could not function as roads or pathways. The basic ontology could abstract the gaps between buildings to a graph and consider the relations between buildings and roads (for example, access) (Campari, 1996).

5.9.4. SPATIAL ONTOLOGY FOR LANGUAGE

What are the basic spatial notions apparent in language? What are the categories used in the explanation of language? As a starting point, I would select the spatial image schemes from the list by Johnson (1987) and use the detailed analysis of Herskovits (Chapter 6).

5.9.5. ONTOLOGICAL PROBLEMS OF DATABASES

In current applications of database technology two (at least two) fundamental ontological problems appear as real and vexing problems:

- How do entities assume a role? How do we separate between objects and the roles they assume?
- How long does an object remain the same? When does it become a new one?
- How to determine when the normal closed-world assumption applies to application domains and when it does not?

5.10. Conclusions

This chapter lists a smörgåsbord of problems for which I see links with the standard ontological and mereological questions. I have listed some examples where I sense that current GIS technology is hindered by a lack of clear ontological bases, following the tradition of a study in 1983, which already pointed to the connection between the lack of theory and the difficulties encountered in the practical application (Smith et al., 1983).

What a software engineer building a GIS or any other information system would expect is a set of small theories capturing the behavior of certain parts of reality. The software technology to combine reusable pieces of code is spreading rapidly with names like rapid application development (RAD), OLE, and applets. What is missing is the theoretical (ontological) foundation for these coded objects.

To make such small theories usable, there must exist a method to combine them and to predict their interaction. Combinable theories should be available for the same parts of reality, seen from a physical or engineering point of view, and also considering a cognitive aspect or sociocultural perspective. The engineering point of view is necessary to integrate engineering knowledge in the system; the cognitive position is necessary to make it understandable to the user at the interface. Finally, the third, the sociocultural perspective, serves to achieve integration with the social and cultural systems, such as the law and administrative tradition, which are more based on folk theories or commonsense reasoning.

The current literature fulfills this requirement only partially. To be useful for software engineers, contributions must be in a format corresponding to standard software engineering practice. In particular, formalisms must use modern symbolism and terminology (engineers do not appreciate being confused with the Aristotelian senses of substance or accident). Engineers have very little interest in reviews of historical development of an idea: only the "correct" solution warrants much attention. Consequently, there is hardly any discussion of historic development in engineering. The difference in discussion style between ontology as a philosophy-influenced discipline and mathematics documents this aspect: historical development is at best reduced to footnotes, and the history of mathematics is a subdiscipline with very few disciples. To make a contribution useful for an engineer does not only exclude a lengthy historical treaty but also requires a view toward the consistent part, not the differences between views: the search is for a "useful piece", not discrimination between different people's contribution. To allow effective cooperation and transfer of knowledge from ontologists to software engineers these differences of attitude need to be respected.

Efforts to build a single, unified, and encompassing ontology (the grand, unifying theory) appear to be impractical. Understanding the differences in the ontologies of different applications is more important.

A goal could be a standard catalog of ontologies, with a corresponding taxonomy, with description of assumptions and pointers to possible interaction with incompatible assumptions that other theories may make. In software engineering, such catalogs have been produced for data structures (Booch, 1987). They are useful and have led to standard implementations as software libraries after the necessary changes were included in programming languages and software engineering practice.

Acknowledgments

I wish to thank the organizers of this symposium for the opportunity they provided. They have shown a broad concern, which goes substantially beyond the usual scientific disciplinary point of view, and the resulting discussion has demonstrated, once again, the potential of interdisciplinary discussion to transcend the ordinary course of science. It has also led to new insight not only in particular ontologies, but also in the methods different researchers have used, in the different types of problems posed and the limitations of the results achieved.

It is a pleasure to acknowledge the numerous and profound discussions with Barry Smith. He made extensive comments on an earlier draft of the manuscript, which contributed enormously to the clarity of the exposition of these ideas here. I further appreciate Mag. Roswitha Markwart's efforts to make my presentation clear and easy to read.

6. Language, Spatial Cognition, and Vision

Annette Herskovits

6.1. Introduction: Speaking About the Spatial World

One essential function of language is to refer to objects and situations in the world. This process is mediated by nonlinguistic mental representations, most prominently by perceptual representations in different modalities. Human minds have the ability to establish systematic relationships between linguistic forms and perceptually based knowledge. This *grounding* of linguistic symbols in perceptual representations (Harnad, 1990), though often overlooked in linguistics and artificial intelligence, is essential to understanding linguistic abilities and linguistic structure. And a good way to examine it is to investigate our ability to talk about space; the spatial world seems amenable to precise and objective description – unlike, say, the world of smells and feelings – and much is known about visual and spatial perception.

As this chapter shows, close semantic analysis of spatial expressions opens a window onto the interplay of faculties that supports our ability to describe the spatial world. There are several kinds of spatial expressions, but spatial relation terms are key elements in a large proportion of them, as they are the principal means available to speakers for the description of location and path. So, in this chapter, I examine the meaning and use of spatial prepositions in English against the background of current knowledge on vision and spatial cognition and infer the consequences of this exploration for the processes linking language and spatial knowledge.

In speaking about the spatial world, we tap several sources of knowledge: linguistic knowledge; conceptual knowledge; world knowledge; perceptual knowledge (particularly the output of visual perception); and nonperceptual spatial representations. I offer brief characterizations of these before sketching the connections between semantic facts and spatial cognition brought out in this study.

6.1.1. LINGUISTIC AND CONCEPTUAL KNOWLEDGE

The conceptual system consists in the set of concepts and principles of conceptual combination by which we categorize our experience. The semantic system of a language cannot be identical with the conceptual system because we think and reason with concepts that have no ordinary linguistic expression – mathematical ones, for instance. But are semantic structures simply a subset of conceptual structures – that is, the linguistically expressible subset? Some linguists assume this is the case (Jackendoff, 1983; Langacker, 1991); others (Bierwisch, 1988; Pinker, 1989) propose separate conceptual and semantic systems, assigning distinct semantic and conceptual structures to a sentence.

The linguistic analyses of Pinker differ significantly from those of Bierwisch, but both are moved to distinguish two levels of structure by the assumption that nonlinguistic conceptual thought is universal. Given that semantic distinctions can be language-specific, "equating linguistic semantic representations with the conceptual categories underlying nonlinguistic thought is tantamount to a very strong and implausible Whorfian claim" (Pinker, 1989, p. 357). Yet the evidence so far for a language-independent, universal conceptual system is rather weak. Bowerman (1996), Langacker (1991), and Levinson (1993) describe differences between languages that would be hard to reconcile with a common underlying conceptual base.

This study assumes only one level of meaningful structure, which I call indifferently semantic or conceptual. Collapsing semantic and conceptual structure compels us to assume that conceptual systems are significantly shaped by the language one speaks, a position congruent with the views of lexical knowledge advocated in this chapter.

6.1.2. COMMONSENSE KNOWLEDGE OF THE WORLD

Commonsense knowledge of the world includes general knowledge about location, shape, gravity, time, motion, and causality; about the properties of liquids, solids, gases, and various particular substances; about the many kinds of objects with which we interact (people, animals, plants, buildings, lakes, rivers, and so on); and about the self and its range of behaviors. This commonsense world is the world "as it is," the reality in the background of our linguistic productions; it is the default reference world, the one we typically talk about; it is "objective," not in any scientific sense but according to our naive ontology.

Work in artificial intelligence typically assumes that a representation of commonsense knowledge is the key to semantics, that the meaning of a lexical item corresponds to some structural configuration in the knowledge representation. The semantics of a language is thus definable as a mapping from lexical items to such configurations. But, in fact, world knowledge can take us only so far toward understanding semantics. Languages manifest subjective ways of structuring the objective, commonsense world, and much of this chapter is concerned with understanding that structuring in the domain of space.

6.1.3. SPATIAL COGNITION

Spatial cognition – the collection of mental structures and processes that support our spatial behavior – involves a complex and various set of abilities:

- *Visual abilities*: Vision is a primary source of spatial information.
- *Other perceptual abilities*: The aural, kinesthetic, haptic, and olfactory systems all deliver spatial information.
- *Motor abilities*: Walking, reaching, interacting with, and using various objects (avoiding an obstacle, sitting in a chair, putting a cap on a bottle, and so on) depend on coordinating perceptual and general knowledge to direct motion.
- *Navigational abilities*: When moving through medium- to large-scale spaces, we use *cognitive maps* as guides (Kuipers, 1983). Unlike real maps, these representations are fragmented – some regions are rich in detail, others only roughly characterized – and distorted. They may include visual memories, but encode essentially the location of landmarks and routes connecting the landmarks.
- *Mental imagery*: We can evoke in our minds scenes observed from a specific viewpoint, imaginary or remembered scenes. Kosslyn (1980) and Finke (1989) claim these mental images are functionally similar to perceptual representations.
- *Spatial mental models*: As we attempt to comprehend linguistic spatial descriptions, we create models of the situations described (Johnson-Laird, 1983; Tversky, 1993b). These share properties with mental images (they are in part analog) but are apparently three-dimensional rather than dependent on a particular vantage point.
- *Spatial memory*: This complex ability involves several distinguishable mechanisms (Wadell and Rogoff, 1987; Stiles-Davis et al., 1988). It

intersects with mental imagery and cognitive maps.

- *Spatial reasoning and problem solving*: To plan a trip or design an appropriate configuration of furniture in a room, one must engage in spatial problem solving. This joins logical reasoning with the ability to create and manipulate various mental images and models.

6.1.4. FROM SPATIAL COGNITION TO LANGUAGE

Spatial cognition, then, includes many abilities and distinguishable representations. Which representations can language access? One possible answer is that it has access to a veridical (but partial) three-dimensional map of the environment – a map constructed from perceptual representations and world knowledge, yet consistent with cognitive maps and with the representations guiding motion. Such a map would explain our ability to coordinate different spatial operations – for instance, when we use both a cognitive map and sights along the route to find our way. Moreover, some such view of the *real world* – whether explicitly represented or not – is always in the background of our utterances. Otherwise there would be neither truth nor reference, and hence no communication.

But we refer using linguistic categories (of objects, spatial relations, actions, and so on). A sentence is not a *copy* of a scene; it is a statement that the scene belongs to a certain category, which every part of the sentence helps specify. The categories available in languages are only partially determined by the world; they can be defined in many different ways as shown by variation among languages. Thus, this (presumably essentially universal) view of the *real* physical world does not determine what concepts are used to describe a scene. And, as we will see, the categorizing of scenes by spatial relations does in fact show that language accesses representations distinct from this hypothetical veridical map.

The question of how scenes are categorized by spatial relations is tied to the question of *schematization*. A phrase like *the tree lying across the road* reduces the rich information contained in the referent scene to the mention of two object categories (tree and road), and the assertion that the axis of the tree leads from one edge of the road to the other. The relation expressed is based on simple geometric descriptions of two complex entities – the tree as an axis and the road as a ribbon – and their detailed arrangement reduced to a very simple geometric relation. This is schematization.

It seems sensible to assume that schematization is based on general spatial cognitive processes and that the geometric representations of objects in spatial expressions are clues to the spatial representations accessed by language. It is therefore essential to examine schematization closely; to see exactly which schematizations are used in which contexts. For example, it is often assumed that schematization means that the actual arguments of a preposition are always simple geometric representations of the objects: points, lines, planes, or blobs. A close look shows that such reduction happens sometimes but not always. Where reduction does occur, it reveals a great deal indeed about the representations accessed by language. For example, it provides evidence that spatial expressions often invoke cognitive maps, in which landmarks and moving objects are seen as points. But at times fully detailed close-up representations of scenes, including precise representations of objects' shape, are needed to decide whether a preposition is applicable. In fact, for many prepositions, there is evidence of two categories of use: one in which the objects are close to each other and requiring full representations of objects shape and placement, and one in which the objects are far apart, when a representation analogous to a cognitive map is used.

Objects are represented as points in almost all descriptions of motion (Section 6.3.3). Other representations accessed by language include a two-dimensional representation homologous to the visual array, and two-dimensional ground maps for small-scale environments (those for large-scale environments are simply cognitive maps). In some cases, Gestalt processes of perceptual organization provide the applicable schematic representations of objects. One may not want to consider each of these as distinct, but it is important to be precise about which object representations are used in spatial expressions and about their origin.

Schematization also sheds light on a hypothesis proposed by Landau and Jackendoff (1993), which posits a division of spatial language and ascribes it to a division in the processing of spatial information in the brain. The hypothesis, based on a mistaken view of schematization, is shown to be invalid (see 6.5.2).

The representations accessed by language are part and parcel of nonlinguistic spatial cognition, but the spatial relations expressed need not be explicit elements of these representations. In the last part of the chapter (6.5.3), I argue that perceiving and expressing a spatial relation requires, at least at times, visual processing beyond a simple act of attention. The related objects must be configured together, and their configuration assigned to a prepositional category. These operations might not take place without a linguistic goal; thus, there are language-induced percepts.

The balance of this chapter is divided into four main parts. Section 6.2 presents the English system of spatial prepositions and general patterns in the way they are used to specify spatial characteristics; Section 6.3 examines schematization; Section 6.4 concerns the striking fluidity of prepositional meaning and questions of polysemy and prototypicality; and Section 6.5 looks at the interface between language and spatial cognition.

6.2. Usages of the Prepositions

Prepositions denote spatial relations, which are principally used to predicate constraints on such attributes as location, trajectory, orientation, direction, and disposition. Most prepositions are polysemous (Herskovits, 1986; Brugman, 1988), but one finds patterns in the polysemy that allow one to classify them. Thus, the *location prepositions* (Table 6.1) have only location senses; the prepositions can be used in motion sentences, but these do not require defining additional (motion) senses. The *primarily motion* prepositions, on the other hand, have distinct motion senses and stationary senses, some of which are systematically related to the motion senses. For convenience, I term these prepositions the *motion prepositions*. The prepositions labeled *misfits* follow patterns of their own.

6.2.1 BASIC USAGES OF THE LOCATION PREPOSITIONS

The prepositions in the first column fit in a syntactic frame:

NP is preposition NP

as in

> The ball is ...
> ... on the table / against the wall / among the stones / at the store / behind the wall / ...

In these expressions, the location of the first object (the ball) is constrained with respect to the second by the spatial relation .denoted by the preposition. Following Talmy (1983), I will call the located object the *Figure* and the reference object – the object of the preposition – the *Ground*:

The ball   is on   the table

Figure   *Ground*

Located object   *Reference object*

It is often assumed that the [Preposition + Ground] phrase defines a region of space, and the meaning of a locative sentence is an assertion that the Figure is located in that region. This is often the case, but not always:

> The milk is in the cup.
> The cat is under the bed.

These statements do mean that the milk is located in the interior of the cup, and the cat in the region *under the bed*. But prepositions implying contiguity – such as *on, against,* and *on top of* – cannot be defined in terms of inclusion in a region, however the region is defined: contiguity cannot be reduced to inclusion in the surface of the object, or in the region above the object, or in the region around it. An object *on the desk* is not in the

Table 6.1. English spatial prepositions

Location	Primarily Motion	Misfits
at/on/in	across	over
upon	along	about
against	alongside	throughout
inside/outside	around	after/before
within/without	away from	ahead of
near/ (far from)	toward	for
next	up/down	
beside	to/from	
by	into/ (out of)	
between	onto/off	
beyond	past	
opposite	through	
amidst	via	
among		
above/below		
under		
beneath		
underneath		
on top/bottom of		
on the top/bottom of		
behind		
in front/back of		
at the front/back/right/left of		
on/to the left/right of		
left/right of		
north/east/west/south of		
to the east/north/south/west of		

surface of the desk; inclusion in the regions above or surrounding the desk does not entail contiguity with the desk.

6.2.2. BASIC USAGES OF THE MOTION PREPOSITIONS

Every motion preposition fits in a syntactic frame:

NP [activity verb][1] Preposition NP

as with

The ball rolled ...

...across the room / along the street / toward the boy / away from the curb / ...

Here the Figure is the moving object; the Ground is still the referent of the object of the preposition; the preposition constrains the trajectory, or path of the Figure.

The ball   rolled across   the street

Figure   *Ground*

Moving object   *Reference object*

To illustrate how these prepositions constrain the Figure's path:

1. One sense of *across* implies motion from one side to the opposite side of a ribbonal Ground (such as a road). The directed lines in Figure 6.1a show possible paths satisfying the description *across the road.*
2. *Along*, in one main sense, requires a linear Ground (Figure 6.1b); the path may be in, on, or alongside (parallel to and outside) the Ground. Since the Ground need not to be straight, we must extend the notion of parallelism to lines of any shape.
3. *Around*, in one main sense, requires that the Ground be a region bounded by a closed line; the trajectory can be any closed line either circumnavigating the Ground or within it at a short distance from the boundary (Figure 6.1c).
4. *Toward* applies to any path leading in the direction of the Ground (Figure 6.1d), though not necessarily reaching it. So in *Walk toward the tower for half a mile, then turn right!*, the turn may be any distance from the tower. The path need not be straight; it may be the customary, or the only possible, route to the Ground. Thus, interpretations of *toward* and *away from* must take into account the geography of the earth.
5. *Through* describes any trajectory whatsoever within a three-dimensional Ground.

In conclusion, a motion preposition defines a *field of directed lines* with respect to the Ground. A motion sentence using such a preposition asserts that the path of the Figure coincides with one of the directed lines of the field defined by preposition and Ground.

The [Preposition + Ground] phrase does not refer to a path; it is a *predicative* phrase, which can be used to express a constraint on a path referred to by other means.[2] So in

Jim walked across the street.

Jim walked implies the existence of a particular path. *Across the street* predicates that this path satisfies a constraint: it is one of the continuous infinity of paths defined by *across the street*. The "extension" of *across the street* is not one path, but a field of paths. A prepositional phrase alone does not specify "one" path.

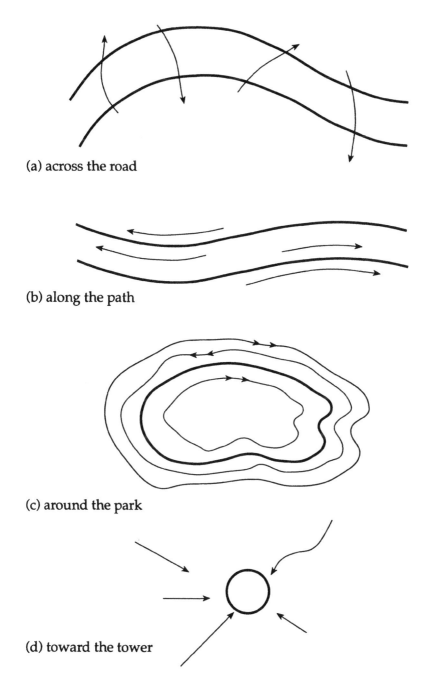

(a) across the road

(b) along the path

(c) around the park

(d) toward the tower

Figure 1.   Fields of directed lines associated with various motion prepositions

Although it is often said that motion prepositions specify the orientation of a path, this is not generally the case, for any reasonable and consistent definition of orientation. Since a trajectory can be a directed line of any shape, no single value of orientation can be called "its" orientation. Orientation can be defined in accord with usual intuitions for straight lines: all straight parallels have the same orientation; thus parallel straight trajectories running in opposite directions have the same orientation – mathematically, orientation is an equivalence class of parallel lines. But if a trajectory twists and curves, its orientation changes at every point.

6.2.3. MOTION USES OF THE LOCATION PREPOSITIONS

Location prepositions are used in motion sentences in three ways:

1. To constrain the location of the entire trajectory:

    The butler was walking ...
        ... among the guests.
        ... on the floor.
        ... under the trees.
        ... near the park.

This class of motion uses has an interesting property, which differentiates it from the basic uses of the motion prepositions; at every point of its trajectory, the figure satisfies the relation denoted by preposition and Ground. So the walking butler remains always *among the guests, on the floor*, and so on. But a man walking to the store is not always *to the store*; a chicken running across a road is not always *across the road*.

2. To constrain the endpoint of the trajectory:

    The cat ran ...
        ... under the bed.
        ... outside the room.
        ... between the two chairs.
        ... behind the curtain.

These sentences can also mean that the entire path is *under the bed, outside the room*, and so on, though that interpretation is pragmatically somewhat less natural.

3. To constrain the location of a point or segment internal to the path:

    Jack walked by the house.
    The cart passed in back of the house.
    The geese flew over the house.

This interpretation may be triggered by the verb (pass) or by the preposition (*by* strongly favors this interpretation). Or it may be suggested by pragmatic factors (the geese probably did not fly in a minimal arc over the house).

I think it more appropriate to assume here different types of use rather than three additional senses. The different interpretations involve locating the event referred to by the clause, or a part of that event, using the same sense of the preposition as is used to locate objects; it seems therefore more natural to attribute the differences to different syntactical meanings associated with the clause structure – as is easily done in a construction grammar approach (Goldberg, 1995) – than to different senses of the preposition.

6.2.4. STATIONARY SENSES OF THE MOTION PREPOSITIONS

Though most of the motion prepositions have several motion senses, one usually stands out as highly salient; and two stationary senses systematically related to that motion sense – the *Figure disposition* and *vantage point* senses – are frequently associated with the preposition.

6.2.4.1. Figure disposition senses
They are illustrated by

The snake lay...
> ... across the road.
> ... along the wall.
> ... around the tree.

The Figure must be a linear object coaxial with one of the directed lines of the field defined by preposition and Ground object. These are sometimes called *Figure orientation* uses, but *disposition* seems a better term; just as a motion preposition does not define "the" orientation of a trajectory, it does not define the orientation of objects whose shape is not fixed by their category, such as snakes and pathways.

There are restrictions on the Figure disposition uses of the motion prepositions. Consider

The snake lay ...
> ... ♮ up/down the tree trunk.[3]
> ... * up to the edge of the ditch.
> ... * from the rock to the tree.
> ... ♮ past the stone.[4]

The two first sentences cannot mean that the snake's body is aligned vertically with the tree trunk. The last cannot mean that the snake's body is like a path running past a stone. It is not clear why these are not acceptable. Acceptability depends on subtle factors, as shown by the following sentences, which are analogous to the ones above:

He has bangs down to his eyebrows.
His arm is scarred from the elbow to the shoulder.[5]

All the motion prepositions can be used in instances of *virtual motion* such as

The road runs ...
    ... up to the top of the hill.
    ... past the stone.
    ... from the rock to the stream.

It is as if these expressions included an instruction to mentally scan along the road.[6]

6.2.4.2. *Vantage point senses*

These involve asserting that the Figure is located at the end of a (virtual or real) path constrained as specified by preposition and Ground.

The car is ...
    ... across the street.
    ... across the corner.
    ... up the hill.

In every such use, there is an implicit vantage point where the virtual path starts. So *across the street* is across from some contextually defined vantage-point, usually associated with the speaker.

Here also we find restrictions, but they are clearly motivated:

The car is ...
    ... * to the church.
    ... * onto the hill.
    ... * from the church.

Saying * *The car is to the church* to mean *The car is at the end of a path leading to the church* is needlessly indirect: *The car is at the church* says the same thing. The unacceptability of the other two examples can be explained in a similar way.

Different senses, rather than different usages of the same sense, are involved here. The primary sense of the preposition (the salient motion sense) cannot be used in describing the meaning of sentences with the corresponding stationary senses, unless one brings in a "hypothetical" path; but one would not want such a notion to be introduced as part of the meaning associated with clause structure.

6.2.5. THE MISFITS

Over is one preposition that has a highly salient location sense but an equally salient motion sense:

The lamp is over the table.

He walked over the hill.

Over in the second example does not mean the same as in the first; the path is not only above (on) the hill: it leads from a point at the base of the hill to a point opposite by way of the summit. *Over* has the Figure disposition and vantage point senses derived from that motion sense:

The rope goes over the wall.

The post-office is over the hill.

About and *throughout* also have equally salient motion and location senses:

There were newspapers about/throughout the room.

He walked about/throughout the apartment.

and do not fit in the frame [NP is Preposition NP]. They require an existential or a verb implying a *distributed* configuration – that is, a collection of objects scattered through space with an approximately uniform distribution:

*Newspapers were about/throughout the room.

Newspapers were strewn about/throughout the room.

As for *ahead*,

Jack walked ahead of Mary.

does not constrain the trajectory of Jack with respect to Mary; instead its semantic contribution includes the presupposition that Jack and Mary were simultaneously walking on the same path in the same direction, and the assertion that Jack preceded Mary on that path. *Before* and *after* have similar spatial meanings. *Before*, but not *after* and *ahead*, has also a simple locative sense:

Before me was my long-lost friend.

For can specify spatial extent:

Jane walked for six miles.

For expository purposes, this section was organized in terms of patterns found in the polysemy of English prepositions. But these patterns manifest only tendencies, not necessity, logical or other, since the misfits are exceptions.

6.2.6. FIGURE AND GROUND ASSIGNMENTS

The Figure is the object whose location, disposition, or path is at issue (Talmy, 1983); that is to say, it is moving, or *conceptually movable* (which means the same as saying that location or disposition are at issue). The Ground is an object conceived of – perhaps provisorily – as stationary: its location is generally assumed known to the addressee, so that characterizing the location, disposition, or path of the Figure with respect to it will provide adequate localization information.

But what does *knowing the location of an object* mean? Most typically, we assume that the earth is stationary, and knowing an object's location involves knowledge of a place fixed with respect to the earth, as with the living room in

Jack's glasses are in the living room.

But consider

Jack's glasses are on his nose.

The location of Jack's nose is known relative to his body; in this instance, Jack's body is conceived of as stationary, though it can move about. The truth conditions are independent of the location of Jack himself.

In

Jack's glasses are in the next car of the train.

the train, moving or not, is conceived of as stationary, and knowing the location of the car involves only knowledge of a place fixed relative to the train. One could say Jack's glasses are *in the same place as yesterday*, meaning either that they are on his nose (wherever he may be), or in the next train car (even though the train traveled to California). Clearly, what it means to know the location of an object is rather tricky.

Reference objects tend to be – but need not be – larger and less mobile than Figure objects. This is a matter of communication, not spatial cognition; addressees are more likely to know the location of large, fixed objects. But we can say either

The newspaper stand is near Trafalgar Square.

Trafalgar Square is near the newspaper stand.

although in some spatial tasks, Trafalgar Square, but not the newspaper stand, would be a "reference point" (Sadalla et al., 1980).[7] Only when the Ground is considerably smaller and more mobile than the Figure is a sentence odd:

? The house is near the bicycle.

?* The bottle is under the cap.

This may suggest rigid conventional restrictions, but is more likely a product of the workings of a usage-based system – a system affected by practice and by the strength of memory traces, as is true of language (Bybee, 1985). The process of checking size and mobility, practiced innumerable times, is not disabled in these cases, though its original purpose may not apply.

6.3. Schematization

Schematization is characterized in Talmy (1983, p. 225) as

a process that involves the systematic selection of certain aspects of a referent scene to represent the whole, disregarding the remaining aspects

and in Herskovits (1986, p. 2) as follows:

> there is a fundamental or canonical view of the world, which in everyday life is taken as the world as it is. But language does not directly reflect that view. Idealizations, approximations, conceptualizations, mediate between this canonical view and language.

Systematic selection, idealization, approximation, and conceptualization are all facets of schematization, a process that reduces a physical scene, with all its richness of detail, to a sparse and sketchy semantic content. This reduction is often said to involve applying some abstract spatial relation to simple geometric objects. So

> The village is on the road to London.

would imply contiguity between a point (*the village*) and a line (*the road*).

Schematization   has   been   discussed   mostly
in linguistics and psycholinguistics; no artificial intelligence work provides explicit computational accounts of it. There are two sets of questions here:

1. Which schematic representations of the objects are used in which contexts? How are objects and trajectories related to their schematic representation? Is it true that objects in the context of a preposition are always represented as either points, lines, planes, or blobs?

2. Is schematization related to language-independent spatial cognitive processes? What precise computational processes underlie linguistic schematization?

6.3.1. ABSTRACTION, GEOMETRIC IDEALIZATION, AND SELECTION

Schematization involves three distinguishable processes: abstraction, idealization, and selection. Abstraction, of course, is an essential characteristic of *all* linguistic meaning. Every linguistic category abstracts from the distinguishing characteristics of its individual members. In saying

> Joe is running.

we abstract away from particular distinguishing characteristics of Joe's running – speed, style, location, goal, and so on. Similarly, in saying

> There is a tree lying across the road.

we abstract away from such characteristics as

- the position of the tree along the road,
- the angle between tree and road axes,
- the positions of the ends of the tree with respect to the the road's edges,
- the width of the road, and

– whether the road is in an horizontal plane or inclines steeply.

The facet of schematization particular to spatial language is *geometric idealization*. We *idealize* features of the real scene so they match simple geometric objects: points, lines, and so on. Idealization goes beyond abstraction: the real geometric features do not exactly match the geometric categories in which we fit them. Thus, the top surface of the road in the above example, though it may be bumpy and of varying width, is (arguably) idealized to a ribbon.

Selection involves using a part or aspect of an object to represent the whole object, as with

the cat under the table

where the top of the table stands for the whole table. Including selections stretches the ordinary meaning of schematization – yet selections do fit Talmy's definition, and they commonly produce the reduced object geometry relevant to spatial expressions.

6.3.2. TREATING OBJECTS AS POINTS: A FALLACIOUS ARGUMENT

Talmy (1983, p. 234) writes that, typically, the prepositions "treat the focal object [the Figure] as a point or related simple form." This is a frequently expressed intuition, but it is not clear what *treating an object as a point* might mean. One justification often given for this view is that if a preposition puts no constraint on the geometry of one of the objects related, then that object is treated as a point. As most prepositions do not restrict Figure shape, it follows that the Figure must generally be treated as a point. Let us examine each step of this argument.

Some stationary senses of the prepositions do in fact put constraints on Figure shape. Figure disposition senses require a linear Figure:

The snake lay across/along the trail.

For one sense of *over*, the Figure must be a surfacy object:

The tablecloth lay over the table.

For one sense of *throughout*, the Figure must be a composite aggregate:

There were blackbirds throughout the tree.

But, other than these few instances, the stationary senses of the prepositions put no constraint on Figure shape. So is the Figure then treated as a point?

There are clearly cases where the Figure is *not* treated as a point. The Figure can be infinite or unbounded:

He contemplated the firmament above him.
The land beyond the river is fertile.

The firmament extends infinitely upward; the land stops somewhere, but this outer boundary is not part of the conceptualization – it is outside the scope of the mental eye. It would be absurd to claim that infinite or unbounded objects are seen or treated as points; only bounded objects can be idealized as points. But even a bounded Figure is not necessarily seen as a point: idealization to a point appears irrelevant to

The orange juice is in the bottle.
The sheets are on the bed.
The Atlantic is between Europe and America.

If the Figure is often not treated as a point, perhaps the problem is with the assumption that when a preposition places no constraints on the shape of one of the objects related, then that object is idealized to a point. And indeed, closer examination shows the assumption to be invalid. The error may stem from the logical misstep: *if a prepositional predicate applies to objects of any shape, then its truth in particular cases can be assessed without referring to the object's shape.* But that is clearly false.

Consider the preposition *in*. It does not restrict the Figure shape in any way; an object of any shape or even any dimensionality will do. The selection restrictions for the Ground are equally loose; any Ground shape will do, except a point (nothing can be "in" a point). But it certainly does not follow that Figure and Ground are treated as points in uses of *in*. Ullman (1985) describes various algorithms for deciding whether a point is in a closed curve. These, as one would expect, require full knowledge of the shape of the curve; hence the Ground (the curve) is not seen as a point. If the Figure is *extended*, we must also know the position of every one of its points to decide whether it is *in* the curve. Therefore we treat neither Figure nor Ground as points.

Perhaps objects are seen as "blobs" rather than points. Blobs may be what Talmy meant by "related simple form." A blob must be how we apprehend an extended object (in two or three dimensions) whose precise shape and extent are not known. Its representation could consist of the position of a center point of the object, together with the assumption that the object extends outward from this center to an indeterminate boundary; the boundary could be additionally known to lie outside a given area surrounding the point. But without the precise extent of the Ground, we cannot in general[8] decide whether an object is in it; in fact, we need also to know the exact region of space occupied by the Figure. So blobs will not do; neither will lines or planes.

The belief that *all* prepositions treat Figure and Ground as points, lines, planes, or blobs is unfounded; some do, and some do not; some do in some uses and not in others (6.3.5). At times, we need to know the precise regions occupied by Figure and Ground to decide whether a preposition applies.

Figure and Ground are then seen (as far as shape is concerned) just as they are.

6.3.3. FIGURE AS A POINT: THE MOTION PREPOSITIONS

While not all prepositions idealize Figures to points, there is some reliable evidence of such a process. The basic meanings of the motion prepositions are all cast in terms of linear paths. Such paths can be traced out by a point, or by a linear, deformable object sliding along its own axis – for instance (ignoring their cross-section), a snake or a train. As the latter objects are not all that common, we must somehow make use of predicates defined in terms of motion of a point to talk about motion of any extended object.

The path of a rigid object undergoing translation has the shape of a generalized cylinder, a kind of snake, but with possible overlaps and not necessarily with a circular cross-section. If the object rotates on itself, changing its orientation as it translates, the volume described is typically too complicated to visualize precisely. Kinematics shows we can analyze this movement as a succession of infinitesimal motions, each combining a translation and a rotation around some axis, but for the most part we lack the ability to represent subcategories of paths involving different such combinations. Fine conceptual distinctions among the possible paths of a *nonrigid* object are of course even harder to make. The restriction is not in our awareness of the object's changing appearance as we watch it move; it is in our ability to analyze the motion, albeit unconsciously and nonverbally – that is, to note separable aspects of it. This ability is needed to form different subcategories of motion and to assign a particular instance to a subcategory.[9]

Because of this limitation, we typically idealize the motion of a three-dimensional object to that of a center point – probably its *centroid* or center of gravity assuming uniform density – ignoring rotations around the centroid. Note, for instance, that there exist no two prepositions that contrast only in that one entails a pure translation and the other translation accompanied by rotation. A few verbs do describe trajectories involving different combinations of these motions – for example, *roll, flip, tumble, turn, twirl, revolve* – but the list is not a long one, which supports the notion that our ability to conceptually distinguish motions along these dimensions is limited.

Consider

The child danced around the Maypole.

Although we would assume that the child rotates on herself, no such notion is expressed by the preposition. The child would still be *dancing around the Maypole* if the pole were on a stage and she continued facing the audience while dancing around it.

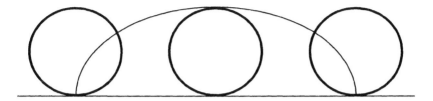

He rolled the log over

Figure 2. Trajectory of a point on the circumference of a rolling log

In some expressions, the preposition does not describe the trajectory of the centroid:

He rolled the log over.

The earth turns around its axis.

use prepositions specifying the motion of a point in a different way. Brugman (1988) provides a nice explanation for the first sentence. As the log rolls along the ground a distance equal to half its circumference (Figure 6.2), the point of the log originally in contact with the ground comes to the top; as the log rolls on another half-circumference, the point goes back to the bottom. Its trajectory is a curve called a *cycloid.* It is as if this point passed *over* the object. In other words, *over* applies to that point only, though we talk about motion of the entire log.

With the earth turning around its axis, each point of the sphere, except the points on the axis, describes a circle around the axis. *Around* constrains the trajectory of every such point.

Consider also

The sea rushed onto the sand.

The water rose up to the roof.

In the first sentence, each wave (a part of a superficial layer of the sea) follows a path constrained by *onto the sand*; in the second, every part of water follows a path leading *up to the roof.* The prepositional phrases then describe the motions of each part (however defined) of the Figure object. Note that this *is* a schematization: the actual motions of the sea and of the rising water are far from so orderly. But it is not idealization of sea and water to a point.

In conclusion,

1. The basic meanings of the motion prepositions are all cast in terms of motion of a point;

2. Most often, such predicates are adapted to the motion of a three-dimensional object by abstracting the rotation components of the motion and reducing the motion to that of the object's centroid. This is effectively idealization to a point, and it follows in part from limitations in spatial cognition.

3. There are a few exceptions to this pattern: idiomatic ones (*roll over*); and cases where the preposition applies to all or most points (or parts) of a two- or three-dimensional Figure.

So far, we have considered the use of motion prepositions from the point of view of perception, but prepositions are not uniquely, or even primarily, for recording perceptual experience; they can be used to describe action – specifically, possible navigation paths.

6.3.4. MOTION PLANNING

The linguistic representation of objects' paths as lines is fundamental to motion planning. In planning to walk across a room, or to move one's hand to reach an object, an essential step is the mental construction of a *line of travel* that leads to the goal while avoiding obstacles. It is certainly a line: the plan would not usually include detailed descriptions of how to move feet and arms – this will happen automatically. Such a line probably still acts as a high-level guide during the execution of the move, while at a lower level, execution relies on modules that coordinate vision and motion and probably operate to a large degree autonomously (Goodale, 1988).

6.3.5. NAVIGATION AND COGNITIVE MAPS

As the question of how to go from here to there is a central concern of human beings, the descriptions of paths in large-scale spaces accounts for a major part of our uses of prepositions. Navigation in large-scale spaces is guided by cognitive maps whose major components are landmarks and routes represented respectively as points and lines. Moreover, in the context of a cognitive map, a moving Figure is conceptualized as a point and its trajectory as a line. Prepositions are frequently used to describe locations, pathways, and trajectories within a cognitive map:

Penny is at the market
Penny walked to the market.
This street goes to the market.

There is much linguistic evidence that a main sense of *at* is "coincidence of a movable point object with a point place in a cognitive map". For instance, *at* cannot be used to describe location in small-scale spaces:[10]

∗ The ashtray is at the bottle.

and

Jack is at the supermarket.

is typically infelicitous if the speaker herself is in the supermarket. A space that surrounds you is not naturally seen as a point; representing a fixed object as a point requires seeing it from a distance. In

I am at the supermarket.

the speaker may be "in" the supermarket, but the sentence evokes a context where he is on the phone and taking the point of view of an addressee located at a distant place.

Consider also

?* She is at the garden.

She is at the community garden.

The first is odd, as the vantage point evoked is from the house adjoining the garden; but the second is fine – the vantage point can be at a place distant from the community garden. The overall geometric context evoked is a cognitive map with landmarks and Figures represented as points.

Finally, one can show that, although the use of *at* requires only close proximity in "real" space, in the geometric idealization of a cognitive map, located object and reference object are collapsed to a point and close proximity becomes coincidence. So if

Jane is at the store.

she may be on the sidewalk next to the store. But in

One focus of the ellipse is at the intersection of the two lines.

the focus of the ellipse is necessarily coincident with the intersection point. Intuitions are very clear; *near* is not enough – the two points must coincide. This supports the meaning of *at* proposed above. One might object that intuitions in the domain of abstract geometry are irrelevant to use of the prepositions with real objects. But *by* means "in close proximity," and it does not shift its meaning when used in the domain of geometry:

Jack was sitting by his sister.

This point is by that one.

So *at* and *by* must differ in meaning. If we assume *at* means coincidence, we have no need to call upon an arbitrary shift in meaning to explain uses in the domain of geometry: with real objects as arguments, coincidence applies in a cognitive map, in which the locations of moving object and landmark are collapsed when they are "very close" to each other.

6.3.6. IDEALIZATION TO A POINT AND DISTANCE BETWEEN FIGURE AND GROUND

The *projective* prepositions (*to the right, above, behind,* and so on) exhibit a dichotomy: when Figure and Ground are far apart, they are viewed as points; when close, their shape and precise relative placement matter. This should come as no surprise. So in Figures 3a and 3b we can decide that *F is to the right of G* by approximating *F* and *G* to points – their shape and orientation are irrelevant. But if Figure and Ground are close together (Figures 6.3c through 6.3e), shape and exact relative placement matter: the rectangle in 6.3c is *to the right of G*, but the rectangle in 6.3d and the cross in 6.3e are not, though the location of the centroid of F is the same in all three cases.

So objects perceivable from a single vantage point (this defines "small-scale" as opposed to "large-scale" environments[11]), but "far" apart, are integrated in a spatial representation quite similar to a cognitive map – they are represented as points.

6.3.7. TREATING AN OBJECT AS A LINE: AXES

Axes play an important role in spatial cognition. Several models of object recognition proposed in computer vision are based on shape representations structured by axes (Binford, 1971; Marr, 1982). Axes also play a role in spatial language. In all Figure disposition uses of the motion prepositions, one can legitimately say that a preposition treats an object as if it were a line, that is, reduced to its major axis. The Figure is then elongated, and the only object knowledge required to check the preposition's applicability is the position and shape of the axis. But note that shape is not fully abstracted. The elongation axis may not be straight, and applicability of the preposition depends on its shape:

The hose lay ...
     ... across the road.
     ... around the flower bed.
     ... along the trail.

Moreover, except with *along*, the Ground cannot be reduced to a line. With *across the road*, we cannot judge whether the hose leads from side to side if the road is reduced to a line, and we must know the exact region covered by the flower bed to decide whether the hose goes around it. Only with *along the trail* do the median axes of trail and hose suffice to decide whether the sentence is true. So again, it is not the case that prepositions always treat objects as if they were points, lines, or blobs.

The kind of axis selected to represent an object supports Marr's 3D-model (1982). Usually, it is the *model axis* for the entire shape.[12] So in

Jack lay across the bed

the model axis of Jack's body is orthogonal to the bed's main axis. But the relevant axis may also be the "principal reference axis" – that is, an axis of the frame of reference used to specify the location and orientation

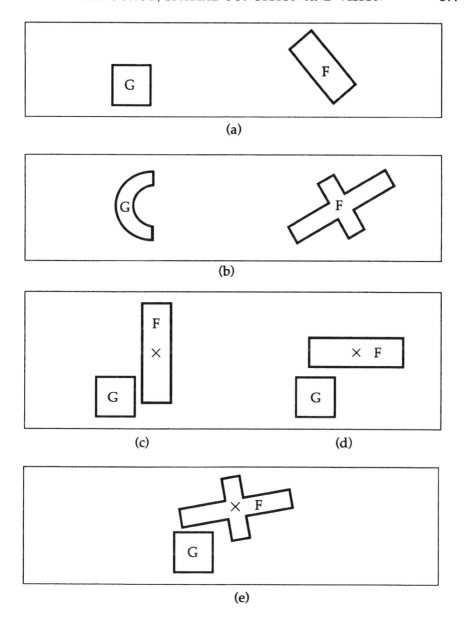

Figure 3.   Effect of the distance between *F* and *G* on the truth of *F is to the right of G*

of the whole object's immediate parts. Model and principal axis need not be identical; Marr suggests that the principal reference axis for the human shape is the torso's axis, as the torso is connected to the greatest number of other parts. This turns out to be the Figure axis relevant to

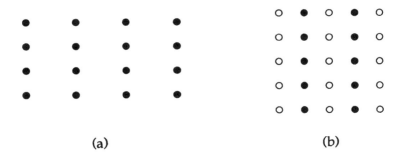

Figure 4. Grouping: effects of proximity and similarity

The driver leaned across the front-seat toward the passenger window.

Here, the axis of the driver's torso projects on the front seat orthogonally to the seat's median plane.

Recent theories of object recognition emphasize viewpoint-dependent knowledge rather than object-based componential representations. Two-dimensional views (especially canonical views) may play an important role in object recognition (Palmer et al., 1981; Tarr and Pinker, 1989), but with rare exceptions (see 6.3.8), what matters to language are parts and axes, not two-dimensional views.

6.3.8. PERCEPTUAL GROUPING, LAYOUT PLANE, AND PLANE OF VIEW

6.3.8.1. Perceptual grouping.

The visual system has a powerful tendency to group objects in the visual field on the basis of proximity, alignment, and similarity (in size, orientation, color, and so on). So in Figure 6.4a, we see vertical lines – the dots being grouped by proximity; in 6.4b grouping is by color similarity.

Some spatial expressions clearly manifest linear grouping:

the lights of the boat along the horizon
the stepping stones across the river
the houses around the lake

Grouping can also involve two- or three-dimensional regions:

the nest in the tree
the brown sugar in the strawberries
The butler made his way through the guests.

Here the Figure is within the global contour of the branches of the tree, the strawberries, the guests – it is in the volume inside the surface bounding the group of objects or parts constituting the Ground. To make sense of *in* or *through*, we must assume that the Ground is viewed as a volume.

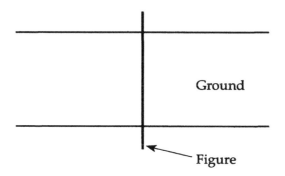

Figure 5.   Diagrammatic representation of Talmy's schema for "across"

6.3.8.2. Layout plane

Shepard and Hurwitz (1985, p. 166) say that "the point of contact with the ground provides the best indicator of an object's location." As creatures bound to the ground, we accord great importance to the ground level arrangement of things and spaces. Thus it is natural to represent the location of an object at some height in terms of its projection on the layout plane together with its height. Language yields evidence of this: frequently, the relations expressed are meant to apply in that plane rather than in three-dimensional space.

Here is an example involving *across*. Figure 6.5 is a diagrammatic representation of Talmy's definition of *across*, a "schema" consisting of a ribbonal Ground and a linear Figure.

Now consider

A curtain hung across the room.

The main discrepancies between this example and the schema are that a curtain is a vertical surface – not a line – and a room is a three-dimensional space – not an area, ribbonal or not. But we get a line and an area – and much closer to the schema – if we project the room-curtain configuration onto the floor. Since Figure and Ground are pretty much restricted respectively to lines and areas in uses of *across* (Section 6.4), it is very likely that projection on the layout plane explains the acceptability of this example.

6.3.8.3. Plane of view

Relations are sometimes meant to hold in the two-dimensional plane of view:

The moon is to the right of the tree.

does not locate the moon in the vicinity of the (ascribed) right axis of the tree; instead, the image of the moon in the plane of view is to the right of the image of the tree. Language has access to the two-dimensional representation of a scene in the plane of view, though in the vast majority of cases, what matters are relations in three-dimensional space.

6.3.9. OBJECT GEOMETRY SELECTION

We have seen that schematization is a finely modulated process, dependent on many cognitive and linguistic variables. In effect, the mappings between real objects and their schematic representations can be accounted for by a set of functions, several of which we have considered in some detail. The argument of these functions is the full region occupied by the object, and their value is the region defining the object's schematic representation. Table 6.2 lists some "schematization functions" or "object geometry selection set of possible mappings.[13] So with

Jane walked across the streaming crowd.

three functions apply in succession: first, individual entities are turned into a volume bound by the "contour" of the crowd; second, this volume is projected on the layout plane to an area; third, directionality – the common direction of motion of the crowd's individual members – is assigned to that area. The final value satisfies the selection restrictions of the Ground for one sense of *across* (directionality intrinsic to an area, see 6.4.3), and we can then compute the Figure's path: it is in the layout plane, orthogonal to the area's directionality.

When use of a preposition depends on full definitions of the shape and placement of Figure (or Ground), then the schematization function for that object is the *identity* (this does sound oxymoronic, hence the rather unwieldy coinage: "object geometry selection function").

The linguistic examples in this chapter show that many factors may play a role in determining the applicable schematizations: the preposition, any sentence element, geometric and functional properties of the objects, contextual factors, and so on. From a linguistic point of view, the application of the functions can be a matter of semantics, of pragmatics, or of both. To fit the objects to the geometric types that a preposition selects for, it may be necessary to employ a pragmatic process of *coercion*.[14] For instance, one sense of *across* selects for a line and an area, which can be obtained by projecting the objects on the layout plane – a transformation best described as a pragmatic process, since it may apply with any preposition. In *The ball rolled across the street*, however, describing the path of the ball by focusing on its centroid is only a matter of the meaning of *across*.

Table 6.2.   Schematization or object geometry selection functions

1. Idealizations to a
       point
       line
       surface
       plane
       ribbon
2. Gestalt processes:
       linear grouping (yields a two- or three-dimensional linear object)
       two- and three-dimensional grouping (yields an area or volume)
       completed enclosure
       normalized shape
3. Selections of axes and directions:
       model axis
       principal reference axis
       associated frame of reference
       direction of motion
       direction of texture
       direction of maximum slope of surface
4. Projections:
       projection on layout plane
       projection on plane of view
5. Part selections (triggered by the high salience of the part):
       three-dimensional part
       oriented free top surface
       base

6.3.10. SCHEMATIZATION AND SPATIAL COGNITION

Relations between objects and their schematic representation can be accounted for by a set of functions, but how are these functions related to spatial cognitive processes? The list in Table 6.2 is heterogeneous in this respect: some functions are specified by spatial cognitive processes (Gestalt processes); others by geometric processes (idealizations and projections); still others by a description of the function's value (all the selections). There is overlap, for example, axis selections are types of idealizations to a line. This heterogeneity appears because we have looked at schematization from different angles. But for every case considered in some depth, we found clear evidence that the functions are grounded in (language-independent) spatial cognitive processes and representations. Sometimes, several spatial representations give rise to a particular mapping; for instance, "idealization to a line" calls on componential axis-based representations for ordinary three-dimensional objects but on cognitive maps for pathways and rivers.

   The functions not described in this chapter are similarly grounded in nonlinguistic spatial cognition. For instance, "associated frame of reference," which refers to the assignment of right, front, back, and so on, axes to an object, is a function that invokes frames of reference motivated by nonlinguistic spatial cognition (Herskovits, 1986); the part selections involve spotlighting a (functionally or interactionally) salient part of an object.

The possible geometric representations of an object are thus strongly constrained by spatial cognition. The list of Table 6.2, arrived at by the consideration of a large number of examples, is probably close to complete, and presumably the same functions apply cross-linguistically. But the simplifications of object geometry in locative expressions are not as drastic as commonly assumed: objects are not always represented as points, lines, planes or blobs – at least for any precise (computational) understanding of this statement; many prepositional uses depend on full representations of the shape and placement of one or both of the objects related.

This deepened understanding of schematization has important implications for the interface between language and spatial cognition. Before we consider this question, it will be worthwhile to discuss the fluidity of prepositional meaning.

6.4. The Fluidity of Prepositional Meaning

Prepositional meaning is very fluid. Introspection is not a good guide to this semantic polymorphism: typically, a couple of senses come quickly to mind when one is asked the meaning of a preposition, but actual texts yield a wealth of examples that do not fit the senses accessed in this "zero" context. This section uses the example of one preposition, *across*, to examine whether polysemy and/or prototypicality are useful in accounting for this fluidity and for the salience of particular usage types.

6.4.1. ACROSS: TALMY'S SCHEMA

Talmy (1983) defined *across* as follows:

  (F = the Figure object; G = the Ground object)

a. F is linear (and generally bounded at both ends).
b. G is ribbonal (a two-edged plane).
c. The axis of F is (and the axis of G is typically, but not necessarily) horizontal.
d. The axes of F and G are roughly perpendicular.
e. F is parallel to the plane of G.
f. F is adjacent to (not in) the plane of G.
g. F's length is at least as great as G's width.
h. F touches both of G's edges (without this stipulation, the conditions so far would also fit this configuration: $|+$)
i. Any extension of F beyond G's edges is not enormously greater on one side than on the other, nor than the width of G itself.

(Figure 6.5 contains a diagrammatic representation of this definition; being a view from above, it does not represent the fact that the Figure is just above the Ground.)

The object geometry selection functions represent one dimension of the flexibility of prepositional meaning. We can view Figure and Ground in different ways beyond their intrinsic geometry. So we can use *across* with nonlinear Figures and nonribbonal Grounds, provided applicable geometry selection functions allow us to obtain a line and a ribbon from them. But in many cases no applicable geometry selection functions will yield a line and a ribbon arranged as in Talmy's schema:

1. The duck swam across the pond.
2. with his hair combed across the top of his skull
3. The snow was drifting across the land.
4. The man started swimming across the current.
5. One could see children skiing across the slope.
6. Ripples spread across the pond.
7. He searched across the city for an apartment.
8. There were clothes strewn across the floor.

A pond (1) need not be ribbonal. It is hard to relate hair on a skull (2) to the schema (and what accounts for the clear intuition that the hair is combed from side to side?). There are no two edges to "the land" in 3; it is unbounded. In 4, the man need not swim from one edge of a body of water to its opposite edge; the sentence only entails a direction orthogonal to the current. A slope (5) is not horizontal nor is it bounded by two opposite edges (and why is motion approximately along contour lines – compare *along the slope?*). In 6, the path of the ripples is not a line, it is two-dimensional; the advancing "front" could be a straight line, or a circle if the ripples expand in all directions from a center. The most salient interpretation of 7 involves a path distributed over the city – the meaning is the same as *all over*. In 8, the Figure consists of points distributed over a surface, it is a *multiplex*.

So *across* has a great diversity of uses not fitting Talmy's schema. I will show that one can account for almost all the examples I have encountered (in the Brown corpus, Kucera and Francis, 1967, and various readings) using ten distinct senses of *across* obtained by cross-classifying five configurations (or schemas) with the three-way distinction between motion, Figure disposition, and vantage point (Figure 6.6). Five of the fifteen combinations are impossible because of incompatibilities; for instance, there cannot be a vantage point sense with a distributed path.

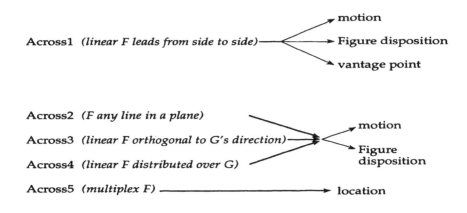

Figure 6.   The senses of *across*

6.4.2. ACROSS1

Across1 is a generalization of Talmy's schema. Talmy (1983, p. 235) defines a ribbon as "a plane bounded along two parallel edges," the complementary boundaries are assumed nonexistent, out of sight, or irrelevant. A road or a river provides a good match for such a geometric object, but *across* can be used with an area of any shape as Ground.[15] Talmy clearly intends his definition to be applicable to any closed-contour objects, but he has not spelled out how his schema is to match such cases and how loose the match can be. As there are difficulties involved here, I will first describe the precise geometry of configurations to which Across1 applies, and then consider whether they can be characterized as rough instantiations of the schema. I will call "ribbons" only those things that are unmistakable ribbons – such as pathways and rivers.

For simplicity, I define only the motion sense of Across1:

1. The Ground is a ribbon or any area bounded by a closed line.
2. The Ground is a plane at any orientation.
   See

   A fly was walking ...
        ... across the window.
        ... across the ceiling.

3. The Path leads from one side to the opposite side of the Ground, starting and ending near the Ground's boundary (within, on, or beyond it).

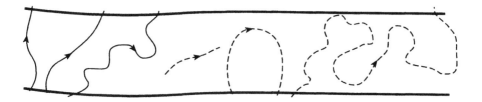

Figure 7.   Acceptable and unacceptable paths *across* a ribbon

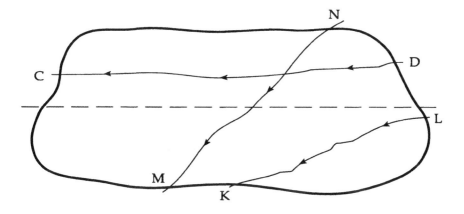

Figure 8.   Acceptable paths *across* an elongated shape

Since in *He walked across the room*, the path need not reach the walls of the room, conditions *g* and *h* of Talmy's schema do not hold.

The last condition – that the Path lead from one side to the opposite side of the Ground – requires some elaboration. Take the case of a "true" ribbon (Figure 6.7; continuous lines represent acceptable paths; dotted lines unacceptable ones). An acceptable path must indeed lead from one side to the opposite side of the ribbon, but it need not be straight nor orthogonal to the ribbon's axis. However, wild zigzagging disqualifies the path as an instance of *across* for some speakers.

Consider a nonribbonal Ground (Figure 6.8). The most natural way to divide a shape into two opposite sides is to cut it along its major axis, here an elongation axis. And indeed, MN is an excellent path across; but so are KL and CD, although they do not intersect the major axis.

In fact, the function that discriminates between instances and non-instances of *across* appears to depend on two factors: (1) how good opposites the endpoints of the path are and (2) the straightness of its average heading. A path becomes more acceptable as its endpoints become better opposites and its average heading is closer to a straight line. If the end-points are very good opposites, the path can go off-track; if not, the

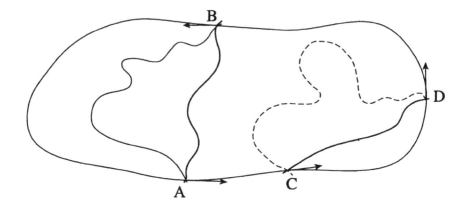

Figure 9.   Acceptable and unacceptable paths *across* an elongated shape

path must go straighter to the goal. So A and B (Figure 6.9) are very good opposites and the circuitous path from A to B is acceptable. C and D are not such good opposites, so an "across" path joining them must go more or less straight: the curving C to D path, though quite similar to the acceptable A to B path, is not acceptable. Finally, A and C are very bad opposites; no "across" path can join them.

What is a measure of how "good opposites" two points on a boundary are? Assuming a smoothed out (no small irregularities) and smoothly curving (no deep concavities or singularities) contour, the angle between the tangents at the points provides such a measure: if the angle of the tangents is 180 degrees (when all tangents are oriented counterclockwise, say), the points are perfect opposites (Figure 6.9); as the angle decreases, the points become worse opposites until 0 degrees, where the points are not opposites at all. Subjects asked to rate different paths across an ellipse (Herskovits et al., 1996) confirmed the validity of this measure.

Note that the measure defining the goodness of across paths is a continuous function of the two factors mentioned (the straightness of the path heading and the opposition of the path's endpoints). To decide whether or not to use *across*, we need a threshold, and there will naturally be cases where no clear-cut decision is possible.

This measure works well for all shapes with a smoothly varying curvature and no deep concavities. If there are singularities in the curvature (vertices), judgments may be "bistable": for instance, a path joining adjacent vertices in a rectangle might look good if viewed as linking opposite sides, but unacceptable if viewed as linking adjacent sides. For shapes with deep concavities and several lobes, judgments become uncertain and unstable. The difficulty is analogous to that found when trying to assign width and length to such shapes. Clearly, parallelepipedic and rectangular shapes play a central role in our conceptual system. Systems of dimensional adjectives (*high, deep, wide, long*) are based on assuming objects not too dissimilar to these.

In any case, division of the Ground shape into opposite sides, very flexibly interpreted, is the principal idea underlying Across1. This flexibility, however, disappears if geometric or interactional properties produce a salient division of the Ground; then, the Path or Figure must lead from one side of the dividing axis to the other and be loosely orthogonal to that axis, as the following illustrations show:

- *Elongation:* If there is great disparity between the Ground's width and length, then Figure or Path must be orthogonal to the Ground's long axis:

    She walked across the vegetable row
    The road leads across the ridge.

- *Canonical use:* If the Ground is primarily used for travel along a given direction, then the Path must be orthogonal to it:

    She walked across the pier.

    Similarly, there is a canonical way to sit on a saddle and lie on a bed: *across* in

    to sit across the saddle
    He was lying across the bed.

    is orthogonal to that canonical direction.

- *Symmetry:*

    She laid the stick across her lap.
    with his hair combed across the top of his skull

    The stick is orthogonal to the symmetry plane of the lap, and the hair combed orthogonally to the symmetry plane of the head.

- *Verticality:* A vertical plane could be generated by the sweep of an horizontal or a vertical line, but we think of it as made up of verticals; we conceptualize it as having a vertical intrinsic orientation. So across a vertical plane is (loosely) horizontal:

    He drew a line across the blackboard.

Does the "goodness" measure of *across* paths measure goodness of fit of Talmy's schema to the Path-Ground configuration? We will return to this question in 6.4.6.

6.4.3. THE OTHER SENSES OF "ACROSS"

6.4.3.1. Across2

1. The Ground is an unbounded plane surface.
2. The Ground has no intrinsic directionality.
3. The Path includes salient segments of straight translation.

Across2 is illustrated by

> They walked across the sand for hours.
> We followed a track across the grass.

where the limits of the sandy area and of the grass are irrelevant. The third condition is meant to explain the following contrasts:

> An ant wandered across the ground.
> She was pacing across the floor.
> * The camel walked in a circle across the sand.
> * He drew a circle across the sand.

One can wander and pace across a surface but not draw a circle or walk in a circle across. The trajectory need not be a single straight line but a circular trajectory is not acceptable. Across2 may be used with a clearly bounded object when those boundaries are deemed irrelevant; the object is then viewed simply as a surface. So in

> She pushed the ashtray across the desk.

the path of the ashtray need not lead from one edge to another – the top of the desk is viewed as a surface. This alternation between a two-dimensional bounded entity and an unbounded surface appears in a surprising example found in the Brown corpus (Kucera and Francis, 1967):

> We did 80 miles an hour across a hard dirt road to a cluster of shacks.

Although the ribbonal geometry of a road appears almost inescapable, it is not impossible to foreground the road as surface; Across2, then, applies instead of Across1. This switch is facilitated by the modifiers *hard* and *dirt*, which bring the road surface into focus.

6.4.3.2. Across3

1. The Ground is an unbounded plane surface.
2. The Ground has an intrinsic directionality.
3. The Path is loosely orthogonal to that directionality.

The Ground may be seen as bounded by edges under certain conditions, yet there is no implication that the Path runs from edge to edge. Intrinsic directionality can arise through

– *Motion*:

cutting across the streaming crowd

swimming across the flow

— *Texture*:

cutting across the grain

— *Inclination*:

skiing across the slope

The intrinsic directionality of a slope is defined by its lines of maximal incline, so motion across a slope is orthogonal to these – along contour lines.

6.4.3.3. Across4

1. The Ground is a bounded plane area.
2. The Path is distributed over the Ground.

One interpretation of

For a whole year, I traveled across India.

involves a path distributed over India.

6.4.3.5. Across5

1. The Ground is a bounded plane area.
2. The Figure is a set of "points" distributed over the Ground.

Across5 applies in

Across the United States, people are listening to the President.

the sprinkle of freckles across her face

6.4.4. RELATIONS BETWEEN SENSES

We can discern relations among the ten senses of across. The senses can be arranged in a network of the kind used by Brugman (1988) and Lindner (1981) to describe prepositional polysemy. Part of the network is represented in Figure 6.10; with the exception of Across4, only motion senses are included.

A link in the network represents close semantic similarity; the two nodes differ minimally in meaning. For instance, Across1 and Across2 entail a punctual Figure moving on a plane; but while in Across1, the path must run between opposite edges of a bounded Ground, with Across2, with the Ground being simply a plane surface, there is no constraint on the position of the path's end-points. An interesting way to think of the link between the two senses is to imagine viewing a case of Across1, and zooming in until the boundaries of the Ground disappear from view; the new configuration will match Across2.

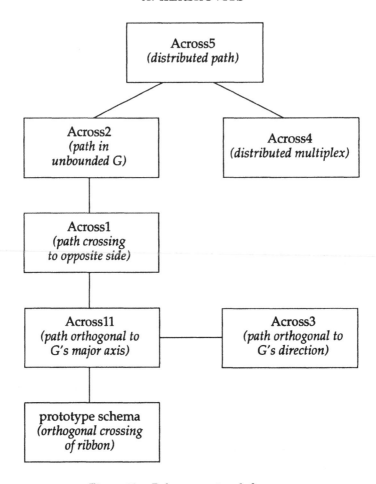

Figure 10. Polysemy network for *across*

Across11 is a specialization of Across1, in which the Path is orthogonal to the major axis of the Ground; it provides a bridge between Across1 and Across3 on one hand, and Across1 and Talmy's schema on the other. Thus Across1 and the schema are separated by two arcs, each representing close similarity; and so are Across1 and Across3. Across5 has one entailment added to Across2 – the path must cover the Ground. Finally, Across4 and Across5 share the feature of distribution over an area. The category is made up of senses related by similarity, but in network fashion, so several "similarity steps" may separate two senses.

The polysemy of *across* parallels that of *over*:

The power line stretches over/across the yard.

He walked carefully across/over the ice.

He traveled across/(all over) India.

His clothes were strewn across/over the floor.

The fact that two prepositions have the same four senses is strong evidence that some natural conceptual plasticity has led to cocategorizing these four geometric patterns. The relations described are plausible explanations for the tendency of these notions to cluster under the same word.

Family resemblance thus makes the different senses cohere. But it does not follow that the entire extension of the category "across" is predictable from a prototype. This is family resemblance but conventionalized. These links need not play a role in comprehension and production; few speakers may even ever be aware of them. Instead, their mental lexicon includes the conventional knowledge needed to use and comprehend all these uses, namely associations of *across* with the various interpretations.

Yet the relations between senses must have been active for some speakers at some time, otherwise there would be no way to explain how these distinct uses came to be expressed by the same word. In other words, I am suggesting that the proper level of understanding for these links is diachronic and statistical: extensions in language change may frequently follow along such links; and a pair of senses tied by a single link will often be expressed by the same word across many languages. Both assumptions, of course, would need to be tested.

6.4.5. IS TALMY'S SCHEMA A PROTOTYPE?

Talmy's schema can be considered a prototype for the category in the sense that it is saliently associated with the form *across* and most frequently accessed in a neutral context. So when subjects were asked to draw a diagrammatic representation of *across* and list five sentences with *across*, half the diagrammatic representations looked like the schema and 39 percent of the sentences involved a ribbon as Ground (Herskovits et al., 1996). But it is clear that membership in the category "across" is not in terms of similarity with Talmy's schema. The similarity between Across5 and the schema is minimal, yet *clothes strewn across the room* is a good example of *across*.

Is the schema a prototype for Across1 in a stronger sense – that is, is the measure of goodness described above (6.4.2) a measure of how similar instances of Across1 are to the schema? Deviations from some schema characteristics (horizontality of the Ground, Path/Figure slightly above the Ground or extending beyond the Ground's edges) do not lead to "worse" instances of Across1:

He drew a line across the blackboard.
the ditch across the road
the curtain across the room

are as good as

the pedestrian overpass across the freeway.

The lexical entry speakers use to judge these examples must be a generalization of Talmy's schema: it is abstracted from the orientation of the Ground plane; from the Path/Figure's precise position within close distance of that plane; and from the precise position of the endpoints of the Path/Figure within close distance of the Ground's boundary. It is not impossible that a process of matching this generalized schema to the situation at hand underlies the measure described, but we would need a better understanding of similarity to decide that point. As the shape of the path can deviate greatly from a straight line, and the edges of the Ground can be far from parallel, the relevant similarity is probably based on function (defined in terms of reaching the other side of a region) rather than perception.

Barsalou (1985) studied variation in typicality among category members. He showed that such "graded structure" depends on (1) the member's similarity to the central tendency of the category, (2) its similarity to the ideal of the category, (3) its frequency of instantiation. The prototype of the category is the member with the highest typicality rating but it need play no role in membership decisions.

The central tendency of Across1 is similar to Talmy's schema, only more abstract, along the three dimensions mentioned above. The ideal of the category would have the symmetry of the schema, the parallelism of the Ground's edges, and also a path extending beyond the Ground's edges, since this "really" takes you across the Ground. And *across* is probably most frequently instantiated by cases of motion on horizontal ground. Thus the schema scores highest on all three counts – no wonder it is the "best" example of Across1. But membership judgments are unlikely to be based on the evaluation of similarity to this "prototype."

6.4.6. CONCLUSIONS

We were able to classify all usages of *across* (excluding some semi-idiomatic forms) by means of ten "related" senses; the relations bring the senses together in a family resemblance network. But what of the mental lexicon itself? What form does the lexical knowledge supporting the comprehension and production of phrases with *across* take? This semantic analysis does not allow precise answers. It is probable that there are many more "entries" than these ten senses, that multiple, more specific "subsenses" have entries of their own, even though they are redundant with the more abstract senses that subsume them (Langacker, 1991). There is even evidence that we use different entries to judge pictures and sentences instantiating the same sense (Herskovits et al., 1996). The precise form of lexical knowledge remains an enduring puzzle, as it is embedded in a complex system of interactions between context-dependent access properties, syntactic and semantic constructional processes, and memorized form-meaning units at various levels of specificity.

6.5. The Interface Between Language and Spatial Cognition

What can we deduce from this detailed study of schematization and category structure concerning (1) the spatial representations accessed by language, and (2) the computations in the interface between language and spatial cognition?

6.5.1. THE SPATIAL REPRESENTATIONS ACCESSED BY LANGUAGE

We found evidence that language may access the following spatial representations:

1. Cognitive maps (large-scale environments),
2. Representations of observable scenes with objects as points (at least in some regions),
3. Representations of motion with objects as points,
4. Representations of observed scenes with objects shapes fully specified,
5. Representations of layout in the ground plane in small-scale environments,
6. Gestalt groupings of objects,
7. Axis-based componential representations of objects, and
8. Representation of plane of view.

These are probably not all distinct. So the first three – in which objects are represented as points – may be integrated into a single seamless representation, but close-up representations of observed scenes (4) with detailed representations of shape ought to be distinguished from it. Layout maps (5), Gestalt groupings (6), and axis-based componential representations of objects (7) could be characterized as aspects of representations of observed scenes (4), but they do provide alternate geometric representations of the objects. Finally, language has access to a two-dimensional representation of the plane of view (8),[16] a representation clearly distinct from the others.

Some authors (such as Bryant, 1993; Landau and Jackendoff, 1993) hypothesize that a single system of spatial representation underlies all spatial activities, as well as language. But this assumption is not confirmed by a careful analysis of schematization. It is true the various representations mentioned are tied together as facets of the "real world"; they are like snapshots taken of the three-dimensional veridical map we believe we sample. We do take a point in a cognitive map and a view of the corresponding landmark to be manifestations of the same object – and, under all circumstances, the object is what we mean to refer to. Yet language calls upon different geometric representations of objects, which are sometimes components of distinct nonlinguistic representations of space.

6.5.2. LANDAU AND JACKENDOFF'S HYPOTHESIS

Landau and Jackendoff (1993) argue for a dichotomy in the expressive power of language: we use detailed geometric properties of the objects when naming them (with nouns); but coarse representations – as points, lines (axial structure), and blobs – when locating them (with the help of a preposition). They suggest that this reflects a division in the way the brain represents spatial information. Assuming object identification and object localization are performed by separate neural subsystems – the "what" and "where" systems (Ungerleider and Mishkin, 1982) – they attribute the contrast between nouns and prepositions to a parallel modular division of the language system: the preposition system accesses only the encoding produced by the "where" system; the noun system only the encoding produced by the "what" system. To quote them directly (Landau and Jackendoff, 1993, p. 257):

> One kind of object description gets through the interface between spatial representations and language for naming (the "whats"), and another kind of object descriptions does so for locating (the "wheres").

The difference between nouns and prepositions would then follow: the "what" system represents fine distinctions of shape; the "where" system represents objects only as place-markers of roughly specified shapes. (The markers are cross-indexed with object representations in the "what" system, so we can know which "what" is at a given "where.")

We have seen that their basic premise is invalid: objects referred to in the context of a preposition are not necessarily represented as points, lines, or blobs; one may need to know their shape and precise placement to decide upon the applicability of a preposition. Landau and Jackendoff confuse the selection restrictions of the preposition with the knowledge of object shape needed for their appropriate use.

As for the interface between language and spatial representations, they skirt the following central question: does it compute abstract spatial relations on coordinate representations produced by the "where" system, or do the encodings produced by the "where" system include all abstract spatial relations necessary to linguistic expression? Either way, the hypothesis cannot hold: If the "where" system computes all relational primitives necessary to linguistic expression, the interface need only focus attention on the relevant combination of primitives and associate it with the right morpheme. Sometimes (as with some uses of *in*), the "where" system must operate with full knowledge of object shape; then, reduction of objects to points or blobs is not needed at any point in the processes leading to the selection of the preposition. If the interface computes the relations, then it must sometimes have access to objects'shapes.

6.5.3. THE COMPUTATION OF LINGUISTIC SPATIAL RELATIONS

We certainly perceive the relations we express. We see that a cup is *on* a table, a chair *to the right of* a door, someone sits *across* a desk. This implies that the relations have a visual (nonsymbolic) representation. But are such abstract relations part of the visual representations constructed in the absence of linguistic goals, or are they (at least sometimes) computed on-line, upon some "command" of the linguistic system? Visual processing may provide different information depending on attention. For instance, a brief look at a scene only yields a sense of its gist – the setting, some awareness of its characteristic objects. Attentional processing of limited regions will lead to more specific shape perception and object recognition. Some elements of information are made available only through sustained attention or scrutiny (Julesz, 1980). Finally, practice improves subjects' abilities to discriminate and note certain characteristics of visual stimuli.

In other words, it is plausible that the perception of certain spatial relations requires special visual processing. It will be useful at this point to look at the relevant work in psychology and computer vision.

6.5.3.1. *Abstract spatial relations in vision.*
Abstract spatial relations could play a role in vision as part of the representation of objects or as part of the representation of location. I consider first object representation.

In componential theories of object recognition (Marr and Nishihara, 1978; Biederman, 1987), objects are represented as assemblies of parts. The parts' boundaries are determined by geometric features of the objects' surface (Hoffman and Richards, 1985a). The parts themselves are represented by shape primitives, such as generalized cones (Marr and Nishihara, 1978), or "geons" (Biederman, 1987). There is very little specific about the encoding of relations between parts, other than the suggestion that abstract spatial relations would solve the problem nicely, since the resulting representations for articulated objects would be stable (Marr and Nishihara, 1978; Kosslyn et al., 1989). For instance, in any position, the arm is connected to the shoulder – *connected* is an invariant under normal motion. However, fully abstract relations will not in general suffice: for instance, we know that an arm can move only within a certain solid angle, and we can immediately recognize an arm at an odd angle. So *connected* by itself will not do; some measure of angle must be added.

Biederman (1987) proposes a set of spatial relations to represent the connections between geons:

- For any pair of connected geons, whether one is greater than, equal to, or smaller than the other;
- Whether a geon is above, below, or at the same height as another;
- Whether two geons are joined end-to-end, end-to-side and centered, or end-to-side and uncentered;
- Whether a geon is joined to another's "long" or "short" surface.

This is a very short catalogue and unlikely to account for all needed distinctions between shapes, but the relevant point here is that, except for the second, these relations do not appear fundamental to language. They are not lexicalized in English or even easy to express (see the fourth), and it seems unlikely that any language lexicalizes them – although English lexicalizes a great many other relations, as do most other languages.

Ullman (1985, p. 98) suggests that "objects are often defined visually by abstract shape properties and spatial relations among components." He illustrates this with a representation of a face in which the internal features have been shuffled; the resulting picture is not recognizable as a face. Yet, it is unclear that a set of abstract spatial relations of the kind used in language is what brings features together into a face. It is the simultaneous satisfaction of many spatial relations – at least some of which must be in terms of metric parameters – that makes a face into a face, and this simultaneity might be better captured by a pattern-matching process than some articulated (proposition-like) representation. In short, there is no strong support for the assumption (expressed in Kosslyn et al., 1989 and Hayward and Tarr, 1995) that linguistic spatial relations originate in those used in object representations.

Abstract spatial relations may also play a role in location representation. But researchers (such as Shepard and Hurwitz, 1985; Pinker, 1985; Sedgewick and Levy, 1986; Hinton and Parsons, 1988) have usually assumed that location is represented by means of metric coordinates (or some equivalent) within three types of reference frames:

1. Egocentric, based on the top, bottom, front, back, right, and left of the perceiver;
2. Allocentric, anchored on prominent landmarks in the environment (for example, the walls of a room);
3. Object-based.

Coordinate representations yield the precision evident in visual representations. Moreover, any abstract relationship can be computed from coordinate representations.

So there is little substantive evidence that visual representations include explicit representations of the spatial relations we express – except when we are specifically prompted to compute such relations. Yet the question is certainly not settled. It looks intuitively plausible, for instance, that simple spatial relations between proximate objects, such as contiguity, inclusion, or "immediately above," would be explicitly encoded in visual representations independently of higher-level cognitive activities.

6.5.3.2.   Perceiving for speaking.

There are definitely cases where some "extra" visual processing – beyond a simple act of attention – is needed to extract a spatial relation from visual representations. I will give five arguments to support the proposition that visual processing beyond that accompanying the attentional, but not goal-directed, apprehension of a scene is needed to compute and perceive at least some linguistic spatial relations (see Logan, 1994, for supporting psychological evidence). The arguments are based on careful examination of the processing needed to compute a given relation, and on introspective evidence that such processing takes application, effort, and time.

Assume a scene of moderate scope (such as a desk top supporting some objects); in looking at it at leisure but with no particular goal in mind, we construct a visual representation.

1. It is implausible that all the relational primitives needed to ascertain any lexically expressible relation would be encoded in that representation. There would have to be one or more primitives for every pair of objects – not only proximate objects but distant ones. It is highly unlikely that we have explicit representations of every expressible relation between distant objects. If asked to describe the relationship between one book among several between book ends at one corner of the desk and a cup at a diagonal corner I may produce *The book is to the left of the cup.* But that requires "configuring" the book and cup together in an act of attention[17] that ignores the objects in between, and then evaluating the degree of fit of the configuration with *to the left.* There is no reason to perform these operations absent a linguistic goal – and clear introspective evidence that it requires a special effort.

2. The evaluation of some spatial relations requires configuring *virtual structures* with visible ones. These processes are sometimes clearly language dependent.

Assume a speaker looking obliquely at the TV in Figure 6.11a who says *The basket is to the right of the TV.* Ascertaining the truth of the relation required her to establish which side of the TV is its canonical front; imagine the symmetry axis leading from the center of the TV toward the

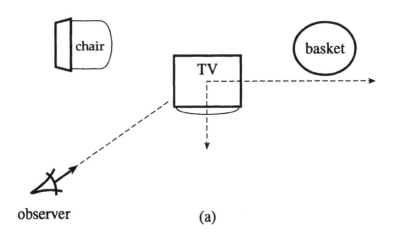

observer   (a)

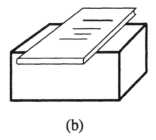

(b)

Figure 11.   Perceiving spatial relations

front; imagine the line orthogonal to that axis running through the center; choose the appropriate half of this orthogonal; and ascertain the presence of the basket within a cone centered on that half-axis (Gapp, 1995). While egocentric right and left are relatively easy to access,[18] the right and left directions intrinsic to an object rotate with it; keeping track of the divisions of surrounding space induced by these directions is unlikely to be done at all times by automatic vision processes.

3. In describing a configuration of two objects, we can often express either of two converse relationships, provided the objects' size and mobility are not disproportionate. It is unlikely that these converse relationships are both encoded in visual representations. The perception of non-symmetric spatial relations must be anchored on one of the objects. One might perceive two

objects as *near each other*, but it is hard to imagine how one would perceive simultaneously that *The chair is to the left of the TV* and *The TV is in front of the chair* (Figure 6.11a).

4. Categorizing a configuration by a spatial relation may require approximate fitting and yield uncertain results; this is a high-level operation, not the kind performed by undirected, unintentional vision processes.

Several lexically expressible relations can generally categorize a given configuration of two objects. So in Figure 11b, one could say any of the following:

The book is ...

      ... on the box
      ... on top of the box.
      ... on the top of the box.
      ... over the box.
      ... across the box.

The box is under the book.

The choice between these is a matter of what is most salient and/or relevant in the context. For the first three expressions, the only relational primitives that need be accessed are contiguity and support – relations so basic they may well be encoded in "minimal" visual representations. But consider *over* and *across*: *over* highlights the fact that the book *almost* covers the box; *across* the fact that the long (top-bottom) axis of the book is *almost* orthogonal to the long axis of the box. Prepositional categories, like many linguistic categories, are fuzzy. Why perform such an act of categorization, an act involving approximate fitting, in the absence of a high-level cognitive goal? The complex computations underlying some uses of *across* (6.4.2) certainly support this point.

5. The basic purpose of the motion prepositions is to describe navigation paths. Their use in describing static configurations in visual scenes is derivative. It is improbable that we would "see" relations like *across* or *along* in a visual scene, were it not that language makes them available, prompting us to look for the patterns that define them (between and within objects; see *the carving across the handle of the knife*).

To compute a spatial relation between two objects, one must:

1. Configure them together – that is, select them for attention in a way that makes it possible to apprehend the applicable spatial relations; and

2. Categorize the configuration.

Each of these steps may require visual processing beyond that involved in observing the scene in undirected fashion.

Thus, we can look at a scene, even focus on two particular objects, and not see the spatial relations between them that we later express. This means there are *language-induced percepts*. Slobin (1996) gives evidence of "thinking for speaking," a special kind of thinking used on line in the act of speaking, which is evanescent and does not affect the way we think outside the act of speaking.[19] There must also be "perceiving for speaking." I do not doubt that speakers of Dyirbal and of Thai see essentially the same thing when they simply look at a scene; the basic processes of vision are certainly universal. But using language involves a kind of "visual cognition" beyond these basic processes. Here, perceptual and conceptual operations cease to be clearly distinguishable (Talmy, 1996), and language prompts the visual system to constructive operations that are not a necessary part of undirected perception.

Ullman (1985) addresses the question of the computation of abstract spatial relations from coordinate representations, and proposes a set of operators that can be assembled to construct "visual routines." I am not concerned here with the details of his architecture, but with the design constraints he posits: visual routines would not apply throughout the image but operate on selected locations of particular interest when triggered by high-level (possibly linguistic) goals. They would constitute a task-specific vision system. This system would allow the computation of an open-ended variety of abstract predicates – thus enabling perceptual learning. Ullman bases these design constraints on the requirements of object recognition, but they are clearly useful for the extraction and perception of the abstract relations used in language[20] and spatial problem-solving.

6.6. Conclusions

We have examined the semantics of English prepositions, the schematization processes involved in their use, and the forms of nonlinguistic spatial cognition underlying these processes. This exploration has taken us a step closer to understanding the interface between language and spatial cognition, showing that the flexible choice of object representation employed in descriptions of location is tied to access to various nonlinguistic spatial representations; and that the expression of at least some spatial relations requires processes of configuration and categorization beyond those performed by automatic visual perception.

Rather than a closed system with limited access to nonlinguistic representations, language seems to be flexibly connected to a variety of spatial representations. This does not mean that spatial cognition puts no restriction on the spatial relations languages can express: we brought out one such restriction relating to the perception and representation of motion. Also, given the importance of cognitive maps in spatial cognition, it is likely that every system of spatial relation terms will have a significant subset used primarily with objects represented as points. But the conceptual system is not restricted to these. The visual system has the ability to compute an extended variety of linguistic relations, requiring a flexible computational process controlled by linguistic goals.

This study of schematization and of the structure of prepositional categories also provides a first sketch of the complex way spatial linguistic categories are grounded in perception. The problem of object recognition has driven much of the research in computer vision in the last thirty years; other, less transparent connections between vision and conception have been neglected – those having to do with relations, actions, and events. The basic categories that the visual system must compute to identify these are not as clearly apparent as Rosch's (1977) "basic-level" object categories. They need to be brought out by fine-grained semantic analysis and psycholinguistic studies. This chapter sets the stage for such developments.

Notes

[1] Activities are one of the "aspectual classes"; the others are states, achievements, and accomplishments (Vendler, 1967). An activity extends over time (contrary to achievements, such as *reach*, which are punctual events), but does not specify a completion point (in contrast with accomplishments, such as *cross* in *Jo crossed the road*).

[2] In Jackendoff's conceptual structure (Jackendoff, 1983; 1990), phrases such as *from the bridge* are said to refer to trajectories. The motion prepositions are Path-functions that map a reference object onto a trajectory. It is actually impossible to define such functions; given a preposition, there is no way to assign a unique trajectory to every given reference object.

[3] Examples preceded by ♯ are acceptable, but do not have the intended intepretation. So *The snake lay up the tree trunk* is acceptable but with the whole snake located toward the top of the tree trunk.

[4] The sentence is acceptable with the entire snake located past the stone. These examples are adapted from Talmy (1983).

[5] The difference in acceptability may be due to Figure and Ground being body parts, which frequently are treated differently from other kinds of objects in spatial sentences (Herskovits, 1986).

[6] Again, Talmy (1983) uses very similar examples. See also Talmy (1996) on fictive paths.

[7] Sadalla et al. (1980) found that some locations in cognitive maps are *anchors*; other places are seen in relation to them. One of the facts associated with the role of anchor is that subjective distance is asymmetric; subjects judge the distance from A to B longer than the distance from B to A, if A is an anchor and B is not.

[8] *Inness* is certainly often inferred rather than directly assessed; the location of every point of the Figure need not always be checked. So ascertaining that an object is *in a room* often only requires making sure it is visible.

[9] Rock (1972, p. 671) defines perception "to mean what is 'noted,' 'described,' attended to, or apprehended about a figure, albeit unconsciously and nonverbally." There can be awareness without perception. Experiments show that perception, so defined, is necessary for memory formation. It must also be a condition for the formation of conceptual categories dividing the range of shapes (or motions) considered.

[10] One sense of *at* entails a canonical interaction between Figure and Ground:

Jane is at the desk.

This sense can be extended to chairs but not to objects playing no role in the canonical interaction:

The chair/*vase is at the desk

[11] "A large-scale environment is one whose structure is revealed by integrating local observations over time" (Kuipers, 1983, p. 347).

[12] Marr's 3-D model (1982) is hierarchical: the whole shape is divided into its "immediate" parts, which are in turn divided into parts, and so on down. The location of parts is represented only with respect to the entity immediately above in the hierarchy, which allows for stability in the representation of articulated objects: the representation of a finger will be with respect to a frame of reference attached to the hand, not to the whole body. The entire shape and each part have a model axis, which gives coarse information about length and orientation.

[13] The list here is a revised and augmented version of a similar list in Herskovits (1986) where examples of application of the functions not considered in this chapter can be found. See also Section 6.5 for additional illustrations.

[14] Hays (1987) uses the term *coercion*, from programming language theory, to indicate the "forced" matching of the argument(s) of a linguistic predicate to its selection restrictions. It is always associated with metonymy (Herskovits, 1986), since the actual arguments of the predicate are geometric constructs distinct from the primary referents of the complement noun phrases.

[15] I will, for conciseness, talk about Figure and Ground in what follows, when actually meaning "coerced Figure" and "coerced Ground" – that is, the values of the applicable geometry selection functions (the actual arguments of the relation *across*).

[16] Levinson (1994) makes a similar point, using examples from Tzeltal.

[17] Niyogi (1995) proposes a model of the computation of spatial relations in which the location of the focus of attention itself serves as input to the "daemons" carrying out the computation; configuring, then, would involve moving the focus from one object to the other.

[18] Egocentric relations are stable under projective transformations; so, from a given vantage point, right and left in three-dimensional space always correspond to right and left in the plane of view. We can easily judge whether two objects are to the right of another; they both appear on the same (right) side of it. By contrast, two objects to the intrinsic right of a TV could project in the plane of view right and left of the TV, given that the Figures are not required to be exactly on the axes.

[19] But Levinson's study of Guugu Yimidhirr (1993) shows that not all spatial thought supporting language use is without consequences for spatial thought outside language.

[20] Chapman (1991) and Niyogi (1995) use visual routines in artificial intelligence models of linguistic abilities; they argue against vision models that involve processing an entire retinal image, and assume that relational knowledge is computed only when needed by higher-level cognitive processes.

Part III

Temporal Reasoning

7. Actions and Events in Interval Temporal Logic

James F. Allen and George Ferguson

7.1. Introduction

Representing and reasoning about the dynamic aspects of the world — primarily about actions and events — is a problem of interest to many different disciplines. In Artificial Intelligence (AI), we are interested in such problems for a number of reasons — in particular, to model the reasoning of intelligent agents as they plan to act in the world and to reason about causal effects in the world. More specifically, a general representation of actions and events has to support the following somewhat overlapping tasks:

- *Prediction*: Given a description of a scenario, including actions and events, what will (or is most likely to) happen?
- *Planning*: Given an initial description of the world and a desired goal, find a course of action that will (or is most likely to) achieve that goal.
- *Explanation*: Given a set of observations about the world, find the best explanation of the data. When the observations are another agent's actions and the explanation desired is the agent's plan, the problem is called *plan recognition*.

Our claim in this chapter is that in order to adequately represent actions and events, one needs an explicit temporal logic, and that approaches with weaker temporal models, such as state spaces (for example, STRIPS-based approaches) and the situation calculus, either cannot handle the problems or require such dramatic extensions that one in effect has grafted an explicit temporal logic onto the earlier formalism. Furthermore, if one of these formalisms is extended in this way, the temporal logic part will dominate and the original formalism plays little role in the solution. We will primarily defend this position by proposing a specific temporal representation and showing that it can handle a wide range of situations that are often problematic for other formalisms. In particular, here are some properties of actions and events that we feel are essential to any general representation:

- Actions and events take time. During this time, they may have a rich structure. For instance, the event of driving my car to work involves a wide range of different actions, states of the world, and other complications, yet the activity over that stretch of time is appropriately described as a single event.
- The relationship between actions and events and their effects is complex. Some effects become true at the end of the event and remain true for some time after the event. For example, when I put a book on the table, this has the effect that the book is on the table for at least a short time after the action is completed. Other effects only hold while the event is in progress — for example, holding an elevator open by pressing the "open door" button. Other effects might start after the beginning of the event and end before it does, such as my being on a bridge while driving to work. This is an effect of the action even though it is not true at the end of it. Finally, it may be the case that the effects of actions are wholly independent of the action once the action is performed, as in a rock rolling down a hill after I nudge it out of place.
- External changes in the world may occur no matter what actions an agent plans to do and may interact with the planned actions. Possible external events should be an important factor when reasoning about what effects an action might have. Certain goals can be accomplished only by depending on external events, whether they are a result of natural forces (sailing, for example, needs wind) or the actions of other agents (needed cargo arrives when a vehicle arrives).
- Actions and events may interact in complex ways when they overlap or occur simultaneously. In some cases, they interfere with certain effects that would arise if the events were done in isolation. In other cases, the effects may be additive. And in still other cases, the effect of performing the two actions may be completely different from the effects of each in isolation.
- Knowledge of the world is necessarily incomplete and unpredictable in detail. Thus, reasoning about actions and events can be done only on the basis of certain assumptions. No plan is foolproof, and it is important that a formalism makes the necessary assumptions explicit so that they can be considered in evaluating plans.

Our aim is to develop a general representation of actions and events that supports a wide range of reasoning tasks, including planning, explanation, and prediction but also natural language understanding and commonsense reasoning in general. Most previous work tends to address only a subset of these problems. The STRIPS-based planners — TWEAK (Chapman, 1987), SIPE (Wilkins, 1988), and SNLP (McAllester and Rosenblitt, 1991), for instance — only address the planning problem, while work in the situation calculus such as (McCarthy and Hayes, 1969; Baker, 1991) has primarily focused on the prediction problem or on using it as an abstract theory for planning (for example, (Cordell, 1969)). Natural language work, on the other hand, typically deals only with commonsense entailments from statements about actions and events, sometimes with a focus on plan recognition and explanation (see, for example, (Allen, 1994; Hobbs et al., 1993; Schubert and Hwang, 1989)). Our representation is intended to serve as a uniform representation to support all these tasks. As a result, we try to avoid introducing any specific syntactic constructs that support only one reasoning task. Knowledge should be encoded in a way so that it is usable no matter what reasoning task is currently being performed.

Section 7.2 outlines our intuitions about actions and events and briefly explores the two predominant models of action: the situation calculus and the state-based STRIPS-style representations. As typically formulated, neither is powerful enough for the issues described above. Section 7.3 then introduces interval temporal logic, first defining the temporal structure and then introducing properties, events, and actions. Section 7.4 demonstrates how the interval logic can be used to solve a set of simple problems from the literature in order to facilitate comparison with other approaches. The key place where other approaches have difficulty is in representing external events and simultaneous actions. Section 7.5.1 explores the implications of external events in detail, and Section 7.5.3 explores interacting simultaneous actions.

7.2. Representing Actions and Events

Before starting the formal development, we attempt to describe the intuitions motivating the representation. We then consider why the most commonly accepted representations of action in AI do not meet our needs.

7.2.1. INTUITIONS ABOUT ACTIONS AND EVENTS

The first issue concerns what an event is. We take the position that events are primarily linguistic or cognitive in nature. That is, the world does not really contain events. Rather, events are how agents classify certain useful and relevant patterns of change. As such, there are very few restrictions on what an event might consist of except that it must involve at least one object over some stretch of time or involve at least one change of state. Thus, the very same circumstances in the world might be described by any number of events. For instance, consider a circumstance in which a glass fell off a table and broke on the floor. This already is one description of what actually happened. The very same set of circumstances could also be described as the event in which a glass broke or in which someone was woken by the noise of the breaking glass. Each of these descriptions is a different way of describing the circumstances, and each is packaged as a description of an event that occurred. No one description is more correct than the other, although some may be more informative for certain circumstances, in that they help predict some required information or suggest a way of reacting to the circumstances.

Of course, the "states" of the world referred to above are also ways of classifying the world and are not inherent in the world itself either. Thus, the same set of circumstances described above might be partially described in terms of the ball being red. Given this, what can one say about the differences between events and states? Intuitively, one describes change and the other describes aspects that do not change. In language, we say that events occur and that states hold. But it is easy to blur these distinctions. Thus, while the balling falling from the table to the floor clearly describes change and hence describes an event, what about the circumstance where an agent John holds the door shut for a couple of minutes. While the door remains shut during this time and thus doesn't change state, it seems that John holding the door shut is something that occurred and thus is like an event. These issues have been studied extensively in work on the semantics of natural language sentences. While there are many proposals, everyone agrees on a few basic distinctions (see, for example, (Vendler, 1967; Mourelatos, 1978; Dowty, 1986)). Of prime relevance to us here are sentences that describe *states* of the world, as in *The ball is red*, or *John believes that the world is flat*, and sentences that describe general ongoing *activities* such as *John ran for an hour*, and *events* such as *John climbed the mountain*. Each of these types of sentences has different properties, but the most important distinctions occur in their relation to time. All these sentences can be true over an interval of time. But when a state holds over an interval of time t, one can conclude that the state also held over subintervals of t. Thus, if the ball is red during the entire day, then it is also red during the morning. This property is termed *homogeneity* in the temporal logic literature. Events, on the other hand, generally have the opposite property and are antihomogeneous: if an event occurs over an interval t, then it doesn't occur over a subinterval of t, as it would not yet be completed. Thus, if the ball dropped from the table to the floor over time t, then over a subinterval of t is would just be somewhere in the air between the table and floor. Activities, on the other hand, fall in between. They may be homogeneous, as in the holding the door shut example above, but they describe some dynamic aspect of the world like events. This type of distinction must appreciated by any general purpose knowledge representation for action and change.

Finally, a word on actions. The word *action* is used in many different senses by many different people. For us, an action refers to something that a person or robot might do. It is a way of classifying the different sorts of things that an agent can do to affect the world, thus it more resembles a sensory-motor program than an event. By performing an action, an agent causes an event to occur, which in turn may cause other desired events to also occur. For instance, I know how to perform an action of walking that I may perform in the hope of causing the event of walking to my car. Some theories refer to the event that was caused as the action, but this is not what we intend here. Rather, we will draw on an analogy with the robot situation and view actions as programs. Thus, performing an action will be described in terms of running a program.

7.2.2. THE SITUATION CALCULUS

The situation calculus means different things to different researchers. In its original formulation ((McCarthy and Hayes, 1969)), which we will call the general theory of the situation calculus, situations are introduced into the ontology as a complete snapshot of the universe at some instant in time. In effect, the situation calculus is a point-based temporal logic with a branching time model. In its most common use, which we will call the *constructive situation calculus*, it is used in a highly restricted form first proposed by Green (Cordell, 1969), in which the only way situations are introduced is by constructing them by action composition from an initial state. This practice has attracted the most attention precisely because the formalism is constructive — specifically, it can be used for planning. To construct a plan for a goal G, prove that there exists a situation s in which G holds. In proving this, the situation is constructed by action composition, and thus the desired sequence of actions (the plan) can be extracted from the proof. As others have pointed out (see, for example, (Schubert, 1990)), most of the criticisms about the expressibility of the situation calculus concern the constructive form of it rather than the general theory. Our position is that the constructive situation calculus is a limited representation, especially in dealing with temporally complex actions and external events. The general theory, on the other hand, is much richer and can be extended to a model much closer to what we are proposing, but at the loss of its constructive aspect. This is explored further after the interval temporal logic has been introduced.

```
STACK(a,b)
        preconds: (Clear a) (Clear b)
        delete:   (Clear b)
        add:      (On a b)
```

Figure 1.   Actions as state change in STRIPS

7.2.3. THE STRIPS REPRESENTATION

The STRIPS representation ((Fikes and Nilsson, 1971)) adds additional constraints to the situation calculus model and is used by most implemented planning systems built to date. In STRIPS, a state is represented as a finite set of formulas, and the effects of an action are specified by two sets of formulas: the delete list specifies what propositions to remove from the initial state, and the add list specifies the new propositions to add. Together, they completely define the transition between the initial state and the resulting state. Figure 1 shows a simple Blocks World action that involves placing one block on top of another (the STACK action). The preconditions on an action indicate when the action is applicable: in this case, it is applicable whenever both blocks are clear. The effects state that one block is now on top of the other (the add list) and that the bottom block is not clear (the delete list). The operation for constructing a resulting state applies the delete list first and then asserts the add list.

Like the situation calculus, STRIPS-style actions are effectively instantaneous, and there is no provision for asserting what is true while an action is in execution. Also, since the state descriptions do not include information about action occurrences, such systems cannot represent the situation where one action occurs while some other event or action is occurring. Such a case would violate the STRIPS assumptions, which assume that the world only changes as the result of a single action by the agent and that the action definitions completely characterize all change when an action is done. Of course, these assumptions would not be valid if simultaneous actions or external events were allowed.

The STRIPS assumptions appear to be fundamentally incompatible with interacting simultaneous actions and external events. They hold only in worlds with a single agent, who can do only one thing at a time, and where the world changes only as the result of the agent's actions. However, they are so ingrained in the planning literature that many researchers don't even acknowledge their limitations. In some sense, they have become part of the definition of the classical planning problem.

7.3. Interval Temporal Logic

Having described our motivations, we now start the development of the temporal logic. We start by describing the basic temporal structure to be used in the logic — namely the interval representation of time developed by Allen (Allen, 1983; Allen, 1984) and discussed in detail in (Allen and Hayes, 1989). We then describe the temporal logic used to represent knowledge of properties, events, and actions. We conclude this section with a comparison of related formalisms. Subsequent sections explore how the representation supports reasoning about events and actions, especially in complex situations with external events and simultaneous actions.

7.3.1. THE STRUCTURE OF TIME

The temporal structure we assume is a simple linear model of time. Notions of possibility that are introduced in branching time models or the situation calculus would be handled by introducing a separate modal operator to represent possibility explicitly. Since such a modal operator is needed in general anyway, there seems no need to build it into the temporal structure. The temporal theory starts with one primitive object, the time period, and one primitive relation: $Meets$.

A time period intuitively is the time associated with some event occurring or some property holding in the world. Intuitively, two periods m and n meet if and only if m precedes n, yet there is no time between m and n, and m and n do not overlap. The axiomatization of the $Meets$ relation is as follows, where i, j, k, l, and m are logical variables restricted to time periods. The axioms are presented graphically in Figure 2. First, there is no beginning or ending of time, and there are no semi-infinite or infinite periods. In other words, every period has a period that meets it and another that it meets:

$$\forall i \,.\, \exists j, k \,.\, Meets(j, i) \wedge Meets(i, k). \tag{1}$$

Second, periods can compose to produce a larger period. In particular, for any two periods that meet, there is another period that is the "concatenation" of them. This can be axiomatized as follows:

$$\forall i, j, k, l \,.\, Meets(i, j) \wedge Meets(j, k) \wedge Meets(k, l) \supset \tag{2}$$
$$\exists m \,.\, Meets(i, m) \wedge Meets(m, l).$$

As a convenient notation, we will often write $j + k$ to denote the interval that is the concatenation of intervals j and k. This functional notation is justified because we can prove that the result of $j + k$ is unique ((Allen and Hayes, 1989)).

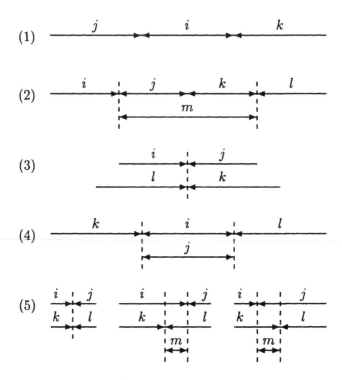

Figure 2.   The axiomatization of time periods

Next, periods uniquely define an equivalence class of periods that meet them. In particular, if i meets j and i meets k, then any period l that meets j must also meet k:

$$\forall i,j,k,l \, . \, Meets(i,j) \wedge Meets(i,k) \wedge Meets(l,j) \supset Meets(l,k). \qquad (3)$$

These equivalence classes also uniquely define the periods. In particular, if two periods both meet the same period, and another period meets both of them, then the periods are equal:

$$\forall i,j,k,l \, . \, Meets(k,i) \wedge Meets(k,j) \wedge Meets(i,l) \wedge Meets(j,l) \supset i = j. \quad (4)$$

Finally, we need an ordering axiom. Intuitively, this axiom asserts that for any two pairs of periods, such that i meets j and k meets l, then either they both meet at the same "place," or the place where i meets j precedes the place where k meets l, or vice versa. In terms of the meets relation, this can be axiomatized as follows, where the symbol "$\otimes$" means "exclusive-or":

$$\forall i,j,k,l \, . \, (Meets(i,j) \wedge Meets(k,l)) \supset \qquad\qquad (5)$$

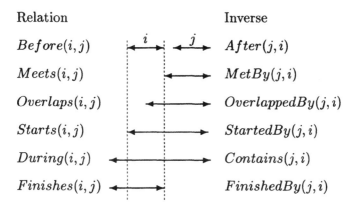

Figure 3.   The possible relations between time periods (equality not shown)

$$Meets(i, l) \otimes (\exists m . Meets(k, m) \wedge Meets(m, j)) \otimes$$
$$(\exists m . Meets(i, m) \vee Meets(m, l)).$$

Many of the properties that are intuitively desired but have not yet been mentioned are actually theorems of this axiomatization. In particular, it can be proven that no period can meet itself, and that if one period i meets another j then j cannot also meet i (that is, finite circular models of time are not possible).

With this system, one can define the complete range of the intuitive relationships that could hold between time periods. For example, one period is before another if there exists another period that spans the time between them — for instance,

$$Before(i, j) \equiv \exists m . Meets(i, m) \wedge Meets(m, j).$$

Figure 3 shows each of these relationships graphically (equality is not shown). We will use the following symbols to stand for commonly used relations and disjunctions of relations:

$Meets(i, j)$ $i : j$
$Before(i, j)\ i \prec j$ $Before(i, j) \vee Meets(i, j)\ i \prec: j$
$During(i, j)\ i \sqsubset j$ $During(i, j) \vee i = j$ $i \sqsubseteq j$

Finally, an important relationship between two periods is *Disjoint*: two intervals are disjoint if they do not overlap in any way. We write this as "$i \bowtie j$" and define it by

$$i \bowtie j \equiv i \prec: j \vee j \prec: i.$$

The computational properties of the interval calculus and algorithms for maintaining networks of temporal constraints are presented in (Allen, 1983; Vilain and Kautz, 1986; Vilain et al., 1990).

A period can be classified by the relationships that it can have with other periods. For example, we call a period that has no subperiods (that is, no period is contained in it or overlaps it) a *moment* and a period that has subperiods, an *interval*. In addition, we can define a notion of time point by a construction that defines the beginning and ending of periods. It is important to note that moments and points are distinct and cannot be collapsed. In particular, moments are true periods and may meet other periods, and if $Meets(i, m) \land Meets(m, j)$ for any moment m, then i is before j. Points, on the other hand, are not periods and cannot meet periods. Full details can be found in (Allen and Hayes, 1989).

Any semantic model that allows these distinctions would be a possible model of time. In particular, a discrete time model can be given for this logic, where periods map to pairs of integers $\langle I, J \rangle$ where $I < J$. Moments correspond to pairs of the form $\langle I, I + 1 \rangle$, and points correspond to the integers themselves. A similar model built out of pairs of real numbers does not allow moments. A more complex model can be specified out of the reals, however, that does allow continuous time, or models that are sometimes discrete and sometimes continuous are possible. Ladkin and Maddux (Ladkin and Maddux, 1988b) have characterized the set of possible models as precisely the arbitrary unbounded linear orders.

7.3.2. INTERVAL TEMPORAL LOGIC

The most obvious way to add times into a logic is to add an extra argument to each predicate. For example, in a nontemporal logic, the predicate *Green* might denote the set of green objects. Thus, a formula such as *Green*($frog13$) would be true only if the object named by the term, $frog13$, is in the set of green objects. To make this a temporal predicate, a time argument is added and *Green* now denotes a set of tuples consisting of all green objects with the times at which they were green. Thus, the proposition *Green*($frog13, t1$) is true only if the object named by $frog13$ was green over the time named by $t1$.

By allowing time intervals as arguments, we open the possibility that a proposition involving some predicate P might be neither true nor false over some interval t. In particular, consider a predicate P that is true during some subinterval of t and also false in some other subinterval of t. In this case, there are two ways we might interpret the negative proposition $\sim P(t)$. In the weak interpretation, $\sim P(t)$ is true if and only if it is not the case that P is true throughout interval t, and thus $\sim P(t)$ is true if P changes truth-values during t. In the strong interpretation of negation, $\sim P(t)$ is true if and only if P is false throughout t, and so neither $P(t)$ nor $\sim P(t)$ would be true in the above situation. Thus, a logic with only strong negation has truth gaps.

We take the weak interpretation of negation as the basic construct, as do Shoham (Shoham, 1987) and Bacchus, Tenenberg, and Koomen (Bacchus et al., 1989), to preserve a simple two-valued logic. Weak negation also seems to be the appropriate interpretation for the standard definition of implication. In particular, the formula $P(t) \supset Q(t')$ is typically defined as $\sim P(t) \vee Q(t')$. Since we want the implication to mean "whenever P is true over t, then Q is true over t'," this is best captured by the weak negation form of the equivalent formula. With weak negation, $\sim P(t) \vee Q(t')$ says that either P is not true throughout t (but might be true in some subintervals of t), or Q is true over t'. This seems the right interpretation. Of course, we can still make assertions equivalent to the strong negation. The fact that P is false throughout t can be expressed as

$$\forall t' . t' \sqsubseteq t \supset \sim P(t').$$

This is a common enough expression that we will introduce an abbreviation for the formula — namely $\neg P(t)$ (that is, the symbol "$\neg$" means strong negation). This way we obtain the notational convenience of strong negation while retaining the simpler semantics of a logic with no truth gaps.

There are several characteristics of propositions that allow them to be broadly classified based on their inferential properties. These distinctions were originally proposed by Vendler (Vendler, 1967), and variants have been proposed under various names throughout linguistics, philosophy, and artificial intelligence ever since (see, for example, (Mourelatos, 1978; Allen, 1984; Dowty, 1986; Shoham, 1988b)). For the most part we are not concerned with all the distinctions considered by these authors. However, one important property mentioned previously is homogeneity. Recall that a proposition is homogeneous if and only if when it holds over a time period t, it also holds over any period within t. In the current formulation, this property is defined by a family of axiom schemata, one for each arity of predicate.

7.3.2.1 Homogeneity axiom schema
For all homogeneous predicates P of arity $n + 1$:

$$\forall x_i, t, t' . P(x_1, \ldots, x_n, t) \wedge t' \sqsubseteq t \supset P(x_1, \ldots, x_n, t').$$

All predicates will be homogeneous in what follows except when explicitly noted. The following useful theorem follows from the definition of strong negation and the homogeneity property, for any homogeneous predicate P:

DISJ $\forall t, t' . P(t) \wedge \neg P(t') \supset t \bowtie t'.$

That is, two intervals over which a predicate has different truth values (with respect to strong negation) must be disjoint.

There is still one aspect of the relationship between time and properties that remains to be addressed. This issue is crucially important to our subsequent development of mechanisms for reasoning about change. Thus far, we have not been concerned with whether the temporal structure is modeled on the real line or on some more restricted domain. However, once we start considering properties changing value in time, we are immediately confronted with the possibility of various sorts of infinities if the underlying model is the reals. For example, the definition of weak negation allows intervals over which $\sim P$ holds but for no subinterval of which does $\neg P$ hold. In such a case, we would have an infinite intermingling of P and $\sim P$ intervals.

While such strange situations are mathematically possible, they are clearly not what would expect from a commonsense theory. We therefore explicitly rule them out with a axiom schema of "discrete variation," adapted from Hamblin (Hamblin, 1972):

7.3.2.2 *Discrete variation axiom schema*

$$\forall t . \sim P(t) \supset \exists t' . t' \sqsubseteq t \wedge \neg P(t').$$

This states that any interval over which a property P is weakly false has (at least) a strongly false "core." Hamblin states that this schema, together with homogeneity, defines the "phenomenal" predicates — those corresponding to natural phenomena.

It turns out that this is not in fact strong enough to draw all the commonsense conclusions one would expect.[57] For example, consider that we know of two intervals t and t' where $t \prec: t'$, such that $P(t)$ and $\neg P(t')$. A desirable (indeed fundamental) conclusion that we would like to draw from this premise is that there is a "transition point" between P and $\neg P$ — that is,

$$\exists T, T' . P(T) \wedge \neg P(T') \wedge T : T' \wedge t' \sqsubseteq T'.$$

That is, there exist two intervals that meet where the property changes truth value, and these intervals are related to the original ones by inclusion on the left (there is a similar statement for the right). This conclusion, however, does not follow from discrete variation and homogeneity. The reason is that although the discrete variation schema rules out infinite intermingling, we can still have an infinite sequence of intervals of the *same* truth value telescoping toward a point, as in Zeno's paradox.

This problem is, of course, familiar to mathematicians from the theory of continuous functions. It led Galton (Galton, 1990) to introduce additional axioms to explicitly eliminate such telescoping intervals. More generally in AI, Davis (Davis, 1992) has pointed out several related problems with the relationship between continuous functions and AI theories of knowledge representation. Van Bentham (van Benthem, 1983) is the definitive treatment of these questions as regards temporal logic. For our part, we believe that it would be possible to import and adapt appropriate pieces of the theory of functions such that, with appropriate assumptions about, for example, continuity and density, we could derive the desired conclusions. The details are complicated, and in any event would mostly be a recapitulation of prior mathematical analysis. Not only are we not really qualified for the task, our purpose here is a commonsense theory, which the theory of functions certainly is not. We will therefore add the following "transition point" axiom schema to our temporal logic:

7.3.2.3 *TRPT*

$$\forall t, t' \, . \, P(t) \wedge \neg P(t') \wedge t \prec: t' \supset$$
$$\exists T, T' \, . \, P(T) \wedge \neg P(T') \wedge T : T' \wedge t' \sqsubseteq T'.$$

What price have we paid for axiomatizing away this difficulty? Davis (Davis, 1992, p. 48) quotes Russell as stating that "the method of 'postulating' what we want has many advantages; they are the same as the advantages of theft over honest toil." In our own defense, we believe that our axiomatization is intended to produce a commonsense theory — one whose conclusions are those sanctioned by "common sense." The onus is therefore on the critics of the axioms to produce commonsense examples that violate the axioms. Davis argues that ruling out the use of some standard physical theories (as TRPT does) is too high a price to pay. Van Bentham, however, in his discussion of "linguistic" aspects of temporal logic (that is, using the logic in descriptions of the world), comments that "There is a lesson to be learnt here. Nature makes no jumps; but our linguistic descriptions can." (van Benthem, 1983, p. 229)

7.3.3. THE LOGIC OF EVENTS

The logic developed thus far is still insufficient to conveniently capture many of the circumstances that we need to reason about. In particular, we need to introduce events as objects into the logic. There are many reasons for this, and the most important of these are discussed in the remainder of this section.

Davidson (Davidson, 1967) argued that there are potentially unbounded qualifications that could be included in an event description. The issue of reifying events is not only an issue for representing natural language meaning, however. A sophisticated plan reasoning system also needs to represent and reason about events of similar complexity. In addition, in many forms of plan reasoning, the system must be able to distinguish events even though it does not have any information to distinguish them.

We use a representation that makes event variables the central component for organizing knowledge about events. In particular, events are divided into types, and each type defines a set of role functions that specify the arguments to any particular event instance. The event of Jack lifting the ball onto the table at time $t1$ would be represented as

$$\exists e . \text{LIFT}(e) \wedge agent(e) = jack34 \wedge$$
$$dest(e) = table5 \wedge theme(e) = ball26 \wedge time(e) = t1.$$

Event predicates will always be written in SMALL CAPS to distinguish them from other functions and predicates.[58]

This representation is somewhat verbose for presenting examples. When needed to make a point, the representation using only functions on events will be used. At other times, however, we will use the more standard predicate-argument notation as a convenient abbreviation. Thus, we will usually abbreviate the above formula as

$$\exists e . \text{LIFT}(jack34, ball26, table5, t1, e).$$

The arguments in this predicate-argument form will depend on the predicate, but the last two argument positions will always be the time of the event and the event instance, respectively. Finally note that event predicates are antihomogeneous (that is, they hold over no subinterval of the time over which they hold) as discussed in Section 7.2.1.

Because of the representation based on role functions, an event instance uniquely defines all its arguments. This is important to remember when the predicate-argument abbreviation is used. In particular, if we asserted that both $\text{LIFT}(a_1, b_1, c_1, t_1, e)$ and $\text{LIFT}(a_2, b_2, c_2, t_2, e)$ were true, then this would entail that $a_1 = a_2$, $b_1 = b_2$, $c_1 = c_2$, and $t_1 = t_2$, a fact not obvious when using the predicate-argument form but clear from the functional form.

We will represent knowledge about events in several ways. The first is by defining necessary conditions on the event occurring. For instance, consider the event of one block being stacked on another by a robot. This could be described by an event predicate of form $\text{STACK}(x, y, t, e)$. Axioms then define the consequences of this event occurring. For instance, one might assert that whenever a stack event occurs, the first block is on the second block at the end of the action. In the predicate-argument notation, this could be written as

$$\forall x, y, t, e . \text{STACK}(x, y, t, e) \supset \exists t' . t : t' \wedge On(x, y, t').$$

In the functional form, the same axiom would be

$$\forall e . \text{STACK}(e) \supset \exists t' . time(e) : t' \wedge On(block1(e), block2(e), t').$$

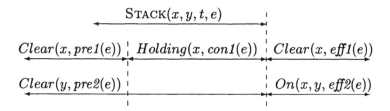

Figure 4.   Necessary conditions for stacking x on y

Of course, there are many other necessary conditions in order for a stacking event to occur. For instance, we might say that the block moved ($block1(e)$) must be clear when the event starts, that the agent must be holding that block some time during the event (actually up to the end of the event), and that the other block ($block2(e)$) is clear just before the end of the event and has $block1$ on it immediately after the event completes. The event terminates at the time when $block1$ is on $block2$. This information can be expressed directly using the temporal logic by the following axiom, also shown graphically in Figure 4:

$$\forall x, y, t, e . \text{STACK}(x, y, t, e) \supset$$
$$\exists j, k, l, m, n . Clear(x, j) \wedge Overlaps(j, t) \wedge$$
$$Holding(x, k) \wedge Finishes(k, t) \wedge j : k \wedge$$
$$Clear(x, l) \wedge t : l \wedge Clear(y, m) \wedge SameEnd(t, m) \wedge$$
$$On(x, y, n) \wedge t : n.$$

A more useful form of this axiom for planning uses temporal functions on each event that define the structure of the temporal intervals needed for its definition. For example, for the class of stacking events, we need functions to produce times corresponding to the existential variables in the axiom given above. Using new function names, we might define the temporal structure of the stacking event as follows:

$$\forall t, e . \text{STACK}(t, e) \supset$$
$$Overlaps(pre1(e), t) \wedge Finishes(con1(e), t) \wedge pre1(e) : con1(e) \wedge$$
$$t : eff1(e) \wedge SameEnd(t, pre2(e)) \wedge t : eff2(e).$$

The temporal functions are named to informally suggest the three classes of conditions that arise in an event definition. The "preconditions" — conditions that must hold prior to the event's occurrence — have the prefix *pre*, the "effects" — conditions that must hold following the event — have

the prefix *eff*, and the other conditions that must hold during the event have
the prefix *con*. The temporal functions can be viewed as Skolem functions
justified by the original axiom. The only aspect that will seem puzzling
is that we will use the same Skolem functions in several axioms. This
should be viewed as a notational convenience that allows a large conjunctive
axiom (with a single universally quantified event variable) to be presented
as several smaller axioms. With this temporal structure defined for every
stacking event, the axiom defining the necessary conditions for the event's
occurrence now can be expressed as follows:

$$\forall x, y, t, e \,.\, \text{STACK}(x, y, t, e) \supset$$
$$Clear(x, pre1(e)) \wedge Holding(x, con1(e)) \wedge Clear(x, eff1(e)) \wedge$$
$$Clear(y, pre2(e)) \wedge On(x, y, eff2(e)).$$

Again, the combination of this axiom and the temporal structure axiom is
shown graphically in Figure 4.

This axiom asserts what is true whenever a stacking event occurs,
independent of the situation. Other knowledge about events is relevant
only in certain situations (that is, the event has conditional effects). For
instance, if the block being moved in a stacking action was initially on
another block, then this other block becomes clear. This is expressed in the
logic by the following axiom, which states that if block x was initially on
another block z, then z becomes clear when x is moved:

$$\forall x, y, z, t, e, t' \,.\, \text{STACK}(x, y, t, e) \wedge On(x, z, t') \wedge Overlaps(t', t) \supset$$
$$\exists T, t'' \,.\, t' \sqsubseteq T \wedge On(x, z, T) \wedge T : con1(e) \wedge Clear(z, t'') \wedge T : t''.$$

Of course, if the only events we needed to represent were simple events
such as occur in the blocks world, then the temporal logic would be overkill.
But we are interested in much more realistic events, where we may have
significant knowledge about how the world changes as the event occurs. As
a quick example, consider the event of a cup filling up with water. At the
end the cup is full, but while the event is occurring, the level of the water is
continually increasing. Commonsense knowledge about this event is easily
captured in the interval logic. For instance, the fact that the level of the
water continues to rise throughout the event is captured by the following
axiom:

$$\forall c, e, t \,.\, \text{FILL}(c, t, e) \supset$$
$$\forall t', t'' \,.\, (t' \sqsubset t) \wedge (t'' \sqsubset t) \wedge (t' \prec: t'') \supset$$
$$level(c, t') < level(c, t''),$$

where $level(c, t)$ is now an interval-valued function that gives the range of
level of the water in the cup over time t. This axiom captures the intuition

that the water continually rises quite simply and directly without making a commitment to a continuous model of change. In order to draw conclusions from axioms such as this one, we would need to develop the mathematics of interval-valued functions in some detail. Van Bentham (van Benthem, 1983) presents several definitions of continuous functions in interval-based theories. Dealing with events that involve such "continuous change" is not the focus of this chapter, however, and most of our examples will involve the very simple actions that are common in the literature on planning and reasoning about action.

Finally, some might wonder why the logic has no separate mechanism for describing processes, as was present in (Allen, 1984). While this may ultimately be necessary, the existing formalism already supports a wide range of "process-like" predicates. In particular, you can define a property that is true only when an event is occurring. In the above example about the cup, we could define a predicate $CupFilling$ as

$$\forall c, t \,.\, CupFilling(c, t) \equiv \exists t', e \,.\, t \sqsubseteq t' \wedge \text{FILL}(c, t', e)$$

Note that by this definition, $CupFilling$ is a homogeneous predicate, as expected for properties. The place where problems arise with this simple approach is in dealing with the imperfective paradox. For instance, you might want to say that a person was crossing the street at some time t, even if they changed their mind at the last minute and went back to the original side. This problem has been studied extensively in the philosophical literature, but has not been a focus for our work as it does not seem to arise naturally in the planning domains we have studied.

7.3.4. THE LOGIC OF ACTIONS

The representation of events described in the previous section does not adequately capture knowledge of causality. In particular, the formulas above do not state what properties are caused by the stacking action or what properties simply must be true whenever the action succeeds. This is the distinction that STRIPS makes between preconditions and effects. Intuitively, it is evident that the stacking action causes block A to be on block B in situations where both blocks are clear at the start of the action. Furthermore, the stacking action causes block B to become not clear while it does not affect the condition that block A is clear.

To encode such knowledge, we need to be able to reason about attempting to perform an action. To do this, we need to better define the distinction between events and actions. So far, we have only talked about events occurring. The assertion that Jack lifted the ball onto the table describes an event in which Jack performed some action that resulted in the ball being lifted onto the table. The action Jack performed — namely, the lifting — was realized by some set of motions that Jack performed in order to lift the ball. If Jack were a robot, the action would be the execution of a program that involved the correct control sequences given perceptual input. Thus, in a robot world the action corresponds to the program, whereas the event corresponds to a situation in which the program was executed successfully.

As noted in Section 7.2.1, for every action there is a corresponding event consisting of an agent performing that action. We will often exploit this by using the same names for events and actions. Thus the STACK(x, y, t, e) predicate presented in the previous section might correspond to the action term $stack(x, y)$ that denotes a program where x and y correspond to the blocks being stacked. Of course, there are other events that do not involve actions. For example, natural forces (such as the wind blowing) result in events but do not involve action in the sense we are using it. Actions may be arbitrarily complex activities and can be decomposable into other less complex actions, which themselves may be decomposable, until a certain basic level of action is attained. The primitive actions are called the *basic* actions following (Goldman, 1970).

The predicate Try is defined on programs, such that $Try(\pi, t)$ is true only if the program π is executed over time t.[59] As with event predicates, Try is antihomogeneous. We can now assert an axiom defining the conditions sufficient to guarantee successful action attempts. In the case of stacking, whenever the agent tries to stack x on y starting in a situation where x and y are clear, then a stacking event occurs that is temporally constrained by the initial conditions:

$$\forall x, y, t, j, k \,.\, Try(stack(x, y), t) \wedge Clear(x, j) \wedge Overlaps(j, t) \wedge$$
$$Clear(y, k) \wedge SameEnd(k, t) \supset \exists e \,.\, \text{STACK}(x, y, t, e)$$

More realistic versions of this axiom might include duration constraints, and our theory can also have constraints on t such that $Try(\pi, t)$ is true (for example, that it is tried for long enough).

It is important to consider why the information about stacking is captured by two different sets of related axioms: one capturing the necessary conditions whenever a stacking event occurs (Section 7.3.3), and the other relating action attempts to event occurrences (above). This is because the two sets of axioms represent two very different sources of knowledge. The first defines knowledge about what the world is necessarily like whenever the event occurs successfully, while the second defines the abilities of the agent in causing events. In many situations, an agent may know the former but not the latter. For example, we all can recognize that the mechanic fixed our car, even if we have no idea what enabled the mechanic to do the job. Knowledge of this sort is also essential for much of natural language semantics, where many verbs are defined and used without the agent's knowing the necessary causal knowledge. Allen (Allen, 1984) discusses this at length.

To summarize the development thus far, we can partition our axioms describing events and actions into three broad categories:

- *Event definitions* (EDEF): These are axioms of the form

$$\forall e \,.\, E(e) \wedge \phi \supset \psi,$$

where E is an event-type predicate and ϕ and ψ contain no event predicates. The necessary conditions for stacking given in the previous section fall into this category.

- *Action definitions* (ETRY): These are axioms of the form

$$\forall t, \ldots \,.\, Try(\pi, t) \wedge \phi \supset \exists e \,.\, E(e) \wedge t \circ time(e) \wedge \psi,$$

where again E is an event predicate. In this case, ψ represents constraints on e, and can involve other quantified variables. The symbol "o" stands for the temporal relation between the action and the event, typically "*Equal*" or "*Meets*", as discussed above.

- *Event generation axioms* (EGEN): These are of the form

$$\forall e \,.\, E(e) \wedge \phi \supset \exists e' \,.\, E'(e') \wedge \psi.$$

Again, E and E' are event-type predicates and ϕ and ψ represent constraints on the events. The classic example of event generation is represented in English using the "by" locution — for example, signaling a turn by waving one's arm, under appropriate conditions. More concrete examples will be presented in later sections.

Examples of all three classes of axioms will be presented in the next section when we describe application of the formalism to a set of problems from the literature on reasoning about action.

7.3.5. DISCUSSION

Having introduced our representation of time, actions, and events, we can now compare it to other formalisms. Note that this comparison is based on the expressiveness and simplicity of the logic for capturing commonsense knowledge. Dealing with prediction is a separate issue for most of these formalisms and will be discussed at the end of the next section.

As discussed previously, most formalisms have not included an explicit model of time but base their model on states or situations. To handle explicit temporal relations in the situation calculus, a function can be defined that maps a state or situation to a timepoint. In this way, the situation calculus defines a point-based branching time model. A duration function on actions can be defined that allows one to compute the time of the resulting situation given the initial situation (Gelfond et al., 1991). Within the constructive models, however, the range of temporal reasoning that can be performed is severely limited. First, note that there are no situations defined during the time an action is executing. This means that you cannot assert anything about the world during an action execution. Rather, all effects of an action must be packaged into the resulting situation. As a consequence, all effects start simultaneously. Since situations correspond to time points, the formalism also has no mechanism for representing knowledge about how long an effect might hold, as time only moves forward as a result of an action. The only way around this seems to be to allow null actions that move time forward but have no effect, which is neither convenient or intuitive.

As a consequence, the only worlds easily represented by the constructive situation calculus are those that remain static except when the agent acts, and where nothing important happens while actions are being executed. Of course, if one abandons the requirement of a constructive theory, then more complicated scenarios can be represented. In fact, in some approaches (for example, (Shanahan, 1990)) even continuous change has been represented. The primary mechanism that enables this, however, is the exploitation of the mapping from situations to times, and the introduction of situations that are not the result of any actions. Given these radical extensions, it is not clear to us what the advantage is in retaining the situation calculus as the underlying theory, rather than moving to the simpler, more direct, explicit temporal logic. Temporal logic gives properties, actions, and events equal temporal status, allowing complex situations to be captured quite directly in a manner similar to how they are intuitively described.

There is no explicit representation of events in the situation calculus, which makes it difficult to represent knowledge of the actual world. For instance, it is not possible to directly assert that an event E will occur tomorrow or even that the agent will perform an action A tomorrow. In the constructive situation calculus, one would have to quantify over all action sequences and ensure that the event or action was present. This does not seem workable, and recent attempts to represent the actual events generally abandon the constructive approach and have to introduce an explicit new construct for events (see, for example, (Miller and Shanahan, 1994)). The resulting formalism is again closer to what we propose, and we question the advantage of retaining the original situation calculus framework.

The event calculus (Kowalski and Sergot, 1986) has an explicit notion of event that corresponds more closely to our notion of events. This is not surprising as both this formalism and our own development of the temporal logic are based on intuitions about the close relationship between time and events. The event calculus does not seem to have a separate notion of actions, although formulas of the form $act(E, give(a, x, y))$ are used that suggest they might. As far as we can tell, however, this is only a syntactic mechanism for naming events. Reasoning in the event calculus is driven by the events that occur, as it is in our approach, but the relationship between the behaviors that an agent might perform and the events that the agent causes is not explored.

Closest to our representation is that described by McDermott (McDermott, 1985). He does distinguish between actions (which he calls *tasks*) and events and uses an explicit model of time. As a result, he can define notions such as a successful action attempt and explicitly reason about an agent's actions and what events they will cause. His representation of time has many similarities to the work that extends the situation calculus with a time line (Pinto, 1994), and he explores the consequences of adding explicit time to such a model in depth. A significant difference between our approaches is that we use an interval-based logic, while McDermott uses a continuous point-based model. These differences have been discussed in detail elsewhere (see, for example, (van Benthem, 1983; Allen, 1984; Shoham, 1988b)).

7.4. Reasoning About Action in Simple Domains

As mentioned in the introduction, there are three major reasoning tasks we require the logic of events and actions to support: prediction, planning, and explanation. Of these, prediction is the most basic capability: given a description of the world and a set of actions and events that will occur, what can we conclude about the past, present, and future? With a temporal logic, the initial world description might already contain some information about the past or the future — say, some external events that will occur or future actions that the agent knows it will perform. The prediction task reduces to predicting the effects of new actions and events that are posited to occur, and updating the world model accordingly. Neither planning nor explanation can be accomplished without a model of prediction. In planning, for instance, the task is to find a set of actions that will accomplish a given set of goals. This can be divided into two abstract tasks: generating a candidate set of actions and evaluating whether the plan will succeed. This latter task is exactly the prediction task. Explanation can be similarly decomposed into generating a possible set of events that might explain the observations and then verifying whether the events would actually cause the observed effects. Of course, any particular algorithm might not divide the reasoning into two explicit steps. In fact, most planning algorithms exploit a specific prediction model in order to suggest actions likely to produce a good plan, but all systems are based on some prediction model, which typically is based on the STRIPS assumptions (for example, (Nilsson, 1980; Chapman, 1987; McAllester and Rosenblitt, 1991)).

7.4.1. FRAME AXIOMS AND EXPLANATION CLOSURE

The problem is that the STRIPS assumptions do not hold in most realistic situations that one needs to reason about. The situation calculus and temporal logic-based approaches do not have to operate with such assumptions. As a result, these theories themselves make little commitment to how the state resulting from an action relates to the state before the action. Rather the properties of the resulting state must be specified axiomatically, and the frame problem involves how best to specify these properties. The original proposal for the situation calculus (McCarthy and Hayes, 1969) was to use *frame axioms*, which explicitly stated which properties are not changed by the actions. Explicit frame axioms have come under criticism, primarily because there are too many of them, both to write down explicitly and to reason with efficiently.

There are several ways to try to overcome this problem. Many researchers abandon frame axioms altogether and have built models that use persistence or inertia assumptions (see, for example, (Lifschitz, 1987a; Shoham, 1988b)). These approaches assume that all changes caused by an action are specified and every property not asserted to change does not change. This technique has much to recommend it, as it eliminates the need to enumerate frame axioms, but in its simple form it tends to be too strong. In particular, if there is uncertainty as to whether a property might change or not, techniques based on this approach will often incorrectly assume that the change does not occur. Other approaches work instead by minimizing event or action occurrences. Properties are assumed to change only as a result of events defined in the representation, and logically unnecessary events do not occur (for example, (Georgeff, 1986b; Georgeff, 1986a; Morgenstern and Stein, 1988)). These approaches show more promise at handling more complex situations and have many similarities to our work.

The approach we take, however, retains the flavor of explicit frame axioms. Rather than specifying for each action whether each property changes or not, however, one specifies for each property what events can change it. The problem of reasoning about changes then reduces to the problem of reasoning about what events may or may not have occurred. This technique is called the *explanation closure* approach and was proposed by Haas (Haas, 1987) and Schubert (Schubert, 1990). Schubert has shown that such a technique can dramatically reduce the number of frame axioms required to produce a workable set of axioms for a problem. Of course, assumptions must still be made. As in other approaches, we assume that unnecessary events do not occur, but this is specified axiomatically rather than being built into the semantic model. This has several advantages. Most important, the resulting axioms can be interpreted with the standard semantics of the first-order predicate calculus, meaning that there are well-defined notions of entailment and proof. We can show that our representation handles a particular class of examples by showing a proof of the desired consequences, without needing to appeal to model-theoretic arguments in a nonstandard semantics. In addition, various forms of uncertainty are handled using the standard methods in logic with disjunction and existential quantification. Finally, the assumptions that are made appear explicitly as axioms in the system. While not exploited in this chapter, this allows for explicit reasoning about the assumptions underlying a line of reasoning (see

(Ferguson and Allen, 1994; Ferguson and Allen, 1993; Allen, 1991; Ferguson, 1992)).

If you are willing to reinstate strong assumptions about the domain, roughly equivalent to the STRIPS assumptions, then Reiter (Reiter, 1992) has shown that the explanation closure axioms can be computed automatically using predicate completion techniques. But this close correspondence breaks down in more complex domains. Schubert (Schubert, 1990) argues that explanation closure is distinct from predicate completion or biconditionalization and thus that the axioms cannot be generated automatically. Specifically, he argues that any automatic procedure will produce axioms that are too strong in cases where knowledge of the world is incomplete and actions may have conditional effects. In addition, he argues that explanation closure axioms have "epistemic content" and are independently motivated by other problems such as language understanding. As such, they form a crucial body of knowledge necessary for many commonsense reasoning tasks.

The development to follow in the rest of this section does not demonstrate the full power of our approach, as it does not consider simultaneous actions and external events. This will facilitate the comparison of our work to other approaches. More complex cases are considered in detail in (Allen and Ferguson, 1994). Because of the simple nature of the problems, the closure axioms can be classified into two classes, corresponding to two assumptions: no properties change unless explicitly changed by an event occurring, and no events occur except as the result of the actions. Although these are difficult to precisely describe schematically, they look something like the following following:

- *Strong closure on properties* (EXCP): Every property change results from the occurrence of an instance of one of the event types defined in the axioms. These axioms are of the form:

$$\forall t, t' \,.\, P(t) \wedge \neg P(t') \wedge t : t' \supset \exists e \,.\, (E_1(e) \vee E_2(e) \vee \ldots) \wedge time(e) : t',$$

where the E_i are the event-type predicates that (possibly) affect the truth value of P. These axioms are derived from the event definition axioms (EDEF).

- *Strong closure on events* (EXCE): Every event that occurs does so as a result of some action being attempted, possibly indirectly via event generation. These axioms are of the form: "$\forall e \,.\, E(e) \supset \phi_1 \vee \phi_2 \vee \ldots,$" where ϕ_i is either of the form

$$\exists t \,.\, Try(\pi, t) \wedge t \circ time(e) \wedge \psi,$$

for π an action term and "$\circ$" a temporal relation (typically "$=$"), or of the form

$$\exists e' \,.\, E'(e') \wedge time(e) \circ time(e') \wedge \psi,$$

for E' an event-type predicate. These axioms can often be derived from the action definition (ETRY) and event generation (EGEN) axioms.

7.4.2. EXAMPLE

By way of illustrating the application of the logic and the explanation closure technique, we now present the formalizations of one of the standard problems from the literature on reasoning about action, taken from the Sandewall Test Suite (Sandewall, 1994a). In (Allen and Ferguson, 1994), we consider a much wider range of problems from the test suite.

Consider our formulation of the basic Yale shooting problem (YSP). The scenario involves a hapless victim, Fred, who apparently sits idly by while an adversary loads a gun, waits some period of time, and shoots (at Fred). The question is whether Fred is dead or not, or rather whether an axiomatization of the problem in some logical system allows the conclusion that Fred is dead to be derived. This simple problem has generated an extensive body of literature (see (Brown, 1987)). In most cases, the issue is that while the loadedness of the gun ought to persist through the waiting (and then the shooting succeeds in killing Fred), Fred's "aliveness" ought not to persist through the shooting (indeed, cannot, without risk of inconsistency), although it should persist through the loading and waiting. On the other hand, there might be nonstandard models where the gun somehow becomes unloaded, in which case the shooting would fail to kill Fred.

Figure 5 shows the axioms for the YSP in our logic; they are depicted graphically in Figure 6. Recall that the EDEF axioms describe the necessary conditions for event occurrence and the ETRY axioms describe the sufficient

EDEF1 $\forall e \, . \, \text{LOAD}(e) \quad \supset \quad Loaded(eff1(e)) \wedge time(e) : eff1(e)$

EDEF2 $\forall e \, . \, \text{SHOOT}(e) \supset$
$\qquad Loaded(pre1(e)) \wedge SameEnd(pre1(e), time(e)) \wedge$
$\qquad \neg Loaded(eff1(e)) \wedge time(e) : eff1(e) \wedge$
$\qquad \neg Alive(eff2(e)) \wedge time(e) : eff2(e)$

ETRY1 $\forall t \, . \, Try(load, t) \quad \supset \quad \exists e \, . \, \text{LOAD}(t, e)$

ETRY2 $\forall t \, . \, Try(shoot, t) \wedge Loaded(t) \quad \supset \quad \exists e \, . \, \text{SHOOT}(t, e)$

Figure 5.   Basic axioms for the Yale shooting problem

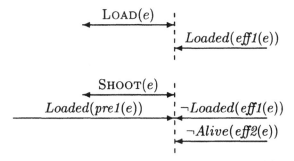

Figure 6.   The LOAD and SHOOT event definitions

conditions relating program executions (actions) and events. For loading, these are both almost trivial: any attempt to load will cause a LOAD event (ETRY1), and this will entail that the gun is loaded immediately thereafter (EDEF1). A successful SHOOT event, on the other hand, entails that the gun is loaded beforehand, that it is unloaded afterwards, and also that Fred is dead afterwards (EDEF2). Attempting the shooting action will be successful in causing such an event if the gun was loaded at the time of the shooting (ETRY2). Of course, the example axioms are very simple: there are only temporal roles, and there are no generation axioms (yet).

Figure 7 gives the explanation closure axioms corresponding to the event and action axioms in Figure 5. Given the simple actions and strong assumptions made in the problem formulation, an automatic procedure could probably devised to generate them. But notice that the closure axioms are not simply a strengthening of the implication to a biconditional. In particular, the EXCP2b axiom does not say that every SHOOT event causes a transition from alive to dead, just that every such transition is the result of a SHOOT. This would allow one to shoot things that are already dead, for example.

We can now present the axiomatization of the YSP scenario. Initially

EXCP1 $\forall t, t'$. $\neg Loaded(t) \wedge Loaded(t') \wedge t : t' \supset$
$$\exists e . \text{LOAD}(e) \wedge time(e) : t'$$

EXCP2a $\forall t, t'$. $Loaded(t) \wedge \neg Loaded(t') \wedge t : t' \supset$
$$\exists e . \text{SHOOT}(e) \wedge time(e) : t'$$

EXCP2b $\forall t, t'$. $Alive(t) \wedge \neg Alive(t') \wedge t : t' \supset$
$$\exists e . \text{SHOOT}(e) \wedge time(e) : t'$$

EXCE1 $\forall e . \text{LOAD}(e) \quad \supset \quad \exists t . Try(load, t) \wedge t = time(e)$

EXCE2 $\forall e . \text{SHOOT}(e) \quad \supset \quad \exists t . Try(shoot, t) \wedge t = time(e)$

Figure 7. Explanation closure axioms for the YSP

a turkey (taking the role of Fred) is alive, and the gun is not loaded. The agent loads the gun, waits, and shoots. We are to show that the turkey is dead sometime after the shooting. At issue is the persistence of loadedness through the waiting and the nonpersistence of aliveness through the shooting. The following axioms describe the scenario:

AX0 $t0 \prec t1 \prec t2 \prec t3$

AX1 $Alive(t0)$

AX2 $\neg Loaded(t0)$

AX3 $Try(load, t1)$

AX4 $Try(shoot, t3)$

AX5 $\forall a, t . Try(a, t) \equiv (a = load \wedge t = t1) \vee (a = shoot \wedge t = t3)$

The final axiom is the important assumption that we attempt only the given actions. With the EXCE axioms, this ensures that "nothing else happens," which drives the explanation closure method. Note that the formalism does not require such an assumption. Rather, we are making explicit an aspect of the scenario that is usually implicit and accomplished via some form of semantic minimization.

To Prove: $\exists t . \neg Alive(t) \wedge t3 \prec: t$

Since there are no preconditions for loading, AX3 and ETRY1 give

$$\exists e_1 . \text{LOAD}(t1, e_1),$$

then EDEF1 gives

$$Loaded(\mathit{eff1}(e_1)) \wedge t1 : \mathit{eff1}(e_1).$$

That is, the loading succeeds, and the gun is loaded, at least immediately afterward. Now, suppose that

$$Loaded(t3) \qquad \qquad (*)$$

— that is, the gun remains loaded until the shooting is attempted. In that case, AX4 and ETRY2 give $\exists e_3$. SHOOT($t3, e_3$), and then EDEF2 gives

$$\neg Alive(\mathit{eff2}(e_3)) \wedge t3 : \mathit{eff2}(e_3).$$

That is, the shooting also succeeds, and the turkey is dead afterward, as required.

To show the persistence (∗), suppose otherwise that $\neg Loaded(t3)$. The interval temporal logic theorem DISJ (Section 7.3.2) gives $\mathit{eff1}(e_1) \bowtie t3$, then AX0 and the fact that $t1 : \mathit{eff1}(e_1)$ give $\mathit{eff1}(e_1) \prec: t3$. We apply interval temporal logic axiom TRPT to get

$$\exists T, T' . Loaded(T) \wedge \neg Loaded(T') \wedge T : T' \wedge t3 \sqsubseteq T'.$$

Then, EXCP2a gives

$$\exists e . \text{SHOOT}(e) \wedge time(e) : T'.$$

That is, if the gun became unloaded it must have been because of a shooting. Note that $time(e) \prec: t3$ since $t3 \sqsubseteq T'$ and $time(e) : T'$. Then from EXCE2 we get

$$\exists t . Try(shoot, t) \wedge t = time(e),$$

— that is, if there was a shooting then someone must have tried to shoot. Since $t = time(e) \prec: t3$, we have $t \neq t3$, contradicting AX5.

7.4.3. DISCUSSION

Work on the frame problem investigates methods of making assumptions about the world to predict the likely consequences of actions. There are therefore two separable issues to consider, which have been called the "epistemological" and "computational" aspects of the problem (see (Kowalski, 1992), but also (McCarthy and Hayes, 1969) regarding epistemological and heuristic adequacy). The epistemological aspect concerns what assumptions one makes about the world, while the computational aspect concerns how to compute and use these assumptions in the formalism. For example, it is an epistemological issue whether to make assumptions about property changes as in the persistence-based approaches or to make assumptions about event occurrences. On the other hand, it is a computational issue whether to use minimization techniques in the model theory to implement assumptions or to use explicit axioms, as in the original situation calculus or with the explanation closure technique. We discuss each of these issues separately, although they are, of course, closely related.

Our approach is based on making assumptions about event occurrence, both events caused by actions and external events. In this way, it is similar to work by Morgenstern and Stein (Morgenstern and Stein, 1988), Haas (Haas, 1987), Schubert (Schubert, 1990), and Kowlaski and Sergot (Kowalski and Sergot, 1986). In such approaches, properties do not change unless there is some event that causes them to change. Approaches based on STRIPS-style representations can be viewed in this way as well, except that the assumptions are not a separable part of the formalism. Rather, the representation makes sense only when these assumptions are made. The other major approach focuses on minimizing property change, with additional constraints based on the temporal ordering of properties (see, for example, (Shoham, 1988b; Kautz, 1986)) or minimizing causal relationships (for example, (Lifschitz, 1987a)). Sandewall (Sandewall, 1994a) examines the advantages and limitations of each of these approaches in detail. Most of the approaches that minimize property change cannot handle Sandewall's test suite of problems, let alone be extended to handle external events and simultaneous actions. We find that basing the assumptions on events leads to much more intuitive characterization of problems, where each statement in the logic is closely related to an intuitive fact about the world. In addition, in (Allen and Ferguson, 1994) we show how this approach naturally handles a wide range of more complex problems.

The second issue is what mechanism is used to make the assumptions. There are two main approaches here: explicitly adding axioms that encode the assumptions (for example, (Cordell, 1969; Schubert, 1990)) or using a nonmonotonic model theory that defines a new notion of entailment that includes the assumptions (for example, (McCarthy, 1980; Shoham, 1988b; Baker, 1991; Sandewall, 1994a)). Of course, the work on circumscription shows that model-theoretic techniques always have an equivalent axiomatic formulation, although it may require going beyond standard first-order logic. This equivalence suggests that there is really a continuum of approaches here. Everyone must make assumptions. Some prefer to pack it all in the model theory, others use axioms to capture much of the complexity and use only simple minimization assumptions, while others prefer to encode everything in axioms. Many of the issues come down to ease of formalization, an issue that is bound to vary from researcher to researcher. The reason we prefer explanation closure axioms is that they give us a very flexible system that is easily extended to handle complex issues in representing actions. In addition, the resulting representation is a standard first-order logic, so it is relatively straightforward to tell if certain consequences follow from the axioms. The same cannot be said for approaches based on specialized reasoners or specialized semantic theories that solve one problem at the expense of the others. Schubert (Schubert,

1990) provides an excellent discussion of the advantages of the explanation closure approach.

7.5. External Events and Simultaneous Actions

We now turn our attention to more interesting and complex cases of reasoning about action. This section gives a brief overview of how our formalism handles external events and simultaneous actions — two problems that are beyond the scope of many representations. There is not the space for detailed examples and discussion. The interested reader should see (Allen and Ferguson, 1994) for more detail.

7.5.1. EXTERNAL EVENTS

External events arise for different reasons. Some simply occur as a result of natural forces in the world, whereas others are set into motion by the action of the planning agent. Some external events are predictable: we know, for instance, that the sun will rise tomorrow and that many of the central events of a normal workday will occur. But even when we are certain that a particular event will occur, we are often still uncertain as to when it will occur. Most of the time, for instance, I can only roughly estimate when the sun will rise, but this uncertainty doesn't generally affect my plans. Rather, I know that by a certain time, say 6 a.m. at this time of year, the sun will be up. In most realistic applications, the planning agent will not have complete knowledge of the world and its causal structure, and thus there will be many external events for which it cannot reliably predict whether they will occur or not. Assuming that such events do not occur will lead to highly optimistic plans. Rather, an agent should be able to plan given the uncertainty of external events.

The logic presented in Section 7.3 already provides the formalism for representing external events. In fact, the only way to distinguish external events from events caused by the agent's acting is by the presence of an axiom involving the predicate $Try(\pi, t)$ that states that the event was caused by an action attempt. But there is no requirement that all events have axioms relating them to action attempts.

The complications arise in characterizing the appropriate explanation closure axioms. In particular, if one makes the strong event closure assumptions (as in the previous section), that all events are ultimately caused by some action, then external events caused solely by natural forces or other agents cannot be represented. Of course, the explanation closure approach doesn't require such a strong assumption. If fact, we could simply not have closure axioms for some event classes that are caused by natural forces. But this would then allow such events to interfere with the prediction process at every possible opportunity, as you could never prove that the event didn't occur. While this might be the right result in some situations, usually external events are more constrained.

There are two orthogonal aspects of external events that affect the representation. The first relates to uncertainty about whether the event will occur. A nonprobabilistic logic can only easily represent the two extremes on this scale: either the event definitely will occur, or it may or may not occur. The second relates to the conditions for an event's occurrence. Again, there is a continuum here between a complete lack of constraints on when the event may occur and cases where the event will only occur under specific conditions, such as being caused by the agent's actions. Somewhere in the middle of this scale would be events that may only occur within a certain time period but that are independent of the agent's actions. There are three simple combinations that appear frequently in many domains. These are

- *Triggered events*: The external event will not occur unless it is specifically triggered by an agent's actions (for example, the microwave will heat my coffee only if someone presses the "on" button).
- *Definite events*: The external event will definitely occur, independent of the agent's actions, although the exact time may be uncertain (for example, the sun will rise between 5:30 and 6:30 a.m.).
- *Spontaneous events*: The external event may or may not occur during some time period (for example, I might win the lottery tonight).

Our representation can also handle more complex cases, such as triggered spontaneous events, which become possible only as a result of some action by the agent. We only have space here to consider a simple example of a triggered event. In (Allen and Ferguson, 1994), we present examples showing how definite and spontaneous events are handled.

Triggered events are actually already handled by the development so far. In fact, all events in the last section can be viewed as triggered events that characterize the agent's actions. The same approach can be used to handle other triggered external events.

Sandewall's hiding turkey scenario is quite naturally handled as a simple case of reasoning about triggered external events. In this setting, the turkey may or not be deaf. If it is not deaf, then it will go into hiding when the gun is loaded and thus escape death from the shooting. That is, we are given information about how the turkey will respond to a certain situation — namely, that it will hide if it hears the gun being loaded. We must conclude that after the shooting, either the turkey is alive and not deaf, or it is dead.

Many formalizations of this problem treat the turkey hiding as an conditional effect of loading the gun rather than as an external event. If this approach worked for all triggered external events, then it might be justified. But unfortunately, it works only in the simplest of cases — namely, when the event caused has no structure or temporal complexity and so can be characterized as a static effect. For example, consider a situation where the only place the turkey might hide is in a box, and the box has a door that can be closed by the agent. A natural formalization of this would include the following facts:

- If the turkey is not deaf, it will try to hide when the gun is loaded.
- If the box door is open when the turkey tries to hide, it will be hidden in 30 seconds.

You could capture some of this situation by adding a new effect rule about loading that if the box door is open, the turkey will hide. But it is not clear how you might encode the fact that the turkey is not hidden for 30 seconds, so if you shoot quickly you could still hit it. As the scenario becomes more complicated, more and more information would have to be packed into the loading action rather than the hiding event. Even if this could be done, it would very unintuitive, as it would not allow you to reason about the turkey hiding except in this one case when the agent loads the gun. What if the turkey may hide for other reasons as well, or might spontaneously decide to hide, or always hides between 6 p.m. and 7 p.m.? Clearly, hiding is just as valid an event as any other event (such as loading) and requires similar treatment.

Given all this, let's return to the simple example as originally formulated. Taking $Deaf$ to be an atemporal predicate, the triggering of hiding by loading is captured with a conditional generation axiom:

EGEN3 $\forall e . \text{LOAD}(e) \wedge \neg Deaf \supset \exists e' . \text{HIDE}(e') \wedge time(e) = time(e')$

To capture the simplicity of the original problem and other solutions in the literature, we assume that the hiding is simultaneous with the loading. The more natural formulation would complicate the proof as we would need to reason about whether the agent could shoot while the turkey was trying to hide.

Next, we need to add axioms for hiding events to the YSP axioms from Figure 5. These are

EDEF3 $\forall e . \text{HIDE}(e) \supset Hidden(eff1(e)) \wedge time(e) : eff1(e)$
EXCP3 $\forall t, t' . \neg Hidden(t) \wedge Hidden(t') \wedge t : t' \supset$
$$\exists e . \text{HIDE}(e) \wedge time(e) : t'$$
EXCE3 $\forall e . \text{HIDE}(e) \supset \neg Deaf \wedge \exists e' . \text{LOAD}(e') \wedge time(e') = time(e)$

The EDEF3 axiom simply states that a HIDE event results in the turkey being hidden. EXCP3 is a closure axiom that says that things become hidden only as a result of a HIDE event occurring. Closure axiom EXCE3 is justified by the important information implicit in the problem statement that the turkey does not hide unless it hears the gun being loaded.

We then need to modify the definition of shooting (EDEF2) so that it only kills the turkey if it's not hidden:

EDEF2a $\forall e \,.\, \textsc{Shoot}(e) \supset$
$$Loaded(pre1(e)) \wedge SameEnd(pre1(e), time(e)) \wedge$$
$$\neg Loaded(eff1(e)) \wedge time(e) : eff1(e)$$

EDEF2b $\forall e \,.\, \textsc{Shoot}(e) \wedge \neg Hidden(time(e)) \supset$
$$\neg Alive(eff2(e)) \wedge time(e) : eff2(e)$$

Note that this characterization of a SHOOT event means "the bullet leaving the gun," presumably in the direction of the turkey. It does not mean "kill the turkey," which is rather a conditional effect of the shooting (EDEF2b). The action *shoot* is "pulling the trigger" on this account.

The axioms describing the problem are then as follows (the YSP axioms plus new axioms AXH1 and AXH2):

AX0 $t0 \prec t1 \prec t2 \prec t3$
AX1 $Alive(t0)$
AX2 $\neg Loaded(t0)$
AXH1 $\neg Hidden(t0)$
AXH2 $\forall t, t' \,.\, Hidden(t) \wedge t \prec: t' \supset Hidden(t')$
AX3 $Try(load, t1)$
AX4 $Try(shoot, t3)$
AX5 $\forall a, t \,.\, Try(a, t) \equiv (a = load \wedge t = t1) \vee (a = shoot \wedge t = t3)$

Note that axiom AXH2 simply states that once the turkey is hidden it remains hiding forever. A more realistic axiomatization might allow the possibly of an UNHIDE event, and then provide explanation closure axioms for when it might occur. The details are irrelevant for purposes of the example.

To Prove: $\exists t \,.\, t3 \prec: t \wedge ((Deaf \wedge \neg Alive(t)) \vee (\neg Deaf \wedge Alive(t)))$

The following is a sketch of the proof, since many of the details are similar to the previous proof.

(a) Suppose *Deaf*, so we need to show that the turkey is killed. The issue is whether the turkey is hiding at the time of the shooting — that is, whether $Hidden(t3)$. Suppose it is. Then, from AX0, AXH1, and TRPT we get

$$\exists T, T' \,.\, \neg Hidden(T) \wedge Hidden(T') \wedge T : T' \wedge t3 \sqsubseteq T'.$$

Then EXCP3 gives

$$\exists e \,.\, \textsc{Hide}(e) \wedge time(e) : T'.$$

But then EXCE3 gives $\neg Deaf$, a contradiction, since the turkey only hides if it is not deaf. Thus $\neg Hidden(t3)$. Since the turkey is not hidden when the shooting occurs, axiom EDEF2b allows us to conclude that the turkey is killed afterward, as required assuming that reincarnation is ruled out axiomatically.

(b) Suppose instead $\neg Deaf$, so we need to show that the turkey is not killed. AX3 and ETRY1 give

$$\exists e \, . \, \text{LOAD}(e) \wedge time(e) = t1$$

and then EGEN3 gives

$$\exists e' \, . \, \text{HIDE}(e') \wedge time(e') = t1.$$

That is, the loading succeeds and the turkey hides, since it is not deaf. This is consistent with EXCE3, and then EDEF3 yields $Hidden(eff1(e')) \wedge t1 : eff1(e')$. This persists indefinitely (AXH2), in particular until $pre2(e_3)$, so the shooting fails to kill the turkey (EDEF2b doesn't apply). Thus $Alive$ persists indefinitely starting at $t0$ (EXCP2b, AX5), from which we can derive the desired result.

Triggered events are very useful for characterizing many domains. For example, whenever you press a button to start a machine, you trigger an event. Our formalism allows you to define the behavior of the machine using the full power of the language to describe events. Thus, pressing one button could trigger a complex sequence of events that greatly affects the domain for extended periods of time. A simple example could involve making a simple meal of reheated pizza. The plan is to put the pizza in the microwave oven and then press the start button. While it is cooking, you take a beer out of the refrigerator and get out the dishes. When the microwave beeps, you take out the pizza and eat. The fact that the microwave is running could constrain other actions you can perform during that time. For instance, you couldn't also reheat some coffee using the microwave, as it is in use. Or if the electric service is limited, you might not be able to run the toaster oven at the same time without blowing a fuse. As simple as this scenario sounds, representing it is beyond the capabilities of most formalisms.

7.5.2. DISCUSSION

Most formalisms prohibit external events. For example, action definitions in STRIPS-based systems must encode all changes in the world, so external events are fundamentally banned from analysis. Similarly, the constructive situation calculus has the same problem: since there is no way to express information about what the state of the world is while the action is happening, there is no mechanism for allowing an event to occur while an action is being performed. Lifschitz and Rabinov (Lifschitz and Rabinov,

1989) present a limited mechanism to handle this by allowing "miracles" to occur while an action is performed to explain why its effects are not as expected. But this does not allow external events to occur independently of actions, nor does it give events the first-class status required to represent complex situations. In addition, by minimizing the number of miracles, the approach makes it difficult to handle uncertainty about whether some external event will occur or not. Another possibility would be to encode external events as pseudo-actions so that they can be used in the result function, although they are clearly different from normal actions (for example, the agent couldn't plan to execute them).

Work based on the situation calculus that addresses external events typically rejects the constraints of the constructive approach and uses the more general formalism. In these approaches situations are arbitrary states of the world, not necessarily related to a particular action sequence. In addition, situations can be associated with times from a time line and one can quantify over situations. With this, one can introduce an *Occurs* predicate that asserts that a particular action occurs at a specific time and that is defined by an axiom that quantifies over all situations at that time (see, for example, (Pinto, 1994; Miller and Shanahan, 1994)). This development moves the formalism closer to what we are proposing.

Ultimately, the main difference between our approach and these extended situation calculus representations with explicit time will probably be one of approach. We start from a representation of the actual world (or an agent's beliefs about the world) and must introduce mechanisms to allow reasoning about the effects of possible actions. The situation calculus starts from a representation based on possible futures based on the actions and must introduce mechanisms for dealing with information about the actual world.

7.5.3. SIMULTANEOUS ACTION

There are several levels of difficulty in dealing with simultaneous actions. The model described so far already handles some cases of simultaneous actions — namely,

- When two actions cannot occur simultaneously,
- When they occur simultaneously and are independent of each other, and
- When they together have additional effects that neither one would have individually.

The more difficult case is when two actions partially or conditionally interfere. After first describing how the basic approach handles the three cases above, we discuss some approaches to reasoning about interference.

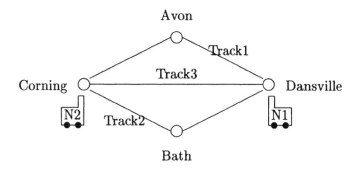

Figure 8.   Example TRAINS domain map

We prefer to use a more complex domain than that of the YSP to illustrate these cases. The TRAINS domain is a transportation and manufacturing domain developed for use in the TRAINS project (Allen and Schubert, 1991; Allen et al., 1995). The goal of the project is to build an intelligent planning assistant that is conversationally proficient in natural language. The domain involves several cities connected by rail links, warehouses, and factories at various cities, and engines, boxcars, and so on to transport goods between them. In this domain, interacting simultaneous actions and external events are unavoidable aspects of the domain.

When actions are independent of each other, the existing formalism does exactly the right thing. The effect of the two actions is simply the sum of the effects of actions individually, a result you get directly from the axioms. When there are simple interactions, such as mutual exclusion of actions under certain circumstances, this behavior typically naturally falls out of a reasonable axiomatization of the domain.

Consider the simple TRAINS domain scenario shown in Figure 8. Now consider simultaneously sending engine N1 to Corning via Bath and sending N2 via Avon to Dansville. A reasonable axiomatization of the move actions will allow us to conclude that both get to their destinations. Now let's assume that, in this domain, only one train can be on a track at a time and that this constraint is captured by an axiom. For instance, we might require that a track be clear for an engine to successfully move along it. With such an axiomatization, if we try to send N1 to Corning via Avon and N2 to Dansville via Avon simultaneously, then one of the move actions will not succeed since one of the tracks along the route will not be clear when needed. More details are given in (Allen and Ferguson, 1994).

Notice that the fact that the actions were attempted is still true. In general, we do not limit action attempts in any way, reflecting a belief that an agent may attempt most actions at any time. If the conditions are not appropriate, the actions simply won't cause the desired events. Of course, we could add additional axioms describing what happens when action attempts interact. For instance, we could add a dramatic axiom that asserts that if two move actions are attempted simultaneously on the same track, the engines crash. More realistically, we might predict a deadlock situation or predict that one will wait while the other passes. The point here is that the temporal logic provides a fairly natural way to axiomatize the knowledge in this domain so as to capture the desired behavior.

Another form of interaction between simultaneous action attempts are resource conflicts. For instance, in the TRAINS domain, an engine requires fuel to make trips. If two engines are planning trips but there is only enough fuel at the station for one, then only one engine can succeed. Many of these cases require reasoning about quantities, which would introduce many complications not necessary to make the points in this chapter. But some resources can be modeled as unitary: either you have the resource or you don't. In these cases, the techniques used above can be adapted to resources. In fact, you can view the track in the previous example as a resource required by an engine to make a trip and the problem where the engines try to use the same track as a resource conflict.

Other constraints on simultaneous action arise because of limitations on the part of the agent. While often such restrictions can be cast in terms of resource conflicts, the temporal logic also allows specific axioms about action co-occurrence. For instance, say a engineer cannot try to couple one car and decouple another at the same time. This constraint can be simply captured by the axiom

$$\forall n, c, c', t, t' \,.\, Try(couple(n, c), t) \wedge Try(decouple(n, c'), t') \supset t \bowtie t'.$$

This axiom would make a set of assertions where an agent simultaneously attempted to couple one car and decouple another inconsistent. Axioms like this can be very useful in defining simple planning systems similar to nonlinear planners (see, for example, (Allen and Koomen, 1983)).

It is also easy to define additional synergistic effects that occur when two actions occur simultaneously. For instance, you can define events that occur only when several actions are performed simultaneously. Thus, if one agent lifts one end of a piano while another agent lifts the other end, then the entire piano is lifted off the floor. Such situations are easily described in our representation. For example, assuming axioms for a *lift* action that causes LIFT events, we could specify how the simultaneous lifting of both ends o. .he piano results in the piano being lifted using a generation axiom such as

$$\forall p, t, e1, e2 \,.\, \text{LIFT}(left(p), t, e1) \wedge \text{LIFT}(right(p), t, e2) \supset \exists e3 \,.\, \text{LIFT}(p, t, e3).$$

Complications in handling simultaneous actions arise when they partially interfere with each other or interfere under certain conditions. Note that with our view of events as classifications of patterns of change, it makes no sense to talk about events interfering with each other. The same world cannot be characterized by two events whose definitions are mutually inconsistent. Interference makes sense only when talking about actions. For instance, if an agent is trying to open a door, then it is performing a *push* action hoping to cause an OPENDOOR event. If, simultaneously, another agent pushes on the door the other way, then the first agent will still have performed the *push* action, but the OPENDOOR event will not have occurred. Thus, we say that the two *push* actions interfered with each other. In this case, they cancelled each other out. Of course, action attempts might also be affected by external events that are occurring simultaneously.

When an action interacts with other events that are occurring, the interaction can be treated much the same as we handled conditional effects of action attempts when different properties hold. This technique formalizes the problem in terms of events, and the different effects result from synergistic interaction between events. For example, consider a situation where we want to load a boxcar from an automatic hopper. If we push the start button, the hopper tips and dumps its cargo into the boxcar. This, of course, requires that the boxcar be in the appropriate location under the hopper. If the boxcar was not under the hopper to start with, it is clear that the loading of the car would not occur although the hopper would still be emptied. The more interesting case occurs when the boxcar is initially under the hopper but then moves away while being loaded. Intuitively, we say that the moving of the boxcar interferes with the loading of the car. Again, the hopper would still end up empty, but the boxcar would not contain all the cargo. An axiomatization of this example can be found in (Allen and Ferguson, 1994).

7.5.4. DISCUSSION

For the most part, treatments of simultaneous actions in the literature are limited. As mentioned earlier, STRIPS-based systems (see, for example, (Tate, 1977; Vere, 1983; Wilkins, 1988)) allow simultaneity only when the actions are independent. A few others (such as (Pednault, 1986)) allow for synergistic effects cast in terms of domain constraints on states (for example, in any state s, if the left side of the piano is lifted, and the right side is lifted, then the piano is lifted).

The situation calculus shows more promise with the introduction of action composition operators. For instance, given two actions a_1 and a_2, then the action $a_1 + a_2$ is the action of performing the two simultaneously (see, for example, (Gelfond et al., 1991; Schubert, 1990)). Explicit axioms can then be given for these complex actions, and mechanisms can be introduced to automatically derive such axioms from the individual actions if they are independent of each other (see (Lin and Shoham, 1992)). If the actions are not independent of each other, some reasonable solutions can be found and, as long as actions are instantaneous, it appears that the theory can remain constructive. But these approaches do not seem to be easily extended to handle the more complex cases in which actions have duration and may be temporally related in complex ways. Pelavin (Pelavin, 1991) contains an extensive analysis of the problems that arise in general with simultaneous interacting actions.

Our approach provides a range of techniques for representing information about interacting actions. In cases where one has detailed knowledge of the causal structure of a domain, the problems can usually be reduced to a level of independent events, and knowledge about interactions is captured by event generation axioms. In other cases, it is more natural to have explicit knowledge about how certain actions interact with events. We believe this flexibility is important for building comprehensive knowledge bases that contain information about a wide range of situations and that are applicable for different reasoning tasks. In addition, we have shown that we can handle these complex cases without introducing any new mechanisms beyond the basic logic discussed in Section 7.3.

7.6. Problems and Future Work

One of the most significant open issues in this chapter has to do with temporal durations. A realistic characterization of almost all the examples in this chapter would require such a capability. For instance, it is not realistic to say that if an agent tries to turn the ignition on the car for any length of time, then the engine will start. If the action is tried for too short a time, the engine probably won't catch. And if the action is tried for too long a time, the starting motor will burn out. So durations play a critical role. At first glance, adding durations does not pose a problem. One simply defines a function that, given an interval, returns a value on some metric scale. A small number of axioms are required to define the appropriate properties of this function. We have not pursued this here as it would further complicate the examples and remove attention from our main points, and in any case, this simple metric model doesn't solve the problem. Consider the action of starting the engine again. There is no minimum time or maximum time within which the engine is guaranteed to start. The duration required depends on the condition of the car, the weather, and many other factors that the agent simply won't have access to. A better formalization of the durational constraints would be that the agent turns the ignition until the engine starts, or a certain time elapses and the agent gives up for fear of burning out the motor, or the battery runs flat. The logic we propose offers no direct solution to this problem, and it remains an important challenge.

Another important issue is the introduction of probabilistic knowledge. By staying within standard first order logic, for example, we are restricted to saying that an event will definitely occur or that it might possibly occur. We cannot say that an event is very likely to occur, or that it is very unlikely to occur. Such knowledge is crucial for predicting the likely effects of actions and thus for evaluating the likelihood of success for proposed plans. Further, since all formalisms must make assumptions, the ultimate evaluation should be based on how likely the assumptions are to hold. This is another motivation for favoring the explanation closure technique. It makes the assumptions that are made explicit, and thus potentially available for probabilistic analysis. Some initial work on this is described in (Martin, 1993; Martin and Allen, 1993). It is much more difficult to see how techniques that build the assumptions into the semantic model could be extended to support probabilistic reasoning.

Finally, it needs to be acknowledged that formalizing knowledge using the more expressive temporal representation can be difficult. Subtle differences in meaning and interactions between axioms may be more common than in less powerful representations, and more experimentation is needed in building knowledge bases based on our representation. But it seems to us that this is the price to pay if we want to move beyond Yale shooting and the blocks world. Our representation is based on intuitions about the way people describe and reason about actions in language, which we believe makes it more natural, intuitive, and grounded in common sense.

7.7. Conclusion

Many of the techniques we have proposed have appeared in various forms previously in the literature. What makes this work novel is the combination of the techniques into a unified and what we think is an intuitive and relatively simple framework. This logic has the following features:

- It can express complex temporal relationships because of its underlying temporal logic.
- It supports explicit reasoning about action attempts and the events they cause, which allows explicit reasoning about success and failure of attempted actions, and subsumes work on conditional effects.
- It handles external events in a natural way, making only minimal distinctions between external events and events caused by the acting agent.
- It handles simultaneous actions in a direct manner, including cases of simultaneously interacting actions.

By using an explicit temporal logic with events, we have been able to handle all these problems within a standard first-order logic. We believe this formalism to be more powerful than competing approaches. We also believe that it is simpler than these other formalisms will be once they are extended to handle the temporal complexities of realistic domains, assuming they can be successfully extended.

The second contribution of this chapter has been to add to the argument that explicit frame axioms, based on the explanation closure approach, produce a viable theory of prediction with some attractive formal and practical properties. On the formal side, this approach does not require the introduction of specialized syntactic constructs into the language or the use of nonmonotonic semantic theories. On the practical side, the closure axioms capture knowledge that is required in any case as part of the specification of the domain. Note that the formulation of the temporal logic and the use of explanation closure are separable issues. We would not be surprised if the nonmonotonic techniques in the literature could be adapted to our temporal logic. Whether this could be done without extending the syntax with special operators specifically introduced to enable the right minimizations is more questionable, however. The risk is that such operators might subtly affect the range of situations that can be handled and may require nonintuitive formulations of problems.

While this chapter has focused on formal issues, it is important to remember that our goal is actually the development of practical planning and natural language understanding systems. As a result, another key requirement on this model is that it provides insight and guidance in developing effective knowledge representation systems. We are using this formalism in the TRAINS project (Allen and Schubert, 1991; Ferguson and Allen, 1994; Allen et al., 1995). We have found that it allows us to express the content of natural language utterances quite directly and supports plan reasoning algorithms similar to those in the planning literature. The use of explicit assumptions and closure reasoning is essential in such an interactive system where plans are formed based on assumptions and where those assumptions are often the subject of the conversation.

Acknowledgments

A longer version of this chapter originally appeared in *Journal of Logic and Computation* 4(5), 531–579 (1994). This material is based on work supported by the National Science Foundation under Grant number IRI-9003841. This work was also supported by ONR/ARPA research grant no. N00014-92-J-1512 and by Air Force – Rome Air Development Center research contract no. F30602-91-C-0010.

Notes

[57] We are indebted to Nort Fowler for making this clear.

[58] The logic containing reified events also allows one to discuss events that do not occur. In particular, asserting that an event instance exists does not necessarily entail that it occurred. A new predicate *Occurs* can be introduced and the assertion that Jack lifted the ball (at time $t1$) would be represented as $\exists e \,.\, \text{LIFT}(jack34, ball26, t1, e) \wedge Occurs(e)$. Using an explicit *Occurs* predicate allows events to exist even if they do not actually occur, or could never occur. We will not need this expressive power in this chapter so will proceed under the interpretation that only events that occur exist. Not having to put the *Occurs* predicate in each formula will simplify the presentation.

[59] In previous work (such as, (Allen, 1991)), we included the event "caused" by attempting the action as an argument to the *Try* predicate. The problem with this is that we might want to categorize the "caused" event in several ways (that is, using several event predicates).

8. Probabilistic Projection in Planning

Drew McDermott

8.1. The Problem

Automated planners need to do temporal reasoning— that is, to decide what will be true at various times if their plans are executed, in support of planning operations (such as reordering plan steps) that depend on when various facts become true or false during plan execution. The main line of research in this area is to represent a plan as a partially ordered list of events, and to attempt to infer what must be true before or after each event. In many such efforts, it is assumed that the events' effects are all known and context-independent, so that the fact P is true after event e if and only if there is some event e' preceding or coinciding with e that has P as an effect, and such that for every event e'' with $\neg P$ as an effect, e'' precedes e' or follows e (McAllester and Rosenblitt, 1991; Dean and McDermott, 1987; Chapman, 1987; Allen, 1984; van Beek, 1992).

However, in general the effects of an event depend on what is true before the event, and in this more general setting the problem becomes much harder (Dean and Boddy, 1988a). One way to cope with the complexity is to stop trying to work with a partial ordering representing a set of possible total orderings. Instead, decouple the plan from the temporal database completely. Given a plan, we can generate several *projections* of the plan, each of which is a totally ordered possible execution scenario. Now, instead of asking, What must be true in all projections?, we can ask, What is true in the sample of projections generated so far? There are several advantages to this approach:

- Plans can remain partially ordered. In fact, they can become arbitrary programs, as long as it is possible to predict how they might be executed at some level of detail.

- The inference machinery for each projection can be fast and simple.
- The more projections the planner generates, the more it learns about the current plan. Under time pressure, it can generate fewer projections.
- Probabilistic world models can be handled.

In this chapter, I describe an algorithm for probabilistic, totally ordered database management. The planning algorithm this fits into is described in (McDermott, 1992b; Beetz and McDermott, 1994). Here is a brief description of how this planning system is supposed to work: we assume the existence of a *plan library,* a collection of *default plans* that can make progress toward goals, even in the presence of some disturbances. Default plans to carry out users' commands can be assembled quickly just by retrieval from this plan library. However, in the presence of multiple commands or special circumstances, the default plan assemblage may not be optimal or even correct. It is the job of the planner to try to improve it, by *projecting* the current best version of the plan and using the resulting *projections* to suggest ways the plan might be improved. The suggestions come from *critics,* specialized programs that look for particular patterns of degraded performance and couple them to standard *plan transformations* that can often eliminate those patterns. For example, there is a critic that looks for instances where the subplan P_1 for one user command causes a proposition Q to become false that some other subplan P_2 for another command is trying to keep true. The critic suggests imposing ordering relations among the steps that require or delete Q. Critics are responsible for providing estimates for how much the plan will improve as a result of carrying out the transformations they recommend. These estimates are used by the planner to decide which transformations to try first.

My focus in this chapter is on the module that generates the projections. Its job is to take a plan and produce a sequence of dated events. Each event occurs at a single time instant. (Events with duration are modeled as beginning at one instant and ending at another.) The job of the temporal inference system is to build a data structure called a *timeline* that records the events and their effects. It starts with a set of initial conditions— that is, facts true before the projection begins. At any point before or after the event sequence is complete, we must be able to give the system a query and a time point, and it will return a list of all instances of the query that are true at that point. For a given timeline, it always returns the same answer for a given query and time point, but exactly which answer is determined by the probabilities in the laws of physics. That is, if a new timeline were constructed from the same event sequence, the same query could give different results.

This is not the first work in the area of probabilistic projection. The formalism I develop here takes off from the work of Hanks (Hanks, 1990b; Hanks, 1990a; Hanks and McDermott, 1994), who developed a theory of temporal representation, plus an algorithm that generated all possible timelines with their associated probabilities. The present work achieves more representational power at the cost of finding only approximations to the true probabilities of different outcomes. Other works, notably Kanazawa (Dean and Kanazawa, 1989; Kanazawa, 1992), have reduced probabilistic temporal reasoning to reasoning about Bayes nets (Pearl, 1988b) whose nodes represent the occurrence of different events and propositions at different times. Unfortunately, the resulting nets are not particularly manageable. The present work may be thought of as an application of stochastic simulation to a specialized Bayes net, extended to allow for the generation of spontaneous random events. However, my goal is not to evaluate probabilities accurately but instead to generate plausible scenarios for plan execution. It may well be more valuable for plan debugging to be able to inspect samples of actual causal chains than to have an accurate assessment of probabilities.

There have been several other stabs at formalizing and carrying out probabilistic temporal reasoning. Thiébaux and Hertzberg (Thiébaux and Hertzberg, 1992) have a formalism similar to mine (more expressive in some ways, less expressive in others) that allows them to treat plans as Markov processes. See also (Haddawy, 1990).

8.2. An Idealized System

In a temporal setting, propositions are not merely true or false. They become true at a time point, persist for a while, become false at a time point, and so forth. I use the word *occasion* to denote a stretch of time over which a proposition is true.[60] When an occasion becomes false, it is said to be *clipped*. Each occasion corresponds to an atomic formula, such as $loc(box1, coords(5, 6))$,[61] called the *proposition* of the occasion. Negation, variables, and such are not allowed as occasion propositions.

There are several entry points to the system:

1. START-TIMELINE: Creates a new timeline.
2. TIMELINE-ADVANCE: Adds new *exogenous* events to the timeline. They are called exogenous because from the point of view of the timeline manager, they are arbitrary and unmodeled. In the course of adding a new exogenous event, it may randomly spawn some *endogenous* events— that is, events whose occurrence is modeled by rules in the timeline manager's model.
3. TIMELINE-RETRIEVE: Used to infer what's true at the end of the timeline. Both TIMELINE-ADVANCE and TIMELINE-RETRIEVE use an

internal routine called TL-RETRIEVE, which can determine what's true at an arbitrary point in the timeline.

4. PAST-RETRIEVE: Direct entry point to TL-RETRIEVE.

All these routines make and record random choices, based on the probabilities in the rules described below.

It is important to realize that in this chapter I am speaking only of the temporal-reasoning system, not the overall planning system it is a part of (described in (McDermott, 1992b)). Some of the ways the narrower system is described will seem parochial or warped. For example, the labels *exogenous* and *endogenous* applied to events seem backward from the point of view of the overall planner. What I call exogenous events are those due to the planner's own actions, while endogenous events are the autonomous events that occur in the part of the world outside the planner's control. However, even though they are outside the agent's control, there is a probabilistic model of them, so the timeline system knows how to generate them; it has no model of the agent's actions.

Another possible point of confusion is that the timelines generated by the projection system are totally ordered, while the plans being projected are not. For example, our plan language, called RPL, allows for loops and parallel combinations of events. The plan (N-TIMES K (PAR (P) (Q))) specifies doing P and Q each K times, in no particular order on each iteration. K is a RPL variable, whose value can vary from execution to execution. A typical projection, with K=2, might look like

$$Q.1.A \rightarrow Q.1.B \rightarrow P.1.A \rightarrow Q.1.Z$$
$$\rightarrow P.1.Z \rightarrow P.2.A \rightarrow Q.2.A \rightarrow Q.2.Z \rightarrow P.2.Z$$

where $X.i.Y$ is an event in the ith execution of X. Events are labeled A, B, ..., Z. For instance, the first execution of Q has events $Q.1.A$ $\rightarrow Q.1.B \rightarrow Q.1.Z$ The events of P.1 are interleaved with the events of Q.1, and similarly for P.2 and Q.2. But although the interleavings differ from projection to projection, for any given projection the events are totally ordered. Finally, in this chapter I do not explain how the action P generates events like P.1.A and P.1.Z. I'll just take events as given. Consult (McDermott, 1992b) for the linkage.

8.2.1. PROBABILISTIC RULES

There are several forms of rule for expressing the laws of physics in a given domain:

- $precond/event \overset{prob}{\rightarrow}{}_{-} effect$: Whenever an event of the form *event* occurs, when *precond* is true, then, with probability *prob*, create and clip occasions as specified by *effect*. Used whenever an event is added.

The *effect* can be a conjunction of atomic formulas and expressions of the form $\neg A$, where A is an atomic formula. The $\neg$ symbol in an *effect* is not interpreted as ordinary negation but means that an occasion of A comes to an end with this event. We can read $\neg A$ as "clip A."

- *effect* $\underset{}{\overset{prob}{\_\leftarrow|}}$ *event\precond*: Same meaning as $|\rightarrow \_$, but used to answer a query about *effect*.
- *precond* $\underset{}{\overset{elap}{\_\rightarrow|}}$ *event*: Over any interval where *precond* is true, generates random endogenous events, "Poisson-distributed," with an average spacing of *elap* time units. (The exact nature of the distribution is explained below.)
- $p_\_ \leftarrow \_q$: If q is true at a time point, so is p. Used to answer queries about p. p is an atomic formula; q is a conjunction of literals.

Rules with connective $|\rightarrow \_$ or $\_\rightarrow|$ are called *forward-chaining rules*. Rule with connective $\_\leftarrow|$ or $\_\leftarrow\_$ are called *backward-chaining rules*. The *consequent* of a rule is the part on the same side of the connective as the arrowhead. The part on the other side (*precond* or q) is called the *antecedent*.

Rules and queries may contain variables, and the implementation uses unification to match queries with rules, but in the technical sections of this chapter we avoid thinking of the system as being a full first-order logic. Instead, I treat each rule as a schema standing for all its ground instances. Because occasions cannot contain variables, we impose the requirement that if a variable occurs in the *consequent* of a forward-chaining rule, then it must also occur in the *antecedent* of that rule, or in its *event* if it has one. Similarly, if a variable occurs in the *antecedent* of a backward-chaining rule, it must also occur in the *consequent* or *event*. And if a variable occurs in the *prob* of a $|\rightarrow \_$ or the *elap* of a $\_\rightarrow|$, it must occur in the antecedent (or the event if it's a $|\rightarrow \_$); if it appears in the *prob* of a $\_\leftarrow|$, it must occur in the consequent.

In each case, the antecedent can be a conjunction of literals— that is, atomic formulas and expressions of the form $\neg A$, where A is atomic. The empty conjunction can be written **true**, or omitted. As I show, this system is simple enough that $\neg$ can be implemented by the device of "negation as failure" (Clark, 1978). Because of this, I impose the restriction that any variable that occurs in a negated part of an antecedent must also occur in an unnegated part.

A rule instance is said to be *firable* at a time point if its precondition is true at that time point. It is said to *fire* if it is firable and its probabilistic test comes up true. *The probabilistic test for a given firable rule instance is performed at most once at a given time point.* (In the case of a $\_\leftarrow|$ rule, if the query never occurs, the test is never performed.)

TIMELINE-ADVANCE uses $_- \rightarrow|$ rules to add endogenous events to the timeline. It calls TL-RETRIEVE to verify the preconditions of these rules, using $_- \leftarrow|$ and $_- \leftarrow _-$ rules. For every event added by TIMELINE-ADVANCE, $|\rightarrow _-$ rules are used to infer the consequences of the event.

Every timeline begins with an event of the form START. We can use this event to set up initial conditions,[62] as shown in the following example:

;*Initially,* nugget1 *is at 10,0, and...*

$$\text{START} \; |\overset{1}{\rightarrow} _- \; \text{loc}(\text{nugget1}, \text{coords}(10, 0))$$

;*T1000, an enemy robot, is at 0,0*

$$\text{START} \; |\overset{1}{\rightarrow} _- \; \text{loc}(\text{T1000}, \text{coords}(0, 0))$$

;*Roughly every 10 seconds, T1000 moves right.*

$$_- \overset{10}{\rightarrow}| \; \text{move}(\text{T1000}, 1, 0)$$

;*When an agent moves, its location changes.*

$$\text{loc}(b, \text{coords}(x, y)) / \text{move}(b, \Delta x, \Delta y)$$
$$|\overset{1}{\rightarrow} _- \; \text{loc}(b, \text{coords}(x + \Delta x, y + \Delta y)) \land \neg \text{loc}(b, \text{coords}(x, y))$$

;*(We don't really notate addition in rules this way;*
;*see Section 8.3.)*
;*Whenever T1000 and the nugget are in the same place,*
;*T1000 grasps the nugget, typically within 1 second.*

$$\text{loc}(\text{T1000}, \text{coords}(x, y)) \land \text{loc}(\text{nugget1}, \text{coords}(x, y))$$
$$_- \overset{1}{\rightarrow}| \; \text{grasp}(\text{T1000}, \text{nugget1})$$

;*Grasping succeeds with a probability of 80%.*

$$\text{holding}(a, b)$$
$$_- \overset{0.8}{\leftarrow}| \; \text{grasp}(a, b) \backslash \text{loc}(a, \text{coords}(x, y)) \land \text{loc}(b, \text{coords}(x, y))$$

This little model of the world might be useful if the planner had to predict the chances of preventing an enemy robot from stealing a gold nugget. The planner could project the plan by initializing the timeline, then using TIMELINE-ADVANCE to add the agent's own successive actions as exogenous events, then using TIMELINE-RETRIEVE with query

$$\text{loc}(\text{nugget1}, \text{coords}(10, 0))$$

to find out if the nugget is still at 10,0 at the end. The enemy will take about 100 seconds to get to 10,0, then repeatedly try to grasp the nugget, until it succeeds, when $\text{loc}(\text{nugget1}, \text{coords}(10, 0))$ will be clipped and grasping will cease. Given these rules, the only way to stop the T1000 is to move it to a location where it will not reach the nugget.

The only difference between $|\rightarrow _-$ and $_- \leftarrow|$ rules is when they are called. $_- \leftarrow|$ rules have the advantage that they are called only when the query they answer arises. I call the application of $\_\leftarrow|$ rules "backward chaining," and the application of $|\rightarrow\_$ rules "forward chaining" by analogy with their static counterparts. In the present example, there was really no reason to use a $\_\leftarrow|$ rule, because the $|\rightarrow\_$ rule is going to require querying loc(nugget1, coords(...)) repeatedly anyway. This pattern, where the same query is repeated at many time points, distinguishes temporal inference from routine backward chaining, and leads to the optimizations described in Section 8.3.

8.2.2. FORMAL SEMANTICS

So far my exposition of the meanings of the various types of rule has been informal. But below I introduce some fairly intricate algorithms for making inferences using those rules, and we want to verify that the algorithms work. Hence, I need to be more formal about the semantics of the rules.

Definition 1 A *world state* is a function from proposition symbols to $\{\#T, \#F, \perp\}$.

A world state s can be considered an assignment of truth values to every proposition symbol. I use $\#T$ and $\#F$ to denote boolean values; $\perp$ means "undefined," or "inconsistent." The state $\mathbf{F}$ assigns $\#F$ to every proposition symbol.

I extend the meaning of states so that they apply to boolean combinations of propositions in the obvious way. In this chapter, propositions are notated as ground atomic formulas, but that notation is mainly a frill. All we require is a supply (possibly infinite) of symbols for propositions, which I $\mathcal{P}$. Similarly, we need a supply of event symbols, which I call $\mathcal{Q}$.

Definition 2 An *occurrence* is a pair $\langle e, t \rangle$, where e is an event (type) and t is a particular *time,* a nonnegative real number. The *event* of the occurrence is e and the *date* is t. We write such an occurrence as $e{\downarrow}t$.

Definition 3 An *occurrence sequence* is a sequence of occurrences, ordered by date. If C is a finite occurrence sequence, then we write its length as $length(C)$. If the dates in C are bounded, we write $duration(C)$ to mean the least upper bound of those dates.

Obviously, if C is finite, $duration(C) = date(C_{length(C)})$.

Definition 4 A *world of duration* L, where L is a real number > 0, is a complete history of a stretch of time of duration L. That is, it is a pair $\langle C, H \rangle$, where C is an occurrence sequence, such that the date of the last occurrence is $\leq L$, and H is a function from $[0, L]$ to world states. in which all proposition symbols $\mathcal{P}$ are false. If $t_1 < t_2$ and $H(t_1) \neq H(t_2)$, then there must be an occurrence $e{\downarrow}t \in C$ with $t_1 \leq t < t_2$.

If $W = \langle C, H \rangle$ is a world of duration L and A is a proposition, and t is a date $\leq L$, I write $(A{\downarrow}t)(W)$, read "A after t in W," to mean that there is some $\delta > 0$ such that for all t', $t < t' < t + \delta$, $H(t')(A)$. Similarly, I write $(A{\uparrow}t)(W)$, read "A before t in W," to mean that there is some $\delta > 0$ such that for all t', $t - \delta < t' \leq t$, $H(t')(A)$. If c is an occurrence, I write $A{\uparrow}c$ and $A{\downarrow}c$ to mean $A{\uparrow}\,date(c)$ and $A{\downarrow}\,date(c)$.

It should be obvious that in any world $W = \langle C, H \rangle$ where c and d are consecutive occurrences $\in C$, and for any proposition A, $(A{\uparrow}d)(W) = (A{\downarrow}c)(W)$, and for all t, $date(c) < t < date(d)$, $(A{\downarrow}t)(W) = (A{\uparrow}t)(W) = (A{\downarrow}c)(W)$.

The next step is to attempt to define the idea of a model of a probabilistic theory.

Definition 5 *(Actually, an attempted definition)* If $\mathcal{T}$ is a set of rules as described in Section 8.2.1, C is an occurrence sequence of length n (the exogenous occurrences), and L is a real number $\geq duration(C)$, then an L-*model* of $\mathcal{T}$ and C is a pair $\langle \mathcal{W}, \mathcal{M} \rangle$, where $\mathcal{W}$ is a set of worlds of duration L such that for each $\langle C, H \rangle \in \mathcal{W}$, $C \subset \mathcal{C}$; and $\mathcal{M}$ is a probability measure (Breiman, 1969) on $\mathcal{W}$ that obeys certain restrictions, which I now describe.

We can consider $A \uparrow t$, $A \downarrow t$, and $e \downarrow t$ to be boolean random variables, defined on the "outcome set" $\mathcal{W}$. As usual, we can combine random variables, letting $\mathcal{M}(\neg A) = 1 - \mathcal{M}(A)$, $\mathcal{M}(A|B) = \frac{\mathcal{M}(A \wedge B)}{\mathcal{M}(B)}$, and so on. Define $\overline{A}$, the *annihilation* of A, where A is a conjunction, to be the conjunction of the negations of the conjuncts of A. (Example: $\overline{P \wedge \neg Q} = \neg P \wedge Q$.) For $\langle \mathcal{W}, \mathcal{M} \rangle$ to be a model, the measure $\mathcal{W}$ must be constrained to fit the rules $\mathcal{T}$ as follows:

- *Initial blank slate:* For any proposition $A \in \mathcal{P}$, $\mathcal{M}(A{\uparrow}0) = 0$.
- *Event-effect rules when the events occur:* If $\mathcal{T}$ contains a rule instance $A/e \mid\!\overset{r}{\to}_- B$ or a rule instance $B \;_-\!\overset{r}{\leftarrow}\mid E\backslash A$, then for every date t, require that, for all nonempty conjunctions C of literals from B:

$$\mathcal{M}(C{\downarrow}t \mid E{\downarrow}t \wedge A{\uparrow}t \wedge \overline{B}{\uparrow}t) = r.$$

- *Static backward-chaining rules:* If $\mathcal{T}$ contains a rule instance $B_-\!\leftarrow_-A$, then

$$\mathcal{M}(B{\downarrow}t \mid A{\downarrow}t) = 1.$$

- *Event-effect rules when the events don't occur:* Suppose B is an atomic formula, and let $R = \{R_i\}$ be the set of all instances of $\mid\!\to_-$ or $_-\!\leftarrow\mid$ rules whose consequents contain B or $\neg B$. If $R_i = A_i/E_i \mid\!\overset{p_i}{\to}_- C_i$ or

$C_i \overset{p_i}{\text{-}\leftarrow\!|} E_i \backslash A_i$, then let

$$D_i = A_i \wedge \overline{C_i}.$$

Let S be the set of all the $\text{-}\leftarrow\text{-}$ rules in whose consequents B occurs, and let

$$A = \bigvee_{r \in S} (antecedent(r)).$$

(The D_i or A may be identically **false**, e.g., in the case where R or S is empty.) Then

$$\begin{aligned}
\mathcal{M}(B{\downarrow}t \mid B{\uparrow}t \wedge N) &= 1 \\
\mathcal{M}(B{\downarrow}t \mid \neg B{\uparrow}t \wedge N) &= 0,
\end{aligned}$$

where

$$\begin{aligned}
N &= (\neg E_1{\downarrow}t \vee \neg D_1) \\
&\wedge (\neg E_2{\downarrow}t \vee \neg D_2) \\
&\wedge \ldots \\
&\wedge \neg A.
\end{aligned}$$

- *Event-occurrence rules:* For every time point t such that no occurrence with date t is in $\mathcal{C}$, and every event type E, let R be the set of all rule instances of the form $\ldots \text{-} \rightarrow\!| E$ in $\mathcal{T}$, and suppose that S is an arbitrary nonempty subset of R, and let $A = \bigwedge_{R_j \in S} A_j$, and let $\lambda_S = \sum_{R_j \in S} 1/d_j$, where $R_j = A_j \overset{d_j}{\text{-}\rightarrow\!|} E$. Then if $\mathcal{M}(A \uparrow t) \neq 0$, require that

$$\mathcal{M}(\text{ some occurrence of } E \text{ between } t \text{ and } t + dt \mid A{\uparrow}t) = \lambda_S\, dt.$$

If $N = \bigwedge_{R_j \in R} \neg A_j$, then

$$\mathcal{M}(\text{some occurrence of } E \text{ between } t \text{ and } t + dt \mid N{\uparrow}t) = 0.$$

In most theories, R contains zero or one rule instance. In the former case, we require

$$\mathcal{M}(\text{ some occurrence of } E \text{ between } t \text{ and } t + dt) = 0.$$

In the latter case, with just one instance $A \overset{d}{\text{-}\rightarrow\!|} e$, we require

$$\begin{aligned}
\mathcal{M}(\text{ some occurrence of } E \text{ between } t \text{ and } t + dt \mid A{\uparrow}t) &= dt/d \\
\mathcal{M}(\text{ some occurrence of } E \text{ between } t \text{ and } t + dt \mid \neg A{\uparrow}t) &= 0.
\end{aligned}$$

- *Conditional independence:* If one of the previous clauses defines a conditional probability $\mathcal{M}(\alpha \mid \beta)$, which mention times t, then α is conditionally independent, given α, of all other random variables mentioning times on or before t. That is, for an arbitrary γ mentioning times on or before t, $\mathcal{M}(\alpha \mid \beta \wedge \gamma) = \mathcal{M}(\alpha \mid \beta)$.

Clause 5 of this definition is stated tersely but imprecisely. To make it rigorous, we must replace all statements of the form $\mathcal{M}$(some occurrence of e between t and $t + dt \ldots$) $= x\,dt$ with

$$\lim_{\Delta t \to 0} \frac{\mathcal{M}(\text{ some occurrence of } e \text{ between } t \text{ and } t + \Delta t \ldots)}{\Delta t} = x.$$

This quantity has the character of a *probability density*, and it is well defined only if $\mathcal{M}$ is defined over any small interval around almost every point t. There is a time point associated with every real number, so, if a theory contains $\_\to\!|$ rules, each of its models must have an uncountably infinite set of worlds.

In what follows, I refer to this probability density with the slightly misleading notation $\mathcal{M}(e \downarrow t \ldots)$. So, even more tersely, we can state the constraint on a theory with one rule $A \overset{d}{\_\to\!|} E$ governing occurrences of E as:

$$\mathcal{M}(E{\downarrow}t \mid A{\uparrow}t) = 1/d$$
$$\mathcal{M}(E{\downarrow}t \mid \neg A{\uparrow}t) = 0.$$

In fact, I already made use of this notation in clauses 5 and 5 of Definition 5. The meaning of $\mathcal{M}(\ldots \mid c)$, where $c = E \downarrow t$, can be rigorously specified only by using limits if $\mathcal{T}$ includes $\_\to\!|$ rules.

Because of this infinity, we cannot assume that Definition 5 makes sense without putting in a little more work to show that there is exactly one $\mathcal{M}$ that satisfies it. The work is what you would expect: a limit process that defines $\mathcal{M}$ as the limit of a series of discrete approximations. The details are important but somewhat tortuous. Please see (McDermott, 1994) for the details. For our purposes, we just assume that Definition 5 defines a unique probability distribution.

Let me point out some consequences of Definition 5 that are fairly obvious even without the detailed analysis. Please attend to the role of negation in the clauses of Definition 5. Suppose we have a rule $e \overset{r}{|{\to}\_} \neg A$. Then clause 5 says that $\mathcal{M}(\neg A \downarrow e \mid e \wedge A \uparrow e) = r$. Because the truth values of propositions can change only at occurrences, this formula means that any occasion of A that persists to an occurrence of e gets clipped with probability r.

Clause 5, with its negated annihilations, may sound daunting, so I give an example. Suppose we have three rules:

$$P \wedge Q/\text{squirt} \quad \overset{0.8}{\mapsto}_{-} \quad B \wedge C$$
$$P/\text{squirt} \quad \overset{0.6}{\mapsto}_{-} \quad \neg B \wedge D$$
$$B \quad {}_{-}\!\leftarrow_{-} \quad E.$$

Then clause 5 states that

$$\mathcal{M}(B{\downarrow}t \mid B{\uparrow}t \wedge N) = 1$$
$$\mathcal{M}(B{\downarrow}t \mid \neg B{\uparrow}t \wedge N) = 0,$$

where N is defined as

$$(\neg\text{squirt}{\downarrow}t \vee \neg P{\uparrow}t \vee \neg Q{\uparrow}t \vee B{\uparrow}t \vee C{\uparrow}t)$$
$$\wedge \quad (\neg\text{squirt}{\downarrow}t \vee \neg P{\uparrow}t \vee \neg B{\uparrow}t \vee D{\uparrow}t)$$
$$\wedge \quad \neg E{\downarrow}t.$$

One consequence of these rules is that if $\mathcal{T}$ contains two rule instances that specify different probabilities for their consequents in some worlds for an event sequence $\mathcal{C}$, then there is no model of $\mathcal{T}$ and $\mathcal{C}$. Such a theory, event-sequence pair is said to be *inconsistent*. A theory is *consistent* if it is consistent for all event sequences. For example, the theory

$$\text{START} \quad \overset{0.5}{\mapsto}_{-} \quad A$$
$$A/\text{bang} \quad \overset{0.8}{\mapsto}_{-} \quad B \wedge C$$
$$A/\text{bang} \quad \overset{0.6}{\mapsto}_{-} \quad B \wedge D$$

is inconsistent for event sequence $\langle \text{START} \downarrow 0, \text{bang} \downarrow 1 \rangle$ because half the worlds in any model must have $A \downarrow \text{START}$, and those worlds assign two different probabilities to B after **bang**. For event sequences not containing **bang**, the theory is consistent. Observe the impact of assigning probability to every *subset* of the consequent of a rule.[63] If A is true before a **bang**, then the second rule states that B, C, and B∧C must all have probability 0.8 afterward. If we simply assigned a probability to B∧C, then the theory would be consistent after all, but the probabilities of the individual occasions would be underdetermined. For example, we could assign probabilities 0.6 to BCD, 0.2 to BC$\overline{\text{D}}$, and 0.2 to B$\overline{\text{CD}}$, so that the probability of B alone was 1. Other assignments would give B different probabilities. My semantics avoids such indeterminacies.[64]

Compare the previous theory to this one:

$$\text{START} \quad \overset{0.5}{\mid\rightarrow}{}_{\_} \quad \text{A}$$

$$\text{A/bang} \quad \overset{0.8}{\mid\rightarrow}{}_{\_} \quad \text{B}$$

$$\neg\text{A/bang} \quad \overset{0.6}{\mid\rightarrow}{}_{\_} \quad \text{B}.$$

This theory is consistent for $\langle\text{START}\!\downarrow\!0, \text{bang}\!\downarrow\!1\rangle$ because only one of the B rules is ever firable.

Another way for inconsistency to develop is for a $\_\!\leftarrow\!\_$ rule to disagree with a $\mid\rightarrow\_$ rule. However, the following theory is *consistent:*

$$\text{bang} \quad \overset{0.8}{\mid\rightarrow}{}_{\_} \quad \text{A}$$

$$\text{bang} \quad \overset{0.6}{\mid\rightarrow}{}_{\_} \quad \neg\text{A}$$

If a sequence of **bangs** occurs, then there are worlds where both rules fire. However, the first rule causes occasions of A to be created, and the second causes them to be clipped. Hence the two rules can never fire at the same eventinstant.

8.2.3. AN ABSTRACT ALGORITHM

In a later section, I discuss the actual implementation of the algorithm. Here I describe an idealized version that makes it clear how the algorithm works. One of the idealizations I make is to ignore $\_\!\leftarrow\!\_$ rules, which clutter the exposition. I return to them in Section 8.3. An idealization I do *not* make is to ignore $\_\!\leftarrow\!\mid$ rules. If we got rid of backward chaining, then TL-RETRIEVE would never have to look before the time point it had been asked about, and TIMELINE-ADVANCE would do all the inferential work. However, that would require us to initialize the timeline with every proposition the system believes. As I discuss in greater depth in Section 8.3.1, that's an awkward requirement to meet. Hence we must adopt a style of "lazy projection" in which points along the timeline, especially the initial point, are constructed incrementally as queries are posed about them. (Cf. (Hanks, 1990b).)

A timeline keeps track of events and the occasions that they delimit. The events are totally ordered, and no proposition changes in truth value between two adjacent events. Hence we can implement timelines, essentially, as lists of *eventinstants,* defined thus. An eventinstant is a record that contains:

- A *date:* The time of occurrence of the eventinstant, relative to the beginning of the timeline,

- *Happenings:* The events that occur here (zero or one),
- *Overlapping occasions:* Occasions that are true here (that is, they overlap this eventinstant, either because they begin here, or because they begin before and are not clipped here or before),
- *Clipped ocasions:* A list of occasions that were clipped at this eventinstant,
- *Established queries:* A list of atomic queries that have been tested at this eventinstant, and
- *Clipnotes:* A table of ⟨ atomic-formula, boolean ⟩ pairs, where the boolean records whether the decision was to clip or not to clip the atomic formula at this eveninstant.

The actual structure of an eventinstant is more complex, but this will do for now.

Each occasion is a record that contains:

- *A proposition:* a ground atomic formula,
- *Begin:* The eventinstant where the occasion begins to be true, and
- *End:* The eventinstant where the occasion ceases to be true, or #F if that eventinstant is not yet known.

The fact that we store a list of occasions, each associated with an atomic formula, means that we are making the *closed-world assumption* for occasions: if no occasion for proposition A overlaps a time instant, then the algorithm will take A to be false at that time instant.

The established-queries list and the clipnotes table of an eventinstant play a crucial role. Once a query has been processed at an eventinstant, the inferred instances must be stored in this list. Such a query is said to have been *established at* this eventinstant. There are two good reasons for saving this information. First, it serves as a cache. When backward-chaining for answers to a query, the system must check previous eventinstants to see if the query can be infered there and shown to persist to the point of interest. If a query is repeated at every time point, which is a common occurrence in our application, this check will propagate back to previous eventinstants many times. The cache saves repeating rule application. Second, and even more important, we simply cannot run a probabilistic rule more than once at a given eventinstant. Once the answer to a query has been randomly selected, we must record the outcome and avoid doing another random selection later.

A timeline is then essentially a list of eventinstants. In the Lisp implementation, the list is kept in reverse chronological order, so that adding to the timeline requires CONSing a new eventinstant on, and backward chaining requires CDRing through the list.

I use the term *time point* to refer to a position in this list. The *initial* time point corresponds to the beginning of the list. Every noninitial time point is associated with an eventinstant, namely— the one that just occurred (the CAR of the list in the implementation). Because of this near one-to-one correspondence between time points and eventinstants, I refer to the date, happenings, and so on of a noninitial time point, meaning the date, happenings, and so on of the associated eventinstant. The *past* of a noninitial time point is the time point that is its immediate predecessor (its CDR in the implementation). Because no occasion changes in truth value between eventinstants, we do not really have continuous time, but in reasoning about endogenous events the system will have to choose real-valued dates at which to place the next event. In describing this part of the system, I use the term *time instant* to describe one of the uncountable number of anonymous points between two eventinstants.

TL-RETRIEVE is the basic entry point to the temporal-inference system, so I start by describing it. It takes as argument a query, a time point, and a timeline. It returns two values: a list of substitutions that answer the query (possibly empty), and a list of new occasions created while answering it (usually empty). This second value is quite important. Even though a query may have been asked at a point late in a timeline, answering it may require running a _←| rule at a point arbitrarily early in the timeline. An important special case is rules that trigger off START.[65] When a rule fires, it creates new occasions, which persist for a while but may get clipped eventually. Getting TL-RETRIEVE right requires synchronizing this activity with backward chaining. When new occasions are created, the system will be in the midst of exploring answers to a query at a future time point. See Figure 1. It will be several layers down in a recursion involving possibly a cascade of _←| rules. If the system tried to figure out the lifetime of an occasion as soon as it was created, it would end up starting several new backward-chaining computations in the same place in the timeline as the existing computation, and inconsistent answers and infinite recursion would ensue. On the other hand, if it postponed figuring out the lifetime until the dust had settled on the current computation, then the current computation might not see the correct lifetime when it resumed at later time points.

The only solution is to interleave backward chaining with creation of new occasions. When TL-RETRIEVE returns, it guarantees that the timeline is in a consistent state up through the given time point, and that the new occasions it is returning persist that far. If it was called recursively, its caller must check whether the occasions persist to the next time point. If they do, they get returned up the line to the next caller; otherwise, they get clipped. This persistence check is calling *bringing the occasions forward.*

I present algorithms in a pseudo-code style with vaguely Algol-like syntax. Italics are used for comments, and for parts of the code that are not worth going into detail about. I notate multiple-value return with angle

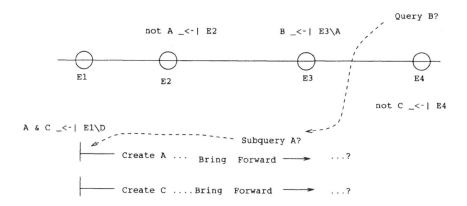

Figure 1. Interleaving backward chaining and occasion creation

brackets. If a function F returns an expression like $\langle x_1, x_2, \ldots \rangle$, then its caller can capture those values by saying

Let $\langle v_1, v_2, \ldots \rangle = F(\ldots)$
—*body-of-Let*—

As this example shows, scope is indicated with indentation wherever possible. To indicate random binary choices, I write a call to a procedure random-choice(*prob*).

Here is the code:

```
TL-RETRIEVE(query,timepoint,timeline)
```
  If **query** *is a conjunction,*
  then *call* **TL-RETRIEVE** *on each conjunct and combine the results,*
  ordering the conjuncts so "¬" conjuncts occur last.
  Else if timepoint *is the initial timepoint of* timeline
  then <if query=true or ¬A for some A
  then *(empty substitution)*
  else (),
  ()>

  Else if query is of form ¬Q,
  then Let < anses, newoccs >
  = TL-RETRIEVE(Q,timepoint,timeline)
  <if anses = () then *(empty substitution)*
  else (),
  newoccs>
  else Let newoccs =
  Maybe-establish-query(query,timepoint,timeline)
  <Match-against-occasions(query,timepoint),

```
newoccs>
```

Match-against-occasions(query,timepoint)
  Match query *against all occasions in*
  overlapping-occasions(timepoint)
  Return a list of substitutions, one for each successful match

Maybe-establish-query(query,timepoint,timeline)
  If query *is a variant of some member of*
  established-queries(timepoint)
  then ()
  else Establish-query(query,timepoint,timeline)

Establish-query(query,timepoint,timeline)
  If timepoint *is initial time point of timeline*
  then ()
  else Let from-past
  = Bring-forward(Maybe-establish-query
  (query,
  past(timepoint),
  timeline),
  timepoint,timeline)
  from-past
  ∪ Establish-after(query,timepoint,timeline)

Establish-after(query,timepoint,timeline)
  Let newoccs = '()
  For each rule $Q_1 \wedge Q_2 \wedge \ldots \wedge Q_n \overset{p}{\text{-}\leftarrow|} e \backslash C$,
  where query unifies with a Q_i,
  and event of timepoint unifies with e
  with unifier θ
  newoccs := newoccs
  ∪ Try-back-chain-rule(*rule*,θ,
  timepoint,timeline);
  add query to established-queries(timepoint);
  newoccs

Try-back-chain-rule(rule,substitution,timepoint,timeline)
  ;rule *is of form* $Q_1 \wedge Q_2 \wedge \ldots \wedge Q_n \overset{p}{\text{-}\leftarrow|} e \backslash C$
  Let precond = *Apply* substitution *to* C
  Let <anses,occs> = TL-RETRIEVE(precond
  $\wedge \neg Q_1 \wedge \ldots \wedge \neg Q_n$,
```
```

```
past(timepoint),timeline)
Let newoccs = Bring-forward(occs,timepoint,timeline)
For each ρ in anses
newoccs := newoccs
∪
Conclude-from-rule(rule,ρ,
timepoint,timeline);
```
Note that query *is established at* timepoint;
```
newoccs
```

```
Conclude-from-rule(rule,substitution,timepoint,timeline);rule
```
is of form

$$Q_1 \wedge Q_2 \wedge \ldots \wedge Q_n \overset{p}{-\!\leftarrow\!|} e \backslash C$$

; *or* $C/e \overset{p}{|\!\rightarrow\!_-} Q_1 \wedge Q_2 \wedge \ldots \wedge Q_n$

Let $D_1 \wedge D_2 \wedge \ldots \wedge D_n$

= *Apply* substitution *to* $Q_1 \wedge Q_2 \wedge \ldots \wedge Q_n$

and prob = *Apply* substitution *to* p

and newoccs = '()

If random-choice(prob) ; *(rule fires)*

then For each D_i

If *of form* ¬A

then if *no entry* $\langle A, \ldots \rangle \in$ clipnotes(timepoint)

; *No previous decision has been made whether*

; *A is clipped at* timepoint

then add $\langle A, \#T \rangle$

to clipnotes(timepoint)

Else if $D_i \notin$ established-queries(timepoint)

then ; *Note that* D_i *is established at* timepoint

add D_i

to established-queries(timepoint);

Let occ = *Create new occasion*

with proposition=D_i

and begin=timepoint

and end=#F

add occ to

overlapping-occasions(timepoint);

newoccs := cons(occ,newoccs)

else For each D_i

If *of form* ¬A

then if *no entry* $\langle A, \ldots \rangle \in$ clipnotes(timepoint)

; *No previous decision has been made whether*

; *A is clipped at* timepoint

```
then add ⟨A, #F⟩
to clipnotes(timepoint)
else ; Note that D_i has been established at timepoint
add D_i
to established-queries(timepoint);
newoccs
```

Notice how the **established-queries** and **clipnotes** tables are used by these routines. The basic idea is that, for a given time point, no query is processed more than once, and no decision to create or clip an occasion is made more than once. Every time one of these things happens, it is recorded in the appropriate table to prevent its happening again. It would be possible to suppress the established-queries manipulations in **Maybe-establish-query** and **Establish-after**, although it would be less efficient. It is not possible to avoid the establish-queries manipulations in **Conclude-from-rule**, because consideration of the same literals can arise from consideration of different queries. For example, the rule

$$B(x,y) \overset{0.8}{\_\leftarrow|} E\backslash A(x,y)$$

can lead to consideration of the literal $B(a, b)$ from both the query $B(a, y)$ and the query $B(x, b)$.[66]

Unlike the established-queries table, the clipnotes table records the outcome of the clipping decision as well as the fact that it was made. As we will see when considering $|\rightarrow\_$ rules, when the system notices whether a proposition is clipped at a time point, it may or may not know whether an occasion with that proposition overlaps that time point. So the algorithm must save the clipping-decision result for future reference. **Bring-forward** then retrieves the outcome from the table to see what is clipped. Here's the code:

```
; This procedure is responsible for bringing new occasions
        forward
; and checking whether they survive through timepoint
Bring-forward(occasions,timepoint,timeline)
 Let to-future = () ; The list of survivors we're going to asemble
 For each occ ∈ occasions
 Let <clipped,newoccs>
 = Been-clipped(occ,timepoint,timeline)
 to-future := to-future ∪ newoccs;
 If clipped
 then end(occ) := timepoint
 else (Add occ to overlapping-occasions(timepoint);
```

```
to-future := cons(occ,to-future));
to-future
```

; *Test for whether* occasion *gets clipped at* timepoint
; *Return two values: boolean indicating whether it got clipped,*
; plus *(subtle requirement) new occasions created when deciding*
; *whether this one is clipped(!)*
Been-clipped (occasion,timepoint,timeline)
  Let prop = proposition(occasion)
  and newoccs = '()
For each rule of the form   ·
$$Q_1 \wedge Q_2 \wedge \ldots \wedge Q_n \ \_\leftarrow| \ \overset{p}{} e\backslash C$$
  where some Q_i is of form $\neg P$,
  and prop unifies with P
  and event of timepoint unifies with e
  with unifier θ
newoccs := newoccs
∪ Try-back-chain-rule(rule,θ,
timepoint,timeline);
<if *There is an entry* $\langle$prop,c$\rangle$ *in* clipnotes(timepoint),
then c
else #F,
newoccs>

The following lemma is obvious but useful:

Lemma 1 Conclude-from-rule makes a decision about creating or
clipping an occasion at a time point only if the decision has not been made
before.

Proof: Each such decision is recorded in the **established-queries** or
clipnotes table for the time point, and blocks repetitions.
To prove that **TL-RETRIEVE** works, I first state two definitions.

Definition 6 A timeline is *properly established through time point t* if
and only if t is initial or for every time point p before or coinciding
with t, and every occasion $n = \langle A, c_1, c_2 \rangle$ in any eventinstant's
overlapping-occasions list, $n \in$ overlapping-occasions(p) if and only
if $date(c_1) \le date(p) < date(c_2)$, taking any date to be $< date(c_2)$ when
$date(c_2) = $ #F.

Definition 7 A timeline is *properly clipped through time point t* if for every
time point p before or coinciding with t, except the initial one, if $c \in$
overlapping-occasions(past(p)), where c has proposition A, then

- There is an entry $\langle A, \#\mathrm{T} \rangle \in$ clipnotes(p) if and only if

$$c \notin \text{overlapping-occasions}(p);$$

- If there is no entry for A in clipnotes(p) then there is no $|\rightarrow\_$ or $\_\leftarrow|$ rule whose consequent includes a literal $\neg A'$, where A' unifies with A.

Now to state that TL-RETRIEVE works correctly:

Lemma 2 If a timeline L for a consistent theory $\mathcal{T}$ is properly established and properly clipped through time point t, then TL-RETRIEVE(q, t, L) will

1. Make a decision about creating or clipping an occasion at a time point only if the decision has not been made before;
2. Make and record decisions about occasions whose propositions are subsumed by atomic formulas occuring in q, such that the truth value of all instances of q at t will be decided and recorded;
3. Make all decisions based on the correct conditional probabilities, as laid out in Definition 5;
4. Leave L properly established and properly clipped through t;
5. Return all answers that follow from the decisions made, plus a list of all occasions created that overlap t, each of which will be of the form $\langle A, c, \#\mathrm{F} \rangle$.

Proof: The first clause follows from the fact that Conclude-from-rule is the only routine that creates occasions, and Bring-forward is the only one that clips them. Both respect the decisions taken by Conclude-from-rule, so clause 1 follows by Lemma 1.

Clause 2 will follow if we can show that it holds for any atomic query, because TL-RETRIEVE breaks a compound query down into atomic pieces.

Clauses 2 to 5 are proven by induction on the number of eventinstants up through t, taking the query to be atomic as just mentioned. If t is the initial time point of L, then L will vacuously remain properly clipped and established through t. No probabilistic decisions will be made or recorded, and only formulas of the form true or $\neg A$ will be taken as true. No occasions will be created or returned, and the empty substitution or nothing will be returned.

Now assume clauses 2 to 5 of the theorem are true up to t, and consider t's successor t' in L.

Suppose that the algorithm is about to make a decision, in Conclude-from-rule, about whether to clip or create an occasion n with proposition A. Conclude-from-rule is called in Try-back-chain-rule, after a call to TL-RETRIEVE with

$$\mathtt{query} = \textit{precondition of rule} \wedge \overline{\textit{consequent of rule}}$$

and `time point` $t = <$ past(*current time point*). This query must have succeeded, thus finding a firable rule instance whose consequent contains A or $\neg A$. (Because $\mathcal{T}$ is consistent, there will be just one such rule instance.) By the induction hypothesis, the recursive call to `TL-RETRIEVE` will make enough decisions about this subquery to fix the truth values of all its instances at t and will return the list P of all newly created occasions that persist through t. In particular, to get to this point in `Conclude-from-rule`, it must have found the substitution corresponding to A. Hence when it makes a random choice, it uses the probability from the rule instance obtained using this substitution, so that the chance of creating or clipping A is as described in clause 5 of Definition 5.

Now consider an occasion of A in `overlapping-occasions`(t), such that no rule involving A or $\neg A$ ever becomes firable at t' as a result of decisions made by recursive calls to `TL-RETRIEVE`. Because L was properly established and clipped through t' when we started, and, by induction, it is properly clipped through t after all recursive calls to `TL-RETRIEVE`, then either $n \in$ `overlapping-occasions`(t') or $n \in$ some new-occasions list returned by a recursive call to `TL-RETRIEVE`. In the latter case, `Bring-forward` will have been called on the new-occasions list, and, by the induction hypothesis, decisions will have been made that fix at `false` the truth value of the formula corresponding to D in clause 5 of Definition 5. Hence `Bring-forward` will add n to the overlapping-occasions list of t'.

To prove clause 5, notice that the occasions returned by `TL-RETRIEVE` come from two sources: those created in `Conclude-from-rule` and those returned by recursive calls to `TL-RETRIEVE`. The former category all get returned, and all have `end=#F`. The latter category also have `end=#F` (by induction hypothesis), but they get passed through `Bring-forward`, which either clips them and resets their ends, or returns them, still with `end=#F`.

Finally, we need to show that the timeline remains properly established and clipped through t'. Let n be an occasion $\in$ `overlapping-occasions`(t). If n was present before this call to `TL-RETRIEVE`, then its status in `overlapping-occasions`(t') and `clipnotes`(t') will not be changed. So suppose that n is a newly created occasion of A. Because it is new, and doesn't start at t', it will have been returned by some recursive call to `TL-RETRIEVE`. It will then be checked by `Been-clipped`, and will be omitted from `overlapping-occasions`(t') if only if an entry $\langle A, \#T \rangle$ is added to the clipnotes for t'. Hence the timeline will remain properly clipped. To show it remains properly established, we also need to consider occasions that begin at t'. But these are always put in `overlapping-occasions`(t').

The other main entry point to the system is `TIMELINE-ADVANCE`, which adds a single new eventinstant to a timeline. The easy part of its job is to run $| \rightarrow {}_-$ rules for the new eventinstant. The tricky part is to run ${}_- \rightarrow |$ rules.

Recall that the meaning of $A \xrightarrow[\ ]{\overset{d}{}} \mid e$ is that over any tiny interval (duration "dt") where A is true, events of type e tend to occur with probability dt/d. What this entails is that, over an interval of length l, the probability that an e does not occur is $\exp(-\lambda l)$, where $\lambda = 1/d$ ((Breiman, 1969; Feller, 1970).[67] In simple cases, such a rule should generate a random series of e events, according to a Poisson distribution. But every time an event occurs, $\mid \rightarrow \_$ rules can change the set of true propositions. Consider these rules:

$$A \quad \xrightarrow[\ ]{\overset{10}{}} \mid \quad E$$

$$E \quad \mid \xrightarrow[\ ]{\overset{1}{}} \_ \quad \neg A$$

the first rule suggests that any occasion of A is punctuated by random occurrences of E every 10 time units (on the average). But the second makes it clear that in fact the first such occurrence will be the last.

The best way to think of the meaning of $\_ \rightarrow \mid$ rules is this: at any time instant, there is a set of firable $\_ \rightarrow \mid$ rules. Each is like a ticking time bomb, with random elapsed times until they fire or until the next exogenous event occurs. If one of the rules fires, a new event is created, the set of firable rule instances gets recomputed, and the process resumes. In a sense, this process never stops, but the system does not bother to model past the last exogenous event. Hence the job of TIMELINE-ADVANCE is to tack on a new exogenous eventinstant, then fill in with endogenous events the time interval between the eventinstant's predecessor and the new eventinstant. I call this the *time-passage interval.*

It is a well known fact (see, for example, (Breiman, 1969)) that a set of independent processes, each of which behaves as described by a $\_ \rightarrow \mid$ rule instance with frequency λ_i, can be modeled as a single process with $\lambda = \sum_i \lambda_i$. Hence the chance that no endogenous event occurs in a time-passage interval of length l is $\exp(-\sum_i \lambda_i)l$. If an event does occur, then the chance that it is of the type belonging to process i is λ_i/λ.

I now present the algorithm. I use the notation date(L) to denote the date of the last eventinstant in timeline L.

```
; Add a new eventinstant at the end of timeline, after
elapsed
; time units. Put an event of type event at the new eventinstant.
TIMELINE-ADVANCE (event,elapsed,timeline)
  Let advdate = date(timeline) + elapsed
  Pass-time(timeline,advdate);
  Add-eventinstant(advdate,timeline);
```

```
Add-event(event,timeline)
```

; This routine fills in a time-passage interval with endogenous events
```
Pass-time(timeline,nextdate)
 Let rl = Event-rule-instances(timeline)
 If not empty(rl)
```
then Let $\lambda = \sum(\lambda_i)$ for every rule instance in rl
Let prob = $1 - e^{-\lambda(\text{nextdate}-\text{date}(timeline))}$
```
 if random-choice(prob)
 then Let x = random real number
 between 0 and 1
```
Let when = $\frac{-\log(1-x\times\text{prob})}{\lambda}$
Let which = *pick rule i from* rl
with probability $\frac{\lambda_i}{\lambda}$
```
 One-endogenous-event
 (which,timeline,
 date(timeline)+when,
 nextdate)
```

```
Event-rule-instances(timeline)
 Let instances=()
```
For every rule $A \xrightarrow{d}\mid E$
```
 Let <anses,newoccs> =
 TL-RETRIEVE(A,last-time-point(timeline),timeline)
```
Ignore newoccs — *they'll be picked up by the call to*
```
 Check-clipping;
 For a in anses
 add instance of rule for a to instances;
 instances
```

; Add event from rule-instance *to* timeline *at time* newdate,
; then pass time until thendate
```
One-endogenous-event(rule-instance,timeline,newdate,thendate)
 Add-eventinstant(newdate,timeline);
 Add-event(event from rule-instance,timeline);
 Pass-time(timeline,thendate)
```

```
Add-eventinstant(date,timeline)
```
Add one more eventinstant, with date date, *to the list in*
```
timeline
```

```
Add-event(event,timeline)
```

```
Add event to happenings(last eventinstant of timeline);
Forward-chain(event,timeline);
Check-clipping(timeline)
```

```
Forward-chain(event,timeline)
                      p
For every rule  A/e |→_ B,
where e unifies with event
with substitution θ
Let <anses,newoccs>
= TL-RETRIEVE(θA,
penultimate-time-point(timeline),
timeline)
Ignore newoccs (see comment in Event-rule-instances);
For a in anses
Conclude-from-rule(rule,a,
last-time-point(timeline),
timeline)
```

```
Check-clipping(timeline)
For each occ
∈
overlapping-occasions(penultimate-time-point
(timeline))
If Been-clipped(occ,last-time-point(timeline),timeline)
then end(occ) := timepoint
else add occ
to overlapping-occasions(last-time-point
(timeline))
```

This algorithm is somewhat unusual in that its termination condition is probabilistic. It can in principle loop, interpolating new events, forever, as Pass-time calls One-endogenous-event and One-endogenous-event calls Pass-time. Of course, the probability of this happening is zero.

Lemma 3 If a timeline L for a consistent theory $\mathcal{T}$ is properly ended, and properly established and properly clipped through its last time point, then TIMELINE-ADVANCE(e, l, L) will

1. Make a decision about creating or clipping an occasion at a time point only if the decision has not been made before;
2. Make all decisions based on the correct conditional probabilities, as laid out in Definition 5;
3. Leave L properly established and properly clipped through t.

Proof: TIMELINE-ADVANCE adds eventinstants only to the end of a timeline, using Add-eventinstant. Add-event then runs forward chaining rules, calling TL-RETRIEVE on the past of the new timeline (which = the last time point of the old timeline). By Lemma 2, TL-RETRIEVE leaves the timeline in the proper state up through that time point. So all I have to do is show that the later machinations of Add-event obey clauses 1 through 3 of the lemma. Clause 1 follows because Add-event uses Conclude-from-rule (Lemma 1). The proof of clause 2 is essentially the same as for clause 3 of Lemma 2, again because of the use of Conclude-from-rule. The proof of clause 4 is obtained by inspection of Check-clipping, which is essentially the same as Bring-forward, but applies to every element of the overlapping-occasions of the previous time point.

Lemma 4 TIMELINE-ADVANCE creates new events in accordance with clause 5 of Definition 5.

Proof: For simplicity, we consider the case where an event is created by exactly one firable rule instance, of the form $A \xrightarrow{d} | E$, and let $\lambda_1 = 1/d$. What we want to prove is that

$$P(E \text{ occurs in interval } [t, t+dt) \mid A{\downarrow}t) = \lambda_1 dt$$

in accordance with clause 5 of Definition 5. In this formula, P stands for probability defined over execution traces of TIMELINE-ADVANCE for a given set of exogenous occurrences. There are an infinite number of such traces, and, if we wanted to be technical about it, we would define carefully how to impose a measure on them. However, these technicalities would take us far from the topic of the chapter, and would not reveal any unsurprising phenomena, so we will just use common sense.

The only way for TL-RETRIEVE to conclude that A is true at t is for it to conclude that A is true after some previous occurrence G, and for no other events to be added to the timeline from then until t. G must follow or be identical to C, the last exogenous event before t.[68] See Figure 2.

Hence, abbreviating "an occurrence of E is placed in interval $[t, t+dt)$" as "$E \downarrow t$"; and "no event is created between t_1 and t_2 as $N(t_1, t_2)$"; and "the set of firable $\_{\to}|$ rule instances at t_1 is F," as $F{\downarrow}G$, we have

$$
\begin{aligned}
P(E{\downarrow}t \mid A{\downarrow}t) = P(E{\downarrow}t \mid \ \exists G, F \quad & (date(C) \le date(G) < t \\
& \wedge A{\downarrow}G \\
& \wedge F{\downarrow}G \\
& \wedge N(date(G), t)))
\end{aligned}
$$

Consider an arbitrary occurrence G with $date(C) \le date(G) < t <$ nextdate, and consider an arbitrary timeline in which G has just been added, and Event-rule-instances has then picked the set F of all firable rule instances (which it will by Lemma 2). Their frequencies λ_i add up to

λ. (λ_1 is one of them, of course.) Let $\Delta t = \texttt{nextdate} - \texttt{date}(G)$, the size of the interval into which events may or not be placed. If the algorithm creates an event, it creates it with date $\texttt{when}+date(G)$, and the cumulative distribution of $\texttt{when}$ has $P(\texttt{when} + date(G) \le t) =$

$$\frac{1 - e^{-\lambda(t-date(G))}}{1 - e^{-\lambda\Delta t}}.$$

This formula can be verified by finding the cumulative distribution of $\texttt{when}$ given that $\texttt{x}$ is uniformly distributed (the standard "inversion trick" for generating nonuniform random numbers; see, for example, (Bratley et al., 1987)). The probability that the event occurs before t is this number $\times$ the probability that the algorithm creates an event at all, which is $1 - e^{-\lambda\Delta t}$. The resulting cumulative distribution for $\texttt{when}$ is

$$P(\texttt{when} + date(G) \le t) = 1 - e^{-\lambda(t-date(G))}.$$

We are interested in the probability that t is the point the program picks for the first event to occur. This value is of course zero, unless we express it as a probability density:

$$
\begin{aligned}
&\lim_{h\to 0} \frac{1 - e^{-\lambda(t-date(G)+h)} - \left(1 - e^{-\lambda(t-date(G))}\right)}{h} \\
={}&\lim_{h\to 0} \frac{e^{-\lambda(t-date(G))} - e^{-\lambda(t-date(G)+h)}}{h} \\
={}&\lim_{h\to 0} \frac{1}{h}\left(1 - \frac{e^{-\lambda(t-date(G)+h)}}{e^{-\lambda(t-date(G))}}\right) \\
={}&\lim_{h\to 0} \frac{1 - e^{-\lambda h}}{h} \\
={}&\lambda.
\end{aligned}
$$

The probability that our rule fires immediately after t is then $\lambda\, dt \frac{\lambda_1}{\lambda} = \lambda_1 dt$. This value does not depend on the particular timeline or event G, so it is in fact the $P(E{\downarrow}t \mid \exists G, F \ldots)$, so

$$P(\text{ some occurrence of } e \text{ between } t \text{ and } t + dt \mid A{\downarrow}t) = dt/d.$$

Timelines are created with START-TIMELINE:

```
START-TIMELINE()
  Let tl=Create a new timeline
  with one eventinstant with happenings (START)
  Forward-chain('(START),tl);
  tl
```

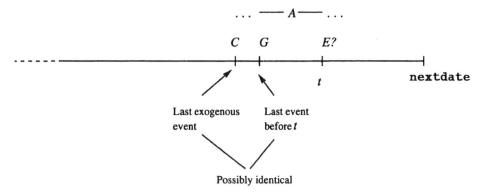

Figure 2. Generating autonomous event $E{\downarrow}t$ given $A{\uparrow}t$

We need an entry point to the system that allows a program to ask about an arbitrary point in the past, not just the last time point:

```
PAST-RETRIEVE (query,timepoint,timeline)
  Let <anses,newoccs>=TL-RETRIEVE(query,timepoint,timeline)
  Bring-forward-until-clipped(newoccs,
  last-time-point(timeline),
  timepoint,timeline);
  anses
```

PAST-RETRIEVE simply calls TL-RETRIEVE, then makes sure any new occasions created get clipped in the right place, using this subroutine:

```
Bring-forward-until-clipped(persisters,endpoint,
  beginpoint,timeline)
  If null(persisters) or endpoint=beginpoint
  then persisters
  else let persisters =
  Bring-forward-until-clipped(persisters,
  past(endpoint),
  beginpoint,
  timeline)
  Bring-forward(persisters,endpoint,timeline)
```

This routine works by bringing persisters forward to past(endpoint) recursively, then using Bring-forward to get them from past(endpoint) to endpoint.

Theorem 5 If a timeline is created by START-TIMELINE, enlarged with TIMELINE-ADVANCE, and queried by TIMELINE-RETRIEVE and

PAST-RETRIEVE, then the resulting timeline state will be properly established, properly clipped, and drawn from the distribution specified by Definition 5.

Proof: START-TIMELINE creates and initializes a timeline (using Forward-chain). Because Forward-chain uses Conclude-from-rule, it generates initial time points with the correct statistics and tidiness, by an argument similar to that in the proof of Lemma 2. TIMELINE-ADVANCE and TIMELINE-RETRIEVE maintain these properties (Lemmas 2, 3 and 4). PAST-RETRIEVE introduces nothing novel, so it can be shown to maintain them, too.

8.3. The Actual Implementation

The actual implementation enhances the idealized algorithm in two ways: greater expressiveness and greater efficiency.

8.3.1. ENHANCEMENTS TO EXPRESSIVENESS

The implemented system is more expressive in several ways:

- $\_\leftarrow\_$ rules are fully implemented. The only change is that Establish-after must call TL-RETRIEVE for the antecedent of such a rule, at the same time point rather than its predecessor.
- In a rule consequent, a conjunct can be of the form $\underline{t}A$, meaning that A becomes true and persists for time t.
- In rule antecedents, it's possible to escape to Lisp for special extensions and low-level computations.
- It is also possible to escape to a simple Prolog-style backward-chaining system for timeless goals. Each rule is of the form $B \leftarrow A_1 \wedge A_2 \wedge \ldots$, where each A_i is handled by another Prolog-style rule or a Lisp handler.
- There is an interface to Lisp for setting up the initial time point.

The implementation is Lisp-based, so rules actually have a Lisp-style syntax. $A \wedge B \ldots$ is actually written (AND A B ...), as usual. Here is a translation table for the special symbols of the system, where typically "$\_$" is replaced by P and "$|$" is replaced by E:

$A \_\leftarrow \_B$	(P<-P A B)
$A/E \mid \overset{r}{\rightarrow} \_ B$	(E->P A E r B)
$B \_\overset{r}{\leftarrow}\mid E \backslash A$	(P<-E r B E A)
$A \_\overset{d}{\rightarrow}\mid E$	(P->E A d E)
$A \leftarrow B$	(<- A B)
$\neg A$ (in antecedent)	(THNOT A)
$\neg A$ (in consequent)	(CLIP A)
$\underline{t}A$	(PERSIST t A)
$A \wedge B \ldots$	(AND A B ...)
$p(a, b, \ldots)$	(P a b ...)
Variable v	?v

Rules are asserted by the use of the construct (DEF-FACT-GROUP *name* — *rules* —). There is currently only one, global, database of temporal rules allowed.

The presence of PERSIST complicates TIMELINE-ADVANCE somewhat. Each occasion must have an optional "expiration date" when it will cease to be true. Before Pass-time can be called, the system must check for occasion expirations during the time-passage interval. If any are found, it must insert an expiration event, then pass the time before the expiration, then pass the time after the expiration.

It is quite valuable to be able to escape to Lisp. Besides being more efficient for doing arithmetic and such, it allows us to transcend the basic formalism in several ways. Here is a list of some of the more useful extensions implemented this way:

- (THNOT p):[69] TL-RETRIEVE doesn't actually have to check for this case specially. It just does a general check for Lisp handlers, and THNOT has one that tries to prove p, hoping to fail.
- (OR A B ...): Disjunction
- (EVAL *exp* *val*): Evaluate *exp* and unify result with *val*.
- (< m n), (> m n), etc.: Inequalities
- (LISP-PRED r —*args*—): Run Lisp predicate r (e.g., MEMBER) on the instantiated *args*. Succeeds if predicate returns #T.
- (START-TIME p t): Succeeds if p is true now and started at dated t.
- (RECENTLY p b e): Succeeds if p is not true now, but on the last occasion of p, it started at date b and ended at date e.

The presence of $\_\leftarrow\_$ and EVAL allows us to express a sort of rule that is missing in the formal theory developed in Section 8.2 and (McDermott, 1994). Suppose we want to express the idea that if a box contains a certain collection of objects, and one is grabbed, then a random object leaves the box. We can do that thus:

```
(P<-E 1.0 (AND (CONTENTS ?BOX ?NEW)
  (CLIP (CONTENTS ?BOX ?L)))
  (GRAB-FROM ?BOX)
  (AND (CONTENTS ?BOX ?L)
  (EVAL (RANDELT ?L) ?OB)
  (EVAL (DELETE ?OB ?L) ?NEW)))
```

This rule states that when GRAB-FROM occurs, the contents of the box change from ?L to ?NEW, where ?NEW is ?L with an object removed. The choice of removed object is made by the Lisp procedure RANDELT. In this way we can eliminate a deficiency in the formalism of this chapter, which has trouble expressing the idea that an event can have one of several mutually exclusive outcomes. Other formalisms (for example, that of Thiébaux and Hertzberg (Thiébaux and Hertzberg, 1992)) allow for this possibility, but only in the case where the possible outcomes can be laid out as alternative rules; I don't know of any formalism that allows for the kind of choice among alternatives computed when the rule is applied that the rule above exemplifies. Here we achieve that choice only by escaping to Lisp, and thus leaving the formal semantics behind.

There are other applications of this ability to generate random numbers in Lisp. Suppose we want a non-Poisson model of the occurrences of event type E. Suppose L is a Lisp function that generates a random interevent interval according to this model. We introduce a proposition S (for "suppress E") such that E occurs immediately whenever S is false:

```
(DEF-FACT-GROUP NON-POISSON

  (P->E (THNOT S) 0 E)

  (E->P (EVAL (L) ?LIFETIME)
  (START)
  1 (PERSIST ?LIFETIME S))
  (E->P (EVAL (L) ?LIFETIME) E 1 (PERSIST ?LIFETIME S)))
```

The last expressiveness enhancement I discuss in this section is one of the most important. A key desideratum for a temporal-inference system is that it connect smoothly to users' representations for what's true in the present. If a program is projecting the future, then its beliefs about the present have to be the starting point. Picture a timeline whose initial state corresponds to that set of beliefs. One way to make this picture a reality is to require all users to represent the present as a "short timeline" consisting of just one instant. But there are two reasons to reject this idea. First, it could be clumsy and constraining. Users design their representations with various goals of efficiency and expressiveness in mind that have nothing to do with temporal inference, and we want them to feel free to focus on those goals. Second, some of the information about the present may be uncertain. The program might know that there are between 2 and 4 balls in box1. Our strategy for probabilistic projection is to generate definite projections with different probabilities. So if the temporal-inference system generates several projections, we would like it to pick two balls in about one-third of the projections, three balls in about one-third, and four balls in about one-third. In each case, there is no uncertainty in the initial state of the timeline.

What we need is an interface between the timeline manager and static representation systems. We provide it with a mutant rule of the form

$$\text{(INITIALIZER } A \ (f \ -args-)),$$

where A is an atomic formula and f is a Lisp function. To compute instances of A true in the initial state, f is called on the given *args*, which are usually just variables bound in A. f is expected to return a list of the form $((p_1 \ l_1)$ $(p_2 \ l_2) \ \ldots)$, where each p_i is an atomic formula and each l_i is a *lifetime*, — that is, a number or #F. An occasion with the given atomic formula will be created starting in the initial state with the given lifetime (#F means "until clipped"). The p_i do not have to be instances of A.

The key feature is that a given f will be called *just once* for a given set of args. f may use random numbers to set the state up.

Here is how we could handle the situation in which there are an unknown number of balls in box1. Suppose that we represent the number of balls in a box by storing a pair "$(l \ h)$" on the property list each box's name, where the actual number of balls lies between l and h. Then we could write the following initialization code:

```
(DEF-FACT-GROUP BALL-BOX-INIT
  (INITIALIZER (IN ?X ?B) (FILL-BOX ?B)))

(DEFUN FILL-BOX (B)
  (LET ((NUMS (GET B 'NUMBALLS)))
  (COND ((NULL NUMS) '())
  (T
  (LET ((L (CAR NUMS)) (H (CADR NUMS)))
  (DO ((N (+ L (RANDOM (+ 1 (- H L)))))
  (- N 1))
  (RES '()))
  ((= N 0) RES)
```

```
(LET ((BALLNAME (GENSYM)))
(PUSH '((IN ,BALLNAME ,B) #F)
RES) )))) )))
```

This example is overly simple and contrived, but you get the idea.[70]

I close this section by explaining how the theory of Section 8.2.1 is really expressed in the system:

```
(DEF-FACT-GROUP EXAMPLE-THEORY

; Initially, NUGGET1 is at 10,0, and...
(E->P (TRUE) (START) 1.0 (LOC NUGGET1 (COORDS 10 0)))


; T1000, an enemy robot, is at 0,0
(E->P (TRUE) (START) 1.0 (LOC T1000 (COORDS 0 0)))


; Roughly every 10 sconds, T1000 moves right.
(P->E (TRUE) 10.0 (MOVE T1000 1 0))


; When an agent moves, its location changes.
(E->P (AND (LOC ?B (COORDS ?X ?Y))
(EVAL (+ ?X ?DX) ?X1)
(EVAL (+ ?Y ?DY) ?Y1))
(MOVE ?B ?DX ?DY)
1.0
(AND (LOC ?B (COORDS ?X1 ?Y1))
(CLIP (LOC ?B (COORDS ?X ?Y)) )))


; Whenever T1000 and the nugget are in the same place,
; T1000 grasps the nugget, typically within 1 second.
(P->E (AND (LOC T1000 (COORDS ?X ?Y))
(LOC NUGGET1 (COORDS ?X ?Y)))
1.0
(GRASP T1000 NUGGET1))


; Grasping succeeds with a probability of 80%.
(P<-E 0.8 (AND (HOLDING ?A ?B)
(CLIP (LOC ?B (COORDS ?X ?Y))))
(GRASP ?A ?B)
(AND (LOC ?A (COORDS ?X ?Y))
(LOC ?B (COORDS ?X ?Y)))))
```

8.3.2. OPTIMIZATIONS

A key observation about temporal inference is that many deductions are repeated several times. The procedure `Establish-query` runs $\_\leftarrow|$ rules at a time point but also calls itself recursively to run them at all previous time points, because a query instance that becomes true earlier could persist until now. Hence the unifications in `Establish-after` will be repeated many times. Similarly, `Check-clipping` will be called every time a new event is added, and it will call `Been-clipped` on every occasion in `overlapping-occasion(last-time-point(`*timeline*`))`, and run through the $\_\leftarrow|$ rules. The same sort of pattern recurs in typical applications of the timeline. A planning algorithm might issue the request (`LOC AGENT ?W`) repeatedly.

Another key observation is that most queries start at the end of a timeline. The reason is that the timeline is built by repeated calls to `TIMELINE-ADVANCE`, which calls `TL-RETRIEVE` on the antecedent of every $|\rightarrow \_$ rule. Furthermore, most occasions true at the end of the timeline remain true when new events are tacked on, and they have to be copied to the new eventinstant. Many of these queries end up being propagated into the past, but action in the present dominates.

On top of this, the idealized versions of the algorithms give no details as to how the system is to perform all the retrievals of rules and occasions that are called for. The idealized versions also do not handle `PERSIST` literals, $\_\leftarrow\_$ rules, or `INITIALIZER`s.

To meet all these challenges, the implemented algorithm differs from the idealized version in several respects:

1 When using $|\rightarrow\_$ and $\_\leftarrow|$ rules, `TIMELINE-RETRIEVE` does not bother to check that the annihilation of the consequent is true before the event. In many cases, the check would be redundant, and usually the rule writer will not mind making the check explicit when necessary. Because of this optimization, it is possible for there to be two overlapping occasions with the same proposition, which is formally meaningless. That means that a program that queries the timeline may have to be careful about duplicate answers. However, one thing we do not have to worry about is the possibility that the multiple occasions will trigger later $|\rightarrow\_$ rules multiply, causing two overlapping occasions to yield four consequences, which then yield eight, and so forth. That's because the first time an occasion is created (by `Conclude-from-rule`) starting at a eventinstant, an entry is made for its proposition in the established-queries table for the eventinstant, so `Conclude-from-rule` will avoid creating a second one starting at the same eventinstant.

2 Occasions are not stored in lists, but discrimination trees (Charniak et al., 1987). I call these *formula trees*. Given a formula with free variables,

one can efficiently retrieve from a formula tree all the occasions it contains whose propositions match that formula.

3 Rules are also indexed, albeit somewhat less efficiently. Different kinds of rules are indexed as they will be retrieved, each associated with one or more symbols. |→ _ (E->P) rules are accessible from the main functor of their events because they will be used in Forward-chain just after an event has been created. _ ←| (P<-E), _ ← _ (P<-P) and ← (<-) rules are indexed by each predicate in their consequents. _ →| (P->E) rules are left unindexed, because they are all tried every time the timeline is extended.

In each case, the system actually stores a pointer from the indexing symbol to a list of all fact-group names that contain a relevant rule. The reason for this is to simplify redefinition of fact groups.

4 A timeline, formerly just a list of eventinstants, acquires several new fields, and now looks like this:

- FIRST: A pointer to the time point for the START eventinstant.
- LAST: A pointer to the last time point (so far).
- INDEFINITE-PERSISTERS: A formula tree containing all occasions that overlap with the last eventinstant of the timeline.
- EARLIEST-EXPIRER: The date when the next occasion in INDEFINITE-PERSISTERS will expire, or #F if all of them will persist until clipped.
- EXPIRERS: A list of all occasions in INDEFINITE-PERSISTERS with definite expiration dates.
- QUERIES: A table, indexed by predicate, of all queries that have ever been issued for this timeline.
- EVENT-RULES: All the _ →| rules, collected once from fact groups when the timeline is initialized.

The QUERIES table can be used to "uniquify" queries. That is, when a query comes into the system, the first action is to see if a variant of this query has been handled before. If not, this one is stored in the table. If a variant is found, TL-RETRIEVE uses the stored variant instead of the original query. This tactic allows us to use EQ to test for whether a query is established, rather than a much more expensive variant test (which needs to happen just once).

The system uses the same table to uniquify occasion propositions, for much the same reason.

5 An eventinstant actually looks like this:

> DATE: When it happens
> TIMESTAMP: A finer-grained time measure, used by applications. (Two consecutive eventinstants can have the same DATE, but not the same TIMESTAMP.)
> HAPPENINGS: Events that happen here; () if nothing happens.

> BEGINNERS: A formula tree containing occasions that start here and are eventually clipped.
> PERSISTERS: A formula tree containing occasions that started before this eventinstant and are clipped at some later eventinstant.
> TEMPS: A formula tree containg occasions derived from _ ← _ rules. These occasions do not persist past the next eventinstant.
> ESTABLISHED: A list of queries that have been established here. The queries are uniquified — that is, they all appear in the QUERIES table for this timeline — so the system can use EQ to search it.
> CLIPNOTES: As before, a table of pairs of the form ⟨atomic-formula, boolean⟩ recording whether any occasion with that formula will be clipped at this eventinstant. These formulas are also uniquified, so an EQ test can be used to check the clip status of an occasion.

We still have some occasions associated directly with an eventinstant, but only those whose endpoints have been seen. Those still true at the end of the timeline (so far) will be stored in the INDEFINITE-PERSISTERS table for the timeline. When a new eventinstant is added, clipped occasions must be moved from this table to the eventinstants they overlap. But most of the table stays the same.

The procedure Match-against-occasions now must check four sets of occasions: the BEGINNERS, PERSISTERS, and TEMPS of the eventinstant in question, plus all elements of INDEFINITE-PERSISTERS that overlap the eventinstant.

6 As rules are defined, the system keeps a table that associates an event functor with all the predicates whose occasions it can possibly clip by way of P<-E rules. E.g., If (MOVE ...) can clip only occasions of the form (LOC ...), then the clip-table entry for MOVE is (LOC). This table enables TIMELINE-ADVANCE to update the INDEFINITE-PERSISTERS formula tree efficiently. Formula trees are discriminated first by predicate, so the only subtrees that need to be touched when an eventinstant $(A \ldots)$ is added to the timeline are those with a predicate in either the clip table for A or the clipnotes for the new eventinstant.

7 An occasion actually looks like this:

* PROPO: The proposition, uniquified using the QUERIES table of the timeline.
* BEGIN: The time point where the occasion begins.
* END: If the end of the occasion is known, this is it. Otherwise, this will be a list of "chainrecs," each of which represents a _←| that could clip it. See below.
* EXPIRATION: If the occasion has a finite lifetime, this is its expiration date. Otherwise, this field is #F.

* JUSTIF: The "justification" for the occasion, a record of how it came to occur. In this chapter, I do not discuss justification structures, but the idea is to set up data dependencies to link events with their effects.

8 To avoid repeating all those unifications, the system employs the new datatype *chainrec* to keep track of a "deduction in progress." For example, whenever an occasion for proposition A is generated, the system finds all P<-E rules that contain a literal unifying with (CLIP A). For each, it makes a chainrec ("chain record") recording the rule, the substitution, and the result of applying the substitution to the event in the rule. It then sets the END field of the occasion to be a list of all such chainrecs. Been-clipped then need not consult the database but simply gets this list from the occasion under consideration. If the list is empty, then the occasion will never be clipped by a P<-E rule.

9 The other use of chainrecs is in backward chaining. The QUERIES table of a timeline is used to associate, with each query Q, a list of chainrecs for all the P<-E, P<-P, and INITIALIZER rules whose consequents contain a literal that unifies with Q. Each such chainrec records the substitution resulting from a successful unification of Q with some literal in the consequent of a rule. Establish-query must then try these rules at every eventinstant.

Actually, Establish-query can do a lot better than that, because what the system stores with each uniquified query is actually two lists, the "start chainrecs" and the "regular chainrecs." The former list is for INITIALIZER rules and rules of the form (P<-E ...(START) ...). There is no point in trying these rules out anywhere except at the beginning of the timeline, and hence no point in running through a deep recursion to get there. These rules are handled specially by jumping to (START) and then working back to the query point using Bring-forward. Regular P<-E rules require repeated calls to Establish-after. If there aren't any, the system skips this phase.

8.4. Experimental Results

In a general rule interpreter like this one, it is impossible to make general statements about run times. It's not hard to make up rule sets that require superexponential times to do projections. However, most rule sets are better behaved. They tend to give rise to the same or similar queries repeated at successive time steps, so many attempts to answer them need only scan back through one eventinstant. Most long scans result from queries that go back to the START event to transfer information from the current world model to the timeline.

Here is an example of a theory. It is contrived, but illustrative, and not as violent as some:

```
(DEF-FACT-GROUP INITIALIZERS

  (P<-E 1.0 (KISSED 0) (START) (ALWAYS))

  (P<-E 1.0 (HUGGED 0) (START) (ALWAYS))

  (P<-E 1.0 (LOC ?X ?X) (START) (ALWAYS))

  (INITIALIZER (PROTECTED ?X) (INITIALLY-PROTECTED ?X)))

(DEFUN INITIALLY-PROTECTED (X)
  (COND ((AND (NOT (HASMVARS X))
  (RANDOM-CHOICE 0.5))
  (VALUES (LIST '(#F (PROTECTED ,X)))
  #'(LAMBDA () '#T)))
  (T '()) ))

(DEF-FACT-GROUP RANDOM-EVENTS

  (P->E (AND (KISSED ?I)
  (EVAL (+ ?I 1) ?I1))
  10.0
  (KISS ?I1))

  (P->E (AND (HUGGED ?I)
  (EVAL (+ ?I 2) ?I2))
  20.0
  (HUG ?I2)))

(DEF-FACT-GROUP KISS-AND-HUG

  (E->P (KISSED ?I)
  (KISS ?J)
  1.0
  (AND (KISSED ?J)
  (CLIP (KISSED ?I))))

  (P<-E 0.8
  (PERSIST 50 (BLUSHING ?I ?J))
  (KISS ?J)
  (AND (HUGGED ?I)
  (KISSED ?I)
  (THNOT (PROTECTED ?I))))

  (E->P (HUGGED ?I)
  (HUG ?J)
  1.0
```

```
(AND (HUGGED ?J)
(CLIP (HUGGED ?I)))))

(DEF-FACT-GROUP KICK-AROUND

(E->P (AND (NEIGHBOR ?L ?N)
(LOC ?X ?N)
(EVAL (+ ?N 8) ?NEW))
(KICK ?L)
1.0
(AND (LOC ?X ?NEW)
(CLIP (LOC ?X ?N)))) )

(DEF-FACT-GROUP NEIGHBOR-DEF

(<- (NEIGHBOR ?L1 ?L2)
(EVAL (- ?L1 2) ?L2))

(<- (NEIGHBOR ?L1 ?L2)
(EVAL (- ?L1 1) ?L2))

(<- (NEIGHBOR ?L1 ?L2)
(EVAL (+ ?L1 1) ?L2))

(<- (NEIGHBOR ?L1 ?L2)
(EVAL (+ ?L1 2) ?L2)) )
```

There are two types of autonomous events, (KISS i) and (HUG i). Initially we have (KISSED 0) and (HUGGED 0); every 5 seconds (on the average) a KICK event occurs, which increments (KISSED i) to (KISSED $i+1$). Similarly for HUGGing, which occurs every 10 seconds on the average, but increments (HUGGED i) by two. If (HUGGED i) and (KISSED i) are ever both true when a (KISS j) occurs and (PROTECTED i) is not true, then an occasion of (BLUSHING i j) begins and persists for 50 seconds. Objects are initially PROTECTED with probability 1/2.

We test the performance of the program by generating exogenous-event streams consisting of $N+1$ events of the form (KICK 5), (KICK 15), ..., (KICK $5+10N$). As N increases, the initial state grows to generate more and more occasions of the form (LOC x x). Here is a table of the execution times that result:

N	Run Time	Number of Events	Time/Event
10	1.0	28	0.03
20	3.4	54	0.06
30	6.2	81	0.08
40	8.8	101	0.09
50	11.8	128	0.09
60	15.0	154	0.10
70	19.0	183	0.10
80	22.9	202	0.11
90	27.5	230	0.12
100	31.7	249	0.13

These numbers are obtained by running each experiment ten times and averaging the results. The key column is Time/Event. This grows linearly with N, indicating that the total time to generate a timeline with N exogenous events is quadratic in N. (See Figure 3.) It's hard to imagine doing much better than that, given that generating a timeline takes many retrievals in order to run $\mapsto$ _ rules, and these retrievals involve a linear component — namely, the time required to check where an occasion added to the beginning of the timeline gets clipped.

Although the shape of this graph is gratifying, we are not too happy with the actual run times. In practice, the projector runs too slowly to do a good job of supporting the kind of planning we are interested in. For realistic-sized plans, we can do no more than two or three projections per minute. If the projector ran an order-of-magnitude faster, it would enable the planner to get larger samples of projections. Currently, projections suffice to tell the planner about almost certain outcomes but cause it to overreact to or overlook less likely outcomes. Whether the time spent by the projector is inherent in the complex job it is doing or just an artifact of the Lisp implementaion, is still under investigation.

8.5. Conclusions

I have presented a formalism for expressing probabilities of outcomes of events and shown that it is possible to use rules expressed in this formalism to generate scenarios — "projections" — of what will result from a given event sequence. The formalism has a formal semantics, and I have proven two main results about it:

1. A broad class of rule sets expressed in this formalism yield well-defined models.
2. The projection algorithm generates a particular projection with the probability specified by the formal semantics.

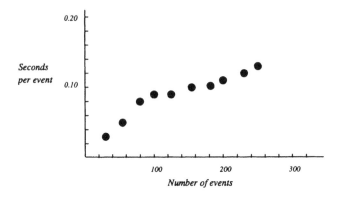

Figure 3.   Time per event required to generate N events

Furthermore, the algorithm appears to be reasonably efficient. The running times given in Section 8.4 are not in themselves impressive, but I hope the growth rate is. As the number of events projected grows, the time to generate one more event grows linearly and slowly. Presumably translating the algorithm from Lisp to C would produce a big absolute speedup, although we have no plans to do that.

This temporal-projection system is now in use in the XFRM planning system being developed at Yale. It is available to interested parties by ftp; please contact mcdermott@cs.yale.edu.

Some enhancements to the system would obviously be worth exploring. The present formalism allows random events to happen at arbitrary real times, but it does not allow for continuous change. For example, we might want to specify that while an agent is moving, its fuel supply depletes continuously with a random slope. It's not hard to see how to alter the implementation to allow for such phenomena, and in fact we have done this on an ad hoc basis. If a quantity is changing continuously toward some threshold (such as an empty fuel tank), then have **Pass-time** check to see if it's gotten there during the time-passage interval being filled in. If it has, then an eventinstant declaring the occurrence of a "reached threshold" event can be added to the timeline. (This is very similar to what happens with expirations of facts with finite lifetimes.)

Unfortunately, as soon as we allow continuous change, the formal analysis will have to be changed significantly. The formal proofs of my results depend crucially on nothing happening between eventinstants, and that assumption will have to be relaxed. Possibly the techniques of Penberthy ((Penberthy, 1993)) will help.

Another class of extensions revolves around allowing rules to make random choices among sets of possibilities. Currently, we can arrange for that only by escaping to Lisp to generate random numbers, and it would be better if the choice was indicated in the rule, and governed by a formal analysis. The problem here is not the formal analysis itself but figuring out a framework that encompasses all the possibilities. One approach might be to introduce a new sort of rule that allows for labeled random choices at a point. (They have to be labeled so that different rules can refer to different random choices at the same eventinstant.) The choice of whether a rule fires or not is then just a special case.

Acknowledgments

I have learned a lot of probability theory in the course of writing this chapter. I thank Dana Angluin, Joe Chang, John Lemmer, and Grigory Matviyenko. Thanks to Matt Ginsberg for suggesting a simpler version of TIMELINE-ADVANCE than the one I originally thought of. Michael Beetz and Wenhong Zhu made many helpful comments about an earlier draft of this chapter.

Notes

[60] In (Dean and McDermott, 1987), these were called *time tokens*." The implementation of occasions is not quite faithful to this formal definition, as we see in Section 8.3.

[61] In the actual implementation, formulas and rules are expressed in a Lispish notation, which is described in Section 8.3.

[62] There are more flexible ways in the actual implementation, described in Section 8.3.

[63] An alternative way to state the condition is to take the consequent of a rule, and generate all possible combinations of "signs" for the atomic formulas in it. Every combination except the one given must have probability zero. For the case at hand, the second rule would assign conditional probability zero to $B \land \neg C$, $\neg B \land C$, and $\neg B \land \neg C$.

[64] Of course, by making additional assumptions, it is possible to assign probabilities in cases like these. One such approach is explored by Thiébaux and Hertzberg (Thiébaux and Hertzberg, 1992). In my experience, it is usually preferable to rewrite rules to avoid inconsistencies.

[65] and, in the actual implementation, timeline initializers, described in Section 8.3.

[66] An alternative idea would be to keep a "used rule instance" table in addition to the established-queries table.

[67] The only reason to use d instead of λ in the rule is that in the implementation, it is occasionally useful to set $d = 0$.

[68] There are execution traces in which an infinite number of events happen after A becomes true (in fact, there are some in which A changes truth value infinitely often just before t), but the set of all such execution traces is of measure 0, and TL-RETRIEVE will run forever in such cases, never concluding that A is true at t.

[69] This negation-as-failure operator was originally named by Sussman et al. in (Sussman et al., 1971).

[70] One simplication is that in the actual system, an initializer must also return a "justification" for its answer. The justification system is not mature enough to talk about in this chapter.

9. Underlying Semantics for Action and Change with Ramification

Erik Sandewall

9.1. Validation of Theories of Action and Change

In earlier publications addressing logics of actions and change, we have developed an underlying semantics for the special case of strict inertia, and used it for assessment of the range of applicability of a number of entailment methods. The case of strict inertia does not allow for ramification, qualifications, or surprises. The present article addresses the problem of ramification using the same systematic methodology as was previously used for strict inertia. We start with a discussion of methodology.

9.1.1. BEFORE THE ADVENT OF VALIDATION: EXAMPLE-BASED METHODOLOGY

There has been much research in recent years on methods for reasoning about actions and change, and on finding solutions of the so-called frame problem. New variants of nonmonotonic logics for common-sense reasoning have been proposed, only to be quickly refuted by counterexamples. Unfortunately, the results that have been obtained in this fashion are notoriously unreliable. According to a common research methodology in the area, the evidence in favor of a proposed logic or theory should consist of intuitive plausibility arguments and a small number of scenario examples for which the theory is proven (or claimed) to give the intended conclusions and no others. This prevailing methodology was summarized by Davis (Davis, 1990) as follows:

> The basic approach used here, as in much of the research on automating commonsense reasoning, is to take a number of examples of commonsense inference in a commonsense domain, generally deductive

inference; identify the general domain knowledge and the particular problem specification used in the inference; develop a formal language in which this knowledge can be expressed; and define the primitives of the language as carefully and precisely as possible...

This methodology has been effective for identifying a range of important problems, such as the qualification and ramification problems. However, since it relies on examples, it is not sufficient for obtaining reliable results of a general nature. One also needs to *validate* a proposed approach and prove that it is correct for the intended type of reasoning about a whole class of scenarios.

9.1.2. VALIDATION OF NONMONOTONIC THEORIES

The quotation from Davis indicates also how each proposed approach to common-sense reasoning must specify the syntax of its language of logical formulae, the conventions for how to use that language for describing actual scenarios, and the methods for drawing conclusions from a scenario description. I shall use the term *method* or (more explicitly) *entailment method* for the formally defined mapping from scenario descriptions to sets of conclusions (or equivalently, models), and reserve the use of the word *logic* for the syntax and the formal semantics which may be used by a particular entailment method, or by several methods jointly. The logic used by an entailment method will be called its *base logic*. The combination of an entailment method, its base logic, and the conventions for their use will be referred to as a *theory*, for example, a theory of actions and change.

We shall only be concerned with validation approaches that apply specifically to the entailment method, while taking the underlying base logic and conventions as given.

The validation of an entailment method must rely, besides the base logic, on a formal definition of the function Σ from a *scenario description* Υ, expressed using logical formulae, to the set $\Sigma(\Upsilon)$ of its *intended models*. If $[\![\Upsilon]\!]$ represents the set of classical models, then it is commonly assumed that $\Sigma(\Upsilon) \subseteq [\![\Upsilon]\!]$, reflecting the possibility of conclusions by default. Once the intended models function has been defined, one can analyze a proposed entailment method in terms of its formulation as a *selection function S* from scenario descriptions to sets of models. The validation consists of proving that the set $S(\Upsilon)$ of *selected models* is equal to $\Sigma(\Upsilon)$ for an interesting and sufficiently large class of scenario descriptions Υ.

The validation criterion can of course be formulated as well in terms of sets of conclusions: if $Cn(\Upsilon)$ is the set of classical conclusions from the given scenario description, $C(\Upsilon)$ is the set of actual conclusions using a proposed entailment method and $Ci(\Upsilon)$ is the set of intended conclusions according to the chosen formal definition, then usually $Cn(\Upsilon) \subset Ci(\Upsilon)$ especially when a nonmonotonic logic is being used, and one requires from C that $C(\Upsilon) = Ci(\Upsilon)$. In this article I use the model-theoretic formulation since it is the more convenient one for analyzing logics based on *preferential semantics*, where the set of selected models is chosen (in the simplest case) as $Min(\ll$, $[\![\Upsilon]\!])$, i.e. as the set of those classical models that are minimal with respect to some preference relation $\ll$. Many of the proposed entailment methods for action and change have this character.

This framework for validation depends on the fact that the base logic is held fixed, so that the notion of intended models can be defined in the terms of that logic. Validation and comparison of whole theories, containing both a logic and an entailment method, is a more complex affair and will not be discussed here.

9.1.3. APPROACHES TO THE VALIDATION OF THEORIES OF ACTIONS AND CHANGE

In the case of reasoning about actions and change, the scenario description is a *chronicle* containing statements about the state of the world at various points in time (the *observations*), about specific actions and their temporal order (the *schedule* of actions), as well as *action laws* defining the effects of actions. Models represent possible histories of the world; those models that satisfy all the statements but violate the "frame" assumption of persistence or inertia are classical but unintended models. Additional types of axioms may also be included for special purposes.

Lin and Shoham (Lin and Shoham, 1991) were probably the first to report a validation of a previously proposed theory of action. They showed that chronological minimization of change is correct for prediction in deterministic situation-calculus theories with strict inertia, i.e. no surprises or qualification, but allowing for ramification. The assumption of determinism applies for the ramification side-effects as well, so the set of intended models is required to be a singleton in their result.

A number of later papers have obtained validations of other theories, and for significantly broader classes of chronicles. Three main approaches have been followed.

9.1.3.1. *Systematic Methodology: "Features and Fluents"*.
The present author has used a *systematic methodology* whereby one can obtain precise results on the *range of applicability* of a number of previously proposed entailment methods, as well as some new ones (Sandewall, 1993a; Sandewall, 1993b; Sandewall, 1994a; Sandewall, 1994b). These results apply, right from the start, to a fairly large class of logics for actions and change, allowing for chronicles with nondeterministic actions and discrete metric time. This includes integer time as a special case, and allows one to represent actions with extended duration, which may be characterized not only in terms of their final effects, but also with respect to changes within their interval of duration. It also allows chronicles where the order of the actions is only partially specified, like in nonlinear planning (Sacerdoti, 1975). Several of the validations generalize trivially to the case of deterministic ramification, but ramification in nondeterministic chronicles is more difficult and was not addressed in those articles.

We have also shown in (Sandewall, 1994a) that these results generalize easily to the case of branching metric time as well, which means that situations calculus is subsumed as a simple special case. Yi (Yi, 1995) generalized some of these results to apply for scenarios with concurrency in the context of explicit metric time.

These validation results are *assessments*, which identify the range of correct applicability of each of a number of methods. We initially define a relatively large class of chronicles, and subdivide the class using a *taxonomy* in terms of a number of properties that chronicles may have. The complete assessment of an entailment method consists of both a lower bound and an upper bound. The lower bound is a family of chronicles within the taxonomy for which the method is provably correct; the upper bound is a family (larger or equal to the lower bound) outside which it is provably impossible that the method is correct. In this way it has sometimes been possible to identify the exact range of applicability of previously proposed theories of action.

The definition of the taxonomy is based on an *underlying semantics* which captures basic notions of intelligent agents, and defines intended models in its terms. This underlying semantics can be viewed as a kind of abstract simulator of the interaction between an intelligent robot and its environment. The same underlying semantics is used both for defining the intended-models function Σ and the taxonomy of chronicles.

9.1.3.2. *Validation Relative to Monotonic Formalizations.*

Other validation results for chronicles in situation calculus with strict inertia have been reported by Lifschitz (Lifschitz, 1991), Reiter (Reiter, 1991), and Kartha (Kartha, 1993). Validations for theories with ramification have been reported by Lin and Reiter (Lin and Reiter, 1994) and by Peppas and Wobcke (Peppas and Wobcke, 1992). Validations for the generalization of situation calculus to theories with concurrent single-timestep actions have been reported by Lin and Shoham (Lin and Shoham, 1992) and by Baral and Gelfond (Baral and Gelfond, 1993).

Different researchers have also used different validation criteria. Lin and Shoham (Lin and Shoham, 1991), Lifschitz (Lifschitz, 1991), and Reiter (Reiter, 1991) relate a nonmonotonic theory over a certain set of "common-sense" axioms, to a monotonic theory over a larger set of axioms which is assumed to capture the full intentions. In other words, they define $\Sigma(\Upsilon)$ as $[G(\Upsilon)]$, where G is an operation that be used as the coordinate system for specifying and comparing the range of applicability of various theories of action.

9.1.3.3. *Validation Relative to an Action Description Language.*

Lifschitz and Gelfond have introduced a separate specification language $\mathcal{A}$ for defining the effects of actions, and used it to define the intended conclusions for reasoning about actions (Gelfond and Lifschitz, 1992). Kartha (Kartha, 1993; Kartha, 1996) applied the same criterion to the theories previously proposed by Baker (Baker, 1991), Pednault (Pednault,

1989), and Reiter (Reiter, 1991). Baral and Gelfond (Baral and Gelfond, 1993) generalized $\mathcal{A}$ to the case of concurrent single-timestep actions and used it for validations as well.

9.1.3.4. *Postulate Oriented Approaches*

Yet another approach, which does not really count as validation, is to constrain the possible choices of the set of intended conclusions through a number of *postulates* for the relation between Γ and $\Sigma(\Gamma)$, or between $[\![\Gamma]\!]$ and $\Sigma(\Gamma)$. Del Val and Shoham (del Val and Shoham, 1992) use the postulates of Katsumo and Mendelzon (Katsuno and Mendelzon, 1989) as the basis, and Peppas and Wobcke (Peppas and Wobcke, 1992) use an extended set of postulates for epistemic entrenchment as the basis for the correctness proof for their system. Since postulates are in principle written to constrain the choice of $\Sigma(\Gamma)$ but not to specify it completely, it seems that their use will lead to intrinsically weaker results.

9.1.3.5. *Equivalence results*

Given this variety of validation criteria one may also consider to what extent they are equivalent and exchangable. A first step towards such an analysis has been reported by Thielscher (Thielscher, 1994), who identified the relationship between the $\mathcal{A}$ language of Gelfond and Lifschitz and a subset of the underlying semantics that is used in the present paper.

9.2. The systematic methodology

The introduction and use of an underlying semantics raises questions of how a proposed logical theory is related to the *meaning* of the formulae that it uses, and of what that very meaning is. Let us now address how these questions are viewed in the systematic methodology.

This methodology proposes to use a two-step process for going from common sense to logic. The first step attempts to capture some characteristics of common sense in terms of a formal definition of $\Sigma(\Upsilon)$; the second step tries to find a theory whose selection function S satisfies $S(\Upsilon) = \Sigma(\Upsilon)$.

What is then the evidence that a proposed definition of Σ itself captures common sense reasoning in an adequate manner?

9.2.1. THE USE OF A PROGRESSION OF UNDERLYING SEMANTICS

In our view, the formalization of common sense can only be achieved as the limiting case in a progression of successively more refined functions Σ_1, Σ_2, and so on. To illustrate the need for several such Σ_i, consider the "stolen car scenario", a very simple example of common-sense reasoning originally proposed by Kautz in (Kautz, 1986). In this chronicle it is assumed that if a certain car is left in the garage overnight then it will still be there the next morning. It is also observed that after the car has been left in the garage for two nights, it is no longer there. What are the common-sense conclusions, or equivalently what should be the set $\Sigma(\Upsilon)$ of intended models for this chronicle?

One possible ontology assumes simple persistence without any exceptions or modifications. I will refer to this case as *strict inertia*. Then the given chronicle is inconsistent, since the car is supposed to remain in the garage after two nights, but it is also stated not to be there. The set of intended models for the stolen car scenario under strict inertia is therefore empty. Another possible ontology allows persistence to be modified by "surprises", and at the same time one makes the *epistemological assumption* that $\Sigma(\Upsilon)$ must be non-empty except in the case where the set $[\![\Upsilon]\!]$ of classical models is itself empty. The set of surprises is minimized subject to the restriction $\Sigma(\Upsilon) \neq \emptyset$. In this case, the given chronicle has two intended models: one where the car vanishes surprisingly during the first night, and one where the car vanishes surprisingly during the second night.

The well-known "qualification" and "ramification" problems concern additional ontological characteristics of common-sense reasoning (CSR) besides surprises. It appears that full CSR involves a considerable number of such difficulties: not only surprises, qualification, and ramification, but also concurrent events, causation chains of events, creation and termination of objects, unreliable observations, and so forth. All of them represent challenges for a logic of common-sense reasoning. However, none of the proposed theories in the current literature gets even close to addressing all of these phenomena, although several of them propose to address more than one phenomenon by one single technical method. In particular, some of the proposed preference relations on models aspire to establish inertia, to minimize side-effects (ramification), and to minimize surprises all at the same time.

It is difficult to compare logics that address different problems and sometimes don't even state exactly what assumptions they make. What I propose, therefore, is to introduce one definition Σ_{IA} for strict inertia, a modified definition Σ_{IAS} for inertia with surprises but without any of the other characteristics, and so on. Unlike the proposed theories, the definitions of the various Σ_i should represent all the characteristics explicitly, so that one can clearly discern each of them.

This proposal has sometimes evoked impatience: why bother with a very simple case such as Σ_{IA} i.e. strict inertia, when other researchers have already thought about more advanced problems such as qualification and ramification? The answer is that the systematic assessment of a theory of action is considerably more complex than finding a few examples where it works, and the assessment is a non-trivial undertaking even for the case of strict inertia. One ought not have to apologize for the strategy of obtaining a solid analysis of the simple cases before one proceeds to the more difficult ones, even though one impatiently feels that the directly useful results will be found in the later stages of the process.

In this perspective, the reason for using the formal definition Σ_{IA} corresponding to strict inertia is not that it is claimed to correspond exactly to common sense – it clearly does not – but because it is the *first step* on a *well structured path* towards the goal of characterizing common sense reasoning; a goal which is very ambitious and which therefore we can not expect to achieve in the near future. For each choice Σ_i of the intended-models function, one obtains a well-defined assessment problem for one or more proposed theories of action, and this is a problem that can be analyzed in an entirely formal fashion.

Although each intended-models function Σ_i is to be *defined* in a formal fashion, the *choice* of that definition for the purpose of CSR is properly outside the scope of formal methods. The traditional methodology in A.I. would leave it to the discretion of the researcher: everyone presumably knows what common sense is? One may speculate whether methods of cognitive psychology could be used for testing the psychological validity of one or the other intended-models functions, but that is not a topic of the present article.

9.2.2. THE METHODOLOGY FOR ASSESSMENT OF RANGE OF APPLICABILITY

Consider a given choice of ontological assumptions, in particular the case of strict inertia represented by its intended-models function Σ_{IA}, and consider also a proposed entailment method viewed as a selection function S. A *direct validation* of S with respect to Σ_{IA} will simply verify whether $S(\Upsilon) = \Sigma_{IA}(\Upsilon)$ for every chronicle Υ that is correctly formed with respect to the chosen ontological assumptions, and the outcome will state whether S is or is not always correct. However, even if S is not always correct, one may be interested in its *range of applicability*, i.e. in a family $\mathcal{Z}$ of chronicles such that $\Upsilon \in \mathcal{Z} \Rightarrow S(\Upsilon) = \Sigma_{IA}(\Upsilon)$. Such results, which I call assessments, have a potential practical interest: it is not evident that a broader-range theory will always be preferred, since an entailment method with a more narrow range of applicability might allow a more efficient implementation. However in order to make use of it, one must have precise knowledge of whether it is correctly applicable for the application one has at hand.

Range of applicability results have a theoretical interest as well: as we proceed to successive new definitions Σ_i of the intended models, a selection function that agrees completely with one version Σ_i can by definition not agree completely with the next one. An understanding of selection functions that are almost correct for one stage may therefore be useful for the next stage of analysis.

The range of applicability may be characterized in terms of various properties of the chronicle, for example whether it contains a nondeterministic action, whether it contains observations for time greater than zero, and so on. I will refer to such properties as *sub-characteristics* since they provide a finer-grain categorization in addition to the one that is obtained from the main characteristics for inertia, surprises, ramification, etc. The collection of characteristics and sub-characteristics together constitute a *taxonomy* of chronicles which may be used as the coordinate system for specifying and comparing the range of applicability of various theories of action.

Notice what is the logical order in which the various definitions must be made:

1. Define the repertoire of main characteristics.
2. Select some class of chronicles $\mathcal{Z}_i$ in terms of the chosen main characteristics.
3. Choose a definition of syntactic structure for chronicles in $\mathcal{Z}_i$.
4. Define the underlying semantics for $\mathcal{Z}_i$, and in particular the selection function Σ_i from well-formed chronicles to their intended model-sets.
5. The underlying semantics is also used for the formal definition of the sub-characteristics that generate a taxonomical structure within $\mathcal{Z}_i$.
6. Proposed theories of action for $\mathcal{Z}_i$ are expressed as selection functions and are assessed with respect to the selection function Σ_i. The results are expressed in terms of the taxonomy defined by the sub-characteristics.
7. Algorithms and other implementation aspects are developed for the theories that have been assessed.

Each definition of Σ_i is merely an approximation to real common sense. When the entailment methods and implementations for one choice of $\mathcal{Z}_i$ are sufficiently well understood, one proceeds to a more refined class and repeats the process. One hopes of course that the analysis of a later class can make use of the results from earlier classes in the progression.

The earlier papers by us and our colleagues showed how this methodology could be applied to the case of strict inertia, allowing for nondeterminism, metric linear time, metric branching time, and concurrent actions. In the present article we begin to extend the same approach to the case of ramification, using a causation-oriented underlying semantics.

9.3. Underlying semantics for strict inertia

Some of the difficulties of the "frame problem" – reasoning about actions and change – relate to how the effects of one particular action are described in terms of the logic at hand. Ramification is an example of such an action-level problem: it has to do with how action laws can be restricted to only specifying the "main effects" or "most significant effects" of actions, whereas other effects are obtained indirectly from more global knowledge.

Other difficulties relate to the structure of the chronicle as a whole, including both action laws, schedule, and observations, as well as other kinds of information which may also be available. The problem that straightforward chronological minimization does not work correctly for postdiction is an example of such a chronicle-level difficulty. This problem was solved by the introduction of filtering (Sandewall, 1989). The correctness and full generality of that solution was formally proved in (Sandewall, 1994a). A reformulation of filtering in terms of circumscription, called nested circumscription, was presented by Lifschitz in (Lifschitz,

1995). Dealing with surprises offers another example of chronicle-level difficulties: presumably, one wishes to make a trade-off between possible surprises early or late during a chronicle, and not merely minimize them chronologically.

Correspondingly, an underlying semantics must characterize the intended models of a chronicle using both the action level and the chronicle level. In this section I shall show how both of these levels are modelled in the underlying semantics for strict inertia. When we proceed to ramification, which is the topic of the present article, it is only the action level that needs to be changed, whereas the chronicle level can be retained unchanged – ramification is intrinsically an action-level phenomenon. Moreover, even the action level for ramification is constructed as a moderate generalization of what was introduced for strict inertia.

We shall start with a basic state-transition semantics which is very simple, and which in particular does not at all reflect the concept of inertia (persistence) that is characteristic of the "frame problem". We then proceed to slightly more detailed semantics which capture the essentials of the frame problem for strict inertia. The further generalization to ramification will follow in the next section.

9.3.1. STATE-TRANSITION SEMANTICS

The following basic concepts are used. Let $\mathcal{R}$ be the set of possible states of the world, formed as the Cartesian product of the finite range sets of a finite number of *state variables*. Also, let $\mathcal{E}$ be the set of possible actions, and let the *main next-state function* $\mathbf{N}(E, r)$ be a function from $\mathcal{E} \times \mathcal{R}$ to non-empty subsets of $\mathcal{R}$. The function $\mathbf{N}$ is intended to indicate the set of possible result states if the action E is performed when the world is in state r. The assumption $\mathbf{N}(E, r) \neq \emptyset$ expresses that every action E can always be executed in every starting state r. (The symbol E is derived from "event"; we consider actions and events to be closely related).

Now, consider a chronicle consisting of action laws, schedule, and observations, where the action laws specify a next-state function $\mathbf{N}$ using some appropriate notation, and where time is assumed to be taken as the non-negative integers. An interpretation for such a chronicle shall be chosen as a history over time, that is, a mapping from timepoints to states. (Assignments of values to constant symbols etc. are also needed, but are of marginal importance for the present purpose). The set of intended models for a chronicle is defined using an *ego-world game*, as follows. First, the observations are removed from the chronicle, so that only the action laws and the schedule remain. The following process is performed using the observation-free chronicle: Start with time = zero and the world in an arbitrary state. At each point in time, perform the move of the "ego" or agent, and the move of the world. The move of the ego is dictated by the schedule, and consists of selecting the action that is indicated by the schedule for the current point in time, or no action if nothing is specified. The move of the world is as follows: if the state of the world at the current time t is r, and the ego has just chosen the action E, then select some r' that is a member of $\mathbf{N}(E, r)$, make it the state of the world at time $t + 1$, and increase the current time by 1. If no move is required, assign the state r to the next timepoint $t + 1$ as well.

The described procedure will non-deterministically generate a set of possible histories of the world. The given definition applies trivially if all actions are specified explicitly by the schedule. Less trivial cases arise if actions are specified in other ways, for example as a disjunction between actions ("either action A or B is performed"), or with an imprecisely specified timing. However, those are technical details, and the general idea remains the same.

Among the world histories that are generated by the ego-world game, one then selects a subset consisting of those histories where all the observations are satisfied. That subset is the set of intended models for the given chronicle.

In this case, which is the simplest one of all, the set of intended models will of course be exactly the set of models for the chronicle, using a conventional concept of models. We now proceed to some less trivial cases, where the characteristic aspects of the frame problem enter the picture.

9.3.2. PARTIAL-STATE TRANSITION SEMANTICS

The purpose of the partial-state transition semantics is to capture the basic assumption of inertia ("no change except as the explicit result of an action") while retaining the general flavor of the state-transition semantics. We use $\mathcal{R}$, $\mathcal{E}$, and $\mathbf{N}$, like before, but we also introduce an *occlusion function* $\mathbf{X}(E, r)$ which is a function from $\mathcal{E} \times \mathcal{R}$ to subsets of the set of state variables. The occlusion function is intended to specify, for a given action E and starting state r, the set of those state variables whose value is affected when the action E is performed in the state r. In other words, it must be the case that any state variable that is not a member of $\mathbf{X}(E, r)$ has the same value in r and in all the members of $\mathbf{N}(E, r)$. (Thus, it would be correct to select $\mathbf{X}(E, r)$ as a the set of all state variables, but it is intended that smaller sets shall be chosen whenever possible).

9.3.2.1. *Action laws and auxiliary next-state functions*
The functions $\mathbf{N}$ and $\mathbf{X}$ together determine the action laws down to the level of semantic equivalence: if these two functions are given, then the action law for an action E shall be constructed so that for each $r \in \mathcal{R}$, it specifies what $\mathbf{N}(E, r)$ says about the possible new values of the state variables in $\mathbf{X}(E, r)$, and it shall not say anything about the new values of other state variables. (Notice, however, that the new values of state variables in $\mathbf{X}(E, r)$ may equally well *depend on* the values of state variables outside $\mathbf{X}(E, r)$ in the starting state r of the action).

Since we are only interested in the set of new states that are permitted by the action law, and not in the actual syntactic form of that action law, it is not necessary to introduce any assumptions about the choice of logical language or about the exact structure of action laws. Using a much simpler approach, we shall introduce two additional, similar but distinct functions $\mathbf{N'}$ and $\mathbf{N}°$ which are derived from the combination of $\mathbf{N}$ and $\mathbf{X}$, and which will be the basis for defining and analyzing the nonmonotonic entailment methods. Of these functions, $\mathbf{N}°$ will be used for strict inertia, and $\mathbf{N'}$ for the analysis of ramification.

The function $\mathbf{N'}$, the *stated next-state function*, is obtained in the following manner. For every result state $r' \in \mathbf{N}(E, r)$, identify the set of all states that agree with r' for all state variables in $\mathbf{X}(E, r)$, but which have arbitrary values elsewhere. Construct $\mathbf{N'}(E, r)$ as the union of all those sets. It follows immediately that $\mathbf{N'}(E, r) \supseteq \mathbf{N}(E, r)$.

This construction should be understood as follows. The action law expresses, in the form of logic formulae, all what $\mathbf{N}$ tells us about the values of state variables in $\mathbf{X}(E, r)$, but nothing about the values of other state variables. We construct the set of models for these logical statements as a subset of $\mathcal{R}$, but using the same vocabulary (the same set of names for state variables) as is used in $\mathcal{R}$. $\mathbf{N'}(E, r)$ has that set of models as its value.

The function $\mathbf{N'}$ that is obtained in this way is therefore a direct counterpart of the usual, logical formulation of an action law that is written as concisely as possible.

Similar to $\mathbf{N'}(E, r)$, the *concise next-state function* $\mathbf{N}°(E, r)$ is obtained as follows. For every E and r, $\mathbf{N}°(E, r)$ is the set of partial states obtained from $\mathbf{N}(E, r)$ by restricting each of its members to be defined for exactly the state variables in $\mathbf{X}(E, r)$.

Notice, therefore, that $\mathbf{N'}$ and $\mathbf{N}°$ are uniquely determined by $\mathbf{N}$ and $\mathbf{X}$, where $\mathbf{X}$ represents the choice as to which state variables to document in the action law. For a given $\mathbf{N}$ and for each choice of $\mathbf{X}$, one obtains a unique $\mathbf{N'}$ and a unique $\mathbf{N}°$. (We do not write $\mathbf{X}$ as an index on $\mathbf{N}$ because we are going to need another index below, and double indices are cumbersome).

Notice, finally, that $\mathbf{N}(E, r) = \emptyset \Leftrightarrow \mathbf{N'}(E, r) = \emptyset$, and similarly for $\mathbf{N}°$. In other words, our assumption of the universal applicability of actions is preserved in the transformations from $\mathbf{N}$ to $\mathbf{N'}$ and $\mathbf{N}°$.

9.3.2.2. *The revised ego-world game*

Once the definition of $\mathbf{N}°$ has been obtained, the partial-state transition semantics is similar to the one defined in the previous section. The following changes are made relative to the case of strict inertia. The move of the ego works like before. The move of the world is now as follows: if the state of the world at the current time t is r, and the ego has just chosen the action E, then select some r' that is a member of $\mathbf{N}°(E, r)$, and construct the state of the world at time $t + 1$ as $r \oplus r'$, that is, as the new state obtained by taking for each state variable the value assigned by r' whenever defined, and otherwise the value assigned by r. At the same time, the current value of time is increased by 1.

9.3.3. TRAJECTORY SEMANTICS

Many applications of actions and change require the use of metric time, and of actions where the world goes through several successive states within the duration of the action. In particular, this is necessary for dealing with concurrent actions in a systematic manner. A corresponding underlying semantics is offered by the *trajectory semantics*, where a trajectory is defined as a finite sequence of partial states over a fixed subset of the state variables, and the function $\mathbf{N}^\circ$ of the previous section is replaced by a function that maps every pair (E, r) to a set of trajectories. The game is modified accordingly: if the world is in the state r and the ego has selected the action E, then the move of the world is to select one member of the set of trajectories for the current (E, r), and to append it to the present history. Thus, the chosen trajectory specifies the outcome of the action both with respect to its duration, and with respect to the sequence of states that the world is in within that duration. The generalization to continuous time is straight-forward.

9.3.4. PREVIOUS RANGE-OF-APPLICABILITY RESULTS

In earlier publications, we have identified the range of applicability of a number of previously proposed entailment methods with respect to the trajectory semantics. In all cases it was possible to obtain both a lower bound and an upper bound on the range of applicability, and in many of the cases these bounds are identical, which means that the range of applicability has been determined completely.

For the details about the trajectory semantics and the range-of-applicability results, please refer to (Sandewall, 1994a) and to the summary in (Sandewall, 1994b).

9.4. Ramification

We proceed now to ramification, which is the main topic of the present article. We shall first make a general review of the problem and of current approaches. Then we develop an appropriate underlying semantics, and analyze current approaches in its terms.

The ramification problem for reasoning about actions and change has been described as follows by Ginsberg and Smith, (Ginsberg and Smith, 1987):

> The difficulty is that it is unreasonable to explicitly record all of the consequences of an action, even the immediate ones. For example [...] For any given action there are essentially an infinite number of possible consequences that depend upon the details of the situation in which the action occurs.

Of course, those "infinite number of consequences" have to be specified to the logical system in some way; the logic can not do magic. More precisely, ramification should provide a solution for at least the following two problems:

- If some regularities in the world at hand are reflected in the consequent side of several of the action laws, then it makes sense to factor out the common parts and to represent them once and for all as "domain constraints". Instead of just applying the action law to determine the effects of an action, one applies the action law plus the domain constraints.
- Consider applications where every scenario describes a number of separate but interconnected objects, different scenarios involve different configurations, and each action has its immediate effects on one or a few of the objects, but indirect effects on other objects which are connected to the first ones, in some sense of the word "connected". Then, it would be completely unreasonable to let the action laws contain different cases which enumerate the possible configurations. Instead, action laws should only specify the "immediate" or "primary" effects of the action, and logical inference should be used for tracing how some changes "cause" other changes across the structure of the configuration at hand.

In both cases, action laws are supposed to specify some of the action's effects, which in some sense are the "primary" effects, and the deductive system shall rely on additional information for inferring other changes that are due to the action. One common approach is to use *domain constraints* that specify what are possible states of the world, and to assume that the total set of changes in state variables that result from the action, consists of those changes that are explicitly stated in the action law, plus a minimal set of other changes that are necessary in view of the domain constraints. Notice that such an approach only makes sense in the second of the two items that were just mentioned: one can imagine that the causational propagation across the scenario configuration obeys some minimization criterion, but if domain constraints have merely been factored out of action laws then there is no particular reason for minimization of the changes.

The *update problem* is in principle the same problem: given a world state before an action, some information about the world state after the action, and certain general restrictions on permissible world states, which are the possible or preferred world states resulting from the action? The main difference is one of presentation: the ramification problem is presented in the context of reasoning about actions and change, where the actions themselves as well as their timing and sequencing is explicit in the logical language being used. For the update problem, by contrast, one generally considers a single update, and leaves aside the question of timing and sequencing of the multiple actions. In othe words, one concentrates on the action-level problem, while disregarding the chronicle-level problems as defined at the beginning of section 3, above.

Even among the methods that use minimization of change, there are a number of different variants which have been proposed by different authors, and which differ in their details. So far, these methods have only been developed using the example-based methodology, where each proposal is motivated on the basis of (1) intuitive and informal reasons why a particular method is the "natural" one, and (2) selected test examples where competing methods do not give intended results. We shall briefly summarize some of these approaches, without going too deeply into the pros and cons of each, and describing only those approaches that will be the subject of assessment later on in this paper. There is no need to be exhaustive since our purpose here is to *characterize properties* of some of these approaches, and not to advocate one of them over the others. The list is not exhaustive; we summarize primarily those approaches that are the subject of assessment below.

9.4.1. PLAIN MINIMIZATION OF CHANGE

The original method, plain minimization of change, is originally due to Winslett (Winslett, 1988), at least in the context of the A.I. literature. The idea is simple: identify a set of *static domain constraints*, that is, restrictions on the possible states of the world. For a given action, the effects specified by the action law are obligatory; a minimal set of additional changes is selected so that the domain constraints are satisfied.

It was observed already by Winslett that plain minimization of change sometimes obtains unintended models, because change in a state variable that was not intended to change may offset change (within the restrictions of the domain constraints) of some other state variables where change is indeed intended. Winslett suggested to solve this problem by imposing a priority ordering on the state variables, but this line of research has apparently not been pursued. The following approaches have been developed instead.

9.4.2. CATEGORIZATION OF STATE VARIABLES

Categorization of state variables is an extension of plain minimization of change: instead of establishing certain changes in the world, and then minimizing changes across all (other) state variables, one divides the state variables into two or more classes which are treated differently with respect to minimization.

One instance of this concept was the introduction of *occlusion* by Sandewall (Sandewall, 1989; Sandewall, 1993b), also represented by the *persists* predicate in (Sandewall, 1988), the *release* operation of Kartha and Lifschitz (Kartha and Lifschitz, 1994) and the *persists* predicate of del Val and Shoham in (del Val and Shoham, 1993). In the simplest case, one separates the state variables into two classes A and B, where the action laws specifying the effects of an action only specify changes in class A, whereas domain constraints are allowed to refer to state variables in both classes. Then, change is minimized for state variables in class B, whereas those in class A are allowed to vary freely to the extent permitted by the action laws.

Another categorization method is to single out some state variables as *dependent* on others, and to stipulate that minimization of change does not apply to dependent state variables. The definitions of the dependencies are part of the domain constraints. This approach was first proposed by Lifschitz as a distinction between frame and non-frame fluents (Lifschitz, 1990), although in implementation terms it goes back to the early STRIPS system (Fikes and Nilsson, 1971).

9.4.3. EXPLICIT SPECIFICATION OF DEPENDENCIES OR CAUSATION

Plain minimization of change is symmetric: a constraint of the form $a \Rightarrow b$, if imposed on a state where a is true and b is false, can be satisfied either by making a false, or by making b true. This does not always correspond to the intentions in the application at hand, since sometimes the influence applies only one way.

The distinction between dependent and independent state variables is often sufficient for dealing with this problem. However, Thielscher (Thielscher, 1995) has shown an example, involving relays, where the distinction between dependent and independent variables is claimed not to be sufficient. In his paper, and in concurrent papers by other authors (McCain and Turner, 1995; Lin, 1995), a "causal" approach is proposed. The basic idea is to express *causal dependencies*, which say that change in one state variable necessitates or enables a change in another state variable. (These links may of course depend on the old and the new value of the first variable, and on current values of other components of the state).

These causal approaches have become popular recently, but one should realize that similar methods have been proposed earlier by Cordier and Siegel (Cordier and Siégel, 1992; Cordier and Siégel, 1995) and by Brewka and Hertzberg (Brewka and Hertzberg, 1993).

However, the proposed causal approaches also have some problems. Their fundamental limitation is that they assume the explicitly stated effects of the action (the effects mentioned in the action law) to be the first ones in a causal chain, and that indirect effects are downstream in that chain. For a counterexample, consider the case of a lamp la that is turned on independently by two different switches: $la \leftrightarrow sw_1 \vee sw_2$. la, sw_1, and sw_2 are the only state variables, and there is no other domain constraint. The action of "turning on the lamp" is defined simply by stating that la becomes true. Presumably, ramification shall allow us to conclude that either sw_1 or sw_2 has become true as well. However, a causal approach will observe that the causal link is from the switches to the lamp, and not vice versa, so it will not deal correctly with this example.

We submit that this is not an odd example: quite generally, it is desirable to characterize actions in terms of their ultimate and main effects, and not in terms of the specifics of how to perform them. Reasoning from main effect to instrumental operations, and from there to other effects of the instrumental operations is therefore an important part of the ramification problem. The underlying semantics that is proposed in the next section is intended to capture that intuition.

It may be argued that the causational approaches can be used in such a way that the formal causation goes in the direction that is opposite to actual causation. However, in this case the approach loses a lot of its intuitive strength, and the need for a formal validation against an underlying semantics becomes even more acute than before.

9.5. Causal propagation semantics

In the case of partial-state transition semantics, there is a function X that identifies all those state variables that are affected for a given combination of action and starting state. The intuition is that action laws shall specify the new values of all those state variables, and that any other state variable is understood to keep its old value.

In the case of ramification, one wishes X to be even more restrictive, so that it only identifies *some of* the state variables that change, whereby the action law can be made even more compact. Changes in other state variables are to be derived from more general information.

In order to capture these intuitions, it is natural to use an underlying semantics that has some notion of direct versus indirect change. We propose to use the following *causal propagation semantics*, which is obtained through an additional modification of the state transition semantics described above. The domain $\mathcal{R}$ of world states and the domain $\mathcal{E}$ of actions are defined like before. A binary non-reflexive *causal transition relation* C between states is introduced; if $C(r, r')$ then r' is said to be the *successor* of r. A state r is called *stable* iff it does not have any successor. The set $\mathcal{R}_c$ of *admitted states* is chosen as a subset of $\mathcal{R}$ all of whose members are stable with respect to C. (It may or may not be chosen to contain all the stable states). The identification of a set of admitted states is equivalent to the introduction of domain constraints.

Furthermore, we assume an *action invocation relation* $G(E, r, r')$ where $E \in \mathcal{E}$ is an action, r is the state where the action E is invoked, and r' is the new state where the instrumental part of the action has been executed. For every E and r there must be at least one r' such that $G(E, r, r')$, that is, every action is always invokable.

An *action system* is a tuple $\langle \mathcal{R}, \mathcal{E}, C, \mathcal{R}_c, G \rangle$ whose five elements have been selected as just described. It is intended to be used as follows.

A *transition chain* for a state $r \in \mathcal{R}_c$ and an action E is a finite or infinite sequence of states

$$r_1, r_2, ... (r_k)$$

where $G(E, r, r_1)$, $C(r_i, r_{i+1})$ for every $i \geq 1$ for an infinite sequence and for every i where $1 \leq i < k$ for a finite sequence, and where r_k is a stable state again in the case of a finite sequence.

The last element r_k of a finite transition chain is called a *result state* of the action E in the situation r.

We intend, of course, that it shall be possible to characterize the result states r_k in terms of E and r, but without referring explicitly to the details of the intermediate states. The following assumptions (or something similar) are needed in order to make this work as intended.

Definition 8 If three states r, r_i, and r_{i+1} are given, we say that the pair r_i, r_{i+1} **respects** r iff

$$r_i(f) \neq r_{i+1}(f) \Rightarrow r_i(f) = r(f),$$

for any state variable f that is defined in $\mathcal{R}$. Then, an action system $\langle \mathcal{R}, \mathcal{E}, C, \mathcal{R}_c, G \rangle$ is said to be **respectful** iff, for every $r \in \mathcal{R}_c$, every $E \in \mathcal{E}$, r is respected by every pair r_i, r_{i+1} in every transition chain, and the last element of any finite chain is a member of $\mathcal{R}_c$.

This condition amounts to a "write-once" or "single-assignment" property: if the action E is performed from state r, the world may go through a sequence of states, but in each step from one state to the next, there cannot be changes in state variables that have already changed previously in the sequence, nor can there be any additional change in a state variable that changed already in the invocation transition from r to r_1.

As a consequence of these definitions, we obtain that if $\langle \mathcal{R}, \mathcal{E}, C, \mathcal{R}_c, G \rangle$ is a respectful action system, if $r \in \mathcal{R}_c$, $E \in \mathcal{E}$, and $G(E, r, r')$ holds for some r', then all the transition chains that emerge from (E, r) are finite and cycle-free. The set of result states will be denoted $\mathbf{N}(E, r)$, using the same notation as in the state-transition semantics. Thus, the main next-state function $\mathbf{N}(E, r)$ which was previously taken as given, is here taken as derived from the elementary relations G and C in the action system. It also follows from the definition that $\mathbf{N}(E, r) \neq \emptyset$.

Respectful action systems are intended to capture the basic intuitions of actions with indirect effects that are due to causation, as follows. Suppose the world is in a stable state r, and an action E is invoked. The immediate effect of this is to set the world in a new state, which is not necessarily stable. If it is not, then one allows the world to go through the necessary sequence of state transitions, until it reaches a stable state. *That whole sequence* of state transitions is together viewed as the action, and the resulting admitted state is viewed as the result state of the action.

The assumption of sequentiality of actions within a chronicle is then taken to mean that the agent or "ego" abstains from invoking any new action before the previous action has run to completion. The exact interpretation of the state transitions may vary. The most obvious is to think of them as spontaneous transitions in the physical world, so that the world actually traverses all the states in the sequence without external intervention. In this case, it is natural to derive a trajectory semantics from the multiple transition semantics. One may also think of the transitions as more or less logical conclusions about a world where all changes happen (or are modelled as happening) concurrently. Finally, one may include the case where additional interventions by the agent (viewed as a controller) are necessary along the path from the starting state to the result state of the action.

For example, in the lamp scenario, if the state variables represent the first switch, the second switch, and the lamp, respectively, the invocation relation G will contain argument sequences such as (E_1, FFF, TFF) for turning on the first switch; the causal transition relation will contain the argument sequence (TFF, TFT) expressing that if the first switch is on, then the lamp goes on as well. The action E_2, which is instrumentally defined as turning on either of the two switches, is true for both $G(E_2, FFF, TFF)$ and $G(E_2, FFF, FTF)$.

The idea with ramification, now, is that one does not wish to specify *all* the effects of an action in the action law; one wishes to restrict the action law to the most important effects, and other effects should be deducible if needed. In other words, the action law shall not specify all components of the result state, and not even all the components that change, but only some of them. Other changes are deduced using information about the relations C and G.

Notice that it is possible, but not necessary, to let the action law characterize the invocation relation G. Alternatively, the action law may characterize some of the later changes along the chain, namely, if the indirect changes are considered to be the most important ones in terms of describing the action. For example, the action law for E_2 in the second-previous paragraph may specify the change in the state variable indicating that "the lamp is lit", leaving the "upstream" change of one or the other of the switches to be inferred. In general, the non-explicit effects of the action may be a combination of changes that are causationally "downstream" as well as "upstream" of the explicit ones.

9.6. Minimization approaches to ramification

With this underlying semantics, we shall begin the analysis of some of the approaches to ramification that have been proposed in recent years. We first address methods for ramification using minimization and categorization.

9.6.1. MEASURE SYSTEMS

The following notation is introduced in order to obtain a common framework within which various minimization-oriented methods can be expressed. A *measure system* is a threetuple

$$\langle \mathcal{Q}, d, \prec \rangle, \tag{1}$$

where $\mathcal{Q}$ is a domain of *quantities*, d is a *difference function* $\mathcal{R} \times \mathcal{R} \to \mathcal{Q}$, $\prec$ is a strict partial order on $\mathcal{Q}$, and where $q \not\prec d(r, r)$ for all r and q. Notice that even $d(r, r') = d(r', r)$ is not required, which is why we call this a "difference" and not a "distance". We shall say that r' is *less remote* than r'' from r if $d(r, r') \prec d(r, r'')$.

Now, let $\mathbf{N}$, $\mathbf{X}$, and a measure system $m = \langle \mathcal{Q}, d, \prec \rangle$ be given, which also means that $\mathbf{N}'$ is defined. Then $\mathbf{N}'_m$ shall be the function such that

$$\mathbf{N}'_m(E, r) \subseteq \mathbf{N}'(E, r) \cap \mathcal{R}_c \tag{2}$$

and where $\mathbf{N}'_m(E, r)$ consists exactly of those members of $\mathbf{N}'(E, r) \cap \mathcal{R}_c$ that are *minimally remote from r according to the measure system m*. Formally, for any member r' of $\mathbf{N}'_m(E, r)$, there must not be any other member r'' of $\mathbf{N}'(E, r) \cap \mathcal{R}_c$ that is less remote than r' from r, and any $r' \in \mathbf{N}'(E, r) \cap \mathcal{R}_c$ having that property must be a member of $\mathbf{N}'_m(E, r)$.

This concept of measure system provides a framework within which it is straightforward to define a number of minimization-of-change methods. For example, the simple case where one partitions state variables into "occluded" and "unoccluded" ones, and minimizes the set of changes in the unoccluded state variables, is obtained by defining $\mathcal{Q}$ as the power set of the set of state variables, $d(r, r')$ as the set of unoccluded state variables where r and r' assign different values, and $\prec$ as the strict subset relation.

A particularly simple case is *strict ramification*, which we shall denote **SR**, where no preference is imposed, and which is written

$$\mathbf{N}'_{SR}(E, r) = \mathbf{N}'(E, r) \cap \mathcal{R}_c. \tag{3}$$

It is easily verified that the approximation $\mathbf{N}'_m$ for arbitrary m satisfies all the Katsuno-Mendelzon postulates (Katsuno and Mendelzon, 1989) **U1** through **U8**, except **U2**. The appropriateness of **U2** has already been cast in doubt by del Val and Shoham in (del Val and Shoham, 1993), where they observed that **U2** is not well chosen in the case of nondeterministic actions.

9.6.2. COMPARISONS OF MEASURE SYSTEMS

With the given definitions, a measure system m is *correct* for a main next-state function $\mathbf{N}$ and occlusion function $\mathbf{X}$ iff $\mathbf{N}(E, r) = \mathbf{N}'_m(E, r)$ for every action E and every $r \in \mathcal{R}_c$. The *range of applicability* of a measure system m is the set of pairs $\langle \mathbf{N}, \mathbf{X} \rangle$ where m is correct.

Notice that in the present section we do not relate the minimization method to the underlying semantics, since we take the function $\mathbf{N}(E, r)$ as given. In the next section, where we start using the underlying semantics, $\mathbf{N}(E, r)$ it will instead be considered as defined along the lines that were introduced in section 5.

If one can not find a correct measure system for a given application, then presumably one prefers a measure system that is *sound* in the sense that it does not allow any unwarranted conclusions. In our framework, the measure system m is *sound* for a main next-state function $\mathbf{N}$ and occlusion function $\mathbf{X}$ iff $\mathbf{N}(E, r) \subseteq \mathbf{N}'_m(E, r)$ for every action E and every $r \in \mathcal{R}_c$.

It is evident that no measure system is correct for all $\mathbf{N}$, and that straight ramification is the only measure system that is sound for all $\mathbf{N}$. (The latter follows by choosing $\mathbf{N}(E, r)$ so that it equals $\mathbf{N}'(E, r) \cap \mathcal{R}_c$, so that no minimization is desired). We have compared different minimization methods with respect to how restrictive they are: a minimization method based on measure system m is *more restrictive* than one based on measure system m' iff $\mathbf{N}'_m(E, r) \subseteq \mathbf{N}'_{m'}(E, r)$ for all E and for all $r \in \mathcal{R}_c$. Thus, a more restrictive method is one that obtains a smaller set of preferred models, and thereby a larger set of conclusions, and a smaller set of pairs $\langle \mathbf{N}, \mathbf{X} \rangle$ for which it is sound. Clearly, straight ramification is the unique least restrictive method. We write $m < m'$ when m is more restrictive than m'.

The following methods are of particular interest. In all cases, the proposed categorization is allowed to depend on the choice of E and r; it does not have to be fixed relative to them.

MSC: Minimal secondary change. State variables are divided into two categories: *occluded* ones specified by $\mathbf{X}$, and *secondary* ones which are the rest. Action laws specify the possible new values for occluded state variables. For given E and r, one selects those members of $\mathbf{N}'(E, r) \cap \mathcal{R}_c$ that minimize the set of secondary state variables that change compared to r. This is the method proposed by del Val and Shoham in (del Val and Shoham, 1993).

MSCC: Minimal secondary change with changeset-partitioning. Similar to MSC for deterministic actions, but differs for nondeterministic actions. In MSCC, one divides $\mathbf{N}'(E, r) \cap \mathcal{R}_c$ into partitions each consisting of those proposed new states that are equal with respect to occluded state variables. In each of the partitions, one selects the subset of those members that are minimally remote from r, using the same criterion as for MSC. Then one forms the union of those closest subsets. It follows at once that MSCC is less restrictive than MSC, although more restrictive than straight ramification.

The intuition behind this alternative is as follows. Consider an action that is nondeterministic already from the point of view of the action law, that is, the action law specifies several alternative outcomes of the action. Then one would like to minimize changes for each of the outcomes separately. For example, the action of playing a game on a gambling machine may result in different states in the machine; let us say just *win* and *lose* for simplicity. Suppose that the action law only specifies this outcome, and there is a static domain constraint specifying that *win* is accompanied by *money-falling-out*. Then MSC will always prefer *lose* over *win* because it minimizes the set of side-effects. MSCC, by comparison, considers *win* and *lose* to be equally preferred. Changeset-partitioning was first proposed by Sandewall in (Sandewall, 1991).

MRC: Minimal remanent change. State variables are divided into three disjoint categories: occluded, remanent, and dependent ones. The occluded state variables are those whose new values are specified in the action laws, like before. Changes in remanent state variables are minimized, whereas changes in dependent state variables are disregarded for the purpose of minimization. This is essentially the method proposed by Kartha and Lifschitz in (Kartha and Lifschitz, 1994), if one identifies "occluded" with "frame released", "remanent" with "frame unreleased", and "dependent" with "non-frame" state variables.

MRCC: Minimal remanent change with changeset-partitioning. Uses the same threeway partitioning as in MRC, but minimizes changes separately for each outcome in occluded state variables, like in MSCC.

The intuition behind the three-way partitioning in MRC and MRCC is as follows: even if one chooses to divide the state variables into two categories, one where change is minimized and one where it is not, there may still be two distinct reasons why a state variable is in the latter category. On one hand, there are those state variables where the outcome or set of possible outcomes is already specified in the action law, so that further minimization is not needed and often not desired (because it may remove some of the intended outcomes of nondeterministic actions). On the other hand, there are those state variables that are functionally dependent on some of the others, and where the dependency is specified by the static domain constraints. In our formulation of the problem, the first subgroup is indicated by $\mathbf{X}$, since $\mathbf{X}$ is used in two ways: it defines $\mathbf{N}'$ from $\mathbf{N}$, and it is part of the definition of minimization. The other subgroup can not be included in $\mathbf{X}$ – the formal account in (Sandewall, 1995) introduces the required notation.

One might think that since the dependent state variables are functionally determined by the others, it would not hurt to bring them along in the minimization. The problem is, as was shown already by Winslett in the 'Aunt Agatha' scenario, that there may be undesired tradeoffs so that an unintended model containing a change in a remanent state variable may be be accepted because it contains a smaller set of changes in dependent variables. In such scenarios it is necessary to exclude dependent state variables from minimization.

Finally, the list should also include the classical method:

MC: Minimization of change. No partitioning of the state variables. One selects the subset of $\mathbf{N}'(E, r) \cap \mathcal{R}_c$ consisting of those members minimizing the set of state variables where the value differs from r. This is the method originally proposed by Winslett (Winslett, 1988).

The formal definitions of these methods in terms of measure systems are straightforward, and can be obtained from (Sandewall, 1995).

9.6.3. RELATIVE RANGE RESULTS

Recalling that $m \leq m'$ means that m is more restrictive than m', and writing **SR** for straight ramification, we have proved the following relative range results:

Theorem 9

$$\mathbf{MC} \leq \mathbf{MSCC} \leq \mathbf{SR} \tag{4}$$

$$\mathbf{MSC} \leq \mathbf{MSCC} \leq \mathbf{SR} \tag{5}$$

$$\mathbf{MRC} \leq \mathbf{MRCC} \leq \mathbf{SR} \tag{6}$$

The proofs are found in our technical report, which is also available on-line (Sandewall, 1995). There does not seem to be any similar result relating e.g. **MSCC** and **MRCC**.

These results suggest at once that, as long as the knowledge of the application domain does not give better evidence, one ought to prefer methods with changeset-partitioning over methods without, that is, MSCC over MSC and MRCC over MRC. This is because one will then obtain a method with a larger range of sound applicability. In other words, although possibly one will fail to obtain some intended conclusions, at least there is a smaller possibility that the system actually infers non-intended conclusions.

Preferably, however, one should be able to use more specific information about the application domain at hand, and obtain an entailment method that is more restrictive but in a way that retains soundness and ideally achieves completeness.

9.7. Assessments of entailment methods based on minimization of change

After having related the various minimization methods to each other, we proceed now to the analysis of how they relate to the underlying semantics. The following results are preliminary ones.

The general problem is viewed as follows. Let the following be given:

- A respectful action system $\langle \mathcal{R}, \mathcal{E}, C, \mathcal{R}_c, G \rangle$. Its corresponding main next-state function will be written $\mathbf{N}$, as before.
- An occlusion function, $\mathbf{X}$.
- A measure system $m = \langle \mathcal{Q}, d, \prec \rangle$.

Informally, it is still the case that $\mathbf{X}$ indicates what are the state variables whose new values are indicated in the action law. The functions $\mathbf{N}$ and $\mathbf{X}$ together define the stated next-state function $\mathbf{N}'$, as described above. The measure system is said to be *correct* for the action system and the occlusion function iff

$$\mathbf{N}'_m(E, r) = \mathbf{N}(E, r)$$

for every E and r. Likewise, the measure system is said to be *sound* for the action system and the occlusion function iff

$$\mathbf{N}'_m(E, r) \supseteq \mathbf{N}(E, r)$$

for every E and r. Notice how the entities in this equation have been derived: $\mathbf{N}$ from the action system alone, $\mathbf{N}'$ from $\mathbf{N}$ and $\mathbf{X}$, and $\mathbf{N}'_m$ from $\mathbf{N}'$ and m.

In particular, given one of the specific measure systems and entailment methods that were described above, for example MRCC, a particular partitioning of the state variables is said to be *correct* for the action system, the occlusion function, and the method at hand iff the corresponding measure system is correct for them. Soundness is defined similarly.

The corresponding *assessment problem* for an entailment method is defined as the following question: what are the requirements on the combination of a respectful action system, an occlusion function, and a partitioning whereby the given entailment method is correct (or sound)?

A broader question, which also is of interest, is for what classes of action systems and occlusion functions is it possible to find a correct measure system at all.

9.7.1. OCCLUSION OF INVOCATION-CHANGED STATE VARIABLES

It turns out that fairly strong restrictions are required in order to get any assessment results at all, and that it is quite easy to construct cases where apparently there is no correct partitioning. The following defines a class of action systems and occlusion functions where the soundness of MSCC has been proved. We consider separately the two cases where action laws describe invocations and where they describe downstream effects.

Definition 10 A respectful action system $\langle \mathcal{R}, \mathcal{E}, C, \mathcal{R}_c, G \rangle$ is said to have **fixed control** iff there is some subset $\mathcal{F}_c$ of the set $\mathcal{F}$ of state variables, such that

$$G(E, r, r') \Rightarrow dom(r - r') \subseteq \mathcal{F}_c$$

and

$$C(r, r') \Rightarrow dom(r - r') \cap \mathcal{F}_c = \emptyset$$

The set $\mathcal{F}_c$ is called the *control set*.

Here and henceforth the following conventions are used: $-$ denotes set subtraction, mappings are viewed as sets of argument/value pairs, and $dom(r)$ maps a mapping (in this case, a partial state) to its domain.

Members of the control set will be called *controlled* state variables; the others will be called *obtained* state variables.

This definition means that invocation transitions can only influence state variables in the control set, and causal transitions can never influence state variables in the control set. Thielscher's relay example in (Thielscher, 1994) is an example of a system that does not have fixed control.

Definition 11 Given a state domain $\mathcal{R}$, a state r'' is said to be a **hybrid** between two states r and r' *with respect to* a set $F \subseteq \mathcal{F}$ of state variables iff

(1) for every state variable f, $r''(f) = r(f) \vee r''(f) = r'(f)$, and
(2) if $f \in F$ then $r'(f) = r''(f)$, and
(3) r'' is different from both r and r'.

Definition 12 A respectful action system is said to be **hybrid free** with respect to a set F of state variables iff no two members r and r' of $\mathcal{R}_c$ have a hybrid with respect to F that is also a member of $\mathcal{R}_c$.

It follows that if an action system is hybrid free with respect to a set F, then it is hybrid free with respect to any superset of F. (Any hybrid with respect to the superset would be a hybrid with respect to F). We immediately obtain:

Theorem 13 MSCC is sound for the combination of a respectful action system $\langle \mathcal{R}, \mathcal{E}, C, \mathcal{R}_c, G \rangle$ and an occlusion function $\mathbf{X}$ if the following conditions are satisfied:

1. The action system has fixed control with a control set $\mathcal{F}_c$
2. The action system is hybrid free with respect to $\mathcal{F}_c$
3. If $G(E, r, r')$ then $dom(r - r') \subseteq \mathbf{X}(E, r)$

Proof We are to prove that $\mathbf{N}'_{MSCC}(E, r) \supseteq \mathbf{N}(E, r)$. Suppose the opposite is the case, that is, for some E and r there is some $r^* \in \mathbf{N}(E, r)$ that is not a member of $\mathbf{N}'_{MSCC}(E, r)$. Since it is a member of $\mathbf{N}(E, r)$, r^* must be a member of $\mathbf{N}'(E, r)$ and of $\mathcal{R}_c$, so its non-membership of $\mathbf{N}'_{MSCC}(E, r)$ must be due to the existence of some $r' \in \mathbf{N}'(E, r) \cap \mathcal{R}_c$ that is less remote than r^* from r.

By the definition of MSCC, r' must agree with r^* in all occluded state variables. By assumptions 1 and 3, r^* agrees with r in all non-occluded controlled state variables, so r' must do so as well. Therefore, r^* and r' agree in all state variables in $\mathcal{F}_c$. But r' differs from r in a subset of the state variables where r^* differs from r. Therefore, either r' is a hybrid between r and r^* with respect to $\mathcal{F}_c$, or $r' = r$. The former case is inconsistent with assumption 2 given that $r' \in \mathcal{R}_c$. The latter, bizarre case requires that r and r^* are equal in all controlled state variables, which means that $\mathbf{N}(E, r) = \{r\}$ and $r^* = r$, making it impossible for any r' to be less remote from r than r^* is.

9.7.2. OCCLUSION OF NON-INVOKED STATE VARIABLES

We proceed now to the case where action laws characterize other changes of state variables than those involved in the invocation.

Definition 14 A respectful action system $\langle \mathcal{R}, \mathcal{E}, C, \mathcal{R}_c, G \rangle$ is **unary controlled** iff $G(E, r, r')$ implies that $dom(r - r')$ is a singleton, for any E, r, and r'.

Note that this property is realistic for low-level actions in engineered systems, where controlled state variables represent the actuators.

Definition 15 Consider the combination of a respectful action system $\langle \mathcal{R}, \mathcal{E}, C, \mathcal{R}_c, G \rangle$ having fixed control, and an occlusion function $\mathbf{X}$. A state $r' \in \mathcal{R}_c$ is called a **shortcut** for (E, r) in this combination, where $r \in \mathcal{R}_c$, if and only if there is some $r'' \in N(E, r)$ such that

(1) for every state variable f, $r'(f) = r(f) \vee r'(f) = r''(f)$, and
(2) r' equals r in all controlled state variables, and
(3) r' equals r'' for all state variables in $\mathbf{X}(E, r)$.

Example 16 The following is an example of a shortcut. Consider an electric circuit consisting of a number of switches, lamps, and relays, where the switches and only them are controlled. In the current state r of the circuit, changing a particular switch s will turn on a lamp l that is presently off; there may also be other effects. Let r'' be the resulting state. An action

E is defined so that $\mathbf{X}(E,r) = \{l\}$ and r'' is a member of $\mathbf{N}(E,r)$, that is, the action is defined in terms of the effect of turning on the lamp, and not in terms of changing the switch. However, there is also a sequence of other actions where different switches are changed in succession, and which ends up in a state r' where all switches are in the same position as in the present state r, the lamp l is on anyway, and only a subset of the changes from r to r'' occur in r'.

It would seem that the property of having a shortcut is not a particularly natural one for an action system to have. However, there is an important special case, involving the combination of an action system and an occlusion function where an action possibly has a null stated effect, that is, there is some $r'' \in N(E,r)$ for which r and r'' are equal for all occluded state variables. In this case, r itself is a shortcut for (E,r).

We immediately obtain:

Theorem 17 MSCC is sound for the combination of a respectful action system $\langle \mathcal{R}, \mathcal{E}, C, \mathcal{R}_c, G \rangle$ and an occlusion function $\mathbf{X}$ if the following conditions are satisfied:

1. The action system has fixed control with a control set $\mathcal{F}_c$.
2. The action system is hybrid free with respect to $\mathcal{F}_c$.
3. $\mathbf{X}(E,r)$ is disjoint from $\mathcal{F}_c$ for every E and $r \in \mathcal{R}_c$.
4. The action system is unary controlled.
5. The combination of the action system and the occlusion function does not have any shortcut.

Proof We are to prove that $\mathbf{N}'_{MSCC}(E,r) \supseteq \mathbf{N}(E,r)$. Suppose the opposite is the case, that is, for some E and r there is some $r^* \in \mathbf{N}(E,r)$ that is not a member of $\mathbf{N}'_{MSCC}(E,r)$. Since it is a member of $\mathbf{N}(E,r)$, r^* must be a member of $\mathbf{N}'(E,r)$ and of $\mathcal{R}_c$, so its non-membership of $\mathbf{N}'_{MSCC}(E,r)$ must be due to the existence of some $r' \in \mathbf{N}'(E,r) \cap \mathcal{R}_c$ that is less remote than r^* from r.

Consider the causation chain leading up to r^*, and its first element r_1. Because of the unary control property, r and r_1 will differ in exactly one state variable; this state variable is a controlled one because of assumption 1, and it is not occluded because of assumption 3. There are two possibilities with respect to r':

(1) r' equals r_1 in all controlled state variables. Then r' is a hybrid between r and r^* with respect to $\mathcal{F}_c$, violating assumption 2.

(2) r' equals r in all controlled state variables. Since r' is a member of $\mathbf{N}'(E,r)$, it must agree with some member r'' of $\mathbf{N}(E,r)$ in all occluded state variables. Therefore, r' is a shortcut for (E,r), which violates assumption 5.

The results of these theorems do not apply in general for MSC because of interference between primary outcomes of the action. Generalization of these results to MRCC encounters technical complications in the generalization of the "hybrid" concept.

9.7.3. COMPARISON WITH CORRECTNESS CRITERIA FOR STRICT INERTIA

The assessments for entailment methods for strict inertia in (Sandewall, 1994a) made use of the concept of minimal-change-compatible, which in the present context may be equivalently defined as follows:

Definition 18 An action system is **minimal-change-compatible** iff it is not the case, for any r, E, r', and r'', that

$$r' \in \mathbf{N}(E, r)$$

$$r'' \in \mathbf{N}(E, r)$$

and r'' is a hybrid between r and r' with respect to $\emptyset$.

We showed in (Sandewall, 1994a) that PCMF (prototypical minimization of change with filtering) is correct for all minimal-change-compatible chronicles with single-timestep actions. We observe that if an action system is hybrid free with respect to $\emptyset$, then it is both minimal-change-compatible and hybrid free with respect to an arbitrary set F.

9.7.4. EXAMPLES

The soundness property means that the entailment method MSCC does not miss any intended models, but it still allows for the possibility of including some unintended models. The following two examples illustrate how unintended models may be included in $\mathbf{N}'_{MSCC}(E, r)$.

Example 19 For the first example, suppose $\mathcal{R}$ is selected as $\{T, F\} \times \{1, 2\} \times \{1, 2\}$, where the first component is controlled and always occluded, and the other two are secondary. Suppose further that the causal transition function C is true for the following pairs:

$$C(T11, T12)$$

$$C(T22, T21)$$

$$C(F12, F11)$$

$$C(F21, F22)$$

and that $T12, T21, F11, F22$ are in $\mathcal{R}_c$. The invocation relation G is supposed to contain

$$G(E_1, F11, T11)$$

$$G(E_1, F22, T22)$$

as well as some suitable transitions when the controlled state variable is initially T. It is clear that $\mathbf{N}(E_1, F11) = \{T12\}$ and $\mathbf{N}'_{MSCC}(E_1, F11) = \{T12, T21\}$, so soundness but not correctness is obtained.

The problem here, of course, is that the entailment method MRCC is based on a notion of minimal change that does not use any of the causal transition information from C.

Example 20 The following example illustrates another possibility for the introduction of unintended models. Suppose now that $\mathcal{R}$ is selected as $\{T, F\} \times \{T, F\} \times \{1, 2\}$, where the first two components are controlled and the third one is obtained. Suppose further that the transition function C satisfies

$$C(TF1, TF2),$$

and that $FF1, FT1, TF2, TT1$ are in $\mathcal{R}_c$. The invocation relation G is supposed to contain

$$G(E_1, FF1, TF1)$$

$$G(E_1, FT1, TT1)$$

as well as some suitable invocation transitions for the other members of $\mathcal{R}_c$. Then $\mathbf{N}(E_1, FF1) = \{TF2\}$. In this case $\mathbf{X}(E_1, FF1)$ needs only contain the first state variable, so both the second and the third state variable can be selected as secondary. Using MSCC with that assumption one obtains $\mathbf{N}'_m(E_1, FF1) = \{TF2, TT1\}$, so again soundness but not correctness is obtained.

In this case, the unintended model entered because $\mathbf{X}(E, r)$ is only required to be a subset of the controlled state variables. This opens the door for admitting some model that satisfies the action laws with respect to occluded variables, but which also includes some change in a controlled, non-occluded variable (in this case, the second state variable), provided that it thereby obtains a smaller set of changes in remanent state variables.

The source of incompleteness that was illustrated here can be removed by requiring that all controlled state variables must be occluded, that is, their new value must be stated in the action law. This means effectively that the action law must not merely specify the new values for some state variables that change their value, but also specify explicitly and un-overridably that some state variables do not change their value in the current action. An additional possibility is to introduce a fourth category for those state variables that *must not* change as the result of an action.

9.8. Causal approaches to ramification

We proceed now to a first account and analysis of so-called causal approaches to ramification. In view of the causation orientation of the underlying semantics that is being used here, one would suppose that causal approaches should enjoy fewer restrictions and a broader range of applicability than the minimization oriented approaches.

Several proposals for causation-oriented methods have been published, first from European research (Cordier and Siégel, 1992; Brewka and Hertzberg, 1993; Cordier and Siégel, 1995) and then from work done in America (Thielscher, 1995; McCain and Turner, 1995; Lin, 1995). Unfortunately, they all use fairly specialized logics, which adds to the difficulties of analyzing them. As a first step, we shall therefore define our own variant of these causal approaches, called **influence-restricted secondary change**, abbreviated **IRSC**, which will then be used for the assessment. IRSC is similar in particular to the approach of Thielscher (Thielscher, 1995), but not equivalent to it.

The entailment methods MRC and MRCC assumed a partitioning of the state variables into three categories: occluded, remanent, and dependent ones. For IRSC, we only retain the distinction between occluded and secondary state variables, like in MSC and MSCC. We also dispense with all minimization. The occlusion function $\mathbf{X}$ is used for characterizing the choice of occluded state variables.

Instead of minimization, IRSC uses an *influence relation* $\mathbf{I}(f, f', r)$ which says that f potentially influences f' in the causal transition chains that emerge from the state r. This relation is a strict partial order with respect to its first two arguments, and we write its non-strict transitive closure as $\mathbf{I}^*$. If F is a set of state variables, then $\mathbf{I}(F, r)$ denotes the superset of F which also contains all state variables f' which satisfy $\mathbf{I}^*(f, f', r)$ for some f in F.

The set of selected new states according to the IRSC method, using an influence relation $\mathbf{I}$, will be written $\mathbf{N}'_{\mathbf{I}}(E, r)$; it is defined as follows:

$$\mathbf{N}'_{\mathbf{I}}(E, r) = \{r' \in \mathbf{N}'(E, r) \cap \mathcal{R}_c \mid dom(r' - r) \subseteq \mathbf{I}(\mathbf{X}(E, r), r)\},$$

with the same usage for $-$ and *dom* as before. This definition says that $\mathbf{N}'_{\mathbf{I}}(E, r)$ is the set of all $r' \in \mathbf{N}'(E, r) \cap \mathcal{R}_c$ that only differ from r in occluded state variables (whose new values are explicitly stated in the action law) and in state variables that are reachable by $\mathbf{I}^*$ from the occluded ones.

As usual, the assessment problem is as follows: given a respectful action system, an occlusion function $\mathbf{X}$, and an influence relation $\mathbf{I}$, to identify restrictions on these structures which guarantee that $\mathbf{N}(E, r) = \mathbf{N}'_{\mathbf{I}}(E, r)$ for all E and r. In particular, we are interested in cases where $\mathbf{X}$ and $\mathbf{I}$ have been derived in a systematic way from the action system.

The following definition captures an obvious way of constructing $\mathbf{I}(f, f', r)$ from the action system and $\mathbf{X}$:

Definition 21 A combination of a respectful action system, an occlusion function $\mathbf{X}$, and an influence relation $\mathbf{I}$ is **invocation based** iff it satisfies the following two conditions for an arbitrary action symbol E and arbitrary state $r \in \mathcal{R}_c$:
  1. If $G(E, r, r')$, then $dom(r' - r) \subseteq \mathbf{X}(E, r)$.
  2. Consider any transition chain

$$r_1, r_2, \ldots r_k$$

where $G(E, r, r_1)$, $C(r_i, r_{i+1})$, and $r_k \in \mathcal{R}_c$, as usual. Write $r_0 = r$. Whenever, for some $i \geq 0$, a state variable f has different values in r_i and r_{i+1}, and a state variable f' has different values in r_{i+1} and r_{i+2}, it must be true that $\mathbf{I}(f, f', r)$.

We immediately obtain:

Theorem 22 IRSC is sound if used for an invocation based combination of an action system, an occlusion function, and an influence relation.

Proof Let r_k be an arbitrary member of $\mathbf{N}(E, r)$, which is determined as such by the transition chain

$$r_1, r_2, ... r_k.$$

Since the combination is invocation based, it follows that $dom(r_1 - r) \subseteq \mathbf{X}(E, r)$, and then that

$$dom(r_k - r) \subseteq \mathbf{I}(\mathbf{X}(E, r), r).$$

Therefore $r_k \in \mathbf{N}'_I(E, r)$, which means that

$$\mathbf{N}(E, r) \subseteq \mathbf{N}'_I(E, r).$$

This concludes the proof.

Thus, unlike the result for the minimization-based approaches, IRSC does not require a strict separation between controlled and obtained state variables. It is possible for a state variable to change in the invocation for some pair (E, r), and to change in the causation chain for some other (E, r). This is typical of the relay example that was put forward by Thielscher in (Thielscher, 1995).

However, there are still two problems with IRSC. First, this result only proves soundness and not completeness, so in gross terms it is no better than MRCC that was analyzed above. The other problem is that it IRSC in a invocation based combination can only work if the action law expresses the invoked changes, that is, those obtained by the G relation. It does not work at all if action laws describe actions in terms of their indirect changes, as in the two-switch lamp example.

There are several possiblities for how one would modify IRSC or its usage in order to eliminate this restriction. As usual, the difficulty is not in proposing the method, but in analyzing its properties. This is a topic for further research.

9.9. Conclusion

As background, we have reviewed current approaches to underlying semantics and range-of-applicability results for logics of actions and change with strict inertia. After that, we have defined and proposed a causation-oriented *causal propagation semantics* for ramification, and we have reported relative range results for minimization-based approaches. Finally, based on the same underlying semantics, we have reported on soundness results both for some of the minimization-based approaches and for a prototypical causation oriented approach to ramification.

The general observation from this study is that one needs to impose fairly strong restrictions and still one obtains relatively weak results (only soundness, no semantic completeness). This suggests that contemporary approaches to ramification are not sufficiently well motivated, and that additional, application-specific information should be used to modify the present methods or to influence how they are used.

Part IV

Between Space and Time

10. Space, Time, and Movement

Antony Galton

10.1. Introduction

Mathematical physics provides an exact, quantitative account of motion which has enabled us to send spacecraft to distant planets and to aim our missiles with deadly accuracy. It becomes unwieldy, perhaps even impotent, when dealing with less tidy situations such as the flow of traffic through the streets of a city, the movement of people about an office, or the procession of weather systems around the globe. The degree of idealization required even to describe these phenomena in mathematical terms inevitably leaves out many factors which are in fact instrumental in determining how they happen. In our everyday life, too, our predictive abilities are sorely limited, yet we have evolved a workable, and in some respects quite refined network of commonsense notions which enable us to get by most of the time. In disciplines such as philosophy and artificial intelligence (Davis, 1990; Hobbs and Moore, 1985) there is an intense interest in laying bare and systematising the conceptual schemes underlying our everyday competence in handling such notions as time, space, and movement, and this chapter is intended to contribute to that enterprise.

A central feature of commonsense reasoning is that it is largely *qualitative*, dealing with broad-brush descriptions of the phenomena it handles rather than exact numerical values. The relationship between quantitative and qualitative descriptions can be viewed as a many-to-one mapping: each qualitative description stands in for an infinite set of distinct quantitative ones. Thus, for example, the qualitative description "It is moving upwards" corresponds to a set of descriptions of the form

$$\left\{ \frac{dz}{dt} = v \mid v > 0 \right\},$$

where z measures the vertical displacement, from the ground up, of the moving object. This view of the relationship between quantitative and qualitative description has proved fruitful within the domain of *qualitative physics* (Weld and de Kleer, 1990), and we make use of it later on when discussing continuity.

The phenomenon of movement consists of the same object occupying different positions in space at different times. A theory of movement must therefore incorporate a theory of time, a theory of space, a theory of objects, and a theory of position. Depending on how these theories are presented, we might end up with very different theories of movement. Let us consider some of the options.

10.1.1. THEORY OF TIME

The essential characteristics of time are *duration* and *direction*. A theory of time articulates raw duration into *times*, which may be considered as chunks of duration. These may be more or less precisely defined. A chunk of duration is an *interval*; it is bounded at either end by *instants*. It is important to note that intervals and instants inevitably exist alongside one another—you cannot have one without the other. An interval is clearly defined only to the extent that its endpoints are, and these are instants. Equally, it is in the nature of an instant to be a place of (actual or potential) division of a stretch of time, and hence of an interval. Formally, we can represent the articulation of temporal duration into instants and intervals either by taking instants as primitive and then defining intervals in terms of their endpoints, or by taking intervals as primitive and defining instants to be their endpoints.

The second element of time, direction, can be represented formally by imposing an ordering relation on the set of times. This is most simply accomplished in the case of instants, which may be regarded as linearly ordered (though for some purposes it is convenient to model the uncertainty of the future by means of a forward-branching partial order). The ordering relations on intervals are rather more complex, but they are well understood.

Another issue that has to be addressed in the theory of time concerns granularity. Any chronometrical device has a certain temporal resolving power, a minimum duration that it is capable of recognizing. In addition, some processes are conveniently conceptualized as proceeding in a discrete, stepwise fashion, the duration of each step being minimal from the point of view of the current conceptualization; an example is the clock cycle of a computer processor. On the other hand, we are familiar with the idea of ever-increasing accuracy in our measurements; we have the idea of being able to make arbitrarily fine discriminations. We know that processes which appear continuous at one level of granularity may appear discrete at a lower level, and then again continuous at a lower level still. A good example is a cinema film, which looks continuous when viewed at normal speed by a human subject, but which we know in fact consists of a sequence of discrete frames — although when looked at more closely still, the replacement of one frame by the next can be seen to involve only continuous motion.

Out of all this complexity there emerge two natural idealizations, each of which can form the basis of a formal theory. One is the idea of *discrete time*, by which temporal duration is articulated into a sequence of minimal steps — atomic intervals or *chronons* — isomorphic in point of ordering with the integers. The other is the idea of *dense time*, by which the articulation of temporal duration allows arbitrarily fine subdivision, so that any interval can be divided further into subintervals — or, equivalently, between any two instants can be found a third, and hence, by iteration, infinitely many. The issue facing us is not so much which of these idealizations paints a true picture of time itself, but rather which of them is best suited to the purpose at hand.

10.1.2. THEORY OF SPACE

Just as the theory of time must articulate raw duration into stretches of time (intervals) and their endpoints (instants), so a theory of space will articulate raw extension into chunks of space and their boundaries. But here we have a richer theory because of the greater dimensionality of space. Space as we ordinarily conceive it is three-dimensional, which means that we have a hierarchy of chunk and boundary articulations as follows. At the highest level, a chunk of three-dimensional space is a *volume*; its boundary is a *surface*. But now a surface also has a kind of extension, but with two degrees of freedom rather than three; a chunk of surface extension is an *area* or *region*, and its boundary is an *edge*. An edge has extension with one degree of freedom; a chunk of edge extension is a *length* or *arc*, and its boundary, analogously to that of a temporal interval, consists of a pair of *points*. We have now reached a spatial element with no extension, and the articulatory process comes to an end.

The standard mathematical model for this hierarchy is *point-set topology*. Here points are taken as fundamental entities; all other spatial entities — lengths, areas, and volumes — are regarded as sets of points. This being the case, it is regarded as perfectly proper to combine elements of different dimension in arbitrary ways. Thus in point-set topology, one might consider such entities as

- The interior of a sphere together with half its surface, or
- An arc together with one endpoint but not the other, or
- A cube with a circle removed from its interior.

Because of such oddities as these, it is sometimes felt that point-set topology offers too rich an ontology of spatial entities to form the basis of a workable common-sense theory of space: put simply, point-set topology enables one to make distinctions that have no meaning in the context of physical space.

In this chapter we take the view that while we want to be able to talk about volumes, surfaces, edges, and points, these entities are each *sui generis*. It does not make sense to combine entities of different dimensions; a surface is an utterly different *kind* of thing from a volume although surfaces are ontologically dependent on volumes (and so on down the hierarchy).

Parallel to the temporal ordering, there exist spatial ordering relations too; but space lacks intrinsic directionality. Directions such as north, south, east, and west or back, front, left, and right are imposed on spatial entities by reference to some privileged point of view (the orientation of the earth's axis in the first case, the position of an observer in the second). But some spatial relations, such as betweenness and contiguity, are absolute.

The distinction between discrete and dense can be applied to space as well as to time, but the higher dimensionality of space leads to complications. Discrete space is composed of atomic regions or *cells*. If, as is natural, we wish space to be homogeneous and isotropic, then this limits the possibilities for discrete space to a small number of three-dimensional tesselations such as a cubic lattice.

10.1.3. THEORY OF OBJECTS

What is an object? For the purposes of a theory of movement, anything must count as an object which it makes sense to ascribe movement to. This covers a multitude of possibilities. We are unable to explore these in detail, but a number of points are worth mentioning.

First, objects may be rigid or non-rigid. A rigid object maintains the same shape and size at all times, whereas a non-rigid one can change in respect of shape, size, or position, complicating the description of its motion. Note, however, that change in size is not motion but growth or shrinkage, and that there is a further important difference, not expressible in terms of purely spatial attributes, between true growth, which involves the accretion of new material, and expansion, which involves only the redistribution of existing material. Again, change in shape is again not motion but deformation. When all three attributes are changing, though, it is not always easy to separate out these components. Absolute rigidity is a physical fiction — yet another of the idealizations we constantly have to make in this business — but many objects in everyday life approach sufficiently near to this state in normal conditions that it is a useful fiction.

Second, objects may have parts, and indeed, rigidity amounts to there being no relative motion of the different parts of a body. Even with a rigid body, though, there can be motions best described in terms of the motions of its parts. For example, a gramophone record rotating on the turntable maintains the same overall position, its motion arising ¿from the fact that each part of the record undergoes a continuous circular displacement.

Third, not all objects, in the sense of "that to which movement can be ascribed", are discrete individuals. At the linguistic level, we have to deal with both count nouns and mass nouns. The flow of water in a river, for example, is certainly a form of movement, which can be described in terms of the changing positions of individual samples of water, but there is no single body of water whose movement can be equated with the river's flow.

Examples like this are notoriously difficult to handle within the object-based framework presupposed by standard logical methods: (Hayes, 1985a) is a classic attempt to do this.

Finally, objects may not be concrete substances at all: an example is *holes*, the subject of a recent study (Casati and Varzi, 1994). Other examples are *waves* and *shadows*. Objects of this kind — *parasitic* or *virtual* objects — can move just as well as concrete objects such as violins and porcupines, though their movement is itself parasitic on the movement of (parts of) the objects they are parasitic on. More generally, a "solid" three-dimensional object will have a two-dimensional surface parasitic on it, and it may have one-dimensional edges and dimensionless corners as well, echoing the dimensional hierarchy we have already recognized for purely spatial entities.

10.1.4. THEORY OF POSITION

The theory of position will bring together the theory of objects and the theory of space by providing the means of specifying where an object is. Following Aristotle, it is natural to define the position of an object as the total region of space occupied by it at a time. An object's position will thus be a region of space precisely congruent, in the geometrical sense, to the body itself.

It is not usually practical, or even useful, to specify the position of an object exactly. Instead we make do with describing its position qualitatively by specifying the spatial relation it bears to some antecedently given region. This relation is typically inclusion, as when we say that something is "in the bathroom" — meaning that its position is a proper part of the region of space identified as the interior of the bathroom — but it might be contiguity ("on the table") or proximity ("near the fireplace"). For this reason, a close study of spatial relationships will be important in our program.

10.1.5. THEORY OF MOVEMENT

With these ingredients in place, we can now define the motion of a body as a mapping from times to positions: for each time t we specify the position of the body at t. This simple statement actually conceals a multitude of complexities. To begin with, what kind of time t are we talking about — an interval or an instant? What kind of position — exact or qualitative? And what difference does it make whether time or space is discrete or dense?

Movement is typically continuous in the sense that to get from one position to another a body has to pass through intermediate positions. It does not make sudden jumps from one place to another. If space is discrete, then positions can be neighbors, which means that an object can move directly from one to the other, there being no intermediate positions in this case. We still have a kind of continuity: let us call it *quasi-continuity*. It means that an object only moves directly between neighboring positions. If time is discrete as well, then there is a fixed upper limit to the speed of quasi-continuous motion: one step per chronon. In discrete time, the position of an object will be specified for each chronon (atomic interval). It does not make much sense to give the position at an instant (the instants in discrete time are the meeting points of neighbouring chronons).

If time and space are both dense, then for continuous motion we have to specify the position of an object at each instant: if an object is in continuous motion throughout some interval, then there is no subinterval of that interval over which the object maintains the same exact position. If this is felt to be unpalatable, then one could define the motion not in terms of exact positions but in terms of *locations*, where the location of an object over an interval is the sum of all the exact positions occupied by the object during the interval.

10.2. Models of Time

As already noted, we can set up our model of time by taking either instants or intervals as primitive elements; the choice between the two approaches is purely practical, since it makes no ultimate theoretical difference which of them we choose. This statement will be justified in what follows.

¿From a practical point of view, it makes good sense to begin with instants, since it is much easier to specify an ordering relation on dimensionless entities than on extended entities which can overlap. We shall suppose, therefore, that we have a set T of instants endowed with an relation $\prec$ of *temporal succession*. If $t, u \in T$ are arbitrary instants, the intended meaning of $t \prec u$ is that instant t precedes instant u. For convenience, we write $t \preceq u$ whenever either $t \prec u$ or $t = u$, and $t \prec u \prec v$ whenever both $t \prec u$ and $u \prec v$.

We specify that the relation $\prec$ defines a total order on T; this is accomplished by means of the three axioms:

- IRReflexivity: For no instant t is it the case that $t \prec t$.
- TRAnsitivity: Whenever $t \prec u \prec v$, then also $t \prec v$.
- LINearity: If $t \neq u$ then either $t \prec u$ or $u \prec t$.

We use the capitalized part of the names as labels for the respective conditions.

An axiom which is sometimes regarded as desirable is

- UNBoundedness: For every instant t there are instants u and v such that $u \prec t \prec v$.

This ensures, if it is required, that there is neither an earliest nor a latest instant.

We now have a choice between dense and discrete time, characterized by the axioms

- DENsity: Whenever $t \prec u$, there is an instant v such that $t \prec v \prec u$.
- DIScreteness: Whenever $t \prec u$, there are instants t' and u' such that $t \prec t'$, $u' \prec u$, and for no instant v is it the case that either $t \prec v \prec t'$ or $u' \prec v \prec u$.

It is noteworthy that discreteness is so much harder to specify than density. For the temporal ordering to be discrete, it is necessary that whenever one instant t precedes another instant u, there is an *earliest* instant t' that t precedes, and a *latest* instant u' that precedes u. (Of course, it could be that $t' = u$ and $t = u'$, or that $t' = u'$—these cases are not ruled out by DIS.) Note that so long as there are at least two instants, DEN and DIS are mutually incompatible.

van Benthem notes that both {IRR, TRA, LIN, UNB, DEN} and {IRR, TRA, LIN, UNB, DIS} form syntactically complete sets of axioms — that is, in each set, any putative first-order property of the ordering relation can be either proved or disproved on the basis of the axioms.

Intervals can now be specified by giving their endpoints. Indeed, for any pair of instants t, u, where $t \prec u$, we can introduce a unique interval $\langle t, u \rangle$, which begins at t and ends at u. We call this the *pair model* of an interval. For short, we say that t begins $\langle t, u \rangle$ and that u ends $\langle t, u \rangle$; and both t and u limit $\langle t, u \rangle$. If $t \prec v \prec u$, then we shall say that v falls within, or divides, $\langle t, u \rangle$, and write $v \in \langle t, u \rangle$.

One frequently identifies an interval with a range of points — namely, all those points which fall within it. For the interval $\langle t, u \rangle$ these are the points v such that $t \prec v \prec u$. The points in the range are thus members of the set

$$\{v \mid t \prec v \prec u\},$$

and it is customary to *identify* the interval with this set. We call this the *set model* of an interval. Unfortunately, people who identify an interval with the set of instants which fall within it very often want at the same time to do something else which is inconsistent with this — namely, to regard the interval as somehow *composed* of the instants which fall within it. This is inconsistent with the set model because a set is an abstract entity to which its members stand in an abstract relation of membership; the set is not composed of its members in the same way that, for example, a table is composed of its constituent atoms. You can see this quite clearly by reflecting on the fact that a table is not at all the same thing as the set of all the atoms which it is composed of: it is not only a different thing, it is a radically different *kind* of thing. The set model of an interval actually has nothing to offer over and above the pair model. And since you need to know the beginning and end points of the interval in order to specify the set of instants which fall in between these, the pair model clearly has logical priority. This is reflected in the very name "interval", which refers to something that lies *between* its extremities.

Intervals inherit temporal succession from instants. But whereas succession of one instant by another always involves an intervening gap, intervals can succeed one another directly, giving us two distinct notions of succession for intervals, as follows:

- *Immediate succession*, also known as *abutment, contiguity*, or *meeting*, is written as $\langle t, u \rangle | \langle v, w \rangle$; a necessary and sufficient condition for this is that $u = v$. We read '|' as *meets*.

- *Delayed succession*, is written as $\langle t, u \rangle < \langle v, w \rangle$, a necessary and sufficient condition being that $u \prec v$.

We shall also write $\langle t, u \rangle \lhd \langle v, w \rangle$ when $u \preceq v$; this is the disjunction of immediate and delayed succession.

We use i, j, k, ... to refer to intervals when we do not wish to specify the endpoints, it being understood, however, that any interval is uniquely characterized by its endpoints. We write $i|j|k$ to mean that both $i|j$ and $j|k$; note that in this case we do *not* have $i|k$, making *meets* an "antitransitive" relation.

Two properties of immediate succession which follow immediately from the definition, without making use of any of the axioms for $\prec$, are:

- M1. If $i|k$, $i|l$, and $j|k$, then also $j|l$.
- M2. If $i|j|l$ and $i|k|l$, then $j = k$.

The transitivity axiom TRA for instants implies the following property of intervals:

- TRA*: If $i|j$ then there is an interval k which meets all and only those intervals which j meets, and is met by all and only those intervals which meet i.

To see why the result holds, let $i = \langle t, u \rangle$ and $j = \langle u, v \rangle$; then put $k = \langle t, v \rangle$. To be able to do this we need to know that $t \prec v$ — but we know $t \prec u$ and $u \prec v$, and we have assumed transitivity. Note that by M2, k must be unique, so we can write $k = i + j$, the *join* or *concatenation* of i and j.

If we now bring in the linearity axiom LIN for instants, we can prove that immediate succession for intervals obeys the rule

- LIN*. If $i|k$ and $j|l$, then exactly one of the following holds: $i < l$, $i|l$, $j < k$.

Next, from the unboundedness axiom UNB we deduce for intervals

- UNB*. For every interval i, there exist intervals j and k such that $j|i|k$.

If we choose the density axiom DEN for instants, then for intervals we have

- DEN*. For every interval i, there exist intervals j and k such that $i = j + k$.

Suppose, on the other hand, we choose discreteness (DIS). We define an *atomic interval* (chronon) as any interval m which cannot be expressed in the form $j + k$ (so the effect of DEN* is simply to rule out atomic intervals). Then we have

- DIS*. For any interval i, either i is an atomic interval or there exist atomic intervals m and m' and intervals j, k such that $i = m + j = k + m'$.

In other words, each non-atomic interval has atomic intervals as initial and final segments. (Note that in DIS*, we could have $m = k$ and $m' = j$; this will occur just in case i is the concatenation of two atomic intervals.)

Further relations on intervals can easily be defined using the + notation. The canonical thirteen interval-to-interval relations of Allen (Allen, 1981; Allen, 1983) are delayed and immediate succession and their converses, equality, and

- *Overlap*, iOj, meaning that there exist intervals i', j', and k such that $i = i' + k$ and $j = k + j'$;
- *Starts*, iSj, meaning that there is an interval k such that $j = i + k$;
- *During*, iDj, meaning that there are intervals k and l such that $j = k + i + l$;
- *Finishes*, iFj, meaning that there is an interval k such that $j = k + i$;

and their converses. In addition, we say that i is a *proper subinterval* of j, written $i \sqsubset j$, if either iSj, iDj, or iFj, and that i is a *subinterval* of j, written $i \sqsubseteq j$, if either $i \sqsubset j$ or $i = j$.

10.2.1. INTERVAL-BASED MODELS

It is often regarded as more satisfactory to base one's temporal model on intervals as the fundamental temporal units rather than instants. Allen and Hayes do this, using equivalents of M1, M2, TRA*, LIN*, UNB*, and DEN* as their axioms for the relation | on intervals. Delayed succession must now be defined by the rule

$$i < j \text{ if and only if there is an interval } k \text{ such that } i|k|j.$$

They also show how instants can be defined in this interval-based system. There are in fact several possibilities.

In the interval-based model, an instant is defined by specifying, for each interval, whether the instant precedes, begins, divides, ends, or follows the interval. We do not need to specify this explicitly for every interval, since we can make use of certain logical connections between these five relations and the immediate succession relation |, as follows (here we use i, j, k for intervals, and t for an instant):

If t ends i and begins j then $i|j$ and, for any interval k,

- t precedes k if $i < k$.
- t begins k if $i|k$.
- t divides k if neither $k \lhd j$ nor $i \lhd k$.
- t ends k if $k|j$.
- t follows k if $k < j$.

It follows that an instant can be defined by giving two intervals — namely i, j as above. These intervals are not uniquely determined by t, however, since i can be replaced by any interval which meets j, and j can be replaced by any interval which i meets, and the same instant will be defined.

For this reason, the pair model of instant is not quite analogous to the pair model of an interval. We have to define an instant not as a single pair of intervals, but as a set of pairs of intervals — namely, an equivalence class of pairs of intervals under the equivalence

$$(i, j) \sim (k, l) \text{ if and only if } i|j, \; k|l, \; i|l, \text{ and } k|j.$$

We write $i][j$ to denote the equivalence class to which the pair (i, j) belongs:

$$i][j = \{(k, l) \mid (i, j) \sim (k, l)\}.$$

Intuitively, $i][j$ is the instant at which i meets j. This model was given by Hamblin (Hamblin, 1969; Hamblin, 1971).

An alternative model for an instant is the set model, which is strictly dual to the set model for an interval. Just as the set model for an interval identifies an interval with the set of instants which divide it, so the set model for an instant identifies an instant with the set of intervals which it divides. Specifically, we can identify the *beginning* of the interval i as the instant

$$Beg(i) = \{j \mid jOi \lor iFj \lor iDj\},$$

and we can identify the *end* of the interval i as the instant

$$End(i) = \{j \mid iOj \lor iSj \lor iDj\}.$$

It can be proved on the basis of the axioms and definitions that $i|j$ if and only if $End(i) = Beg(j)$, and in that case we can identify $End(i)$ and $Beg(j)$ with $i][j$. The set model as given here is closely related, though not quite identical, to that given by Allen and Hayes.

The relationship between the pair model and the set model is that the pair (i, j) is a member of t in the former model if and only if $End(i) = Beg(j) = t$ in the latter model. (But note the equivocation here: the first t is a set of pairs of intervals whereas the second is a set of intervals.)

The temporal succession relation $\prec$ on instants can be defined in the pair model as follows:

$$i][j \prec k][l \text{ if and only if } i < l.$$

Alternatively, in the set model we have

$$t \prec u \text{ if and only if there are intervals } i \in t \text{ and } j \in u \text{ such that } i < j.$$

In either case, it can be proved that if the intervals satisfy M1, M2, TRA*, LIN*, (UNB*,) DEN*/DIS*, then the instants under $\prec$ satisfy IRR, TRA, LIN, (UNB,) DEN/DIS.

It follows that it does not matter very much whether we base our temporal model on instants or intervals. By choosing appropriate definitions we will end up with equivalent systems starting from either choice. It is certainly convenient to be able to use both instant and interval notations!

10.3. Models of Space, Position, and Movement

The spatial analogue of defining an interval in terms of its endpoints would be to define a spatial region in terms of its boundary, which then leaves us with the problem of defining the boundary itself; this is, in general, no less difficult. We shall, in fact, simply avoid the issue of *how* regions are defined — more often than not, a spatial region will be specified as the position of some body — and concentrate instead on defining properties of and relations amongst regions.

Randell et al. have identified a key relation to be that of *connection*, which is best defined in terms of what it is not, by stipulating that two regions are connected if they are not separated, where separation implies that the shortest distance between the two regions is positive. In terms of connection, they are able to define the well-known RCC-8 set of relations:

DC Disconnected

EC Externally connected (that is, touching but not overlapping)

PO Partially overlapping

TPP Tangential proper part

NTPP Non-tangential proper part

TPPi Inverse of TPP

NTPPi Inverse of NTPP

EQ Equal

These relations apply equally well in spaces of one, two, or three dimensions, and they apply to regions of arbitrary complexity, such as scattered regions consisting of two or more mutually disconnected components, regions with various kinds of holes (internal cavities, tunnels, and surface depressions), and even infinite regions.

Essentially the same set of relations was defined by Egenhofer in terms of the intersections between the boundary and interior of one region with those of another (Egenhofer, 1991; Egenhofer and Franzosa, 1991). Egenhofer's system is less general than Cohn's in that it assumes the individual regions are not scattered; but it is otherwise equivalent.

In what follows we assume that the position of an object is specified in terms of the RCC-8 relation that it bears to some known region, such as the position of another object. Sometimes we use a disjunction of RCC-8 regions; a particularly useful case is the the disjunction of TPP, NTPP, and EQ, which is labeled P (for *part*). In this way we can account for a substantial part of the means we use in everyday life for saying where things are, so the restriction to RCC-8 relations and their disjunctions is not as great a limitation as it may seem. And in any case, the principles underlying our exposition are sufficiently general that they can be readily extended to further refinements in the way positions are identified.

10.3.1. MOVEMENTS AND THEIR OCCURRENCE CONDITIONS

10.3.1.1. *Fluents*

We take as our fundamental notion for the analysis of change the idea of a *fluent*. A fluent is something that can take different values at different times (McCarthy and Hayes, 1969). If f is a fluent and a is a value it can take, then $f = a$ is a proposition that can be true or false at different times, in other words a *Boolean fluent* or *state*. Likewise, if A is a set of values, $f \in A$ is also a state.

For a state S, we may say that S holds *at* an instant or *on* an interval. Holding on an interval means holding throughout the interval — that is, at every instant which falls within the interval — and this could be taken as the definition of holding on intervals in terms of holding at instants. An immediate consequence is that S holds on every subinterval of any interval on which it holds.

We sometimes need to refer to the *negation* of a state S, written $-S$. This is the state which holds whenever S itself does not hold. For $-S$ to hold at an instant it is enough that S fails to hold at that instant; but for $-S$ to hold on an interval it is not enough that S fails to hold on the interval: rather, S must fail to hold at any instant within the interval.

We write $pos(a)$ to denote the position of body a. This is a region having exactly the same shape and size as a, so that a can fit into it exactly. Since the position of a can change over time, $pos(a)$ is a fluent. The statement "$pos(a) = r$ holds on i" is to be understood as meaning that, throughout the interval i, the position of a is precisely the region r; and similarly, "$P(pos(a), r)$ holds on i" means that a is within the region r throughout i.

10.3.1.2. *Events*

To handle movement we need to introduce a terminology for referring to events, since a movement is an event (it is not a fluent that is true or false at different times). If e denotes an event type, we say that e occurs on i to mean that there is an occurrence of type e over the interval i. *Allen's rule* for occurrence is that if e occurs on i, then it does not occur on any proper subinterval of i. This rule confers a unitary character on an event: each occurrence has a clear beginning and a clear end, and the interval i marks exactly the stretch of time between these points. The rule does, in fact, restrict the allowable event-types. For example, there cannot be an event-type corresponding to the sentence "The ball falls to the ground", since if this happens over an interval i it is also true to say that it happens over any interval which finishes i. The appropriate event-type to use in this case would correspond rather to "The ball falls to the ground from a resting position".

We also have cause to talk about instantaneous events. For these we say that e occurs *at* an instant t (Galton, 1994).

Our paradigm for analyzing movement will be to specify a movement in terms of its *occurrence conditions*, which will take one of the forms

e occurs on i if and only if ...
e occurs at t if and only if ...

where the "..." should contain no reference to e. We use the standard abbreviation *iff* for *if and only if*. We consider a number of different types of movement event. In each case we give different analyses, corresponding to the choice of dense or discrete models of time and space. Where necessary, we invoke continuity or its discrete analogue (quasi-continuity); but a detailed discussion of continuity in general is deferred to the next section.

10.3.1.3. *Some examples*

Moving from one position to another.   Our first example is "a moves from position r_1 to position r_2 over the interval i".

In discrete time, a must be at r_1 on some interval (possible atomic) which meets i, and it must be at r_2 on some interval which i meets. Moreover, during i itself, a cannot be at either r_1 or r_2, since this would imply that the movement from r_1 to r_2 occurred on a proper subinterval of i, violating Allen's rule. We thus have the following occurrence condition for discrete time:

$Move(a, r_1, r_2)$ occurs on i iff there are intervals j and k such that

- $j|i|k$,
- $EQ(pos(a), r_1)$ holds on j,
- $EQ(pos(a), r_2)$ holds on k,
- $-EQ(pos(a), r_1)$ holds on i, and
- $-EQ(pos(a), r_2)$ holds on i.

In discrete space, the same analysis will apply.

If both time and space are dense, however, there is another possibility. Suppose a moves from position r_0 to r_3, passing through positions r_1 and r_2, in that order, but without stopping at either of them. Then there is no interval over which a is at either r_1 or r_2, yet we can still say that a moves ¿from r_1 to r_2 over the interval between the times at which it is at these positions. To cover this possibility, we must modify our occurrence condition to:

$Move(a, r_1, r_2)$ occurs on i iff

- $EQ(pos(a), r_1)$ holds at $Beg(i)$,
- $EQ(pos(a), r_2)$ holds at $End(i)$,
- $-EQ(pos(a), r_1)$ holds on i, and
- $-EQ(pos(a), r_2)$ holds on i.

Note that for continuous movement in dense time this definition subsumes the previous one, since if a is at position r_1 over an interval meeting i, then by continuity it must be at r_1 at the beginning of i, and likewise with r_2 at the end. We examine this kind of argument in greater detail later when we look more closely at continuity.

Why did we not give the second occurrence condition immediately, given that it subsumes the first? The reason is that in discrete time it is not clear what meaning can be given to the notion of a state holding at an instant. For a state to hold at an instant, it must either hold on some interval within which that instant falls, or it must be the limit of a continuous range of states holding at a range of instants converging on that instant. The former case is adequately handled in terms of states holding on intervals; the latter can only occur in dense time.

Entering a region. Our next example is "*a* enters region *r* over interval *i*". In discrete time, there must be an interval meeting *i* on which *a* is just outside *r*, poised to enter it: the appropriate RCC-8 relation here is EC. Similarly, there must be an interval which *i* meets on which *a* is just inside *r*, the relation in question being TPP. During *i* itself, *a* must be partly inside *r* and partly outside, i.e., PO. We thus have

$Enter(a, r)$ occurs on *i* iff there are intervals *j* and *k* such that

- $j|i|k$,
- $EC(pos(a), r)$ holds on *j*,
- $PO(pos(a), r)$ holds on *i*, and
- $TPP(pos(a), r)$ holds on *k*.

In dense time and space, we can argue as before that *a* does not need to be EC or TPP to *r* for more than an instant: consider, for example, the case where *a* approaches *r* from a distance and enters it without pausing in either the EC or the TPP positions. The occurrence condition we require in this case is therefore

$Enter(a, r)$ occurs on *i* iff

- $EC(pos(a), r)$ holds at $Beg(i)$,
- $PO(pos(a), r)$ holds on *i*, and
- $TPP(pos(a), r)$ holds at $End(i)$.

Leaving a region. The temporal mirror-image of the previous case is "*a* leaves *r* over interval *i*". The occurrence conditions are straightforward modifications of the ones given above, namely, for discrete time or space,

$Leave(a, r)$ occurs on *i* iff there are intervals *j* and *k* such that

- $j|i|k$,
- $TPP(pos(a), r)$ holds on *j*,
- $PO(pos(a), r)$ holds on *i*, and

- $EC(pos(a), r)$ holds on k.

and for dense time and space:

$Leave(a, r)$ occurs on i iff
- $TPP(pos(a), r)$ holds at $Beg(i)$,
- $PO(pos(a), r)$ holds on i, and
- $EC(pos(a), r)$ holds at $End(i)$.

Coming into contact. The next example is an instantaneous event, "a and b come into contact at instant t". In discrete time, t must be the meeting point of two intervals such that throughout the first interval a and b are not in contact and throughout the second they are:

$Connect(a, b)$ occurs at t iff there are intervals i and j such that
- $End(i) = Beg(j) = t$,
- $DC(pos(a), pos(b))$ holds on i, and
- $EC(pos(a), pos(b))$ holds on j.

In dense time and space, we must allow for the possibility that a and b move apart as soon as they have made contact, so that there is no interval over which they are actually in contact; or again, that the two bodies interpenetrate immediately after making contact, so that EC is immediately followed by PO. Both these cases, as well as the original case where the bodies remain in contact over an interval, are covered by the occurrence condition:

$Connect(a, b)$ occurs at t iff there is an interval i such that
- $End(i) = t$,
- $DC(pos(a), pos(b))$ holds on i, and
- $EC(pos(a), pos(b))$ holds at t.

Note the asymmetry in the handling of DC and EC here; one might wonder why one could not instead put

$Connect(a, b)$ occurs at t iff there is an interval i such that
- $Beg(i) = t$,
- $DC(pos(a), pos(b))$ holds at t, and
- $EC(pos(a), pos(b))$ holds on i.

but a little reflection shows that this would violate continuity: if the two bodies are separated at t, then an interval must elapse during which the distance of separation smoothly diminishes to zero before they can make contact (compare the "continuity rule" of Williams).

Moving from one region to another   Our last example is "a moves from r_1 to r_2". This looks very similar to our first example, but there is a subtle, but significant, difference. In the first example, r_1 and r_2 were positions for a — that is, regions of space geometrically congruent to a. Here we attempt to approach more closely to the kind of locutions we use in everyday life, as in "Ann went from the kitchen to the bathroom", or "Bob moved from the desk to the wall". Here Ann is congruent to neither the kitchen nor the bathroom, and Bob is congruent to neither the desk nor the wall.

In the first sentence, Ann is initially located in the kitchen, and ends up located in the bathroom. Maybe she starts off somewhere right inside (NTPP) the kitchen, moves to the door, passes through the doorway, along the passage (up the stairs, and so on, as appropriate), to the door of the bathroom, passes through the door of the bathroom and into the interior. The whole motion takes her from a position that is NTPP to the kitchen to a position that is NTPP to the bathroom. Unfortunately this way of describing the motion violates Allen's rule, since any such motion has a proper part which is also of exactly that kind; if Ann is NTPP to the kitchen at a particular time, then by continuity she must still be NTPP to that room over some interval immediately following that time, and likewise with the bathroom at the other end of the movement. If we are to characterize this motion purely in terms of RCC-8 relations, we have to regard the motion as beginning at the very last instant at which Ann can be said to be in the kitchen, and as ending at the first instant at which she can be said to be in the bathroom. At these instants her position is TPP to the respective rooms. (Here the room is identified with the volume of space bounded by the inward-facing surface of the walls.) This corresponds to the occurrence condition

$Move'(a, r_1, r_2)$ occurs on i iff
- $TPP(pos(a), r_1)$ holds at $Beg(i)$,
- $TPP(pos(a), r_2)$ holds at $End(i)$,
- $-TPP(pos(a), r_1)$ holds on i, and
- $-TPP(pos(a), r_2)$ holds on i.

Note that this condition applies also in the case where the kitchen and bathroom are adjacent rooms, so that during the movement Ann is simultaneously PO to both rooms. If we replace TPP by TP (*tangential part*, the disjunction of TPP and =) throughout, then this subsumes both this occurrence condition and the occurrence condition given in the first example.

Our second example in this section, "Bob moved from the desk to the wall", is different in that Bob is never actually in the desk or the wall. Rather, he moves from a position adjacent to the desk to a position adjacent to the wall. To a first approximation we can assume that "adjacent to" means EC, giving us the occurrence condition

$Move''(a, r_1, r_2)$ occurs on i iff

- $EC(pos(a), r_1)$ holds at $Beg(i)$,
- $DC(pos(a), r_1)$ holds on i, and
- $EC(pos(a), r_2)$ holds at $End(i)$.

with the obvious modification for discrete time.

10.3.1.4. *Further Refinements of the Analysis*

Transitions. The examples given here all adhere more or less closely to a common pattern — or rather pair of patterns. Movement events are *transitions* from one positional state to another. The general pattern for the occurrence of a transition from state S_1 to state S_2 over an interval i is, for discrete time,

$Trans(S_1, S_2)$ occurs on i iff there are intervals j and k such that

- $j|i|k$,
- S_1 holds on j,
- S_2 holds on k,
- $-S_1$ holds on i, and
- $-S_2$ holds on i.

and for dense time,

$Trans(S_1, S_2)$ occurs on i iff

- S_1 holds at $Beg(i)$,
- S_2 holds at $End(i)$,
- $-S_1$ holds on i, and
- $-S_2$ holds on i.

For a general discussion of transitions, see (Gooday, 1994; Gooday and Galton, 1997). It should be noted that in the dense-time version not all states can be substituted for S_1 and S_2 here without violating continuity. We saw above, for example that states involving NTPP cannot be used here, whereas those involving TPP can. The question of which states can, and which cannot, be substituted here will be addressed in the next section.

For instantaneous transitions we have:

$Trans(S_1, S_2)$ occurs at t iff there are intervals i and j such that

- $End(i) = Beg(j) = t$,
- S_1 holds on i, and
- S_2 holds on j.

Nothing is said here about what state, if any, holds at the instant t, so this occurrence condition is usable in discrete time just as well as in dense.

Comparing the general conditions for transitions with our earlier analyses of particular examples, we can immediately identify

- $Move(a, r_1, r_2)$ with $Trans(EQ(pos(a), r_1), EQ(pos(a), r_2))$ and
- $Move'(a, r_1, r_2)$ with $Trans(TPP(pos(a), r_1), TPP(pos(a), r_2))$.

For the other cases we need a little further argumentation. Take $Enter(a, r)$, for instance. We should like to identify this with

$$Trans(EC(pos(a), r), TPP(pos(a), r)).$$

The occurrence conditions for this transition differ from those given for $Enter(a, r)$ only in that the condition that $PO(pos(a), r)$ holds on i is replaced by the condition that both $-EC(pos(a), r)$ and $-TPP(pos(a), r)$ must hold on i. But in the context of the other conditions, these conditions are equivalent, given continuity (or quasi-continuity in discrete time), since the only way of getting from EC to TPP without passing through either of these states in the course of the transition is by being in state PO throughout.

Similar arguments show that, assuming continuity, the conditions we have given enable us to identify

- $Leave(a, r)$ with $Trans(TPP(pos(a), r), EC(pos(a), r))$,
- $Connect(a, b)$ with $Trans(DC(pos(a), pos(b)), EC(pos(a), pos(b)))$, and
- $Move''(a, r_1, r_2)$ with $Trans(EC(pos(a), r_1), EC(pos(a), r_2))$.

If for any reason we wish to allow motion to be discontinuous, then the equivalences just enunciated will break down; and in that case it is the analyses in terms of *Trans* which should be retained. Note, however, that *discontinuous* motion raises grave problems about object identity. Suppose that on interval i each of the positions P_1 and P_2 is occupied by a body of a certain type, the two bodies being similar though not necessarily identical. Now suppose that at an immediately succeeding interval j (where $i|j$), positions P_1 and P_2 are vacant, but positions P'_1 and P'_2, neither of which is adjacent to either of P_1 and P_2, and which were both vacant on i, are now occupied by bodies similar to the bodies that occupied P_1 and P_2 at m. Each of the bodies at j is no more similar to either of the bodies at i than to the other. There seem to be two equally good accounts of what has happened: either the bodies occupying P_1 and P_2 at time i have moved to P'_1 and P'_2 respectively at time j; or they have moved to P'_2 and P'_1 respectively. There is nothing to choose between these alternatives unless each body is supplied with a unique identifier which it carries with it unchanged through time.

Paths.   There are two notable omissions from the above analyses. First, since movements are defined purely in terms of beginning and end positions, nothing is said here about the *path* by which the moving object travels between these places. One way to remedy this in the same spirit as our analyses above is to introduce a three-place *Trans* functor, such that $Trans(S_1, S_2, S_3)$ designates a transition from fluent S_1 to fluent S_2, where fluent S_3 holds throughout the course of the transition. This was introduced, with a different notation, by Gooday. The occurrence condition for durative transitions of this kind in dense time is:

$Trans(S_1, S_2, S_3)$ occurs on i iff
- S_1 holds at $Beg(i)$,
- S_2 holds at $End(i)$,
- $-S_1$ holds on i,
- $-S_2$ holds on i, and
- S_3 holds on i.

The modification required for discrete time is analogous to the case for the two-place version of *Trans*. The fluent S_3 functions as an *invariant*; in principle, any fluent could be used here, but for our present purposes it is natural to use a fluent of the form $P(pos(a), p)$, where p is a region which we can identify with a particular path (typically, it will be a "long thin" region, but it need not be).

Motion and rest.   The second omission is that in defining movements in terms of transitions we have had nothing to say about *motion*. Whereas a movement is a type of event, by motion I understand rather a kind of state: we speak of a body's being *in motion* or *at rest*, and these are states which can hold or not hold at different times: we could notate them in our usual function-and-argument style as $Moving(a)$ and $Resting(a)$. Our occurrence conditions for $Move(a, r_1, r_2)$ have nothing explicit to say concerning the holding or not holding of $Moving(a)$ and $Resting(a)$ during the interval on which the movement takes place; indeed, if over an interval i_1 the body a moves away ¿from r_1 to a position r_3, say, then stays at r_3 throughout an immediately succeeding interval i_2, and finally moves from r_3 to r_2 over the interval i_3, then $Move(a, r_1, r_2)$ holds on the interval $i_1 + i_2 + i_3$, even though a is at rest (at r_2) during a subinterval of that interval — and indeed i_2 could amount to a high proportion of the total length of the interval. On the other hand we know that, if motion is continuous, a cannot be at rest throughout the entire interval during which it moves from one position to another.

How are the states $Moving(a)$ and $Resting(a)$ to be defined? The latter is straightforward: a body is at rest at a position if it remains in that position over an interval. Note that this excludes cases where a body has velocity zero for an isolated instant, for example the case of a vertically thrown projectile at the highest point of its trajectory. If we wanted to include such cases, the definition of *Resting* would have to be much more complicated. Excluding these, then, we can say that

Resting(a) holds on i iff there is a region r such that $pos(a) = r$
    holds on i.
Resting(a) holds at t iff t falls within an interval on which
    Resting(a) holds.

We can now define motion as the absence of rest: that is, a body is
considered to be in motion over an interval so long as it is not at rest
over any subinterval of that interval:

Moving(a) holds on i iff there is no interval $j \sqsubseteq i$ on which
    Resting(a) holds.
Moving(a) holds at t iff t falls within an interval on which
    Moving(a) holds.

Only on the assumption that time is dense do these definitions succeed
in capturing our intentions; in discrete time, no object is ever moving,
according to these definitions, since every object is at rest on every atomic
interval. Motion occurs whenever there are intervals i and j such that $i|j$, a
is at rest over i and at rest over j but not over $i + j$ — a phenomenon that
is impossible with continuous motion in dense time. In a certain sense, one
could say that in discrete time *movement* can occur without *motion*; it is
perhaps puzzling *how* movement gets to occur in this case. It is not too hard
to adopt a frame of mind in which this same sense of puzzlement carries
over to the case of continuous time — which is the source of Zeno's arrow
paradox, according to which, in the words of Paul Jennings, "a flying arrow
can't really be moving because at any given moment it must *be* somewhere"
(Jennings, 1959, p. 80).

10.4. Continuity

Mathematics provides us with an account of the two different notions of
continuity suggested by our experience of the physical world. On the one
hand, there is the continuity of space and time, which we are accustomed
to regard as "seamless" continua admitting arbitrary fine subdivision and
no "gaps". On the other hand, there is the continuity of *change*, according
to which measurable physical magnitudes such as the position, velocity,
acceleration, or temperature of a body vary smoothly in time, again
presenting an appearance of seamlessness, with no instantaneous jumps. It
is with the latter kind of continuity that we are mainly concerned, though
the former will inevitably play a part in our deliberations.

10.4.1. QUASI-CONTINUITY

Before embarking on a detailed examination of continuity proper, let us
first dispose of the phenomenon I call *quasi-continuity* that can occur in
discrete space. By way of illustration we take as a model for discrete space

and time the game of chess, where "space" consists of the discrete 8×8 array of the chessboard, and "time" consists of the sequence of states of play that constitute the game.

We should distinguish at the outset between a game of chess as a mathematical abstraction and its physical realization as the motion of wooden pieces on a board. It is perfectly possible for two competent players to conduct a game entirely verbally, while walking down the street, say. The physical movement of wooden pieces on a board, which is a continuous process in dense space and time, is thus inessential to the game itself, and must be regarded as a simulation of the abstract game whose time and space are, as noted above, both discrete.

Considered *in abstracto*, then, the game consists of a discrete sequence of states

$$s_1, s_2, s_3, \ldots, s_n,$$

each state being characterized by the distribution of pieces on the board together with such information as which player has the next move, whether each king has moved (determining whether castling is possible), and so on. Nothing that happens outside this sequence of states has any reality as far as the game is concerned. In particular, states of the game may be considered to follow on from one another without a gap. A move in the game is an instantaneous transition from one state to the next in the sequence.

In the chessboard, although there is no continuous movement in the strict sense, we can nevertheless distinguish between, for example, the movement of the king, which is always between neighbouring squares (except when castling), and the movement of the queen, which can move directly between remote squares. Admittedly, for the queen to move between two squares, there must be a clear path between them; one might think that in some sense the queen traverses this path, but it does not do so within the discrete time of the chess game. One might contrast this with the knight, which also moves between non-neighboring squares, in this case without any requirement of there being a free path. We describe the movement of the king, as opposed to that of the queen or knight, as *quasi-continuous*.

Quasi-continuity is a phenomenon that can occur only in discrete space: it characterizes movement in which every change of position is from one spatial location to an adjacent one. By adjacent positions we mean positions between which the displacement is exactly one cell-width: this covers both positions which are themselves minimal cells (as in the positions of chess pieces, which occupy only one square of the board at a time) and positions of objects which cover more than one minimal cell at a time. This notion of adjacency is, of course, defined only in discrete space. The "law of quasi-continuous motion" for discrete space is then:

If $pos(a) = r_1$ holds on i and $pos(a) = r_2$ holds on j, where $i|j$, then r_1 is either equal or adjacent to r_2.

If time is discrete too, then, as observed above, we obtain an interesting effect: namely, *there is a maximum speed for quasi-continuous motion*. The maximum speed is one cell-width per chronon, where the cell-width is the maximum distance between adjacent positions, and the chronon is the indivisible unit of time. In chess, this maximum speed is the speed of the king and the pawns; that these are in fact the slowest-moving chess pieces is merely indicative of the circumstance that the other pieces do not move in a quasi-continuous fashion.

10.4.2. CONTINUITY PROPER

We are here concerned with continuous variation in the value of a fluent: that is, we have a fluent f taking different values at different times, and we want to model the idea that the value of f changes in a continuous, "seamless" fashion, without any instantaneous jumps between separate values. Intuitively, continuity is a property that a fluent has over an interval of time; it does not make much sense to say that a fluent exhibits continuous variation at an isolated instant. Despite this, the standard mathematical treatment of continuity is point-based: continuity of a fluent over an interval is defined as continuity at each instant in the interval. (Of course, the mathematical treatment covers functions over arbitrary continua, not just over time.) A fluent f taking real-number values is defined to be continuous at the instant t so long as, for every positive real number ϵ, there is an (open!) interval i containing t such that the value of f at each instant in i differs from its value at t by less than ϵ. The interval i that is chosen will in general depend on the value of ϵ.

This definition does not assume that time instants are ordered like the real numbers, but we get some very odd results if this is not the case. Consider, for example, the function

$$f(t) = \left\{ \begin{array}{ll} 0 & \text{if } t^2 < 2 \\ 1 & \text{if } t^2 > 2 \end{array} \right.$$

If the times t are allowed to be arbitrary real numbers, then whatever value is given to this function at $t = \sqrt{2}$, it is discontinuous there; but if times are only allowed to be rational numbers (so that there is no time corresponding to the value $\sqrt{2}$), the function becomes continuous! At first sight this looks desperately counterintuitive, but that is only because we tend to imagine the rational numbers as simply an attenuated version of the real numbers, whereas in fact the ordering of the rationals is utterly different in kind from that of the reals, with infinitely many inbuilt discontinuities — one of which successfully accommodates the "jump" we perceive in our function f, so that viewed from within the rationals themselves the jump is totally invisible. In short, the rational numbers do not form a good model for a continuous space such as we often conceive the time dimension to be.

Because mathematical continuity is defined primarily at points rather than over intervals, we get bizarre results even if we stick to the real numbers for both the range and domain of our functions. An infamous example is the "pathological" function p defined by

$$p(x) = \begin{cases} 1/n & \text{if } x \text{ is rational, with denominator } n \text{ in lowest terms} \\ 0 & \text{if } x \text{ is irrational} \end{cases}$$

which comes out as continuous at irrational points but not at rational ones. From an intuitive point of view this is distinctly odd, since we do not normally regard continuity as something which can exist at isolated points. One way of reacting to this would be to say "Isn't mathematics wonderful!" and treat it as a substantial discovery about the inadequacy of our everyday notion of continuity; but one could equally well be skeptical about the mathematical claim and regard it as revealing a "bug" in its handling of continuity. My own inclination is to favor the latter reaction — much as I love and respect mathematics, I do not believe it has a greater claim to infallibility that any other discipline (something that is occasionally forgotten by its more devoted followers).

The main problem with mathematical continuity, *when considered as a model for the continuity we believe we perceive in the physical world*, is that it starts from the assumption that the values of fluents can in principle be assigned to each instant independently. It would be more in keeping with our everyday notions to start with the assumption that fluents are primarily evaluated over intervals, and that it is only under certain special circumstances that it even makes sense to evaluate them at instants. What are those special circumstances? First, there is obviously no harm in saying that a fluent has a particular value at an instant if it has the same value throughout some interval within which that instant falls — no harm, but also very little to be gained. The only other case where it would seem feasible to evaluate a fluent at an instant is precisely when the fluent exhibits continuous variation in the neighborhood of that instant. A continuously varying fluent cannot be assigned values over intervals, since it need never remain at the same value for more than an instant.

This has consequences for one of the oldest problems concerning time and change, the classical *dividing instant* problem, which goes back to Plato and Aristotle. It may be phrased as follows. Let S be a state such that $-S$ holds on i and S holds on j, where $i|j$. The problem is to determine whether S or $-S$ holds at $i][j$.

Now a state is, of course, a Boolean fluent, and the Boolean values true and false do not form a continuum, so it is not possible for a Boolean fluent to exhibit continuous variation (Hamblin, 1969). For this reason, one might suppose that the answer to the dividing instant problem can only ever be that it is meaningless to say that either S or $-S$ holds at $i][j$. An example which is frequently cited in this connection is that of a lamp, which is on during an interval ending at midnight and off during an interval beginning at midnight; to the question whether the lamp is on or off *at* midnight, it is often said that either answer would be meaningless since fluents like "the lamp is on" and "the lamp is off" take values only over intervals, and not at instants. This approach has become prominent in AI, largely owing to the influence of Allen. Allen's work was prefigured by that of Hamblin (Hamblin, 1969; Hamblin, 1971) in philosophy. Hamblin was very much motivated by the dividing instant problem. His response to it, in effect, is that that problem is much ado about nothing, that it simply is not necessary to say anything at all about the truth value of S at the instant of change (or as van Benthem puts it, "one only has the ... problem if one insists on having it" [by requiring Dedekind continuity]).

In fact, there are cases where we can give a clear answer to the dividing instant problem, and these are precisely the cases where there is a continuously varying fluent underlying the Boolean fluent that is explicitly mentioned in the problem. An example of such a clear case is the following: let S be the state $pos(a) = r$. We are supposing that $pos(a) \neq r$ holds on i and $pos(a) = r$ holds at j, where $i|j$. Underlying the Boolean fluent $pos(a) = r$ there is a position-valued fluent $pos(a)$, and the latter, unlike the former, can be presumed to exhibit continuous variation.

For $pos(a) \neq r$, it is enough that the space occupied by some part of a is disjoint from r — in other words, a does not have to be right outside r to count as not being at r. Assuming that the motion of a is continuous, then for a to move to r from any position r' distinct from r it must pass through a range of intermediate positions forming a path from r' to r. Suppose, then, that a is not at r at the instant $t = i][j$. Let u be any instant dividing j: since a is at r thoughout j, it is at r at u. So a moves from r' at t to r at u. Hence, by continuity, it must occupy positions along a path joining r' to r at some times in the interval $\langle t, u \rangle$. But this is a subinterval of j. Hence there are times during j when a is not at r — contradicting our assumption that a is at r throughout j. It follows that a must be at r at instant t as well. There is an asymmetry between the states represented by "a is at r" and "a is not at r", which could be expressed by saying that the former must be true on closed sets of instants, the latter on open sets.

In general, if the state S describes the state of the world with respect to some continuously variable property (such as the position of a body), then it is possible, case by case, to determine a solution to the dividing instant problem. One thing we look at later is a systematic way of doing this. In this light, it is worth reconsidering the example of the lamp.

Suppose the lamp is off over the interval $i = \langle t_1, t_2 \rangle$ and on over $j = \langle t_2, t_3 \rangle$. The problem is whether the lamp is on or off at the instant $t_2 = i][j$. Both of the possible answers can be made sense of on the assumption that there is a continuously variable fluent underlying the Boolean fluents "The lamp is on" and "The lamp is off". The fluent in question, which we denote b, measures the brightness of the lamp. It varies continuously over the range $0 \leq b \leq B$, where B is the maximum brightness, which the lamp has when it is fully on. We assume that when the lamp is switched on, the value of b increases continuously from 0 to B. If we now stipulate that "The lamp is off" means $b = 0$, and "The lamp is on" means $b > 0$, then we obtain the answer that the lamp is off at t_2. If, on the other hand, we stipulate that

"The lamp is off" means $b < B$, and "The lamp is on" means $b = B$, then we obtain the answer that the lamp is on at t_2.

Another possibility is to reject the premises and deny that it is possible for an interval over which the lamp is off to be immediately followed by an interval over which it is on. To justify this, one must deny that "The lamp is off" is the negation of "The lamp is on". In view of the previous two cases, it is easy to see how to do this: we define "The lamp is off" to mean $b = 0$, and "The lamp is on" to mean $b = B$. Now in order for the lamp to change from being off to being on, it has to pass over the range of values for which $0 < b < B$, and this must take time. So the true picture, on this view, would be that the lamp is off over some interval $\langle t_1, t_2 \rangle$, on over an interval $\langle t_3, t_4 \rangle$, and neither on nor off over the interval $\langle t_2, t_3 \rangle$, which we may imagine to be of extremely short duration. Of course the dividing instant problem arises again with respect to the instants t_2 and t_3, but this time it is of the relatively harmless continuous variety that we have dealt with already: the lamp is off ($b = 0$) at t_2, and on ($b = B$) at t_3.

For completeness we should mention the admittedly somewhat bizarre possibility that the light is both on and off at t_2. We would get this result if we defined "The lamp is off" to mean, say, $b \leq \frac{1}{2}B$ and "The lamp is on" to mean $b \geq \frac{1}{2}B$, and suppose that $b = \frac{1}{2}B$ at t_2. Once again, this involves denying that "The lamp is off" is the negation of "The lamp is on" — only this time without rejecting the premises of the problem.

10.5. Discrete Representations of Continuous State Spaces

As mentioned in the introduction, qualitative descriptions can be regarded as corresponding to sets or ranges of exact quantitative ones. A qualitative state-space can be thought of as the result of partitioning a quantitative state-space into a discrete set of regions, each corresponding to one qualitative description and covering a (typically) infinite range of quantitative ones. The lamp example discussed in the previous section provides a simple illustration of this. Each statement of the form "$b = k$", for values of k ranging between 0 and B, corresponds to a distinct quantitative state of the lamp. We considered various possible ways of partitioning this state-space into qualitative descriptions such as "on", "off" and "neither on nor off". The important point for our present purposes is that the underlying quantitative state-space is conceptualized as continuous — this is implicit in the assumption that b can take *any* real-number value in the range $[0, B]$ — whereas the qualitative state-space into which it is partitioned is necessarily discrete. For example, if we define "off" as $b < k$ and "on" as $b \geq k$ then there is no state intermediate between "on" and "off"; if we define "off" as $b = 0$ and "on" as $b = B$, then $0 < b < B$ corresponds to the state "neither on nor off", and there is no state intermediate between "off" and "neither on nor off", nor between "neither on nor off" and "on".

A more complicated example of a discrete qualitative state-space derived by partitioning an underlying continuous state-space is the set of RCC-8 relations discussed earlier. The set of all possible mutual configurations of two variable regions R_1 and R_2 forms a continuous state-space: between any two such configurations a whole path of intermediate configurations can be found. Each of the regions can vary continously as regards shape, size, and position, and the result of this variation in the regions is a continuous variation in the exact mutual configuration of the two together. This enormously complex state-space is partitioned by RCC-8 into a discrete set of just eight qualitative relations.

Earlier, when presenting occurrence conditions for movement events, we noted that, for example, it is possible for two bodies (or rather, their positions) to be EC for a single instant (in the context of a transition from DC to PO, or ¿from DC back to DC again), whereas if they are DC at an instant they must be DC over an interval within which that instant falls. These facts can be derived ¿from a consideration of the nature of the underlying continuous space; essentially it is to do with the fact that the qualitative state EC corresponds to a lower-dimensional *boundary* between DC and PO. If the qualitative space is treated on its own, however, without consideration of the underlying continuous space, this kind of information will be lost unless specific provision is made to retain it. In this section we examine the nature of that provision, and see that it can provide us with a powerful tool for the investigation of discrete representations of continuous state-spaces.

10.5.1. PERTURBATION AND DOMINANCE

We shall say that a state S' is a *perturbation* of state S if and only if at least one of the following situations can occur:

1. S holds on an interval, and S' holds at one of its endpoints.
2. S' holds on an interval, and S holds at one of its endpoints.

If only the first of the above situations can occur, then we say that state S' *dominates* state S, written $S' \succ S$, whereas if only the second can occur, S' is dominated by S, written $S' \prec S$.

To illustrate the notions of dominance and perturbation, consider the example in which the state-space for a single real variable is divided into the three qualitative states positive, negative and zero, which we here abbreviate to P, N, and Z, respectively. Assuming continuous variation, we know that

If Z holds on i, then Z holds at the endpoints of i,

which means that neither of the situations

$^*Z$ holds on an interval and P holds at one of its endpoints
$^*Z$ holds on an interval and N holds at one of its endpoints

can occur (it is convenient here to adopt from linguistics the convention of attaching an asterisk at the beginning of a disallowed form). On the other hand, if our variable increases uniformly over the interval $\langle -1, 1 \rangle$ so that its value is 0 at time 0, then we have

N holds on the interval $\langle -1, 0 \rangle$ and Z holds at 0, an endpoint of the interval.

P holds on the interval $\langle 0, 1 \rangle$ and Z holds at 0, an endpoint of the interval.

It follows that Z dominates both N and P.

We also know from continuity that

if N holds on i then either N or Z holds at the endpoints of i.

if P holds on i then either P or Z holds at the endpoints of i.

This rules out both the situations

*N holds on an interval and P holds at one of its endpoints

*P holds on an interval and N holds at one of its endpoints

which means that N and P are not perturbations of each other.

We restrict our attention to state spaces in which all perturbation relations involve dominance in one direction or other, as in the example above. The general definition is as follows:

A *dominance space* is a pair $(S, \succ)$, where

- S is a finite set of *states* and
- $\succ$ is an irreflexive, asymmetric relation on S, where $S_1 \succ_2$ is read "S_1 dominates S_2",

and the following *temporal incidence rule* holds:

- If S holds on i and S' hold at an endpoint of i, then $S' \succeq S$ (where $S' \succeq S$ means that either $S' \succ S$ or $S' = S$).

Clearly the example $(\{N, Z, P\}, \succ)$, which we looked at above, forms a dominance space. Indeed, it is very nearly the simplest possible such space.

The key fact about dominance spaces is that a set of such spaces can be combined into a composite dominance space, as shown by the following theorem.

Theorem 1. The Composition Theorem for Dominance Spaces
Let $(S_1, \succ_1), (S_2, \succ_2), \ldots, (S_n, \succ_n)$ be dominance spaces. Then

$$(S_1 \times S_2 \times \cdots \times S_n, \succ)$$

is also a dominance space, where $\succ$ is defined by the rule

$(S_1, \cdots, S_n) \succ (S'_1, \cdots, S'_n)$ if and only if
$S_i \succeq S'_i$ for $i = 1, \ldots n$ and $(S_1, \cdots, S_n) \neq (S'_1, \cdots, S'_n)$.

(Note: the ordered n-tuple $(S_1, S_2, \ldots, S_n)$ is to be understood as representing the simultaneous conjunction of the states $S_1, S_2, \cdots, S_n$, defined to hold at/on a time if and only if each of the individual components holds at/on that time.)

Proof. First, since $S_1, S_2, \ldots, S_n$ are all finite, so is $S_1 \times S_2 \times \cdots \times S_n$. Next, we must check the properties of $\succ$:

(a) $\succ$ is irreflexive. This is immediate from the condition

$$(S_1, S_2, \cdots, S_n) \neq (S'_1, S'_2, \cdots, S'_n)$$

appearing in the definition.

(b) $\succ$ is asymmetric. Suppose that both $(S_1, \ldots, S_n) \succeq (S'_1, \ldots, S'_n)$ and $(S'_1, \ldots, S'_n) \succeq (S_1, \ldots, S_n)$. Then for $i = 1, 2, \ldots, n$, both $S_i \succeq_i S'_i$ and $S'_i \succeq_i S_i$, so by asymmetry of $\succ_i$, $S_i = S'_i$. It follows that $(S_1, \cdots, S_n) = (S'_1, \cdots, S'_n)$. Hence if we have $(S_1, \ldots, S_n) \succ (S'_1, \ldots, S'_n)$, then we do *not* have $(S'_1, \ldots, S'_n) \succ (S_1, \ldots, S_n)$.

Finally, we must check the temporal incidence rule. Suppose that

$(S_1, S_2, \ldots, S_n)$ holds on i, and $(S'_1, S'_2, \ldots, S'_n)$ holds at an endpoint of i.

Then for $k = 1, 2, \ldots, n$ we have

S_k holds on i and S'_k holds an endpoint of i,

which by the kth temporal incidence rule implies that $S'_k \succeq_k S_k$. We thus have

$$S'_1 \succeq_1 S_1 \wedge S'_2 \succeq_2 S_2 \wedge \cdots \wedge S'_n \succeq_n S_n$$

that is, $(S'_1, S'_2, \ldots, S'_n) \succeq (S_1, S_2, \ldots, S_n)$, as required. The significance of this theorem is that it is very often possible to describe a qualitative state-space that one is interested in as the product of simpler such spaces, which — if they are dominance spaces — allows one to use the theorem to determine the dominance and perturbation structure of the product space. We shall illustrate this with the RCC-8 relations in the next section.

10.5.2. APPLICATION OF THE DOMINANCE THEOREM

Suppose we wish to know what kinds of transition are possible between different elements of the RCC-8 state-space. One way of tackling this problem is to express RCC-8 as a dominance space derived as a product of simpler spaces for which the possible transitions are known. This presupposes that the RCC-8 set can be regarded as a partition of an

underlying continous space, as discussed in the previous section. Provided
that any pair of spatial regions can be continuously deformed into any other
pair, this is an entirely reasonable assumption. This is certainly the case
if the regions in question are topologically equivalent to discs (if we are
working in two dimensions) or balls (if we are working in three). If we allow
regions with scattered parts (like the old Welsh county of Flintshire), or
regions with interior cavities (like South Africa, with its 'cavity' Lesotho),
then we need a more liberal notion of continuous deformation which allows
"tearing" and "gluing" operations as well as topological homeomorphism.

The underlying continuous state-space is in fact extremely complex,
since it must contain separate points for each possible shape that each
region can have. Shape, thus unconstrained, has infinitely many degrees
of freedom. We are thus confronted with an infinite-dimensional space, of
which the RCC-8 set is a partition. It would clearly be impractical to work
with such a space, but luckily it is possible to abstract away from almost all
the dimensions of variation within this space to obtain a three-dimensional
continuous space within which the RCC-8 set can still be defined as a
partition.

Each point in this space is determined by a triple of real numbers
(α, β, γ), where

- α measures the proportion of region A that overlaps with region B:

$$\alpha = \frac{\text{area of A inside B}}{\text{area of A}},$$

- β measures the proportion of region B that overlaps with region A:

$$\beta = \frac{\text{area of B inside A}}{\text{area of B}},$$

- γ is the minimum distance between a boundary point of A and a
  boundary point of B.

Note that these three measures are not independent. In particular,

- $\alpha = 0$ if and only if $\beta = 0$. Each of these conditions is equivalent to A
  and B not overlapping at all.
- If $\alpha = \beta = 1$ then $\gamma = 0$. The antecedent holds only if A and B are
  coincident, in which case they must share all their boundary points.
- If $0 < \alpha < 1$ and $0 < \beta < 1$ then $\gamma = 0$. This uses the assumption that
  each region consists of a single connected component; the conditions
  on α and β mean that each region lies partly inside and partly outside
  the other; with self-connected regions this can happen only if their
  boundaries cross, giving us $\gamma = 0$.

Each permissible point in $\alpha\beta\gamma$-space corresponds to many distinct
configurations of the regions A and B, which all agree, however, as regards
the measures represented by α, β, and γ: and this is sufficient to determine
the RCC-8 relation between the two regions, as follows:

1. If $\alpha = \beta = \gamma = 0$, then EC.
2. If $\alpha = \beta = 0$ and $\gamma > 0$, then DC.
3. If $0 < \alpha < 1$ and $0 < \beta < 1$, then PO.
4. If $\alpha = \beta = 1$, then EQ.
5. If $0 < \beta < \alpha = 1$ and $\gamma = 0$, then TPP.
6. If $0 < \beta < \alpha = 1$ and $\gamma > 0$, then NTPP.
7. If $0 < \alpha < \beta = 1$ and $\gamma = 0$, then TPPi.
8. If $0 < \alpha < \beta = 1$ and $\gamma > 0$, then NTPPi.

It will be noted that from the point of view of determining the RCC-8 relations, the continuous range of variation of α from 0 to 1 can be considered to be divided up into just the following three qualitatively distinct parts:

$\alpha = 0$ (none of A is inside B)
$0 < \alpha < 1$ (some, but not all, of A is inside B)
$\alpha = 1$ (all of A is inside B)

Let us abbreviate these as $NONE_A$, $SOME_A$, and ALL_A respectively. Moreover, under continuous variation, it is clear that both $NONE_A$ and ALL_A must dominate $SOME_A$: we have a little dominance space $\mathcal{A}$:

$$NONE_A \succ SOME_A \prec ALL_A.$$

Likewise, for β, we can put

$$NONE_B \succ SOME_B \prec ALL_B,$$

defining the dominance space $\mathcal{B}$. The case of γ is even simpler: all we are interested in is whether or not $\gamma = 0$ — that is, whether the boundaries of A and B meet. The case $\gamma = 0$, which we shall designate $MEET$, obviously dominates the case $\gamma > 0$, or $-MEET$, the dominance space being $\mathcal{C}$.

The composition theorem for dominance spaces tells us that $\mathcal{A} \times \mathcal{B} \times \mathcal{C}$ is a dominance space, and the dominance relations are as portrayed in Fig. 1. If the three component spaces were independent, their product would have $3 \times 3 \times 2 = 18$ members, distributed on the grid indicated by the dotted lines. Since, as we have seen, they are not independent, only 8 of the 18 nodes on this grid represent real possibilities, and these correspond to the RCC-8 set, as shown above and indicated by the labels in the figure. The arrows represent dominance. If we were to ignore the arrowheads, then we could still read the shafts of the arrows as representing perturbation — the neighborhood relation on the RCC-8 space. Read in this way, our diagram corresponds exactly to that of (Randell et al., 1992a), as indeed it should.

For each pair of states joined by an arrow in the diagram, direct transitions are possible in either direction: this is the perturbation relation. Not all the perturbations are possible by movement alone: some require growth or deformation for their accomplishment and hence presuppose that

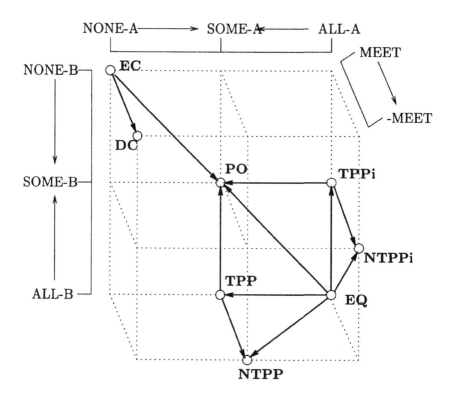

Figure 1. Generation of the dominance space for spatial regions.

at least one of the two regions is non-rigid. The links which imply non-rigidity are those between EQ and all its neighbors apart from PO. All the other transitions are possible for rigid regions on condition that both the states involved are realisable for the bodies in question (for example, $TPP(pos(a), b)$ and $NTPP(pos(a), b)$ are only possible if a is small enough to fit inside b with room to spare). A detailed treatment of the possibilities for rigid motion using the RCC-8 calculus is given in (Galton, 1993), which also gives explicit occurrence conditions for all the possible changes of position of a rigid body with respect to a fixed region.

In addition to giving us the perturbation relations, the dominance diagram encapsulates all the continuity considerations which we used when giving the occurrence conditions of movement events defined as transitions between RCC-8 relations. For example, when giving the occurrence condition of $Move(a, r_1, r_2)$, we noted that "if a is at position r_1 over an interval meeting i, then by continuity it must be at r_1 at the beginning of i". In effect, we are using the fact that EQ dominates $-$EQ, which in turn is a consequence of the fact that EQ dominates *all* its immediate neighbors. In the terminology of (Galton, 1990), EQ is a *state of position*. Again, in giving the occurrence conditions in dense time and space for $Enter(a, r)$, we implicitly used the fact that both EC and TPP dominate PO, and likewise for the occurrence condition of $Connect(a, b)$ we used the fact that EC dominates DC.

10.6. Conclusions

The central thesis of this chapter is that movement events should be specified in terms of their occurrence conditions, necessary and sufficient conditions for the occurrence of a given species of movement at a given time. We considered movement both in dense time and in discrete time, and included both durative and instantaneous movement events in our analyses. Our aim throughout has been to approach the task in a systematic way, with a view to generality.

Considerations of continuity played an important role in our treatment, and we looked in some detail at the implications of continuity for qualitative descriptions of motion. The outcome of this investigation was the introduction of the notion of a dominance space: with this notion, the properties of complex qualitative state-spaces can be derived systematically from those of smaller components, using the composition theorem for dominance spaces. Here we have given only one example of the application of the Composition Theorem. Other examples, including cases from outside the spatial domain, can be found in (Galton, 1995a) and (Galton, 1995c).

List of Authors

James F. Allen
Department of Computer Science
University of Rochester
Rochester, NY 14627
United States
e-mail: james@cs.rochester.edu

Brandon Bennett
Division of Artificial Intelligence
School of Computer Studies
University of Leeds
Leeds, LS2 9JT
United Kingdom
e-mail: brandon@scs.leeds.ac.uk

Roberto Casati
CNRS, Seminaire d'Epistémologie Comparative
Aix-en-Provence
France e-mail: casati@poly.polytechnique.fr

Anthony G. Cohn
Division of Artificial Intelligence
School of Computer Studies
University of Leeds
Leeds, LS2 9JT
United Kingdom
e-mail: agc@scs.leeds.ac.uk

George Ferguson
Department of Computer Science
University of Rochester
Rochester, NY 14627
United States
e-mail: ferguson@cs.rochester.edu

Andrew U. Frank
Department of Geoinformation
Technical University Vienna
Gusshausstrasse 27-29

1040 Vienna
Austria
e-mail: frank@geoinfo.tuwien.ac.at

Antony Galton
Department of Computer Science
University of Exeter
Old Library
Prince of Wales Road
Exeter EX4 4PT
United Kingdom
e-mail: antony@atlas.ex.ac.uk

Alfonso Gerevini
Department of Electronics for Automation
University of Brescia
via Branze 38
25123 Brescia
Italy
e-mail: gerevini@minerva.ing.unibs.it

John Gooday
Decision Solutions
Equifax Ltd.
Capital House
25 Chapel St.
London, NW1 5DS
United Kingdom
e-mail: jgooday@ds.equifax.co.uk

Nicholas M. Gotts
Department of Computer Science
University of Wales Aberystwyth
Penglais
Aberystwyth
Ceredigion
Wales SY23 3DB
United Kingdom
e-mail: nmg@aber.ac.uk

Annette Herskovits
Program in Applied Linguistics
Boston University
Charles River Campus

Boston, MA 02139
United States
current address:
University of California at Berkeley
Institute for Cognitive Science
Berkeley, CA 94705
United States
e-mail: hersko@cogsci.Berkeley.EDU

Drew McDermott
Computer Science Department
Yale University
PO Box 208285
New Haven, CT 06520-8285
United States
e-mail: mcdermott-drew@CS.YALE.EDU

Erik Sandewall
Department of Computer Science and Information Science
University of Linköping
S-581 83 Linköping
Sweden
e-mail: ejs@ida.liu.se

Oliviero Stock
Istituto per la Ricerca Scientifica e Tecnologica (IRST)
38050 Povo (Trento)
Italy
e-mail: stock@irst.itc.it

Achille C. Varzi
Department of Philosophy
Columbia University
MC 4971 Philosophy Hall
1150 Amsterdam Avenue
New York, NY 10027
United States
e-mail: varzi@columbia.edu

Laure Vieu
IRIT-CNRS
Université Paul Sabatier
118 route de Narbonne
31062 Toulouse cedex
France
e-mail: vieu@irit.fr

References

AIJ: 1995, 'Special issue on Planning and Scheduling'. *Artificial Intelligence* **74**(1–2).

Al-Taha, K.: 1992, 'Temporal Reasoning in Cadastral Systems'. Ph.d., University of Maine.

Al-Taha, K. and R. Barrera: 1994, 'Identities through Time'. In: Ehlers (ed.): *International Workshop on Requirements for Integrated Geographic Information Systems*. New Orleans, Louisiana, pp. 1–12.

Allen, J.: 1981, 'An interval-based representation of temporal knowledge'. In: *Proceedings of the Seventh International Joint Conference on Artificial Intelligence*. pp. 221–226.

Allen, J.: 1983, 'Maintaining knowledge about temporal intervals'. *Communications of the ACM* **26**(11), 832–843.

Allen, J.: 1984, 'Towards a general theory of action and time'. *Artificial Intelligence* **23**, 123–154. Also in *Readings in Planning*, J. Allen, J. Hendler, and A. Tate (eds.), Morgan Kaufmann, 1990, pp. 464–479.

Allen, J.: 1991, 'Temporal Reasoning and Planning'. In: J. Allen, H. Kautz, R. Pelavin, and J. Tenenberg (eds.): *Reasoning about Plans*. San Mateo, CA: Morgan Kaufmann, pp. 1–68.

Allen, J.: 1994, *Natural Language Understanding, 2nd ed.* Menlo Park, CA: Benjamin/Cummings Publishing Co.

Allen, J. and G. Ferguson: 1994, 'Actions and events in interval temporal logic'. *Journal of Logic and Computation* **4**(5), 531–579.

Allen, J. and P. Hayes: 1985, 'A common-sense theory of time'. In: *Proceedings of the Ninth International Joint Conference on Artificial Intelligence*. pp. 528–531.

Allen, J. and P. Hayes: 1989, 'Moments and points in an interval-based temporal logic'. *Computational Intelligence* **5**(4), 225–238.

Allen, J., J. Hendler, and A. Tate: 1990, *Readings in Planning*. Morgan Kaufmann.

Allen, J. and J. Koomen: 1983, 'Planning using a temporal world model'. In: A. Bundy (ed.): *Proceedings of the Eighth International Joint Conference on Artificial Intelligence (IJCAI-83)*. Karlsruhe, West Germany, pp. 741–747. Also in *Readings in Planning*, J. Allen, J. Hendler, and A. Tate (eds.), Morgan Kaufmann, 1990, pp. 559–565.

Allen, J. and L. Schubert: 1991, 'The TRAINS Project'. TRAINS Technical Note 91-1, Department of Computer Science, University of Rochester, Rochester, NY, 14627.

Allen, J., L. Schubert, G. Ferguson, P. Heeman, C. Hwang, T. Kato, M. Light, N. Martin, B. Miller, M. Poesio, and D. Traum: 1995, 'The TRAINS Project: A case study in defining a conversational planning agent'. *Journal of Experimental and Theoretical AI* **7**, 7–48.

Amsili, P., M. Borillo, and L. Vieu (eds.): 1995, 'Time, Space and Movement. Meaning and Knowledge in the Sensible World. Workshop Notes of the 5th International Workshop TSM'95'. Toulouse: IRIT, Groupe LRC.

André, E., G. Herzog, and T. Rist: 1988, 'On the simultaneous interpretation of real world image sequences and their natural language description: the system Soccer'. In: *Proceedings of the Eighth European Conference on Artificial Intelligence (ECAI-88)*. Munich.

Antenucci, J., K. Brown, P. Croswell, and M. Kevany: 1991, *Geographic Information Systems: A guide to the techniques*. Van Nostrand Reinold.

Artale, A. and E. Franconi: 1994, 'A computational account for a description logic of time and action'. In: *Principles of Knowledge Representation and Reasoning: Proceedings of the Fourth International Conference (KR'94)*. San Francisco, CA, pp. 3–14.

Asher, N. and J. Lang: 1994, 'When nonmonotonicity comes from distances'. In: *Proceedings of KI'94*. Berlin, pp. 308–318.

Asher, N. and L. Vieu: 1995, 'Toward a Geometry of Common Sense: A Semantics and a Complete Axiomatization of Mereotopology'. In: *Proceedings of the Fourteenth International Joint Conference on Artificial Intelligence (IJCAI-95)*. San Mateo, CA, pp. 846–852.

Aurnague, M.: 1995, 'Orientation in French Spatial Expressions: Formal Representations and Inferences'. *Journal of Semantics* **12**(3), 239–267.

Aurnague, M., A. Borillo, M. Borillo, and M. Bras (eds.): 1993, 'Semantics of Time, Space and Movement, Proceedings of the 4th International Workshop on 'Time, Space and Movement'-TSM'92'. Toulouse: IRIT, Groupe LRC.

Aurnague, M. and L. Vieu: 1993, 'A three-level approach to the semantics of space'. In: C. Zelinski-Wibbelt (ed.): *Semantics of Prepositions in Natural Language Processing*, No. 3 in Natural Language Processing. Berlin: Mouton de Gruyter, pp. 393–439.

Bacchus, F., J. Tenenberg, and J. Koomen: 1989, 'A non-reified temporal logic'. In: R. Brachman, H. Levesque, and R. Reiter (eds.): *Proceedings of the First International Conference on Principles of Knowledge Representation and Reasoning (KR-89)*. Toronto, Ont., pp. 2–10.

Baker, A.: 1989, 'A Simple Solution to the Yale Shooting Problem'. In: R. Brachman, H. Levesque, and R. Reiter (eds.): *Proceedings of the First International Conference on Principles of Knowledge Representation and Reasoning (KR-89)*. pp. 11–20.

Baker, A.: 1991, 'Nonmonotonic reasoning in the framework of the situation calculus'. *Artificial Intelligence* **49**, 5–24.

Ballard, D. and C. Brown: 1982, *Computer Vision*. Englewood Cliffs: Prentice-Hall.

Baral, C. and M. Gelfond: 1993, 'Representing concurrent actions in extended logic programming'. In: *Proceedings of the Thirteenth International Joint Conference on Artificial Intelligence (IJCAI-93)*. pp. 866–871.

Barber, F.: 1993, 'A metric time-point and duration-based temporal model'. *SIGART Bulletin* **4**(3), 30–49.

Barsalou, L.: 1985, 'Ideals, central tendency, and frequency of instantiation as determinants of graded structure in categories'. *Journal of Experimental Psychology: Learning, Memory, and Cognition* **11**, 629–654.

Baykan, C. and M. Fox: 1987, 'An investigation of opportunistic constraint satifaction in space planning'. In: *Proceedings of the Tenth International Joint Conference on Artificial Intelligence (IJCAI-87)*. Los Altos, CA, pp. 1035–1038.

Beetz, M. and D. McDermott: 1994, 'Revising failed plans during their execution'. In: K. Hammond (ed.): *Proceedings of the Second International Conference on AI Planning Systems*. Morgan Kaufmann.

Bell, C. and T. Tate: 1985, 'Use and justification of algorithms for managing temporal knowledge in O-plan'. Technical Report 531, AIAI, Edinburgh, UK.

Bennett, B.: 1994a, 'Some Observations and Puzzles about Composing Spatial and Temporal Relations'. In: R. Rodríguez (ed.): *Proceedings of the ECAI-94 Workshop on Spatial and Temporal Reasoning*.

Bennett, B.: 1994b, 'Spatial Reasoning with Propositional Logics'. In: J. Doyle, E. Sandewall, and P. Torasso (eds.): *Proceedings of KR'94*. San Mateo, CA.

Bennett, B.: 1994c, 'Spatial Reasoning with Propositional Logics'. In: J. Doyle, E. Sandewall, and P. Torasso (eds.): *Principles of Knowledge Representation and Reasoning: Proceedings of the 4th International Conference (KR94)*. San Francisco, CA.

Bennett, B.: 1995, 'Modal Logics for Qualitative Spatial Reasoning'. *Bulletin of the Interest Group on Propositional and Predicate Logics (IGPL)*.

Bennett, B.: 1996a, 'The application of Qualitative Spatial Reasoning to GIS'. In: R. Abrahart (ed.): *Proceedings of the First Int. Conference on GeoComputation*, Vol. I. Leeds, pp. 44–47.

Bennett, B.: 1996b, 'Carving Up Space: steps towards construction of an absolutely complete theory of spatial regions'. In: J. Alfres, L. Pereira, and E. Orlowska (eds.): *Proceedings of JELIA'96*. pp. 337–353.

Benzen, S.: 1959, 'On the Topology of the Genetic Fine Structure'. *Proceedings of the National Academy of Science* **45**(10), 1607–1620.

Bessière, C.: 1996, 'A simple way to improve path-consistency in Interval Algebra networks'. In: *Proceedings of the Thirteenth National Conference of the American Association for Artificial Intelligence (AAAI-96)*. Portland, OR, pp. 375–380.

Biacino, L. and G. Gerla: 1991, 'Connection Structures'. *Notre Dame Journal of Formal Logic* **32**(2), 242–247.

Biederman, I.: 1987, 'Recognition by components: A theory of human image understanding'. *Psychological Review* **94**, 115–147.

Biederman, I.: 1990, 'Higher-Level Vision'. In: D. N. Osherson, S. M. Kosslyn, and J. M. Hollerbach (eds.): *An Invitation to Cognitive Science. Volume 2: Visual Cognition and Action*. Cambridge, MA, and London: MIT Press, pp. 1–36.

Bierwisch, M.: 1988, 'On the grammar of local prepositions'. In: M. Bierwisch, W. Motsch, and I. Zimmermann (eds.): *Syntax, Semantics, and the Lexicon*. Berlin: Akademic-Verlag, pp. 1–65.

Binford, T.: 1971, 'Visual perception by a computer'. In: *Proceedings of the IEEE Conference on Systems and Controls*. Miami, FL.

Bitner, J. and E. Reingold: 1975, 'Backtrack Programming Techniques'. *Journal of the Association for Computing Machinery* **18**, 651–655.

Blum, A. and M. Furst: 1995, 'Fast planning through planning graph analysis'. In: *Proceedings of the Fourteenth International Joint Conference on Artificial Intelligence (IJCAI-95)*. Montreal, CA, pp. 1636–1642. .

Bobrow, D.: 1984, 'Qualitative reasoning about physical systems: an introduction'. *Artificial intelligence* **24**(1-3), 1–5.

Boddy, M.: 1993, 'Temporal Reasoning for Planning and Scheduling'. *SIGART Bulletin* **4**(3), 17–20.

Boddy, M.: 1996, 'Temporal reasoning for planning and scheduling in complex domains: Lessons learned'. In: A. Tate (ed.): *Advanced Planning Technology*. Menlo Park, CA: AAAI Press, pp. 77–83.

Booch, G.: 1987, *Software Components with Ada*. Benjamin Cummings Publ. Co.

Borgo, S., N. Guarino, and C. Masolo: 1996a, 'A Pointless Theory of Space Based on Strong Connection and Congruence'. In: L. C. Aiello and S. Shapiro (eds.): *Proceedings of KR'96, Principles of Knowledge Representation and Reasoning*. San Mateo (CA), pp. 220–229.

Borgo, S., N. Guarino, and C. Masolo: 1996b, 'Towards an Ontological Theory of Space and Matter'. In: *CESA'96, Proceedings of IMACS-IEEE/SMC Conference on Computational Engineering in Systems Applications*. Lille.

Borillo, M. and H. Pensec: 1995, 'From Numerical Observations to Propositional Representations: A Cognitive Methodology to Structure Hybrid Spatial Knowledge'. In: *Proceedings of AISB 95 Conference*. pp. 13–25.

Bowerman, M.: 1996, 'The origin of children's spatial semantic categories: Cognitive vs semantic determinants'. In: J. Gumperz and S. Levinson (eds.): *Rethinking Linguistic Relativity*. Cambridge: Cambridge University Press, pp. 145–176.

Bratley, P., L. Bennet, and L. Schrage: 1987, *A Guide to Simulation*. Springer-Verlag. second edition.

Breiman, L.: 1969, *Probability and Stochastic Processes*. Houghton-Mifflin Company.

Brewka, G. and J. Hertzberg: 1993, 'How to do Things with Worlds: On Formalizing Actions and Plans'. *Journal of Logic and Computation* **5**, 517–532.

Brown, F. (ed.): 1987, *Proceedings of the 1987 Workshop: The Frame Problem in Artificial Intelligence*. Morgan Kaufmann.

Brugman, C.: 1988, *The Story of Over: Polysemy, Semantics, and the Structure of the Lexicon*. New York: Garland.

Brusoni, U., L. Console, and P. Terenziani: 1995, 'On the Computational Complexity of Querying Bounds on Difference Constraints'. *Artificial Intelligence* **74**, 367–379.

Bryant, D.: 1993, 'Frames of reference in the spatial representation system. (Peer commentary on Landau and Jackendoff, 1993)'. *Behavioral and Brain Sciences* **16**, 241–242.

Burger, W. and B. Bhanu: 1992, *Qualitative Motion Planning*. Dordrecht: Kluwer.

Burrough, P. and A. Frank (eds.): 1996, *Geographic Objects with Indeterminate Boundaries*. London: Taylor & Francis.

Bybee, J.: 1985, *Morphology: A Study of the Relation Between Meaning and Form*. Philadelphia: Benjamins.

Bylander, T.: 1993, 'An average case analysis of Planning'. In: *Proceedings of the Eleventh National Conference of the American Association for Artificial Intelligence (AAAI-93)*. Washington, D.C., pp. 480–485.

Bylander, T.: 1994, 'The computational complexity of propositional STRIPS planning'. *Artificial Intelligence* **69**, 165–204.

Campari, I.: 1991, 'Some notes on geographic information systems: The relationship between their practical application and their theoretical evolution'. In: D. Mark and A. Frank (eds.): *Cognitive and Linguistic Aspects of Geographic Space*. Dordrecht: Kluwer, pp. 419–434.

Campari, I.: 1992, 'Human impacts·on coastal regions: An integrated conceptual framework'. In: *Proceedings of EGIS '92*, Vol. 1. Munich, FRG, pp. 791–807.

Campari, I.: 1994, 'GIS Commands as small scale space terms: Cross-cultural conflicts of their spatial content'. In: T. Waugh and R. Healey (eds.): *Sixth International Symposium on Spatial Data Handling*, Vol. 1. Edinburgh, Scotland, pp. 554 – 571.

Campari, I.: 1996, 'Uncertain boundaries in urban space'. In: P. Burrough and A. Frank (eds.): *Geographic Objects with Indeterminate Boundaries*. London: Taylor & Francis.

Campari, I. and A. Frank: 1994, 'Cultural aspects and cultural differences in GIS'. In: T. Nyerges, D. Mark, R. Laurin, and M. Egenhofer (eds.): *Cognitive Aspects of Human-Computer Interaction for Geographic Information Systems - Proceedings of the NATO Advanced Research Workshop*. Dordrecht: Kluwer Academic Publishers.

Car, A. and A. Frank: 1994, 'Modelling a hierarchy of space applied to large road networks'. In: J. Nievergelt, T. Roos, H. Scheck, and P. Widmayer (eds.): *IGIS'94: Geographic Information Sytems. International Workshop on Advanced Research in GIS*. Berlin, pp. 15–24.

Casati, R.: 1995a, 'The Shape Without'. In: *Workshop on Topology and Dynamics in Cognition and Perception*. International Center for Semiotic and Cognitive Studies, San Marino (Italy).

Casati, R.: 1995b, 'Temporal Entities in Space'. In: P. Amsili, M. Borillo, and L. Vieu (eds.): *Time, Space and Movement: Meaning and Knowledge in the Sensible World*. *Proceedings of the 5th International Workshop*. Toulouse: COREP, pp. D66–D78.

Casati, R.: forthcoming, 'Formal Structures in the Phenomenology of Movement'. In: B. Pachoud, J. Petitot, J. M. Roy, and F. Varela (eds.): *Naturalizing Phenomenology: Issues in Contemporary Phenomenology and Cognitive Science*. Stanford: Stanford University Press.

Casati, R. and A. Varzi: 1994, *Holes and Other Superficialities*. Cambridge, MA, and London: MIT Press.

Casati, R. and A. C. Varzi: 1995, 'Basic Issues in Spatial Representation'. In: M. DeGlas and Z. Pawlak (eds.): *Proceedings of the 2nd World Conference on the Fundamentals of Artificial Intelligence*. Paris: Angkor, pp. 63–72.

Casati, R. and A. C. Varzi: 1996, 'The structure of spatial location'. *Philosophical Studies* **82**, 205–239.

Cave, C. B. and S. M. Kosslyn: 1993, 'The Role of Parts and Spatial Relations in Object Identification'. *Perception* **22**, 229–248.

Cervoni, R., A. Cesta, and A. Oddi: 1994, 'Managing Dynamic Temporal Constraint Networks'. In: *Proceedings of the 2nd International Conference on Artificial Intelligence Planning Systems (AIPS-94)*. Chicago, IL, pp. 196–201.

Chapman, D.: 1987, 'Planning for conjunctive goals'. *Artificial Intelligence* **32**, 333–377. Also in *Readings in Planning*, J. Allen, J. Hendler, and A. Tate (eds.), Morgan Kaufmann, 1990, pp. 537–558.

Chapman, D.: 1991, *Vision, Instruction and Action*. Cambridge, MA: MIT Press.

Charniak, E., C. Riesbeck, D. McDermott, and J. Meehan: 1987, *Artificial Intelligence*

Programming. Lawrence Erlbaum Associates. second edition.

Cheeseman, P., B. Kanefsky, and W. Taylor: 1991, 'Where the *really* hard problems are'. In: *Proceedings of the Twelfth International Joint Conference on Artificial Intelligence (IJCAI-91).* pp. 331–337.

Chen, S. (ed.): 1990, *Advances in Spatial Reasoning*, Vol. 1. Norwood: Ablex.

Chou, S.: 1988, *Mechanical Geometry Theorem Proving.* Dordrecht: Reidel.

Ciapessoni, E., E. Corsetti, A. Montanari, and P. Sanpietro: 1993, 'Embedding time granularity in a logical specification language for synchronous real-time systems'. *Science of Computer Programming* 20(1).

Clark, K.: 1978, 'Negation as failure'. In: H. Gallaire and J. Minker (eds.): *Logic and Databases.* Plenum Press, pp. 293–322.

Clarke, B.: 1981, 'A calculus of individuals based on "connection"'. *Notre Dame Journal of Formal Logic* 22(3), 204–218.

Clarke, B.: 1985, 'Individuals and points'. *Notre Dame Journal of Formal Logic* 26(1), 61–75.

Clementini, E. and P. DiFelice: 1994, 'An algebraic model for spatial objects with undetermined boundaries'. In: P. Burrough and A. Frank (eds.): *Proceedings, GISDATA Specialist Meeting on Geographical Entities with Undetermined Boundaries,.*

Clementini, E. and P. DiFelice: 1995, 'A Comparison of Methods for Representing Topological Relationships'. *Information Sciences* 3, 149–178.

Clementini, E., J. Sharma, and M. Egenhofer: 1994, 'Modeling topological spatial relations: strategies for query processing'. *Computers and Graphics* 18(6), 815–822.

Cohn, A.: 1987, 'A more expressive formulation of many sorted logic'. *Journal of Automated Reasoning* 3, 113–200.

Cohn, A.: 1993, 'Modal and Non-Modal Qualitative Spatial Logics'. In: F. Anger, H. Guesgen, and J. van Benthem (eds.): *Proceedings of the IJCAI-93 Workshop on Spatial and Temporal Reasoning.*

Cohn, A.: 1995, 'A Hierarchical Representation of Qualitative Shape Based on Connection and Convexity'. In: A. Frank and W. Kuhn (eds.): *Spatial Information Theory - Proceedings of COSIT'95.* Berlin, pp. 311–326.

Cohn, A.: 1996, 'Calculi for Qualitative Spatial Reasoning'. In: J. Calmet, J. Campbell, and J. Pfalzgraf (eds.): *Artificial Intelligence and Symbolic Mathematical Computation*, Vol. 1138 of *LNCS.* pp. 124–143.

Cohn, A., J. Gooday, and B. Bennett: 1994, 'A Comparison Of Structures In Spatial And Temporal Logics'. In: R. Casati, B. Smith, and G. White (eds.): *Philosophy and the Cognitive Sciences: Proceedings of the 16th International Wittgenstein Symposium.* Vienna.

Cohn, A. and N. Gotts: 1994a, 'Spatial Regions with Undetermined Boundaries'. In: *Proceedings of Gaithesburg Workshop on GIS.* ACM.

Cohn, A. and N. Gotts: 1994b, 'A theory of spatial regions with indeterminate boundaries'. In: C. Eschenbach, C. Habel, and B. Smith (eds.): *Topological Foundations of Cognitive Science.*

Cohn, A. and N. Gotts: 1996a, 'The 'Egg-Yolk' Representation of Regions with Indeterminate Boundaries'. In: P. Burrough and A. Frank (eds.): *Proceedings of the GISDATA Specialist Meeting on Geographical Entities with Undeterminated Boundaries.* Bristol, pp. 171–187.

Cohn, A. and N. Gotts: 1996b, 'A Mereological Approach to Representing Spatial Vagueness'. In: J. D. L.C. Aiello and S. Shapiro (eds.): *Principles of Knowledge Representation and Reasoning, Proceedings of the 5th Conference.* pp. 230–241.

Cohn, A., N. Gotts, D. Randell, Z. Cui, B. Bennett, and J. Gooday: 1997, 'Exploiting Temporal Continuity in Temporal Calculi'. In: R. Golledge and M. Egenhofer (eds.): *Spatial and Temporal Reasoning in Geographical Information Systems.* To appear.

Cohn, A., D. Randell, and Z. Cui: 1995, 'Taxonomies of Logically defined Qualitative Spatial Relations'. *Int. Journal of Human-Computer Studies* 43, 831–846.

Cohn, A., D. Randell, Z. Cui, and B. Bennett: 1993, 'Qualitative Spatial Reasoning and Representation'. In: N. Carreté and M. Singh (eds.): *Qualitative Reasoning and Decision Technologies*. Barcelona, pp. 513–522.

Console, L., A. Rivolin, and P. Torasso: 1991, 'Fuzzy temporal reasoning on Causal Models'. *International Journal of Intelligent Systems* **6**(2), 107–133.

Corbett, J.: 1979, 'Topological Principles of Cartography'. Technical Paper 48, Bureau of the Census, US Department of Commerce.

Cordell, G.: 1969, 'An application of theorem proving to problem solving'. In: D. E. Walker (ed.): *Proceedings of the First International Joint Conference on Artificial Intelligence (IJCAI-69)*. Washington, DC, pp. 741–747. Also in *Readings in Planning*, J. Allen, J. Hendler, and A. Tate (eds.), Morgan Kaufmann, 1990, pp. 67–87.

Cordier, M.-O. and P. Siégel: 1992, 'A temporal revision model for reasoning about world change'. In: *Proceedings of the International Conference on Knowledge Representation and Reasoning*. pp. 732–739.

Cordier, M.-O. and P. Siégel: 1995, 'Prioritized Transitions for Updates'. In: C. Froidevaux and J. Kohlas (eds.): *Proceedings of the European Conference on Symbolic and Quantitative Approaches to Reasoning and Uncertainty*. Springer Verlag, pp. 142–151.

Cormen, T., C. Leiserson, and R. Rivest: 1990, *Introduction to Algorithms*. The MIT Press.

Crawford, J. and L. Auton: 1993, 'Experimental Results on the Cross-Over Point in Satisfiability Problems'. In: *Proceedings of the Eleventh National Conference of the American Association for Artificial Intelligence (AAAI-93)*. Washington, D.C., pp. 21–27.

Cui, Z., A. Cohn, and D. Randell: 1992, 'Qualitative Simulation Based on a Logical Formalism of Space and Time'. In: *Proceedings of the Tenth National Conference of the American Association for Artificial Intelligence (AAAI-91)*. Menlo Park, California, pp. 679–684.

Cui, Z., A. Cohn, and D. Randell: 1993, 'Qualitative and Topological Relationships in Spatial Databases'. In: D. Abel and B. Ooi (eds.): *Advances in Spatial Databases*, Vol. 692 of *Lecture Notes in Computer Science*. Berlin: Springer Verlag, pp. 293–315.

Dague, P. and MQD Group: 1995, 'Qualitative Reasoning: A Survey of Techniques and Applications'. *AI Communications* **8**(3-4).

Davidson, D.: 1967, 'The logical form of action sentences'. In: N. Rescher (ed.): *The Logic of Decision and Action*. University of Pittsburgh Press. Excerpted in *The Logic of Grammar*, D. Davison and G. Harmon (eds.), Dickenson Publishing Co., 1975, pp. 235–245.

Davidson, D.: 1969, 'The Individuation of Events'. In: N. Rescher (ed.): *Essays in Honor of Carl G. Hempel*. Dordrecht: Reidel, pp. 216–234.

Davis, E.: 1988, 'A logical framework for commonsense predictions of solid object behaviour'. *Artificial Intelligence in Engineering* **3**(3), 125–140.

Davis, E.: 1990, *Representations of Commonsense Knowledge*. San Mateo, California: Morgan Kaufmann Publishers, Inc.

Davis, E.: 1992, 'Infinite loops in finite time: Some observations'. In: B. Nebel, C. Rich, and W. Swartout (eds.): *Proceedings of the Third International Conference on Principles of Knowledge Representation and Reasoning (KR92)*. Boston, MA, pp. 47–58.

Davis, E., N. Gotts, and A. Cohn: 1997, 'Constraint networks of topological relations and convexity'. Technical report, Courant Institute, New York University.

de Laguna, T.: 1922, 'Point, Line and Surface as Sets of Solids'. *The Journal of Philosophy* **19**, 449–461.

Dean, T.: 1989, 'Using Temporal Hierarchies to Efficiently Maintain Large Temporal Databases'. *Journal of the Association for Computing Machinery* **36**(4), 687–718.

Dean, T. and M. Boddy: 1988a, 'An analysis of time-dependent planning'. In: *Proceedings of the Seventh National Conference of the American Association for Artificial*

Intelligence (AAAI-88). pp. 49–54.

Dean, T. and M. Boddy: 1988b, 'Reasoning about Partially Ordered Events'. *Artificial Intelligence* **36**(3), 375–399.

Dean, T., R. Firby, and D. Miller: 1988, 'Hierarchical planning involving deadlines, travel time, and resources'. *Computational Intelligence* 4, 381–398.

Dean, T. and K. Kanazawa: 1989, 'A model for reasoning about persistence and causation'. *Computational Intelligence* 5, 142–150.

Dean, T. and M. M. Wellman: 1991, *Planning and Control.* San Mateo, CA: Morgan Kaufmann.

Dean, T. and D. McDermott: 1987, 'Temporal data base management'. *Artificial Intelligence* **32**(1), 1–55.

Dechter, R.: 1992, 'From local to global consistency'. *Artificial Intelligence* 55, 87–108.

Dechter, R., I. Meiri, and J. Pearl: 1991, 'Temporal constraint networks'. *Artificial Intelligence* **49**, 61–95.

del Val, A. and Y. Shoham: 1992, 'Deriving properties of belief update from theories of actions'. In: *Proceedings of the Tenth National Conference of the American Association for Artificial Intelligence (AAAI-91).* pp. 584–589.

del Val, A. and Y. Shoham: 1993, 'Deriving properties of belief update from theories of actions (II)'. In: *Proceedings of the International Joint Conference on Artificial Intelligence.* pp. 732–737.

Delgrande, J. and A. Gupta: 1996, 'A Representation for Efficient Temporal Reasoning'. In: *Proceedings of the Thirteenth National Conference of the American Association for Artificial Intelligence (AAAI-96).* Portland, OR, pp. 381–388.

Dornheim, C.: 1995, 'Vergleichende Analyse topologischer Ansaetze des qualitativen raeuml ichen Schliessens'. Studienarbeit, fachereich informatik, Universitaet Hamburg.

Dousson, C., P. Gaborit, and M. Ghallab: 1993, 'Situation Recognition: Representation and Algorithms'. In: *Proceedings of the Thirteenth International Joint Conference on Artificial Intelligence (IJCAI-93).* San Mateo, CA, pp. 1297–1303.

Dowty, D.: 1986, 'The Effects of Aspectual Class on the Temporal Structure of Discourse: Semantics or Pragmatics?'. *Linguistics and Philosophy* **9**(1).

Drakengren, T. and P. Jonsson: 1996, 'Maximal Tractable Subclasses of Allen's Interval Algebra: Preliminary Report'. In: *Proceedings of the Thirteenth National Conference of the American Association for Artificial Intelligence (AAAI-96).* Portland, OR, pp. 389–394.

du Verdier, F.: 1993, 'Solving Geometric Constraint Satisfaction Problems for Spatial Planning'. In: *Proceedings of the Thirteenth International Joint Conference on Artificial Intelligence (IJCAI-93).* pp. 1564–1569.

Dubois, D. and H. Prade: 1989, 'Processing fuzzy temporal knowledge'. *IEEE Transactions on System, Men and Cybernetics* **19**(4), 729–744.

Edwards, G.: 1993, 'The Voronoi model and cultural space: applications to the social sciences and humanities'. In: A. Frank and I. Campari (eds.): *Spatial Information Theory - A Theoretical Basis for GIS, Proceedings of COSIT'93.* Berlin, pp. 202–214.

Egenhofer, M.: 1989, 'Spatial query languages'. Ph.d. dissertation, University of Maine.

Egenhofer, M.: 1991, 'Reasoning about binary topological relations'. In: O. Gunther and H. Schek (eds.): *Advances in Spatial Databases - SSD'91 Proceedings.* Berlin, pp. 143–160.

Egenhofer, M.: 1994, 'Topological Similarity'. In: *Proceedings FISI workshop on the Topological Foundations of Cognitive Science,* Vol. 37 of *Reports of the Doctoral Series in Cognitive Science.*

Egenhofer, M. and K. Al-Taha: 1992, 'Reasoning about Gradual Changes of Topological Relationships'. In: A. Frank, I. Campari, and U. Formentini (eds.): *Theories and Methods of Spatio-temporal Reasoning in Geographic Space,* Vol. 639 of *Lecture Notes in Computer Science.* Berlin: Springer-Verlag, pp. 196–219.

Egenhofer, M., E. Clementini, and P. DiFelice: 1994, 'Topological relations between regions with holes'. *Int. Journal of Geographical Information Systems* **8**(2), 129–144.

Egenhofer, M. and R. Franzosa: 1991, 'Point-set topological spatial relations'. *International Journal of Geographical Information Systems* **5**(2), 161–174.

Egenhofer, M. and R. Franzosa: 1995, 'On the equivalence of topological relations'. *International Journal of Geographical Information Systems* **9**(2), 133–152.

Elkan, C.: 1994, 'The Paradoxical Success of Fuzzy Logic'. *IEEE Expert* **9**(4), 3–8. Followed by responses and a reply.

Erol, K., D. Nau, and V. Subrahmanian: 1992, 'When is Planning Decidable'. In: *Proceedings of the First International Conference on Artificial Intelligence Planning Systems (AIPS-92)*. pp. 222–227.

Eschenbach, C.: 1994, 'A mereotopological definition of point'. In: C. Eschenbach, C. Habel, and B. Smith (eds.): *Topological foundations of Cognitive Science, Papers from the Workshop at the FISI-CS*. Buffalo, NY.

Eschenbach, C., C. Habel, and B. Smith (eds.): 1994, 'Topological Foundations of Cognitive Science. Papers from the Workshop at the FISI-CS'. Buffalo, NY:.

Eschenbach, C. and W. Heydrich: 1993, 'Classical Mereology and Restricted Domains'. In: N. Guarino and R. Poli (eds.): *Proceedings of the International Workshop on Formal Ontology in Conceptual Analysis and Representation*. Padova, pp. 205–217.

Euzenat, J.: 1995, 'An algebraic approach for granularity in qualitative space and time representation'. In: *Proceedings of the Fourteenth International Joint Conference on Artificial Intelligence (IJCAI-95)*. San Mateo, CA, pp. 894–900.

Faltings, B.: 1990, 'Qualitative Kinematics in Mechanisms'. *Artificial Intelligence* **44**(1-2), 89–119.

Faltings, B. and P. Struss (eds.): 1992, *Recent Advances in Qualitative Physics*. Cambridge, Ma: MIT Press.

Feller, W.: 1970, *An Introduction to Probability Theory and Its Applications, Vol. I*. John Wiley & Sons. (Third edition).

Ferguson, G.: 1992, 'Explicit Representation of Events, Actions, and Plans for Assumption-Based Plan Reasoning'. Technical Report 428, Department of Computer Science, University of Rochester, Rochester, NY.

Ferguson, G. and J. Allen: 1993, 'Generic Plan Recognition for Dialogue Systems'. In: *Proceedings of the ARPA Workshop on Human Language Technology*. Princeton, NJ.

Ferguson, G. and J. Allen: 1994, 'Arguing about Plans: Plan Representation and Reasoning for Mixed-Initiative Planning'. In: *Proceedings of the Second International Conference on AI Planning Systems (AIPS-94)*. Chicago, IL, pp. 43–48.

Fernyhough, J.: 1997, 'Generation of Qualitative Spatio-temporal Representations from Visual Input'. PhD Thesis, submitted.

Fernyhough, J., A. Cohn, and D. Hogg: 1996, 'Real Time Generation of Semantic Regions from Video Sequences'. In: *Proceedings ECCV96*.

Fernyhough, J., A. Cohn, and D. Hogg: 1997, 'Event Recognition using Qualitative Reasoning on Automatically Generated Spatio-Temporal Models from Visual Input'. Unpublished manuscript.

Fikes, R. and N. Nilsson: 1971, 'STRIPS: A new approach to the applicationf of theorem proving to problem solving'. *Artificial Intelligence* **2**, 198–208. Also in *Readings in Planning*, J. Allen, J. Hendler, and A. Tate (eds.), Morgan Kaufmann, 1990, pp. 88–97.

Finke, R.: 1989, *Principles of Mental Imagery*. Cambridge, MA: MIT Press.

Fleck, M.: 1987, 'Representing space for practical reasoning'. In: *Proceedings of IJCAI'87*. pp. 728–730.

Fleck, M.: 1996, 'The topology of boundaries'. *Artificial Intelligence* **80**, 1–27.

Forbus, K.: 1983, 'Qualitative reasoning about space and motion'. In: D. Gentner and A. Stevens (eds.): *Mental models*. Hillsdale (NJ): Erlbaum, pp. 53–73.

Forbus, K.: 1995, 'Qualitative Spatial Reasoning. Framework and Frontiers'. In: J. Glasgow, N. Narayanan, and B. Chandrasekaran (eds.): *Diagrammatic Reasoning. Cognitive and Computational Perspectives*. Menlo Park (CA) and Cambridge (MA):

AAAI Press / MIT Press, pp. 183–210.

Forbus, K., P. Nielsen, and B. Faltings: 1987, 'Qualitative kinematics: a framework'. In: *Proceedings of the Tenth International Joint Conference on Artificial Intelligence (IJCAI-87)*. pp. 430–435.

Forbus, K., P. Nielsen, and B. Faltings: 1991, 'Qualitative Spatial Reasoning: the CLOCK project'. *Artificial Intelligence* **51**, 417–471.

Frank, A.: 1984, 'Computer-assisted cartography: graphics or geometry?'. *ASCE Journal of Surveying Engineering* **110**(2), 159–168.

Frank, A.: 1987, 'Overlay processing in spatial information systems'. In: N. Chrisman (ed.): *Proceedings of the Eighth International Symposium on Computer-Assisted Cartography (AUTO-CARTO 8)*. Baltimore, MD, pp. 16–31.

Frank, A.: 1992a, 'Qualitative Spatial Reasoning about Distances and Directions in Geographic Space'. *Journal of Visual Languages and Computing* **3**, 343–371.

Frank, A.: 1992b, 'Spatial concepts, geometric data models and data structures'. *Computers & Geosciences* **18**(8), 975–987.

Frank, A.: 1994, 'Qualitative temporal reasoning in GIS-ordered time scales'. Technical report, Technical University Vienna, Dept. of Geoinformation.

Frank, A.: 1996a, 'Different types of "times" in GIS'. In: M. Egenhofer and R. Golledge (eds.): *Spatial and Temporal Reasoning in Geographic Information Systems*. Oxford: Oxford University Press.

Frank, A.: 1996b, 'The prevalence of objects with sharp boundaries in GIS'. In: P. Burrough and A. Frank (eds.): *Geographic Objects with Indeterminate Boundaries*. London: Taylor & Francis.

Frank, A.: 1996c, 'Qualitative spatial reasoning: Cardinal directions as an example'. *International Journal for Geographic Information Systems* **10**(3), 269–290.

Frank, A. and I. Campari (eds.): 1993, *Spatial information theory. A theoretical basis for GIS. Proceedings of COSIT'93*, No. 716 in Lecture Notes in Computer Science. Berlin: Springer Verlag.

Frank, A., I. Campari, and U. Formentini (eds.): 1992, *Theories and Methods of Spatio-Temporal Reasoning in Geographic Space, Proceedings of the International Conference GIS - From Space to Territory*, No. 639 in Lecture Notes in Computer Science. Berlin: Springer Verlag.

Frank, A. and W. Kuhn: 1986, 'Cell graphs: A provable correct method for the storage of geometry'. In: D. Marble (ed.): *Second International Symposium on Spatial Data Handling*. Seattle, WA, pp. 411 – 436.

Frank, A. and W. Kuhn (eds.): 1995, *Spatial Information Theory. A Theoretical Basis for GIS. Proceedings of COSIT'95*, No. 988 in Lecture Notes in Computer Science. Berlin: Springer Verlag.

Frank, A. and D. Mark: 1991, 'Language issues for geographical information systems'. In: D. Maguire, D. Rhind, and M. Goodchild (eds.): *Geographic Information Systems: Principles and Applications*. London: Longman Co.

Frank, A., B. Palmer, and V. Robinson: 1986, 'Formal methods for accurate definition of some fundamental terms in physical geography'. In: D. Marble (ed.): *Second International Symposium on Spatial Data Handling*. Seattle, WA, pp. 583–599.

Frank, A. and S. Timpf: 1994, 'Multiple representations for cartographic objects in a multi-scale tree: An intelligent graphical zoom'. *Computers and Graphics, Special Issue on Modelling and Visualization of Spatial Data in GIS* **18**(6), 823–829.

Frederking, R. and N. Muscettola: 1992, 'Temporal planning for transportation planning and scheduling'. In: *International Conference on Robotics and Automation*. Nice, France, pp. 1125–1230.

Freksa, C.: 1991, 'Qualitative spatial reasoning'. In: D. Mark and A. Frank (eds.): *Cognitive and Linguistic Aspects of Geographic Space*. Dordrecht, pp. 361–372.

Freksa, C.: 1992a, 'Temporal reasoning based on semi-intervals'. *Artificial Intelligence* **54**, 199–227.

Freksa, C.: 1992b, 'Using Orientation Information for Qualitative Spatial Reasoning'.

In: A. Frank, I. Campari, and U. Formentini (eds.): *Theories and Methods of Spatio-Temporal Reasoning in Geographic Space, Proceedings of the International Conference GIS - From Space to Territory.* Berlin, pp. 162–178.

Freksa, C. and R. Röhrig: 1993, 'Dimensions of Qualitative Spatial Reasoning'. In: N. P. Carreté and M. Singh (eds.): *Qualitative Reasoning and Decision Technologies.* Barcelona, pp. 482–492.

Friedman, M. and D. Weld: 1996, 'Least-commitment action selection'. In: B. Drabble (ed.): *Proceedings of the 3rd International Conference on Artificial Intelligence Planning Systems (AIPS-96).*

Fujimura, K. and H. Samet: 1989, 'A hierarchical strategy for path planning among moving obstacles'. *IEEE transctions on robotics and automation* 5(1), 61–69.

Galton, A.: 1990, 'A critical examination of Allen's theory of action and time'. *Artificial Intelligence* 42(2–3), 159–188.

Galton, A.: 1993, 'Towards an integrated logic of space, time and motion'. In: R. Bajcsy (ed.): *Proceedings of the Thirteenth International Joint Conference on Artificial Intelligence (IJCAI-93).* San Mateo, CA, pp. 1550–1555.

Galton, A.: 1994, 'Instantaneous Events'. In: Hans Jürgen Ohlbach (ed.): *Temporal Logic: Proceedings of the ICTL Workshop.* Saarbrücken.

Galton, A.: 1995a, 'A qualitative approach to continuity'. In: P. Amsili, M. Borillo, and L. Vieu (eds.): *Time, Space, and Movement: Meaning and Knowledge in the Sensible World.* CNRS, Toulouse. Workshop notes of the 5th International Workshop TSM'95.

Galton, A.: 1995b, 'Time and Change for AI'. In: D. Gabbay (ed.): *Handbook of Logic in Artificial Intelligence and Logic Programming.* Oxford University Press.

Galton, A.: 1995c, 'Towards a qualitative theory of movement'. In: A. Frank and W. Kuhn (eds.): *Spatial Information Theory (Proceedings of the European Conference on Spatial Information Theory COSIT '95)*, Vol. 988 of *Lecture Notes in Computer Science.* Berlin: Springer-Verlag, pp. 377–396.

Galton, A.: 1996, 'Taking dimension seriously in qualitative spatial reasoning'. In: W. Wahlster (ed.): *Proceedings of the Twelfth European Conference on Artificial Intelligence (ECAI-96).* Chichester, pp. 501–505.

Gapp, K.: 1995, 'An empirically validated model for computing spatial relations'. Technical Report 118, SFB 314 (VITRA), Universität des Saarlandes, Saarbrücken.

Gelfond, M.: 1989, 'Autoepistemic Logic and Formalization of Common-sense Reasoning'. In: *Non-Monotonic Reasoning: Second International Workshop* (Lecture Notes in Artificial Intelligence 346). pp. 176–186.

Gelfond, M. and V. Lifschitz: 1992, 'Representing Actions in Extended Logic Programs'. In: *Proceedings of the International Conference on Logic Programming.* pp. 559–573.

Gelfond, M., V. Lifschitz, and A. Rabinov: 1991, 'What are the limitations of the situation calculus?'. In: *Proceedings of the AAAI Symposium on Logical Formalizations of Commonsense Reasoning.* pp. 59–59.

Genesereth, M. and N. Nilsson: 1987, *Logical Foundations of Artificial Intelligence.* Los Altos, CA: Morgan Kaufmann.

Georgeff, M.: 1986a, 'Actions, Processes, and Causality'. In: M. P. Georgeff and A. L. Lansky (eds.): *Reasoning about Actions and Plans: Proceedings of the 1986 Workshop.* Los Altos, CA.

Georgeff, M.: 1986b, 'The representation of events in multiagent domains'. In: *Proceedings of the Fifth National Conference on Artificial Intelligence (AAAI-86).* Philadelphia, PA, pp. 70–75.

Georgeff, M.: 1990, 'Planning'. In: J. Allen, J. Hendler, and A. Tate (eds.): *Readings in Planning.* San Mateo, CA: Morgan Kaufmann, pp. 5–25.

Gerevini, A.: 1997, 'On finding a Solution in Temporal Constraint Satisfaction Problems'. Technical Report 199701-9, Dipartimento di Elettronica per l'Automazione, Università di Brescia, via Branze 34, I-25123 Brescia, Italy.

Gerevini, A. and M. Cristani: 1995, 'Reasoning with Inequations in Temporal Constraint Networks'. In: *Proceedings of the IJCAI-95 workshop on Spatial and Temporal*

Reasoning. Montreal, Canada, pp. 13–23.

Gerevini, A., A. Perini, and F. Ricci: 1996, 'Incremental Algorithms for Managing Temporal Constraints'. In: *Proceedings of the 8th IEEE International Conference on Tools with Artificial Intelligence*. Toulouse, France.

Gerevini, A. and L. Schubert: 1994a, 'An Efficient Method for Managing Disjunctions in Qualitative Temporal Reasoning'. In: *Proceedings of the Fourth International Conference on Principles of Knowledge Representation and Reasoning (KR'94)*. San Francisco, CA, pp. 215–225.

Gerevini, A. and L. Schubert: 1994b, 'On point-based temporal disjointness'. *Artificial Intelligence* 70, 347–361.

Gerevini, A. and L. Schubert: 1995a, 'Efficient Algorithms for Qualitative Reasoning about Time'. *Artificial Intelligence* 74, 207–248.

Gerevini, A. and L. Schubert: 1995b, 'On computing the minimal labels in time point algebra networks'. *Computational Intelligence* 11(3), 443–448.

Gerevini, A. and L. Schubert: 1996, 'Accelerating Partial-Order Planners: Some Techniques for Effective Search Control and Pruning'. *Journal of Artificial Intelligence Research (JAIR)* 5, 95–137.

Gerevini, A., L. Schubert, and S. Schaeffer: 1995, 'The Temporal Reasoning Tools TimeGraph-I-II'. *International Journal of Artificial Intelligence Tools* 4(1–2), 281–299.

Gerla, G.: 1990, 'Pointless Metric spaces'. *The Journal of Symbolic Logic* 55(1), 207–219.

Gerla, G.: 1994, 'Pointless Geometries'. In: F. Buekenhout (ed.): *Handbook of Incidence Geometry*. Elsevier.

Ghallab, M. and A. M. Alaoui: 1989, 'Managing Efficiently Temporal Relations Through Indexed Spanning Trees'. In: *Proceedings of the Eleventh International Joint Conference on Artificial Intelligence (IJCAI-89)*. San Mateo, CA, pp. 1297–1303.

Ginsberg, M. L. and D. E. Smith: 1987, 'Reasoning about Actions I: A Possible Worlds Approach'. In: F. Brown (ed.): *Proceedings of the 1987 Workshop on the Frame Problem in Artificial Intelligence*. Lawrence, Kansas: Morgan-Kaufmann, pp. 233–258.

Glasgow, J.: 1993, 'The Imagery Debate Revisited: A Computational Perspective'. *Computational Intelligence* 9(4), 309–333.

Glasgow, J., N. Narayanan, and B. Chandrasekaran (eds.): 1995, *Diagrammatic Reasoning. Cognitive and Computational Perspectives*. Menlo Park (CA) and Cambridge (MA): AAAI Press / MIT Press.

Glasgow, J. and D. Papadias: 1992, 'Computational Imagery'. *Cognitive Science* 16(3), 355–394.

Godo, L. and L. Vila: 1995, 'Probabilistic Temporal reasoning based on Fuzzy temporal constraints'. In: *Proceedings of the Fourteenth International Joint Conference on Artificial Intelligence (IJCAI-95)*. Montreal, CA, pp. 1916–1922.

Goldberg, A.: 1995, *Constructions: A Construction Grammar Approach to Argument Structure*. Chicago: University of Chicago Press.

Goldman, A.: 1970, *A Theory of Human Action*. Englewood Cliffs, NJ: Prentice-Hall.

Golumbic, C. and R. Shamir: 1993, 'Complexity and algorithms for reasoning about time: a graph-theoretic approach'. *Journal of the Association for Computing Machinery* 40(5), 1108–1133.

Goodale, M.: 1988, 'Modularity in visuomotor control: From input to output'. In: Pylyshyn (ed.): *Computational Processes in Human Vision: An Interdisciplinary Perspective*. Norwood, NJ: Ablex.

Gooday, J.: 1994, 'A Transition-based Approach to Reasoning about Action and Change'. Ph.D. thesis, University of Leeds.

Gooday, J. and A. Cohn: 1995, 'Using Spatial Logic to Describe Visual Languages'. *Artificial Intelligence Review* 10(1–2). Also in *Integration of Natural Language and Vision Processing*, (Vol. IV), P. McKevitt (ed.), Kluwer, 1996.

Gooday, J. and A. Cohn: 1996a, 'Transition-Based Qualitative Simulation'. In: *Proceeding of the 10th International Workshop on Qualitative Reasoning.* pp. 74 – 82.

Gooday, J. and A. Cohn: 1996b, 'Visual Language Syntax and Semantics: A Spatial Logic approach'. In: K. Marriott and B. Meyer (eds.): *Proceedings of Workshop on Theory of Visual Languages.* Gubbio, Italy.

Gooday, J. and A. Galton: 1997, 'The Transition Calculus: A High-Level Formalism for Reasoning about Action and Change'. To appear in *Journal of Experimental and Theoretical Artificial Intelligence.*

Goodchild, M.: 1992, 'Geographical data modeling'. *Computers and Geosciences* **18**(4), 401– 408.

Goodchild, M. and Y. Shiren: 1990, 'A hierarchical data structure for global geographic information systems'. In: K. Brassel and H. Kishimoto (eds.): *Proceedings of the 4th International Symposium on Spatial Data Handling,* Vol. 2. Zurich, Switzerland, pp. 911–917.

Gotts, N.: 1994a, 'Defining a 'doughnut' made difficult'. In: C. Eschenbach, C. Habel, and B. Smith (eds.): *Topological Foundations of Cognitive Science,* Vol. 37 of *Reports of the Doctoral programme in Cognitive Science.* Universität Hamburg, pp. 105–129.

Gotts, N.: 1994b, 'How far can we 'C'? Defining a 'doughnut' using connection alone'. In: J. Doyle, E. Sandewall, and P. Torasso (eds.): *Principles of Knowledge Representation and Reasoning. Proceedings of KR'94.* San Mateo, CA.

Gotts, N.: 1996a, 'An Axiomatic Approach to Topology for Spatial Information Systems'. Technical report, Report 96.25, School of Computer Studies, University of Leeds.

Gotts, N.: 1996b, 'Formalizing Commonsense Topology: The INCH Calculus'. In: *Proceedings of the Fourth International Symposium on Artificial Intelligence and Mathematics - AI/MATH'96.* Fort Lauderdale (FL), pp. 72–75.

Gotts, N.: 1996c, 'Topology from a single primitive relation: defining topological properties and relations in terms of connection'. Technical report, Report 96.23, School of Computer Studies, University of Leeds.

Gotts, N.: 1996d, 'Using the RCC Formalism to Describe the Topology of Spherical Regions'. Technical report, Report 96.24, School of Computer Studies, University of Leeds.

Gotts, N. and A. Cohn: 1995, 'A Mereological Approach to Spatial Vagueness'. In: *Proceedings of the Qualitative Reasoning Workshop (QR-95).*

Gotts, N. M., J. M. Gooday, and A. G. Cohn: 1996, 'A connection based approach to common-sense topological description and reasoning'. *The Monist* **79**(1), 51–75.

Green, C.: 1969, 'Theorem proving by resolution as a basis for question-answering systems'. In: B. Meltzer and D. Michie (eds.): *Machine Intelligence,* Vol. 4. New York: American Elsevier, pp. 183–205.

Greene, D. and F. Yao: 1986, 'Finite-resolution computational geometry'. In: *Proceedings of the 27th IEEE Symp. on Foundations of Computer Science.* pp. 143–152.

Grigni, M., D. Papadias, and C. Papadimitriou: 1995, 'Topological Inference'. In: *Proceedings of the Fourteenth International Joint Conference on Artificial Intelligence (IJCAI-95).* San Mateo, CA, pp. 901–906.

Grzegorczyk, A.: 1951, 'Undecidability of some topological theories'. *Fundamenta Mathematicae* **38**, 137–152.

Guarino, N. and R. Poli (eds.): 1993, *Papers from the International Workshop on Formal Ontology in Conceptual Analysis and Knowledge Representation.* Padova:.

Gueting, R. and M. Schneider: 1992, 'Realms: A Foundation for Spatial Data Types in Database Systems'. Informatik-Report 134, Fern Universitaet Hagen, FRG.

Guevara, J.: 1985, 'Intersection problems in polygon overlay'. In: *Auto-Carto 7.* Washington, DC, March 11-14, 1985.

Güsgen, H.: 1989, 'Spatial reasoning based on Allen's temporal logic'. Report ICSI TR-89-049, International Computer Science Institute, Berkeley.

Guttag, J., J. Horning, and J. Wing: 1985, 'Larch in Five Easy Pieces'. Technical report, Digital Equipment Corporation, Systems Research Center. Reports.

Guttenberg, A.: 1992, 'Toward a behavioral theory of regionalization'. In: A. Frank,

I. Campari, and U. Formentini (eds.): *Theories and Methods of Spatio-Temporal Reasoning in Geographic Space*, Vol. 639 of *Lecture Notes in Computer Science*. Heidelberg-Berlin: Springer-Verlag, pp. 110–121.

Guttenberg, A.: 1993, 'Land, space and spatial planning in three time regions'. In: A. Frank and I. Campari (eds.): *Spatial Information Theory: Theoretical Basis for GIS*, Vol. 716 of *Lecture Notes in Computer Science*. Heidelberg-Berlin: Springer-Verlag, pp. 284–293.

Haas, A.: 1987, 'The case for domain-specific frame axioms'. In: F. Brown (ed.): *Proceedings of the 1987 Workshop: The Frame Problem in Artificial Intelligence*. pp. 343–348.

Habel, C.: 1990, 'Propositional and Depictorial Representations of Spatial Knowledge: The case of Path Concepts'. In: R. Studer (ed.): *Natural Language and Logic*, Lecture Notes in Computer Science. Berlin: Springer Verlag, pp. 94–117.

Habel, C.: 1991, 'Processing of Spatial Expressions in LILOG'. In: O. Herzog and C.-R. Rollinger (eds.): *Text Understanding in LILOG - Integrating Computational Linguistics and Artificial Intelligence. Final report on the IBM Germany LILOG-Project*. Berlin: Springer.

Habel, C.: 1994, 'Discreteness, Finiteness, and the Structure of Topological Spaces'. In: C. Eschenbach, C. Habel, and B. Smith (eds.): *Topological Foundations of Cognitive Science, Papers from the Workshop at the FISI-CS*. pp. 81–90. Buffalo, NY.

Habel, C., S. Pribbenow, and G. Simmons: 1995, 'Partonomies and Depictions; A Hybrid Approach'. In: J. Glasgow, N. Narayanan, and B. Chandrasekaran (eds.): *Diagrammatic Reasoning. Cognitive and Computational Perspectives*. Menlo Park (CA) and Cambridge (MA): AAAI Press / MIT Press, pp. 627–653.

Haddawy, P.: 1990, 'Time, chance, and action'. In: *Proceeding of the Sixth Conference on Uncertainty in Artificial Intelligence*. pp. 147–154.

Haddawy, P.: 1996, 'A Logic of Time, Change, and Action for Representing Plans'. *Artificial Intelligence* **80**, 243–308.

Hamblin, C.: 1969, 'Starting and stopping'. *The Monist* **53**, 410–425.

Hamblin, C.: 1971, 'Instants and intervals'. *Studium Generale* **24**, 127–134.

Hamblin, C.: 1972, 'Instants and Intervals'. In: J. Fraser, F. Haber, and G. Müller (eds.): *The Study of Time*. New York: Springer-Verlag, pp. 324–328.

Hanks, S.: 1990a, 'Practical temporal projection'. In: *Proceedings of the Eighth National Conference on Artificial Intelligence (AAAI-90)*. Boston, MA, pp. 158–163.

Hanks, S.: 1990b, 'Projecting Plans for Uncertain Worlds'. Technical Report 756, Yale Yale Computer Science Department.

Hanks, S. and D. McDermott: 1987, 'Nonmonotonic Logics and Temporal Projection'. *Artificial Intelligence* **33**, 379–412.

Hanks, S. and D. McDermott: 1994, 'Modeling a dynamic and uncertain world I: symbolic and probabilistic reasoning about change'. *Artificial Intelligence* **66**(1), 1–55.

Harnad, S.: 1990, 'The symbol grounding problem'. *Physica* D **42**, 335–346.

Haugh, B.: 1987, 'Simple Causal Minimizations for Temporal Persistence and Projection'. In: *Proceedings of the Sixth National Conference of the American Association for Artificial Intelligence (AAAI-87)*. pp. 218–223.

Hayes, P.: 1978, 'The naive physics manifesto'. In: D. Mitchie (ed.): *Expert Systems in the Microelectronic Age*. Edinburgh: Edinburgh University Press, pp. 242–270.

Hayes, P.: 1985a, 'Naive Physics I: Ontology for liquids'. In: J. Hobbs and R. Moore (eds.): *Formal Theories of the Commonsense World*. Ablex Publishing Corporation, pp. 71–108.

Hayes, P.: 1985b, 'The second naive physics manifesto'. In: J. Hobbs and R. Moore (eds.): *Formal Theories of the Commonsense World*. Norwood, N.J.: Ablex Publishing Corp., pp. 1–36.

Hays, E.: 1987, 'A computational treatment of locative relations in natural language'. Technical Report MS-CIS-87-31, Linc Lab 58, Department of Computer and Information Science, University of Pennsylvania.

Hayward, W. and M. Tarr: 1995, 'Spatial language and spatial representation'. *Cognition* **55**, 39–84.

Hernández, D.: 1993, 'Reasoning with qualitative representations: exploiting the structure of space'. In: N. P. Carreté and M. Singh (eds.): *Qualitative Reasoning an Decision Technologies*. Barcelona: CIMNE, pp. 493–502.

Hernández, D.: 1994, *Qualitative representation of spatial knowledge*, No. 804 in Lecture Notes in Artificial Intelligence. Berlin: Springer Verlag.

Hernández, D., E. Clementini, and P. DiFelice: 1995, 'Qualitative Distances'. In: A. Frank and W. Kuhn (eds.): *Spatial Information Theory - Proceedings of COSIT'95*. Berlin, pp. 45–57.

Herskovits, A.: 1986, *Language and spatial cognition. An interdisciplinary Study of the prepositions in English*. Cambridge, London: Cambridge University Press.

Herskovits, A., A. Levitt, M. Lucas, and L. Wagner: 1996, 'The *across* word puzzle: The category structure of a spatial preposition'. Unpublished manuscript.

Herzog, G. and P. Wazinski: 1994, 'VIsual TRAslator: Linking Perceptions and Natuarl Language Descriptions'. *Artificial Intelligence Review* **8**.

Hilbert, D.: 1971, *Foundations of Geometry*. La Salle (IL): Open Court. Grundlagen der Geometrie, 10th ed., Stuttgart, Teubner, 1968.

Hinton, G. and L. Parsons: 1988, 'Scene-based and viewer-centered representations for comparing shape'. *Cognition* **30**, 1–35.

Hirsh, R.: 1996, 'Relation Algebras of Intervals'. *Artificial Intelligence* **83**(2), 267–295.

Hobbs, J.: 1985, 'Granularity'. In: *Proceedings of the 9th International Joint Conference on Artificial Intelligence*. pp. 432–435.

Hobbs, J., W. Croft, T. Davies, D. Edwards, and K. Laws: 1987, 'Commonsense Metaphysics and Lexical Semantics'. *Computational Linguistics* **13**(3-4), 241–250.

Hobbs, J., W. Croft, T. Davies, D. Edwards, and K. Laws: 1988, 'The TACITUS Knowledge Base'. Technical report, SRI International, Artificial Intelligence Center.

Hobbs, J. and R. Moore (eds.): 1985, *Formal Theories of the Commonsense World*. Norwood, N.J.: Ablex Publishing Corp.

Hobbs, J., M. Stickel, D. Appelt, and P. Martin: 1993, 'Interpretation as abduction'. *Artificial Intelligence* **63**, 69–142.

Hocking, J. and G. Young: 1961, *Topology*. New York: Dover.

Hoffman, D. and W. Richards: 1985a, 'Parts of recognition'. In: S. Pinker (ed.): *Visual Cognition*. Cambridge, MA: MIT Press, pp. 65–96.

Hoffman, D. D. and W. A. Richards: 1985b, 'Parts of Recognition'. *Cognition* **18**, 65–96.

Hogge, J.: 1987, 'TPLAN: A Temporal Interval-based planner with novel extensions'. Technical Report UIUCDCS-R-87, University of Illinois, USA.

Hwang, C. and L. Schubert: 1994, 'Interpreting tense, aspect, and time adverbials: a compositional, unified approach'. In: D. Gabbay and H. Ohlbach (eds.): *Proceedings of the first International Conference on Temporal Logic, LNAI, vol 827*. Berlin, pp. 237–264.

Isli, A.: 1994, 'Constraint-based temporal reasoning: a tractable point-based algebra combining qualitative, metric and holed constraints'. Technical Report 96-06, Inst. Galilee, Univ. 13 Paris Nord, LIPS, URA CNRS 1507, 93430 Villetaneuse, France.

Jackendoff, R.: 1983, *Semantics and Cognition*. Cambridge, MA: MIT Press.

Jackendoff, R.: 1990, *Semantic Structures*. Cambridge, MA: MIT Press.

Jennings, P.: 1959, *Idly Oddly*. London: Max Reinhardt.

JLC: 1994, 'Special Issue on Actions and Processes'. *Journal of Logic and Computation* **4**(5).

Joch, A.: 1995, 'How software doesn't work'. *Byte* **20**(12 (Dec.)), 48–60.

Johnson, M.: 1987, *The Body in the Mind: The Bodily Basis of Meaning, Imagination, and Reason*. Chicago: University of Chicago Press.

Johnson-Laird, P.: 1983, *Mental Models: Towards a Cognitive Science of Language, Inferences and Consciousness*. Cambridge, MA: Harvard University Press.

Jonsson, P. and Bäckström: 1996, 'A linear-programming approach to temporal reasoning'. In: *Proceedings of the Thirteenth National Conference of the American Association for Artificial Intelligence (AAAI-96)*. Portland, OR, pp. 1235–1240.

Jonsson, P., T. Drakengren, and Bäckström: 1996, 'Tractable subclasses of the point-interval algebra: a complete classification'. In: *Proceedings of the Fifth International Conference on Principles of Knowledge Representation and Reasoning (KR'96)*. Boston, MA.

Julesz, B.: 1980, 'Spatial nonlinearities in the instantaneous perception of textures with identical power spectra'. In: C. Longuet-Higgins and N. Sutherland (eds.): *The Psychology of Vision*. B290, Philosophical Transactions of the Royal Society of London, pp. 83–94.

Kahn, K. and V. Saraswat: 1990, 'Complete Visualizations of Concurrent Programs and their Executions'. Technical Report Tech. Rpt. SSL-90-38 [P90-00099], Xerox Palo Alto Research Centre, Palo Alto, California.

Kanazawa, K.: 1991, 'A logic and time nets for probabilistic inference'. In: *Proceedings of the Ninth National Conference on Artificial Intelligence (AAAI-91)*. pp. 360–365.

Kanazawa, K.: 1992, 'Reasoning about Time and Probability'. Technical Report 92-61, Brown University Department of Computer Science.

Kartha, G. and V. Lifschitz: 1995, 'A Simple Formalization of Actions using Circumscription'. In: *Proceedings of the Fourteenth International Joint Conference on Artificial Intelligence (IJCAI-95)*. Montreal, CA, pp. 1970–1975.

Kartha, G. N.: 1993, 'Soundness and Completeness Theorems for Three Formalizations of Action'. In: *Proceedings of the Thirteenth International Joint Conference on Artificial Intelligence (IJCAI-93)*. pp. 724–729.

Kartha, G. N.: 1996, 'On the Range of Applicability of Baker's approach to the Frame Problem'. In: *Proceedings of the Thirteenth National Conference of the American Association for Artificial Intelligence (AAAI-96)*.

Kartha, G. N. and V. Lifschitz: 1994, 'Actions with Indirect Effects (Preliminary Report)'. In: *Proceedings of the International Conference on Knowledge Representation and Reasoning*. pp. 341–350.

Katsuno, H. and A. O. Mendelzon: 1989, 'A unified view of propositional knowledge base update'. In: *Proceedings of the Eleventh International Joint Conference on Artificial Intelligence (IJCAI-89)*. pp. 1413–1419.

Kautz, H.: 1986, 'The logic of persistence'. In: *Proceedings of the Fifth National Conference on Artificial Intelligence (AAAI-86)*. Philadelphia, PA, pp. 401–405.

Kautz, H.: 1987, 'A Formal Theory of Plan Recognition'. Ph.D. thesis, Department of Computer Science, University of Rochester, Rochester, NY. Available as Technical Report 215.

Kautz, H.: 1991, 'A Formal Theory of Plan Recognition and its Implementation'. In: J. Allen, H. Kautz, R. Pelavin, and J. Tenenberg (eds.): *Reasoning about Plans*. San Mateo, CA: Morgan Kaufmann, pp. 69–126.

Kautz, H. and P. Ladkin: 1991, 'Integrating metric and qualitative temporal reasoning'. In: *Proceedings of the Ninth National Conference on Artificial Intelligence (AAAI-91)*. pp. 241–246.

Kautz, H., D. McAllester, and B. Selman: 1996, 'Encoding Plans in Propositional Logic'. In: *Proceedings of the Fifth International Conference on Principles of Knowledge Representation and Reasoning (KR'96)*. Boston, MA.

Kautz, H. and B. Selman: 1992, 'Planning as Satisfiability'. In: *Proceedings of the Tenth European Conference on Artificial Intelligence (ECAI-92)*. Vienna, Austria, pp. 359–363.

Kautz, H. and B. Selman: 1996, 'Pushing the Envelope: Planning, Propositional Logic, and Stochastic Search'. In: *Proceedings of the Thirteenth National Conference of the American Association for Artificial Intelligence (AAAI-96)*. Portland, OR.

Kline, N.: 1993, 'An update of the temporal database bibliography'. *SIGMOD RECORD* **22**(4), 66–80.

Koomen, J.: 1988, 'The TIMELOGIC temporal reasoning system'. Technical Report 231,

University of Rochester, Computer Science Dept., Rochester, NY 14627.

Kosslyn, S.: 1980, *Image and Mind.* Cambridge, MA: Harvard University Press.

Kosslyn, S., O. Koenig, A. Barrett, C. B. Cave, J. Tang, and J. Gabrieli: 1989, 'Evidence for two types of spatial representations: hemispheric specialization for categorical and coordinate relations'. *Journal of Experimental Psychology, Human Perception and Performance* **15**, 723–735.

Koubarakis, M.: 1992, 'Dense Time and Temporal Constraints With $\neq$'. In: B. Nebel, W. Swartout, and C. Rich (eds.): *Proceedings of the Third International Conference on Principles of Knowledge Representation and Reasoning (KR'92).* Cambridge, MA, pp. 24–35.

Koubarakis, M.: 1995, 'From local to global consistency in temporal constraint networks'. In: *Proceedings of the First International Conference on Principle and Practice of Constraint Programming.* Marseilles, France.

Kowalski, R.: 1992, 'Database updates in the event calculus'. *Journal of Logic Programming* **12**, 121–146.

Kowalski, R. and M. Sergot: 1986, 'A logic-based calculus of events'. *New Generation Computing* **4**, 67–95.

Kucera, H. and W. Francis: 1967, *Computational Analysis of Present-day American English.* Providence, RI: Brown University Press.

Kuhn, W.: 1992, 'Paradigms in GIS use'. In: *Proceedings of the 5th International Symposium on Spatal Data Handling,* Vol. 1. Charleston, South Carolina, USA, pp. 91–103.

Kuhn, W.: 1993, 'Metaphors create theories for users'. In: A. Frank and I. Campari (eds.): *Spatial Information Theory,* Vol. 716 of *Lecture Notes in Computer Science.* Springer-Verlag, pp. 366–376.

Kuhn, W.: in press, 'The role of metaphors in task analysis'. In: Y. Waern and M. Tauber (eds.): *Task Analysis and Human-Computer Interaction.* North Holland.

Kuipers, B.: 1978, 'Modelling spatial knowledge'. *Cognitive Science* **2**(2), 129–154.

Kuipers, B.: 1983, 'The cognitive map: Could it have been any other way?'. In: H. Pick and L. Acredolo (eds.): *Spatial Orientation: Theory, Research, and Application.* New York: Plenum Press, pp. 346–359.

Kuipers, B. and T. Levitt: 1988, 'Navigation and Mapping in a Large-Scale Space'. *AI Magazine* **9**(2), 25–43.

Ladkin, P.: 1986, 'Time representation: A taxonomy of interval relations'. In: *Proceedings of the Fifth National Conference of the American Association for Artificial Intelligence (AAAI-86).* Los Altos, pp. 360–366.

Ladkin, P.: 1987a, 'The completness of a natural system for reasoning with time intervals'. In: *Proceedings of the Tenth International Joint Conference on Artificial Intelligence (IJCAI-87).* pp. 462–467.

Ladkin, P.: 1987b, 'Models of Axioms for Time Intervals'. In: *Proceedings of the Sixth National Conference of the American Association for Artificial Intelligence (AAAI-87).* Seattle, WA, pp. 234–239.

Ladkin, P. and R. Maddux: 1988a, 'On Binary Constraint Networks'. Technical Report KES.U.88.8, Kestrel Institute, Palo Alto, CA.

Ladkin, P. and R. Maddux: 1988b, 'Representation and reasoning with convex time intervals'. Technical report KES.U.88.2, Kestrel Institution, Palo Alto, CA.

Ladkin, P. and R. Maddux: 1994, 'On Binary Constraint Problems'. *Journal of the Association for Computing Machinery* **41**(3), 435–469.

Ladkin, P. and A. Reinefeld: 1992, 'Effective solution of qualitative interval constraint problems'. *Artificial Intelligence* **57**(1), 105–124.

Ladkin, P. and A. Reinefeld: forthcoming, 'Fast Algebraic Methods for Interval Constraint Problems'. *Annals of Mathematics and Artificial Intelligence.*

Lakoff, G. and M. Johnson: 1980, *Metaphors We Live By.* Chicago: University of Chicago Press.

Landau, B. and R. Jackendoff: 1993, '*What* and *where* in spatial language and spatial cognition'. *Behavioral and Brain Sciences* **16**, 217–265.

Langacker, R.: 1991, *Concept, Image, and Symbol*. New York: Mouton de Gruyter.

Lascarides, A. and J. Oberlander: 1993, 'Temporal connectives in a discourse context'. In: *Proceedings of the Sixth Conference of the European Chapter of the ACL (EACL-93)*. pp. 260–268.

Latecki, L. and S. Pribbenow: 1992, 'On Hybrid Reasoning for Processing Spatial Expressions'. In: *Proceedings of the Tenth European Conference on Artificial Intelligence (ECAI-92)*. pp. 389–393.

Latecki, L. and R. Röhrig: 1993, 'Orientation and Qualitative Angle for Spatial Reasoning'. In: R. Bajcsy (ed.): *Proceedings of the Thirteenth International Joint Conference on Artificial Intelligence (IJCAI-93)*. San Mateo (CA), pp. 1544–1549.

Latombe, J.: 1990, *Robot Motion Planning*. Dordrecht: Kluwer.

Laurini, R. and D. Thompson: 1991, *Fundamentals of Spatial Information Systems*, APIC Series. New York: Academic Press.

Leban, B., D. Mcdonald, and D. Foster: 1986, 'A representation for collections of temporal intervals'. In: *Proceedings of the Fifth National Conference of the American Association for Artificial Intelligence (AAAI-86)*. pp. 367–371.

Lehmann, F. and A. Cohn: 1994, 'The EGG/YOLK Reliability Hierarchy: Semantic Data Integration Using Sorts with Prototypes'. In: *Proceedings of the Conference on Information Knowledge Management*. pp. 272–279.

Lemon, O.: 1996, 'Semantical Foundations of Spatial Logics'. In: L. C. Aiello and S. Shapiro (eds.): *Proceedings of KR'96, Principles of Knowledge Representation and Reasoning*. San Mateo (CA), pp. 212–219.

Lenat, D., R. Guha, K. Pittman, D. Pratt, and M. Shepherd: 1990, 'Cyc: Toward programs with common sense'. *Communications of the ACM* **33**(8), 30 – 49.

Leonard, H. and N. Goodman: 1940, 'The Calculus of Individuals and its Uses'. *Journal of Symbolic Logic* **5**, 45–55.

Lesniewski, S.: 1927–1931, 'O podstawach matematyki [On the Foundations of Mathematics]'. *Przeglad Filosoficzny [Philosophical Review]* **30-34**.

Levinson, S.: 1993, 'Language and cognition: Cognitive consequences of spatial description in Guugu Yimithirr'. Working paper No. 13, Max Planck Institute of Psycholinguistics, Nijmegen.

Levinson, S.: 1994, 'Vision, shape and linguistic description: Tzeltal body-part terminology and object description'. *Linguistics* **32**, 791–855.

Levitt, T. and D. Lawton: 1990, 'Qualitative navigation for mobile robots'. *Artificial Intelligence* **44**, 305–360.

Lewis, D. K.: 1991, *Parts of Classes*. Oxford: Basil Blackwell.

Lifschitz, V.: 1987a, 'Formal theories of action'. In: F. M. Brown (ed.): *Proceedings of the 1987 Workshop: The Frame Problem in Artificial Intelligence*. pp. 35–58.

Lifschitz, V.: 1987b, 'Pointwise Circumscription'. In: M. Ginsberg (ed.): *Readings in Nonmonotonic Reasoning*. Los Altos, CA: Morgan Kaufmann, pp. 179–193.

Lifschitz, V.: 1990, 'Frames in the Space of Situations'. *Artificial Intelligence* **46**, 365–376.

Lifschitz, V.: 1991, 'Toward a Metatheory of Action'. In: *Proceedings of the International Conference on Knowledge Representation and Reasoning*. pp. 376–386.

Lifschitz, V.: 1995, 'Nested abnormality theories'. *Artificial Intelligence* **74**, 351–365.

Lifschitz, V. and A. Rabinov: 1989, 'Miracles in formal theories of action (research note)'. *Artificial Intelligence* **38**(2), 225–238.

Ligozat, G.: 1990, 'Weak representation of interval algebras'. In: *Proceedings of the Eighth National Conference of the American Association for Artificial Intelligence (AAAI-90)*. Boston, MA USA, pp. 715–720.

Ligozat, G.: 1993, 'Qualitative Triangulation for Spatial Reasoning'. In: A. Frank and I. Campari (eds.): *Spatial Information Theory - COSIT'93*. Berlin, pp. 54–68.

Ligozat, G.: 1996a, 'A new Proof of Tractability for ORD-Horn relations'. In: *Proceedings of the Thirteenth National Conference of the American Association for Artificial Intelligence (AAAI-96)*. pp. 715–720.

Ligozat, G.: 1996b, 'On Generalized Interval Calculi'. In: *Proceedings of the Ninth National Conference of the American Association for Artificial Intelligence (AAAI-91)*. pp. 234–240.

Lin, F.: 1995, 'Embracing Causality in Specifying the Indirect Effects of Actions'. In: *Proceedings of the Fourteenth International Joint Conference on Artificial Intelligence (IJCAI-95)*.

Lin, F.: 1996, 'Specifying the effects of indeterminate actions'. In: *Proceedings of the Fifth International Conference on Principles of Knowledge Representation and Reasoning (KR'96)*. Boston, MA.

Lin, F. and R. Reiter: 1994, 'State Constraints Revisited'. *Journal of Logic and Computation* 4(5).

Lin, F. and Y. Shoham: 1991, 'Provably correct theories of action: Preliminary report'. In: *Proceedings of the Ninth National Conference on Artificial Intelligence (AAAI-91)*.

Lin, F. and Y. Shoham: 1992, 'Concurrent actions in the situation calculus'. In: *Proceedings of the Tenth National Conference on Artificial Intelligence (AAAI-92)*. San Jose, CA, pp. 580–585.

Lindner, S.: 1981, 'A lexico-semantic analysis of verb-particle constructions with UP and OUT'. Ph.D. thesis, University of California, San Diego.

Liskov, B. and J. Guttag: 1986, *Abstraction and Specification in Program Development*. Cambridge, MA: MIT Press.

Logan, G.: 1994, 'Spatial attention and the apprehension of spatial relations'. *Journal of Experimental Psychology, Human Perception and Performance* 20, 1015–1036.

Lozano-Pérez, T.: 1983, 'Spatial planning: a configuration space approach'. *IEEE Transactions on Computers* C-32(2), 108–120.

Maass, W.: 1995, 'How spatial information connects visual perception and natural language generation in dynamic environments: Towards a computational model'. In: A. Frank and W. Kuhn (eds.): *Spatial Information Theory - Proceedings of COSIT'95*. Berlin.

Mackworth, A. K.: 1977, 'Consistency in network of relations'. *Artificial Intelligence* 8(1), 99–118.

Maguire, D., D. Rhind, and M. Goodchild (eds.): 1991, *Geographic Information Systems: Principles and Applications*. London: Longman Co.

Mark, D.: 1992, 'Counter-intuitive geographic "facts": Clues for spatial reasoning at geographic scales'. In: A. Frank, I. Campari, and U. Formentini (eds.): *Theories and Methods of Spatio-Temporal Reasoning in Geographic Space*, Vol. 639 of *Lecture Notes in Computer Science*. Heidelberg-Berlin: Springer-Verlag, pp. 305–317.

Mark, D. and A. Frank (eds.): 1991, *Cognitive and Linguistic Aspects of Geographic Space*, Vol. 63 of *NATO ASI Series D*. Dordrecht: Kluwer.

Mark, D. and A. Frank: 1996, 'Experiential and formal models of geographic space'. *Environment and Planning B* 23, 3 – 24.

Mark, D., A. Frank, W. Kuhn, M. McGranaghan, L. Willauer, and M. Gould: 1992, 'User interfaces for geographic information systems: A research agenda'. In: *Proceedings of the ASPRS/ACSM '92*. Albuquerque, New Mexico.

Marr, D.: 1982, *Vision: a computational investigation into the human representation and processing of visual information*. San Francisco: Freemann.

Marr, D. and H. Nishihara: 1978, *Representation and recognition of the spatial organisation of three-dimensional shapes*. B 200, Proceedings of the Royal Society of London.

Martin, N. G.: 1993, 'Using Statistical Inference to Plan Under Uncertainty'. Ph.D. thesis, Department of Computer Science, University of Rochester, Rochester, NY.

Martin, N. G. and J. F. Allen: 1993, 'Statistical Probabilities for Planning'. Technical Report 474, Department of Computer Science, University of Rochester, Rochester, NY.

McAllester, D. and D. Rosenblitt: 1991, 'Systematic nonlinear planning'. In: *Proceedings of the Ninth National Conference on Artificial Intelligence (AAAI-91)*. pp. 634–639.

McCain, N. and H. Turner: 1995, 'A Causal Theory of Ramifications and Qualifications'. In: *Proceedings of the Fourteenth International Joint Conference on Artificial Intelligence (IJCAI-95)*.

McCarthy, J.: 1963, 'Situations, Actions, and Causal Laws'. Technical Report Memo 2, Stanford Artificial Intelligence Project, Stanford, CA.

McCarthy, J.: 1968, 'Programs with Common Sense'. In: *Semantic Information Processing*. MIT Press.

McCarthy, J.: 1977, 'Epistemological Problems of Artificial Intelligence'. In: *Proceedings of the Fifth International Joint Conference on Artificial Intelligence (IJCAI-77)*. pp. 1038–1044.

McCarthy, J.: 1980, 'Circumscription – A form of non-monotonic reasoning'. *Artificial Intelligence* 13(1,2), 27–39.

McCarthy, J.: 1986, 'Applications of circumscription to formalizing common-sense knowledge'. *Artificial Intelligence* 28, 89–116.

McCarthy, J. and P. Hayes: 1969, 'Some philosophical problems from the standpoint of artificial intelligence'. In: B. Meltzer and D. Michie (eds.): *Machine Intelligence*, Vol. 4. American Elsevier Publishing Co., Inc., pp. 463–502. Also in *Readings in Planning*, J. Allen, J. Hendler, and A. Tate (eds.), Morgan Kaufmann, 1990, pp. 393–435.

McCune, W.: 1990, 'OTTER 2.0 Users Guide'. Technical report, Argonne National Laboratory, Argonne, Illinois.

McDermott, D.: 1982, 'A temporal logic for reasoning about process and plans'. *Cognitive Science* 6, 101–155.

McDermott, D.: 1985, 'Reasoning about plans'. In: J. Hobbs and R. Moore (eds.): *Formal Theories of the Commonsense World*. Norwood, NJ: Ablex Publishing, pp. 269–318.

McDermott, D.: 1992a, 'Reasoning, spatial'. In: E. Shapiro (ed.): *Encyclopedia of Artificial Intelligence*. Chichester: Wiley, 2d edition, pp. 1322–1334.

McDermott, D.: 1992b, 'Transformational planning of reactive behavior'. Technical Report 941, Yale Computer Science.

McDermott, D.: 1994, 'An Algorithm for Probabilistic, Totally-Ordered Temporal Projection'. Technical Report 1014, Yale Computer Science.

McDermott, D.: 1996, 'An Heuristic Estimator for Means-Ends Analysis in Planning'. In: *Proceedings of the Third International Conference on Artificial Intelligence Planning Systems*. Menlo PArk, CA., USA, pp. 142–149.

McKevitt, P. (ed.): 1995–1996, *Integration of Natural Language and Vision Processing*, Vol. I-IV. Dordrecht: Kluwer.

Meiri, I.: 1992, 'Temporal Reasoning: A Constraint-Based Approach'. Technical Report R-173, University of California, LA, Computer Science Dept. Los Angeles, CA 90024.

Meiri, I.: 1996, 'Combining qualitative and quantitative constraints in temporal reasoning'. *Artificial Intelligence* 87(1-2), 295–342. A preliminary version appeared in the *Proceedings of the Ninth National Conference on Artificial Intelligence (AAAI-91)*, MIT Press, pp. 260–267.

Miller, B.: 1990, 'The Rhetorical Knowledge Representation System Reference Manual'. Technical Report 326, The University of Rochester, Computer Science Department Rochester New York 14627.

Miller, R. and M. Shanahan: 1994, 'Narratives in the situation calculus'. *Journal of Logic and Computation* 4(5).

Miller, S. A. and L. Schubert: 1990, 'Time revisited'. *Computational Intelligence* 6, 108–118.

Montanari, U.: 1974, 'Networks of Constraints: Fundamental Properties and Applications to Picture Processing'. *Information Science* 7(3), 95–132.

Morgenstern, L. and L. A. Stein: 1988, 'Why things go wrong: A formal theory of causal reasoning'. In: *Proceedings of the Seventh National Conference on Artificial Intelligence (AAAI-88)*. St. Paul, MN. Also in *Readings in Planning*, J. Allen, J. Hendler, and A. Tate (eds.), Morgan Kaufmann, 1990, pp. 641–646.

Morley, D., M. Georgeff, and A. Rao: 1994, 'A monotonic formalism for events and systems of events'. *Journal of Logic and Computation* **4**(5), 701–720.

Morris, P.: 1988, 'The Anomalous Extension Problem in Default Reasoning'. *Artificial Intelligence* **35**, 383–399.

Morris, R., W. Shoaff, and L. Khatib: 1993, 'Path consistency in a Network of non-convex intervals'. In: *Proceedings of the Thirteenth International Joint Conference on Artificial Intelligence (IJCAI-93)*. pp. 655–660.

Mourelatos, A.: 1978, 'Events, processes and states'. *Linguistics and Philosophy* **2**, 415–434.

Mukerjee, A.: 1989, 'A representation for modeling functional knowledge in geometric structures'. In: Ramani, Chandrasekan, and Anjaneluyu (eds.): *Proceedings of KBCS'89*. New Delhi, pp. 192–202.

Mukerjee, A. and G. Joe: 1990, 'A Qualitative Model for Space'. In: *Proceedings of the Eighth National Conference of the American Association for Artificial Intelligence (AAAI-90)*. Los Altos, pp. 721–727.

Narayanan, N.: 1993, 'Taking issue/forum: The imagery debate revisited'. *Computational Intelligence* **9**(4), 301–435.

Nebel, B.: 1995, 'Computational properties of qualitative spatial reasoning: First results'. In: I. Wachsmuth, C. Rollinger, and W. Brauer (eds.): *Proceedings of KI'95: Advances in Artificial Intelligence*. Berlin, pp. 233–244.

Nebel, B.: 1996, 'Solving Hard Qualitative Temporal Reasoning Problems: Evaluating the Efficiency of Using the ORD-Horn Class'. In: W. Wahlster (ed.): *Proceedings of the Twelfth European Conference on Artificial Intelligence (ECAI-96)*. pp. 38–42.

Nebel, B. and C. Bäckström: 1994, 'On the computational complexity of temporal projection, planning and plan validation'. *Artificial Intelligence* **66**(1), 125–160.

Nebel, B. and H. J. Bürckert: 1995, 'Reasoning about Temporal Relations: A Maximal Tractable Subclass of Allen's Interval Algebra'. *Journal of the Association for Computing Machinery* **42**(1), 43–66.

Nerode, A.: 1990, 'Some Letcures on Intuitionistic Logic'. In: S. Homer, A. Nerode, R. Platek, , G. Sacks, and A. Scedrov (eds.): *Logic and Computer Science*, Vol. 1429 of *Lecture Notes in Mathematics*. Springer-Verlag, pp. 12–59.

Nicod, J.: 1924, 'Geometry in the Sensible World'. Doctoral thesis, Sorbonne. English translation in *Geometry and Induction*, Routledge and Kegan Paul, 1969.

Nielsen, P.: 1988, 'A qualitative approach to mechanical constraint'. In: *Proceedings of the Seventh National Conference of the American Association for Artificial Intelligence (AAAI-88)*. pp. 270–274.

Nilsson, N. J.: 1980, *Principles of Artificial Intelligence*. Los Altos, CA: Morgan Kaufmann Publishers, Inc.

Niyogi, S.: 1995, 'Deducing visual relationships from attentional representations'. In: *Proceedings of the Workshop on Computational Models for Integrating Language and Vision*. AAAI-95 Fall Symposium Series, MIT, Cambridge MA.

Nökel, K.: 1991, *Temporally Distributed Symptoms in Technical Diagnosis*, Vol. 517. Berlin, Heidelberg, New York: Springer-Verlag.

Olivier, P., T. Maeda, and J. Tsuji: 1994, 'Automatic depiction of spatial descriptions'. In: *Proceedings of the Twelfth National Conference of the American Association for Artificial Intelligence (AAAI-94)*. pp. 1405–1410.

Orgun, M.: 1996, 'On Temporal Deductive Databases'. *Computational Intelligence* **12**(2), 235–259.

Özsoyŏglu, R. and T. Snodgrass: 1995, 'Temporal and Real-Time Databases: A Survey'. *IEEE Transactions of Knowledge and Data Engineering* **7**(4), 513–532.

Paivio, A.: 1986, *Mental representations: a dual coding approach*. Oxford: Oxford University Press.

Palmer, S., E. Rosch, and P. Chase: 1981, 'Canonical perspective and the perception of objects'. In: J. Long and A. Baddeley (eds.): *Attention and Perfomance IX*. Hillsdale, NJ: Erlbaum, pp. 135–151.

Pearl, J.: 1988a, 'On the Logic of Probability'. *Computational Intelligence* 4, 99–103.

Pearl, J.: 1988b, *Probabilistic Reasoning in Intelligent Systems: Networks of Plausible Inference*. Morgan Kaufmann.

Pednault, E.: 1988, 'Synthesizing plans that contain actions with context-dependent effects'. *Computational Intelligence* 4(4), 356–372.

Pednault, E.: 1989, 'ADL: Exploring the middle ground between STRIPS and the situation calculus'. In: R. Brachman, H. Levesque, and R. Reiter (eds.): *Proceedings of the First International Conference on Principles of Knowledge Representation and Reasoning (KR-89)*. pp. 324–332.

Pednault, E. P.: 1986, 'Formulating multi-agent, dynamic-world problems in the classical planning framework'. In: M. Georgeff and A. Lansky (eds.): *Reasoning about Actions and Plans: Proceedings of the 1986 Workshop*. Los Altos, CA, pp. 47–82. Also in *Readings in Planning*, J. Allen, J. Hendler, and A. Tate (eds.), Morgan Kaufmann, 1990, pp. 675–710.

Pelavin, R.: 1991, 'Planning with simultaneous actions and external events'. In: J. Allen, H. Kautz, R. Pelavin, and J. Tenenberg (eds.): *Reasoning about Plans*. San Mateo, CA: Morgan Kaufmann, pp. 127–212.

Penberthy, J. and D. Weld: 1992, 'UCPOP: A sound, complete, partial order planner for ADL'. In: B. Nebel, C. Rich, and W. Swartout (eds.): *Proceedings of the Third International Conference on Principles of Knowledge Representation and Reasoning (KR'92)*. Boston, MA, pp. 103–114.

Penberthy, J. and D. Weld: 1994, 'Temporal planning with continuous change'. In: *Proceedings of the Twelfth National Conference of the American Association for Artificial Intelligence (AAAI-94)*. Seattle, WA, pp. 1010–1015.

Penberthy, J. S.: 1993, 'Planning with Continuous Change'. Technical Report 93-12-01, University of Washington Department of Computer Science & Engineering.

Peppas, P. and W. Wobcke: 1992, 'On the Use of Epistemic Entrenchment in Reasoning about Action'. In: *Proceedings of the Tenth European Conference on Artificial Intelligence (ECAI-92)*. pp. 403–407.

Piaget, J. and B. Inhelder: 1948, *La représentation de l'espace chez l'enfant*, Bibliothèque de Philosophie Contemporaine. Paris: PUF.

Pianesi, F. and A. C. Varzi: 1994, 'The Mereo-Topology of Event Structures'. In: P. Dekker and M. Stokhof (eds.): *Proceedings of the 9th Amsterdam Colloquium*. Amsterdam: ILLC, pp. 527–546.

Pianesi, F. and A. C. Varzi: 1996a, 'Events, Topology, and Temporal Relations'. *The Monist* 78, 89–116.

Pianesi, F. and A. C. Varzi: 1996b, 'Refining Temporal Reference in Event Structures'. *Notre Dame Journal of Formal Logic* 37, 71–83.

Pinker, S.: 1985, 'Visual cognition: An introduction'. In: S. Pinker (ed.): *Visual Cognition*. Cambridge, MA: MIT Press, pp. 1–64.

Pinker, S.: 1989, *Learnability and Cognition: The Acquisition of Argument Structure*. Cambridge, MA: MIT Press.

Pinto, J.: 1994, 'Temporal Reasoning in the Situation Calculus'. Ph.D. thesis, University of Toronto, Toronto, Ontario, Canada.

Poesio, M. and R. Brachman: 1991, 'Metric Constraints for Maintaining Appointments: Dates and Repeated Activities'. In: *Proceedings of the Ninth National Conference of the American Association for Artificial Intelligence (AAAI-91)*. pp. 253–259.

Preparata, F. and M. Shamos: 1985, *Computational geometry: an introduction*. Berlin: Springer.

Pylyshyn, Z.: 1985, *Computation and Cognition: Toward a Foundation for Cognitive Science*. Cambridge, MA: MIT Press.

Randell, D. and A. Cohn: 1989, 'Modelling Topological and Metrical Properties of Physical Processes'. In: R. Brachman, H. Levesque, and R. Reiter (eds.): *Proceedings of the 1st International Conference on the Principles of Knowledge Representation and Reasoning*. Los Altos, pp. 55–66.

Randell, D., Z. Cui, and A. Cohn: 1992a, 'A Spatial Logic Based on Regions and Connection'. In: *Proceedings of the Third International Conference on Principles of Knowledge Representation and Reasoning (KR'92)*. San Mateo, pp. 165–176.

Randell, D. A. and A. G. Cohn: 1992, 'Exploiting Lattices in a Theory of Space and Time'. *Computers and Mathematics with Applications* 23(6-9), 459–476. Also appears in F. Lehman (ed.): *Semantic Networks*, Pergamon Press, Oxford, pp. 459-476, 1992.

Randell, D. A., A. G. Cohn, and Z. Cui: 1992b, 'Computing Transitivity Tables: A Challenge For Automated Theorem Provers'. In: *Proceedings CADE 11*. Berlin.

Reiter, R.: 1984, 'Towards a logical reconstruction of relational database theory,'. In: M. Brodie, M. Mylopolous, and L. Schmidt (eds.): *On Conceptual Modelling, Perspectives from Artificial Intelligence, Databases, and Programming Languages*. New York: Springer-Verlag,, pp. 191–233.

Reiter, R.: 1991, 'The frame problem in the situation calculus: A simple solution (sometimes) and a completeness result for goal regression'. In: V. Lifschitz (ed.): *Artificial Intelligence and Mathematical Theory of Computation: Papers in Honor of John McCarthy*. Academic Press, pp. 359–380.

Reiter, R.: 1992, 'The projection problem in the situation calculus: A soundness and completeness result, with an application to database updates'. In: *Proceedings of the First International Conference on AI Planning Systems*. College Park, MD, pp. 198–203.

Reiter, R.: 1996, 'Natural actions, concurrency and continuous time in the Situation Calculus'. In: *Proceedings of the Fifth International Conference on Principles of Knowledge Representation and Reasoning (KR'96)*. Boston, MA.

Reuleaux, F.: 1875, *Theoretische Kinematik: Grundzge einer Theorie des Maschinenwesens*. Braunschweig: Vieweg.

Rit, J.: 1986, 'Propagating temporal constraints for scheduling'. In: *Proceedings of the Fifth National Conference of the American Association for Artificial Intelligence (AAAI-86)*. pp. 383–388.

Rock, I.: 1972, 'The perception and recognition of complex figures'. *Cognitive Psychology* 3, 655–673.

Rosch, E.: 1977, 'Human categorization'. In: N. Warren (ed.): *Advances in Cross-Cultural Psychology*, Vol. 1. London: Academic Press, pp. 1–49.

Sacerdoti, E.: 1975, 'The nonlinear nature of plans'. In: *Proceedings of the Fourth International Joint Conference on Artificial Intelligence (IJCAI-75)*. Tbilisi, Georgia, USSR, pp. 206–214.

Sadalla, E., W. Burroughs, and L. Staplin: 1980, 'Reference points in spatial cognition'. *Journal of Experimental Psychology: Human Learning and Memory* 6, 516–528.

Samet, H.: 1984, 'The quadtree and related hierarchical data structures'. *Computing surveys* 16(2), 187–260.

Samet, H.: 1989, *The Design and Analysis of Spatial Data Structures*. Addison Wesley.

Sandewall, E.: 1988, 'Non-Monotonic entailment for reasoning about time and action, Part I: Sequential actions'. Technical report, IDA.

Sandewall, E.: 1989, 'Filter Preferential Entailment for the Logic of Action in Almost Continuous Worlds'. In: *Proceedings of the Eleventh International Joint Conference on Artificial Intelligence (IJCAI-89)*. pp. 894–899.

Sandewall, E.: 1991, 'Features and Fluents. Review version of 1991'. Technical Report LiTH-IDA-R-91-29, IDA.

Sandewall, E.: 1993a, 'Nonmonotonic temporal logics and autonomous agents: each contributes to the rigorous basis of the other'. In: O. Herzog, T. Christaller, and D. Schütt (eds.): *Grundlagen und Anwendungen der Künstlichen Intelligenz. Proc. German A.I. conference. 17. Fachtagung für Künstliche Intelligenz*, pp. 107–124.

Sandewall, E.: 1993b, 'The range of applicability of nonmonotonic logics for the inertia problem'. In: *Proceedings of the Thirteenth International Joint Conference on Artificial Intelligence (IJCAI-93)*.

Sandewall, E.: 1994a, *Features and Fluents. The Representation of Knowledge about*

Dynamical Systems. Volume I. Oxford University Press.

Sandewall, E.: 1994b, 'The range of applicability of some nonmonotonic logics for strict inertia'. *Journal of Logic and Computation* 4(5), 581–616.

Sandewall, E.: 1995, 'Systematic Comparison of Approaches to Ramification Using Restricted Minimization of Change'. Technical Report LiTH-IDA-R-95-15, IDA.

Sandewall, E. and Y. Shoham: 1995, 'Nonmonotonic Temporal Reasoning'. In: D. Gabbay (ed.): *Handbook of Logic in Artificial Intelligence and Logic Programming.* Oxford University Press.

Schlieder, C.: 1993, 'Representing visible locations for qualitative navigation'. In: N. Carreté and M. Singh (eds.): *Qualitative Reasoning and Decision Technologies.* Barcelona, pp. 523–532.

Schlieder, C.: 1995, 'Reasoning about Ordering'. In: A. Frank and W. Kuhn (eds.): *Spatial Information Theory - Proceedings of COSIT'95.* Berlin, pp. 341–349.

Schmidt, A. and W. Zafft: 1975, 'Programs of the Harvard University Laboratory for Computer Graphics and Spatial Analysis'. In: J. Davis and M. McCullagh (eds.): *Display and Analysis of Spatial Data.* London: John Wiley and Sons, pp. 231–243.

Schmiedel, A.: 1990, 'A Temporal Terminological Logic'. In: *Proceedings of the Eighth National Conference of the American Association for Artificial Intelligence (AAAI-90).* pp. 640–645.

Schubert, L.: 1990, 'Monotonic Solution of The Frame Problem in The Situation Calculus: An Efficient Method for Worlds with Fully Specified Actions'. In: H. Kyburg Jr., P. Ronald, and G. Carlson (eds.): *Knowledge Representation and Defeasible Reasoning.* Dordrecht, The Netherlands: Kluwer Academic Publishers, pp. 23–68.

Schubert, L.: 1994, 'Explanation Closure, Action Closure, and the Sandewall Test Suite for Reasoning about Change'. *Journal of Logic and Computation* 4(5), 679–700.

Schubert, L. and C. Hwang: 1989, 'An episodic knowledge representation for narrative text'. In: R. Brachman, H. Levesque, and R. Reiter (eds.): *Proceedings of the First International Conference on Principles of Knowledge Representation and Reasoning (KR-89).* Toronto, Ont., pp. 444–458.

Schwalb, E. and R. Dechter: 1993, 'Copying with Disjunctions in Temporal Constraint Satisfaction Problems'. In: *Proceedings of the Eleventh National Conference of the American Association for Artificial Intelligence (AAAI-93).* Washington, D.C., pp. 127–132.

Schwalb, E. and R. Dechter: 1995, 'Processing Temporal Constraint Networks'. Technical report, Dept. of Information and Computer Science, Univ. of California, Irvine, CA.

Schwalb, E., K. Kalev, and R. Dechter: 1994, 'Temporal Reasoning with constraints on fluents and events'. In: *Proceedings of the Twelfth National Conference of the American Association for Artificial Intelligence (AAAI-94).* Seattle, WA, pp. 1067–1072.

Sedgewick, H. and S. Levy: 1986, 'Environment-centered and viewer-centered perception of surface orientation'. In: A. Rosenfeld (ed.): *Human Vision II.* New York: Academic Press.

Selman, B., H. Kautz, and B. Cohen: 1994, 'Noice Strategies for Local Search'. In: *Proceedings of the Twelfth National Conference of the American Association for Artificial Intelligence (AAAI-94).* Seattle, WA, pp. 337–343.

Shanahan, M.: 1990, 'Representing continuous change in the situation calculus'. In: L. C. Aiello (ed.): *Proceedings of the Ninth European Conference on Artificial Intelligence (ECAI-90).* Stockholm, Sweden, pp. 598–603.

Shanahan, M. and R. Southwick: 1989, *Search, Inference and Dependencies in Artificial Intelligence.* New York, Chichester,Brisbane, Toronto: Ellis Horwood.

Shaw, M.: 1984, 'The impact of modelling and abstraction concerns on modern programming languages'. In: M. Brodie, J. Mylopolous, and J. Schmidt (eds.): *On Conceptual Modelling, Perspectives from Artificial Intelligence, Databases, and Programming Languages.* New York: Springer-Verlag.

Shepard, R. and S. Hurwitz: 1985, 'Upward direction, mental rotation, and discrimination of left and right turns in maps'. In: S. Pinker (ed.): *Visual Cognition*. Cambridge, MA: MIT Press, pp. 161–193.

Shoham, Y.: 1987, 'Temporal Logics in AI: Semantical and ontological considerations'. *Artificial Intelligence* **33**(1), 89–104.

Shoham, Y.: 1988a, 'Chronological ignorance: Experiments in nonmonotonic temporal reasoning'. *Artificial Intelligence* **36**, 49–61.

Shoham, Y.: 1988b, *Reasoning about change: Time and Causation from the Standpoint of Artificial Intelligence*. Cambridge, MA: MIT Press.

Shoham, Y. and N. Goyal: 1988, 'Temporal Reasoning in Artificial Intelligence'. In: H. Shrobe (ed.): *Exploring Artificial Intelligence: Survey Talks from the National Conference on Artificial Intelligence*. Morgan Kaufmann, pp. 419–438.

Shoham, Y. and D. McDermott: 1988, 'Problems in formal temporal reasoning'. *Artificial Intelligence* **36**, 49–61.

Simons, P.: 1987, *Parts - A study in ontology*. Oxford: Clarendon Press.

Sklansky, J.: 1972, 'Measuring Concavity on a Rectangular Mosaic'. *IEEE Trans. on Computers* **C-21**(12), 1355–1364.

Slack, M. and D. Miller: 1987, 'Path planning through time and space in dynamic domains'. In: *Proceedings of the Tenth International Joint Conference on Artificial Intelligence (IJCAI-87)*. pp. 1067–1070.

Slobin, D.: 1996, 'From "thought and language" to "thinking for speaking"'. In: J. Gumperz and S. Levinson (eds.): *Rethinking Linguistic Relativity*. Cambridge UK: Cambridge University Press, pp. 70–96.

Smith, B. (ed.): 1982, *Parts and Moments*. Munich, FRG: Philosophia.

Smith, B.: 1993, 'Ontology and the logistic analysis of reality'. In: N. Guarino and R. Poli (eds.): *Proceedings of the International Workshop on Formal Ontology in Conceptual Analysis and Representation*. LADSEB-CNR, Padova, pp. 51–68.

Smith, B.: 1995, 'On Drawing Lines on a Map'. In: A. Frank and W. Kuhn (eds.): *Spatial Information Theory-A Theoretical Basis for GIS*, Vol. 988 of *Lecture Notes in Computer Science*. Berlin-Heidelberg-New York: Springer, pp. 475–484.

Smith, B.: 1996, 'Mereotopology: A Theory of Parts and Boundaries'. *Data & Knowledge Engineering* **20**, 287–303.

Smith, B.: forthcoming, 'Boundaries'. In: L. Hahn (ed.): *Roderick Chisholm*, Library of living philosophers. La Salle: Open Court.

Smith, L., A. Boyle, J. Dangermond, D. Marble, D. Simonett, and R. Tomlinson: 1983, 'Final Report of a conference on the Review and Synthesis of Problems and Directions for Large Scale Geographic Information System Development'. Technical report, NASA, report available from ESRI, Redlands CA.

Snodgrass, R.: 1990, 'Temporal databases: status and research direction'. *SIGMOD RECORD* **19**, 83–89.

Song, F. and R. Cohen: 1988, 'The interpretation of Temporal Relations in a Narrative'. In: *Proceedings of the Seventh National Conference of the American Association for Artificial Intelligence (AAAI-88)*. Saint Paul, MI, pp. 745–750.

Song, F. and R. Cohen: 1991, 'Tense interpretation in the context of narrative'. In: *Proceedings of the Ninth National Conference of the American Association for Artificial Intelligence (AAAI-91)*. pp. 131–136.

Song, F. and R. Cohen: 1996, 'A Strengthened Algorithm for Temporal Reasoning about Plans'. *Computational Intelligence* **12**(2), 331–356.

Stevens, A. and P. Coupe: 1978, 'Distortions in judged spatial relations'. *Cognitive Psychology* **10**, 422 – 437.

Stiles-Davis, J., M. Kritchevsky, and U. Bellugi: 1988, *Spatial Cognition: Brain Bases and Development*. Hillsdale, NJ: Erlbaum.

Stillman, J., R. Arthur, and A. Deitsch: 1993, 'Tachyon: A constraint-based temporal reasoning model and its implementation'. *SIGART Bulletin* **4**(3).

Stillman, J., R. Arthur, and J. Farley: 1996, 'Temporal Reasoning for Mixed-Initiative Planning'. In: A. Tate (ed.): *Advanced Planning Technology*. Menlo Park, CA: AAAI

Press, pp. 242–249. Technological Achievements of the ARPA/Rome Laboratory Planning Initiative.

Sussman, G. J., T. Winograd, and E. Charniak: 1971, 'Micro-Planner Reference Manual'. Technical Report 203A, MIT AI Laboratory.

Talmy, L.: 1983, 'How language structures space'. In: H. Pick and L. Acredolo (eds.): *Spatial Orientation: Theory, Research, and Application.* New York: Plenum Press, pp. 225–282.

Talmy, L.: 1996, 'Fictive motion in language and "ception'. In: P. Bloom, M. Peterson, L. Nadel, and M. Garrett (eds.): *Language and Space.* Cambridge, MA: MIT Press, pp. 211–276.

Tarjan, R.: 1972, 'Depth first search and linear graph algorithms'. *SIAM Journal of Computing* 1(2), 215–225.

Tarr, M. and S. Pinker: 1989, 'Mental rotation and orientation-dependence in shape recognition'. *Cognitive Psychology* 21, 233–282.

Tarski, A.: 1938, 'Der Aussagenkalkül und die Topologie [Sentential Calculus and Topology]'. *Fundamenta Mathematicae* 31, 103–134. English translation in A. Tarski, *Logic, Semantics, Metamathematics,* Oxford Clarendon Press, 1956.

Tarski, A.: 1941, 'On the Calculus of Relations'. *Journal of Symbolic Logic* 6, 73–89.

Tarski, A.: 1956, 'Foundations of the Geometry of Solids'. In: *Logic, Semantics, Metamathematics.* Oxford Clarendon Press, Chapt. 2. trans. J.H. Woodger.

Tarski, A.: 1959, 'What is Elementary Geometry?'. In: L. Brouwer, E. Beth, and A. Heyting (eds.): *The Axiomatic Method (with special reference to geometry and physics).* Amsterdam: North-Holland, pp. 16–29. Also in L. Brower, E. Beth, and A. Heyting (eds.): *The Axiomatic Method (with special reference to geometry and physics),* North-Holland, pp. 16–29, 1969.

Tarski, A.: 1972, 'Les fondements de la géométrie des corps'. In: A. Tarski (ed.): *Logique, Sémantique, Métamathématique.* Paris: Armand Colin, pp. 28–34.

Tate, A.: 1977, 'Generating project networks'. In: *Proceedings of the Fifth International Joint Conference on Artificial Intelligence (IJCAI-77).* Cambridge, MA, pp. 888–889.

Tate, A.: 1990, 'A review of AI Planning techniques'. In: J. Allen, J. Hendler, and A. Tate (eds.): *Readings in Planning.* San Mateo, CA: Morgan Kaufmann, pp. 26–49.

Terenziani, P.: 1996, 'Toward an Ontology Dealing with Periodic Events'. In: W. Wahlster (ed.): *Proceedings of the Twelfth European Conference on Artificial Intelligence (ECAI-96).* pp. 43–47.

Thiébaux, S. and J. Hertzberg: 1992, 'A semi-reactive planner based on a possible models action formalization'. In: J. Hendler (ed.): *Proceedings of the First International Conference on AI Planning Systems.* Morgan Kaufmann, pp. 228–235.

Thielscher, M.: 1994, 'An Analysis of Systematic Approaches to Reasoning about Actions and Change'. In: P. Jorrand (ed.): *Proceedings of the International Conference on Artificial Intelligence: Methodology, Systems, Applications (AIMSA).* Sofia, Bulgaria.

Thielscher, M.: 1995, 'Computing Ramifications by Postprocessing'. In: *Proceedings of the International Joint Conference on Artificial Intelligence.*

Timpf, S., P. Burrough, and A. Frank: 1994, 'Concepts and Paradigms for Spatial Data: Geographical Objects with Indeterminate Boundaries'. Specialist meeting report Newsletter Number 4, ESF.

Timpf, S. and A. Frank: 1995, 'A multi-scale dag for cartographic objects'. In: *ACSM/ASPRS,* Vol. 4. Charlotte, NC, pp. 157–163.

Timpf, S., G. Volta, D. Pollock, and M. Egenhofer: 1992, 'A conceptual model of wayfinding using multiple levels of abstractions'. In: A. Frank, I. Campari, and U. Formentini (eds.): *Theories and Methods of Spatio-Temporal Reasoning in Geographic Space,* Vol. 639 of *Lecture Notes in Computer Science.* Heidelberg-Berlin: Springer-Verlag, pp. 348–367.

Tomlin, C.: 1983a, 'Digital Cartographic Modeling Techniques in Environmental Planing'. Doctoral dissertation, Yale University.

Tomlin, C.: 1983b, 'A Map Algebra'. In: *Harvard Computer Graphics Conference.*

Cambridge, MA.

Tomlin, C.: 1989, *Geographic Information System and Cartographic Modeling*. New York: Prentice-Hall.

Tsang, E.: 1986, 'Plan Generation in a Temporal Frame'. In: *Proceedings of the Seventh European Conference on Artificial Intelligence* (ECAI-86). pp. 479–493.

Tversky, B.: 1993a, 'Cognitive maps, cognitive collages, and spatial mental models'. In: A. Frank and I. Campari (eds.): *Spatial Information Theory - A Theoretical Basis for GIS, Proceedings of COSIT'93*. Berlin, pp. 14–24.

Tversky, B.: 1993b, 'Spatial mental models'. In: G. Power (ed.): *The Psychology of Learning and Motivation: Advances in Research and Theory*, Vol. 27. New York: Academic Press, pp. 109–145.

Ullman, S.: 1985, 'Visual routines'. In: S. Pinker (ed.): *Visual Cognition*. Cambridge, MA: MIT Press, pp. 97–159.

Ungerleider, L. and M. Mishkin: 1982, 'Two cortical visual systems'. In: D. Ingle, M. Goodale, and R. Mansfield (eds.): *Analysis of Visual Behavior*. Cambridge, MA: MIT Press, pp. 249–268.

van Beek, P.: 1992, 'Reasoning about Qualitative Temporal Information'. *Artificial Intelligence* 58(1-3), 297–321.

van Beek, P. and R. Cohen: 1990, 'Exact and approximate reasoning about temporal relations'. *Computational Intelligence* 6, 132–144.

van Beek, P. and D. Manchak: 1996, 'The Design and Experimental Analysis of Algorithms for Temporal Reasoning'. *Journal of Artificial Intelligence Research* 4, 1–18.

van Benthem, J.: 1983, *The Logic of Time*. Dordrecht and Boston: D. Reidel and Kluwer.

van Benthem, J.: 1991, *The Logic of Time (second edition)*. Dordrecht, Boston, London: Kluwer Academic Publishers.

Vandeloise, C.: forthcoming, *Langue et physique*.

Varzi, A.: 1994, 'On the boundary between mereology and topology'. In: R. Casati, B. Smith, and G. White (eds.): *Philosophy and the Cognitive Sciences*. Vienna: Hölder-Pichler-Tempsky, pp. 423–442.

Varzi, A.: 1996a, 'Parts, Wholes, and Part-Whole Relations: The Prospects of Mereotopology'. *Data and Knowledge Engineering* 20(3), 259–286.

Varzi, A.: 1996b, 'Reasoning about space: the hole story'. *Logic and Logical Philosophy* 4, 3–39.

Varzi, A.: 1996c, 'Spatial Reasoning in a Holey World'. In: P. Torasso (ed.): *Advances in Artificial Intelligence, Proceedings of the 3rd Congress of the Italian Association for Artificial Intelligence*. Berlin and Heidelberg, pp. 326–336.

Varzi, A. C.: 1997, 'Boundaries, Continuity, and Contact'. *Nous* 31, 1–33.

Vendler, Z.: 1967, *Linguistics in Philosophy*. Ithaca, NY: Cornell University Press.

Vere, S.: 1983, 'Planning in time: Windows and durations for activities and goals'. *IEEE Transactions on Pattern Analysis and Machine Intelligence* 5(3), 246–267. Also in *Readings in Planning*, J. Allen, J. Hendler, and A. Tate (eds.), Morgan Kaufmann, 1990, pp. 297–318.

Vieu, L.: 1991, 'Sémantique des relations spatiales et inférences spatio-temporelles : une contribution à l'étude des structures formelles de l'espace en Langage Naturel'. Phd thesis, Université Paul Sabatier, IRIT.

Vieu, L.: 1993, 'A Logical Framework for Reasoning about Space'. In: A. Frank and I. Campari (eds.): *Spatial Information Theory - A Theoretical Basis for GIS, Proceedings of COSIT'93*. Berlin, pp. 25–35.

Vila, L.: 1994, 'A Survey on Temporal Reasoning in Artificial Intelligence'. *AI Communications* 7(1), 4–28.

Vilain, M.: 1982, 'A system for reasoning about time'. In: *Proceedings of the Second National Conference on Artificial Intelligence (AAAI-82)*. Pittsburg, PA, pp. 197–201.

Vilain, M. and H. Kautz: 1986, 'Constraint propagation algorithms for temporal reasoning'. In: *Proceedings of the Fifth National Conference of the American Association for Artificial Intelligence (AAAI-86)*. Philadelphia, PA, pp. 377–382.

Vilain, M., H. Kautz, and P. van Beek: 1990, 'Constraint propagation algorithms for temporal reasoning: A revised report'. In: *Readings in Qualitative Reasoning about Physical Systems*. San Mateo, CA: Morgan Kaufman, pp. 373–381.

von Wright, G.: 1979, 'A modal logic of space'. In: F. Sosa (ed.): *The philosophy of Nicholas Rescher*. Dordrecht: Reidel.

Wadell, K. and B. Rogoff: 1987, 'Contextual organization and intentionality in adult's spatial memory'. *Developmental Psychology* **23**, 514–525.

Wahlster, W.: 1987, 'One word says more than a thousand pictures. On the automatic verbalization of the results of image sequence analysis systems'. *T.A. Informations - Revue Internationale du Traitement Automatique du Langage* **28**(2). Special issue *Linguistique et Informatique en République Fédérale Allemande*.

Wang, X., S. Jajodia, and V. Subrahmanian: 1995, 'Temporal modules: An approach toward federated temporal databases'. *Information Sciences* **82**, 103–128.

Weida, R. and D. Litman: 1992, 'Terminological reasoning with constraint networks and an application to plan recognition'. In: B. Nebel, W. Swartout, and C. Rich (eds.): *Proceedings of the Third International Conference on Principles of Knowledge Representation and Reasoning (KR'92)*. Cambridge, MA, pp. 282–293.

Weld, D. and J. de Kleer (eds.): 1990, *Readings in Qualitative Reasoning About Physical Systems*. San Mateo, Ca: Morgan Kaufman.

Weld, D. S.: 1994, 'An introduction to least commitment planning'. *AI Magazine* **15**(61), 27–61.

Whitehead, A.: 1920, *The Concept of Nature*. Cambridge: Cambridge University Press.

Whitehead, A.: 1929, *Process and Reality: An Essay in Cosmology*. New York: The MacMillan Company.

Whitehead, A. N.: 1919, *An Enquiry Concerning the Principles of Human Knowledge*. Cambridge: Cambridge University Press.

Wilkins, D.: 1988, *Practical Planning: Extending the Classical AI Planning Paradigm*. San Mateo, CA: Morgan Kaufmann.

Williams, B. C.: 1990, 'Temporal Qualitative Analysis: Explaining How Physical Systems Work'. In: D. S. Weld and J. de Kleer (eds.): *Qualitative Reasoning about Physical Systems*. San Mateo, California: Morgan Kaufmann, pp. 133–177.

Winslett, M.: 1988, 'Reasoning about Actions using a Possible Models Approach'. In: *Proceedings of the Seventh National Conference of the American Association for Artificial Intelligence (AAAI-88)*. pp. 89–93.

Worboys, M. F. and P. Bofakos: 1993, 'A canonical model for a class of areal spatial objects'. In: D. Abel and B. C. Ooi (eds.): *Advances in Spatial Databases: Third International Symposium, SSD'93*, Vol. 692 of *Lecture Notes in Computer Science*.

Yampratoom, E. and J. Allen: 1993, 'Performance of Temporal Reasoning Systems'. *SIGART Bulletin* **4**(3), 26–29.

Yi, C.-H.: 1995, 'Towards the Assessment of Logics for Concurrent Actions'. In: *Proceedings of the AAAI 1995 Spring Symposium*.

Zimmermann, K.: 1993, 'Enhancing Qualitative Spatial Reasoning - Combining Orientation and Distance'. In: A. Frank and I. Campari (eds.): *Spatial Information Theory - COSIT'93*. Berlin, pp. 69–76.

Zimmermann, K.: 1995, 'Measuring without Measures. The Delta-Calculus'. In: A. Frank and W. Kuhn (eds.): *Spatial Information Theory - Proceedings of COSIT'95*. Berlin, pp. 59–67.

SUBJECT INDEX